Contents Table

~ Welcome & What You'll Learn

Section 1: Introduction to Cloud Computing and Microsoft Azure

- Chapter 1: What is Cloud Computing?
- Chapter 2: Why Choose Microsoft Azure?
- Chapter 3: Azure Core Concepts (Subscriptions, Resource Groups, Regions, etc.)
- Chapter 4: The Azure Portal – Your Gateway to Azure

Section 2: Getting Started with Azure

- Chapter 5: Creating Your First Azure Account
- Chapter 6: Navigating the Azure Portal
- Chapter 7: Azure Marketplace: Explore and Deploy Services

Section 3: Azure Compute Services

- Chapter 8: Virtual Machines (VMs): Your Virtual Servers in the Cloud
- Chapter 9: App Services: Building and Hosting Web Applications
- Chapter 10: Azure Functions: Serverless Computing Made Easy
- Chapter 11: Azure Kubernetes Service (AKS): Orchestrating Containers at Scale

Section 4: Azure Storage Services

- Chapter 12: Azure Blob Storage: Storing Unstructured Data
- Chapter 13: Azure File Storage: Shared File Systems in the Cloud
- Chapter 14: Azure Table Storage: NoSQL Storage for Key-Value Data
- Chapter 15: Azure Queue Storage: Asynchronous Messaging and Workflows

Section 5: Azure Networking

- Chapter 16: Virtual Networks: Building Your Private Cloud Network
- Chapter 17: Load Balancers: Distributing Traffic for High Availability
- Chapter 18: Azure DNS: Managing Domain Names and Resolutions
- Chapter 19: Content Delivery Network (CDN): Optimizing Content Delivery

Section 6: Azure Databases

- Chapter 20: Azure SQL Database: Relational Database in the Cloud
- Chapter 21: Azure Cosmos DB: Globally Distributed NoSQL Database
- Chapter 22: Azure Database for MySQL/PostgreSQL: Open-Source Options

Section 7: Azure Identity and Security

- Chapter 23: Azure Active Directory (AAD): Managing Identities and Access
- Chapter 24: Azure Security Center: Protecting Your Resources

- Chapter 25: Azure Key Vault: Securely Managing Secrets and Keys

Section 8: Monitoring and Management

- Chapter 26: Azure Monitor: Gaining Insights into Your Resources
- Chapter 27: Azure Advisor: Recommendations for Optimization
- Chapter 28: Azure Cost Management: Understanding and Controlling Costs

Section 9: Additional Azure Services

- Chapter 29: Azure Machine Learning: Building and Deploying ML Models
- Chapter 30: Azure IoT Hub: Connecting and Managing IoT Devices
- Chapter 31: Azure Cognitive Services: Adding AI Capabilities

Section 10: Advanced Azure Concepts

- Chapter 32: Azure Resource Manager (ARM): Infrastructure as Code
- Chapter 33: Azure DevOps: Continuous Integration and Deployment (CI/CD)
- Chapter 34: Azure Policy: Enforcing Governance and Compliance

Appendices

- Appendix A: Glossary of Azure Terms
- Appendix B: Azure Certifications
- Appendix C: Additional Resources for Learning Azure

~ Conclusion

Welcome & What You'll Learn

Congratulations on taking your first step towards mastering the cloud with Microsoft Azure! If you're new to cloud computing or looking for a clear, structured way to learn Azure, you're in the right place.

Why This Book?

You might be wondering, "Why another book on Azure?" The answer is simple:

- **No Fluff:** We get straight to the point, focusing on the core concepts and skills you need to get started.
- **Hands-On Approach:** We believe in learning by doing. Throughout this book, you'll find practical examples and exercises to reinforce your knowledge.
- **Beginner-Friendly:** We start with the absolute basics and gradually build up your understanding. Even if you have zero cloud experience, you'll be able to follow along.
- **Roadmap to Success:** We'll guide you through a carefully curated learning path, ensuring you build a solid foundation in Azure that prepares you for real-world scenarios and certifications.

What You'll Learn

By the end of this book, you'll be able to:

- **Understand** the fundamentals of cloud computing and why Microsoft Azure is a leading choice.
- **Navigate** the Azure portal like a pro, confidently creating and managing resources.
- **Deploy** virtual machines, web applications, and serverless functions in Azure.
- **Store** and manage different types of data using Azure's diverse storage services.
- **Build** secure and scalable network infrastructure in the cloud.
- **Leverage** Azure's powerful database options for your applications.
- **Implement** essential security practices to protect your cloud environment.
- **Monitor** the health and performance of your Azure resources.
- **Explore** additional Azure services like machine learning, IoT, and AI.
- **Dive into** advanced concepts like infrastructure as code and DevOps.

How This Book is Organized

We've divided this book into sections that take you through a logical progression of learning:

1. **Introduction to Cloud Computing and Microsoft Azure:** We'll demystify cloud computing, explain why Azure is a top choice, and introduce you to essential Azure concepts.
2. **Getting Started with Azure:** You'll create your Azure account, learn to navigate the portal, and discover how to explore and deploy services from the Azure Marketplace.
3. **Azure Compute Services:** We'll cover the different ways you can run applications in Azure, from virtual machines to serverless functions.
4. **Azure Storage Services:** You'll learn how to store and manage various types of data in the cloud.
5. **Azure Networking:** We'll delve into how to build and secure your network infrastructure in Azure.

…and so on, covering databases, security, monitoring, additional services, and advanced concepts.

Are You Ready?

Let's embark on this exciting journey into the world of Microsoft Azure!

Section 1:
Introduction to Cloud Computing and Microsoft Azure

What is Cloud Computing?

Outline

- Defining Cloud Computing
- Cloud Computing Models (IaaS, PaaS, SaaS)
- Benefits of Cloud Computing
- Comparing Cloud Computing with Traditional IT
- Types of Clouds (Public, Private, Hybrid)
- Common Cloud Providers
- Chapter Summary

Defining Cloud Computing

Imagine you're on a road trip. You can either drive your own car, managing all the maintenance, fuel, and directions yourself, or you could hail a taxi or a ride-sharing service. The latter option lets you focus on enjoying the journey while someone else takes care of the logistics.

Cloud computing is like opting for the ride-sharing service of the technology world. Instead of buying and maintaining your own expensive computer servers and data centers (your "car"), you can rent access to computing power, storage, databases, and other IT resources from a cloud provider (your "ride-sharing service"). These resources are hosted in massive data centers and are accessed over the internet.

In essence, cloud computing is:

- **On-demand availability:** You get the computing resources you need, when you need them, like ordering a ride only when you're ready to travel.
- **Pay-as-you-go:** You only pay for what you use, similar to how you pay for the distance and time of your ride.
- **Scalable:** You can easily adjust the amount of resources you use, like upgrading to a larger vehicle if you have more passengers.
- **Accessible:** You can access your cloud resources from anywhere with an internet connection, just as you can request a ride from your phone no matter where you are.

Real-World Examples

You likely already use cloud computing in your everyday life:

- **Email:** Services like Gmail or Outlook store your emails on their servers in the cloud.
- **File storage:** Platforms like Dropbox or Google Drive allow you to store and access your files from anywhere.
- **Streaming services:** Netflix and Spotify stream movies and music from the cloud to your devices.

These are just a few examples of how cloud computing has become an integral part of how we interact with technology.

Cloud Computing Models (IaaS, PaaS, SaaS)

Cloud computing isn't a one-size-fits-all solution. It offers different models that cater to varying needs and levels of control. Let's explore the three main categories:

Infrastructure as a Service (IaaS)

Think of IaaS as renting the building blocks for your IT infrastructure. It's like leasing an empty plot of land where you can build your house according to your specifications. With IaaS, you get access to:

- **Virtual machines:** Virtualized servers in the cloud.
- **Storage:** Scalable storage options for your data.
- **Networking:** Tools to create and manage your network infrastructure.

Example: A startup might use IaaS to quickly set up a development environment without investing in physical servers.

Responsibility: You manage the operating systems, applications, and data. The cloud provider handles the underlying infrastructure like servers, storage, and networking.

Control and Flexibility: You have the most control over your environment in IaaS, but you also have the most responsibility.

Platform as a Service (PaaS)

Imagine PaaS as renting a pre-furnished apartment. It's ready to move in, and you don't have to worry about building or maintaining the structure. PaaS provides a platform for developing, running, and managing applications, including:

- **Runtime environments:** Pre-configured environments for specific programming languages and frameworks.
- **Middleware:** Software that helps applications communicate and share data.
- **Development tools:** Tools for building, testing, and deploying applications.

Example: A development team might use PaaS to quickly build and deploy a web application without worrying about managing the underlying servers or operating systems.

Responsibility: You manage the applications and data. The cloud provider takes care of the operating systems, middleware, and infrastructure.

Control and Flexibility: You have less control than IaaS, but you gain convenience and faster development cycles.

Software as a Service (SaaS)

Think of SaaS as staying in a fully serviced hotel. You don't own or maintain anything; you just use the services provided. SaaS delivers software applications over the internet, such as:

- **Email:** Gmail, Outlook
- **Customer relationship management (CRM):** Salesforce
- **Office productivity:** Microsoft 365

Example: A company might use a SaaS CRM solution to manage customer interactions without installing or maintaining the software on their own servers.

Responsibility: You just use the application. The cloud provider handles everything else, including the software, infrastructure, and maintenance.

Control and Flexibility: You have the least control, but you also have the least responsibility.

Key Differences

Feature	IaaS	PaaS	SaaS
What you manage	OS, apps, data	Apps, data	Nothing
What you get	Building blocks	Platform	Application
Control	Highest	Medium	Lowest
Flexibility	Highest	Medium	Lowest

By understanding these cloud computing models, you can choose the one that best aligns with your specific needs and resources.

Benefits of Cloud Computing

Cloud computing has revolutionized the way businesses and individuals approach IT, offering a wealth of advantages over traditional on-premises infrastructure. Let's delve into the key benefits:

Cost Savings

The Financial Upside: Cloud computing can significantly reduce IT costs. It eliminates the need for upfront capital expenses on hardware, software licenses, and data center maintenance. Instead, you pay for resources on a subscription or pay-as-you-go basis, like paying for electricity based on your usage. This can be particularly beneficial for startups and small businesses with limited budgets.

Real-World Scenario: A small e-commerce business experiences a surge in sales during the holiday season. With cloud computing, they can quickly scale up their server capacity to handle the increased traffic and only pay for the extra resources they use during that period.

Scalability and Flexibility

Effortless Expansion: Cloud computing offers unparalleled scalability. You can easily add or remove resources to meet changing demands. This elasticity allows businesses to adapt quickly to fluctuations in traffic, user needs, or seasonal variations.

Real-World Scenario: A software company launches a new product that becomes an instant hit. With cloud computing, they can rapidly scale their infrastructure to accommodate the influx of new users without worrying about delays or capacity limitations.

Reliability and High Availability

Resilience and Redundancy: Cloud providers typically have multiple data centers located in different geographic regions. This redundancy ensures that even if one data center experiences an outage, your applications and data remain accessible from another location. This leads to higher uptime and improved business continuity.

Real-World Scenario: A news website relies on cloud computing to ensure that its content is available 24/7, even during unexpected events like natural disasters or hardware failures.

Accessibility

Anytime, Anywhere Access: Cloud computing enables you to access your applications and data from anywhere in the world with an internet connection. This is essential for remote teams, mobile workforces, and businesses with a global presence.

Real-World Scenario: A multinational corporation uses cloud-based collaboration tools to enable seamless communication and file sharing between employees across different continents and time zones.

Other Benefits

In addition to the core advantages mentioned above, cloud computing also offers:

- **Increased Innovation:** Cloud providers constantly update and improve their services, giving you access to the latest technologies without requiring expensive upgrades.
- **Enhanced Security:** Cloud providers often have robust security measures in place, protecting your data from threats and ensuring compliance with industry standards.
- **Simplified IT Management:** Cloud computing reduces the burden on your IT staff, allowing them to focus on strategic initiatives rather than routine maintenance tasks.

Cloud computing has become a game-changer for businesses of all sizes. Its numerous benefits empower organizations to be more agile, efficient, and competitive in today's fast-paced digital landscape.

Comparing Cloud Computing with Traditional IT

To understand the advantages of cloud computing, let's compare it with the traditional approach of managing IT infrastructure:

Feature	Cloud Computing	Traditional IT
Infrastructure Ownership	Owned and maintained by the cloud provider	Owned and maintained by the organization
Maintenance	Provider handles maintenance and updates	Requires in-house IT staff for maintenance
Scalability	Easily scalable up or down to meet demand	Scaling requires additional hardware purchase
Cost Structure	Pay-as-you-go or subscription-based model	Upfront capital expenditure and ongoing costs
Deployment Speed	Rapid deployment of resources	Time-consuming procurement and setup process
Accessibility	Accessible from anywhere with internet connection	Limited to on-premises network access
Disaster Recovery	Built-in redundancy and automated backups	Requires manual backup and recovery processes

Key Takeaways

- **Ownership and Control:** In traditional IT, you have complete ownership and control of your infrastructure, but it comes with the burden of maintenance and upgrades. With cloud computing, the provider takes care of the infrastructure, allowing you to focus on your core business.
- **Scalability:** Cloud computing offers unmatched scalability, allowing you to adjust resources based on demand. Traditional IT requires careful planning and significant investments to scale infrastructure.
- **Cost:** Cloud computing operates on a pay-as-you-go or subscription model, reducing upfront costs and offering more predictable expenses. Traditional IT involves high upfront costs and ongoing maintenance expenses.
- **Deployment Speed:** Cloud resources can be provisioned quickly, enabling faster time-to-market for new applications and services. Traditional IT deployments can be slow and cumbersome due to procurement and setup processes.
- **Accessibility:** Cloud resources are accessible from anywhere, promoting remote work and collaboration. Traditional IT is typically restricted to on-premises access.

By comparing these key aspects, it becomes clear why cloud computing has gained such popularity. Its advantages in terms of cost, scalability, speed, and accessibility make it a compelling choice for businesses seeking to modernize their IT infrastructure.

Types of Clouds (Public, Private, Hybrid)

When choosing a cloud computing solution, you'll encounter three main types of cloud environments:

Public Cloud

The public cloud is like a shared apartment building. Multiple tenants (businesses or individuals) share the same infrastructure, resources, and services provided by a third-party cloud provider.

Characteristics:

- **Multi-tenant:** Resources are shared among multiple users.
- **Accessible over the internet:** Anyone can subscribe and access resources.
- **Pay-as-you-go:** Pricing is based on usage.
- **Managed by the provider:** The cloud provider handles all maintenance and updates.

Use Cases:

- **Testing and development:** Public clouds are ideal for experimenting with new technologies and building prototypes.
- **Web applications:** Public clouds offer scalable infrastructure for hosting websites and web applications.
- **Data backup and storage:** Public cloud storage services provide affordable and reliable backup options.
- **Small to medium-sized businesses:** Public clouds are often a cost-effective solution for businesses with limited IT resources.

Example: A startup might use Azure's public cloud to quickly deploy their web application and scale resources as their user base grows.

Private Cloud

A private cloud is like owning your own house. It's a dedicated environment solely for your organization, either hosted on-premises or by a third-party provider.

Characteristics:

- **Single-tenant:** Resources are dedicated to a single organization.
- **Can be on-premises or hosted:** You can build a private cloud in your own data center or have it hosted by a provider.
- **Increased control and security:** You have more control over your environment and data.

Use Cases:

- **Sensitive data:** Private clouds are ideal for storing and processing highly sensitive or confidential data.
- **Regulatory compliance:** Organizations with strict regulatory requirements may prefer private clouds for better control and security.
- **Large enterprises:** Large organizations with extensive IT resources may choose to build their own private clouds for greater customization and control.

Example: A financial institution might build a private cloud to comply with strict data security regulations and maintain control over their sensitive financial data.

Hybrid Cloud

A hybrid cloud combines the best of both worlds, blending public and private cloud environments. It's like having a house with a guest wing.

Characteristics:

- **Combination of public and private:** You can keep sensitive workloads in the private cloud while using the public cloud for less critical applications or to handle spikes in demand.
- **Flexibility:** You can move workloads between public and private clouds as needed.
- **Cost optimization:** You can use the public cloud for cost-effective scalability while maintaining control over critical data in the private cloud.

Use Cases:

- **Data sovereignty:** Organizations can keep sensitive data in their private cloud while using the public cloud for other workloads.
- **Legacy applications:** You can modernize legacy applications in the public cloud while keeping some on-premises for specific needs.
- **Disaster recovery:** A hybrid cloud can provide a reliable and cost-effective disaster recovery solution by replicating critical data and applications to the public cloud.

Example: A retailer might use a hybrid cloud to keep customer data in their private cloud for security reasons while using the public cloud to run their e-commerce website and handle peak traffic during sales periods.

Choosing the Right Cloud

The best type of cloud for your organization depends on various factors, including your budget, security requirements, compliance needs, and the nature of your workloads. Consider the following when making your decision:

- **Cost:** Public clouds are generally more cost-effective than private clouds.
- **Security:** Private clouds offer more control and security, but public cloud providers are also investing heavily in security measures.
- **Flexibility:** Hybrid clouds offer the most flexibility, allowing you to move workloads between public and private environments as needed.
- **Control:** Private clouds give you the most control over your environment, while public clouds offer less customization.

By carefully evaluating your specific needs and priorities, you can choose the cloud environment that best suits your organization.

Common Cloud Providers

The cloud computing landscape is vast and competitive, with several major players vying for market share. Here's a brief overview of three leading cloud providers:

Microsoft Azure

Overview: Azure, the focus of this book, is Microsoft's comprehensive cloud computing platform. It offers a wide range of services, including computing, storage, databases, networking, analytics, AI, and IoT. Azure is known for its seamless integration with other Microsoft products and services, making it a natural choice for organizations already invested in the Microsoft ecosystem.

Strengths:

- **Hybrid capabilities:** Azure excels in hybrid cloud solutions, allowing you to seamlessly integrate your on-premises infrastructure with the cloud.
- **Enterprise-grade features:** Azure offers robust security, compliance, and management tools, making it suitable for large enterprises.
- **Developer-friendly:** Azure provides a variety of developer tools and services, including support for various programming languages and frameworks.

Unique Features:

- **Azure Active Directory:** A comprehensive identity and access management solution that simplifies user authentication and authorization.
- **Azure DevOps:** A suite of tools that streamline software development and delivery, including continuous integration and continuous deployment (CI/CD).

Amazon Web Services (AWS)

Overview: AWS is the pioneer and current market leader in cloud computing. It offers a massive catalog of services, arguably the broadest in the industry, covering virtually every aspect of IT infrastructure and applications. AWS is known for its scalability, reliability, and extensive global reach.

Strengths:

- **Market leader:** AWS has the largest market share and a mature ecosystem of partners and tools.
- **Wide range of services:** AWS offers the most comprehensive set of cloud services, catering to diverse needs.
- **Cost-effective:** AWS provides various pricing models, including reserved instances and spot instances, allowing for cost optimization.

Unique Features:

- **Elastic Compute Cloud (EC2):** A highly scalable and customizable virtual server offering.
- **Simple Storage Service (S3):** A scalable object storage service with high durability and availability.

Google Cloud Platform (GCP)

Overview: GCP is Google's cloud computing platform, known for its strengths in data analytics, machine learning, and artificial intelligence (AI). It offers a wide range of services similar to AWS and Azure, with a focus on innovation and cutting-edge technologies.

Strengths:

- **Data and analytics:** GCP excels in big data processing and analytics, with powerful tools like BigQuery and Dataflow.
- **Machine learning and AI:** GCP offers a suite of machine learning and AI services, including pre-trained models and custom model building tools.
- **Containerization:** GCP has strong support for containerization technologies like Kubernetes, simplifying the deployment and management of applications.

Unique Features:

- **BigQuery:** A serverless, highly scalable data warehouse for analyzing massive datasets.
- **TensorFlow:** An open-source machine learning framework developed by Google, widely used for building and training AI models.

Choosing the Right Provider

The best cloud provider for your organization depends on your specific needs and priorities. Consider the following factors:

- **Services:** Evaluate the breadth and depth of services offered by each provider to ensure they meet your requirements.
- **Pricing:** Compare pricing models and consider using cost optimization strategies to get the best value.
- **Performance:** Consider factors like network latency and data transfer speeds to ensure optimal performance for your applications.
- **Ease of use:** Choose a platform with a user-friendly interface and comprehensive documentation.
- **Support:** Look for providers with responsive customer support and a strong community of users.

By carefully evaluating these factors, you can choose the cloud provider that best aligns with your business goals and technical needs.

Chapter Summary

In this chapter, we explored the fundamental concepts of cloud computing. We defined cloud computing as the on-demand delivery of IT resources over the internet, highlighting its key characteristics of on-demand availability, pay-as-you-go pricing, scalability, and accessibility.

We then delved into the three main cloud computing models:

- **Infrastructure as a Service (IaaS):** Providing the building blocks for IT infrastructure, like virtual machines, storage, and networking.
- **Platform as a Service (PaaS):** Offering a platform for developing, running, and managing applications, complete with runtime environments and development tools.
- **Software as a Service (SaaS):** Delivering software applications over the internet, requiring no installation or maintenance by the user.

We discussed the numerous benefits of cloud computing over traditional IT, such as cost savings, scalability, reliability, accessibility, and increased innovation. We compared cloud and traditional IT infrastructure, highlighting the differences in ownership, maintenance, scalability, cost structure, and deployment speed.

Finally, we explored the three types of cloud environments:

- **Public Cloud:** Shared resources accessible over the internet.
- **Private Cloud:** Dedicated resources for a single organization, either on-premises or hosted.

- **Hybrid Cloud:** A combination of public and private clouds, offering the best of both worlds.

We concluded by introducing major cloud providers like Microsoft Azure, Amazon Web Services (AWS), and Google Cloud Platform (GCP), highlighting their strengths and unique features.

By grasping these foundational concepts, you're well on your way to understanding how cloud computing, and specifically Microsoft Azure, can empower your personal or business endeavors. In the next chapter, we'll delve deeper into why Microsoft Azure stands out as a leading cloud platform and why you might choose it for your cloud journey.

Why Choose Microsoft Azure?

Outline

- Wide Range of Services and Tools
- Global Reach and Reliability
- Security and Compliance
- Integration with Microsoft Ecosystem
- Hybrid Cloud Capabilities
- Pricing and Support Options
- Chapter Summary

Wide Range of Services and Tools

Microsoft Azure isn't just a single product; it's a vast ecosystem of cloud services designed to cater to virtually any IT need. Think of it as a massive toolbox, filled with everything you need to build and run your applications, manage your infrastructure, and analyze your data – all within the cloud.

Here's a glimpse into the diverse categories of services Azure offers:

- **Compute:** Run your applications and workloads on virtual machines, containers, serverless functions, or even dedicated hardware. Azure gives you the flexibility to choose the right compute option based on your specific requirements.
- **Storage:** Store and manage all types of data, from structured to unstructured, with options like blob storage, file storage, and disk storage.
- **Databases:** Choose from a wide range of relational, NoSQL, and in-memory databases to power your applications. Azure supports popular open-source options like MySQL and PostgreSQL, as well as its own powerful offerings like Azure SQL Database and Cosmos DB.
- **Networking:** Build and manage your network infrastructure in the cloud with virtual networks, load balancers, DNS, and content delivery networks (CDNs).
- **Analytics:** Gain valuable insights from your data using Azure's suite of analytics services, including data lakes, data warehouses, stream processing, and machine learning.
- **AI:** Infuse your applications with artificial intelligence capabilities using pre-built AI services or custom machine learning models.
- **IoT:** Connect, monitor, and manage your Internet of Things (IoT) devices at scale using Azure IoT Hub and related services.
- **And much more:** Azure also offers services for security, identity, integration, developer tools, and many other specialized areas.

This extensive portfolio of services gives you the freedom to choose the right tools for the job, whether you're building a simple website, running a complex enterprise application, analyzing massive datasets, or creating intelligent solutions with AI. Azure's breadth ensures that you can find the solutions you need to meet your unique business challenges and objectives.

Global Reach and Reliability

One of Microsoft Azure's standout advantages is its unparalleled global footprint. With data centers strategically located in more regions than any other cloud provider, Azure ensures that your applications and data are always close to your users, no matter where they are in the world.

Worldwide Network of Data Centers

Azure's extensive network of data centers spans across continents and countries, providing a truly global reach. This geographic distribution translates to several key benefits:

- **Improved performance:** By hosting your applications and data closer to your users, Azure reduces network latency and enhances the responsiveness of your services. This means faster load times for websites, quicker response times for applications, and an overall smoother user experience.
- **Low latency:** The proximity of Azure data centers to your users minimizes the time it takes for data to travel between them, resulting in lower latency. This is particularly crucial for real-time applications like online gaming, video conferencing, and financial trading platforms.
- **High availability:** With multiple data centers in different regions, Azure ensures that your applications and data remain accessible even if one data center experiences an outage. This redundancy provides a high level of availability and business continuity.

Availability Zones for Enhanced Resilience

Within each Azure region, you'll find Availability Zones. These are physically separate locations within the same region, each with its own independent power, cooling, and networking infrastructure. Availability Zones act as a safeguard against localized failures, ensuring that your applications and data remain available even if one zone is affected.

By deploying your resources across multiple Availability Zones, you create a fault-tolerant architecture that can withstand hardware failures, network outages, or even natural disasters. If one zone becomes unavailable, your applications can automatically failover to another zone, minimizing downtime and ensuring uninterrupted service.

Azure's Commitment to Reliability

Microsoft invests heavily in ensuring the reliability of Azure. Its data centers are designed with redundancy in mind, featuring backup power supplies, multiple network connections, and robust security measures. Azure also undergoes regular maintenance and updates to keep its infrastructure running smoothly and securely.

In addition, Azure offers various service level agreements (SLAs) that guarantee a certain level of uptime for its services. These SLAs give you peace of mind, knowing that your applications and data are backed by a commitment to reliability from a leading cloud provider.

Security and Compliance

In the cloud, security is paramount. Microsoft Azure takes this responsibility seriously, offering robust security measures and adhering to a wide range of compliance certifications to ensure your data and applications are protected.

Robust Security Measures

Azure employs a defense-in-depth strategy, implementing security controls at multiple layers to safeguard your environment:

- **Physical Security:** Azure data centers are equipped with state-of-the-art physical security measures like perimeter fencing, biometric access controls, video surveillance, and 24/7 security personnel.
- **Network Security:** Azure utilizes advanced network security technologies like firewalls, intrusion detection and prevention systems (IDPS), and distributed denial-of-service (DDoS) protection to protect against unauthorized access and attacks.

- **Data Security:** Azure offers various encryption options to protect data at rest and in transit. It also provides tools for data classification, data loss prevention (DLP), and threat detection.
- **Application Security:** Azure provides services like web application firewalls (WAF) and vulnerability scanners to help you identify and mitigate security risks in your applications.
- **Identity and Access Management:** Azure Active Directory (Azure AD) provides a robust identity and access management solution, enabling you to control who can access your resources and what they can do with them.

Compliance Certifications

Azure holds a wide range of compliance certifications, demonstrating its commitment to meeting the highest security and privacy standards. Some of the key certifications include:

- **ISO 27001:** The international standard for information security management systems (ISMS).
- **SOC 1/2/3:** Reports that attest to the effectiveness of Azure's internal controls over financial reporting, security, and privacy.
- **HIPAA:** The Health Insurance Portability and Accountability Act, ensuring the privacy and security of protected health information (PHI).
- **GDPR:** The General Data Protection Regulation, a comprehensive data privacy law in the European Union.
- **FedRAMP:** The Federal Risk and Authorization Management Program, validating Azure's security for use by U.S. government agencies.

Specific Security Features

Azure offers a variety of security tools and services to help you protect your environment:

- **Azure Security Center:** A unified security management system that provides threat protection, security assessments, and recommendations for improving your security posture.
- **Azure Firewall:** A cloud-native firewall service that protects your Azure resources from unauthorized network traffic.
- **Azure Key Vault:** A secure service for storing and managing sensitive information like encryption keys, passwords, and certificates.

Azure's commitment to security and compliance makes it a trusted platform for businesses and organizations across various industries. By leveraging Azure's robust security features and certifications, you can confidently build and deploy applications while ensuring the protection of your data and compliance with regulatory requirements.

Integration with Microsoft Ecosystem

For organizations already invested in Microsoft technologies, Azure offers a significant advantage: seamless integration with the familiar Microsoft ecosystem. This integration makes it easier to migrate existing applications and data to the cloud, manage resources consistently, and enhance collaboration across teams.

Smooth Transition for Existing Applications

If your organization is running applications on Windows Server, SQL Server, or other Microsoft platforms, you can easily lift and shift those workloads to Azure Virtual Machines or Azure App Services. Azure's compatibility with these platforms minimizes the effort required to move applications to the cloud, reducing the risk of compatibility issues and downtime.

Unified Management with Active Directory

Azure Active Directory (Azure AD) extends your on-premises Active Directory to the cloud. This enables you to manage user identities, access permissions, and security policies consistently across both your on-premises and cloud environments. With a single sign-on (SSO) experience, users can access both cloud and on-premises applications with the same credentials, simplifying authentication and improving productivity.

Enhanced Collaboration with Office 365

Azure integrates seamlessly with Office 365, Microsoft's popular suite of productivity tools. This integration allows you to leverage Azure's capabilities to enhance your Office 365 experience. For example, you can use Azure to:

- **Store and share files:** Azure's storage services can be integrated with SharePoint Online and OneDrive for Business, providing scalable and secure file storage and sharing capabilities.
- **Build custom workflows:** Azure Logic Apps can be used to automate business processes across Office 365 applications, improving efficiency and reducing manual tasks.
- **Gain insights from data:** Azure's analytics services can be used to analyze data from Office 365, such as email usage patterns or collaboration trends, providing valuable insights for decision-making.

Additional Benefits

The integration between Azure and the Microsoft ecosystem extends to numerous other areas, including:

- **Development tools:** Visual Studio and Visual Studio Code seamlessly integrate with Azure, providing a familiar development environment for building cloud-native applications.
- **Management tools:** Microsoft System Center and PowerShell can be used to manage both on-premises and Azure resources, simplifying IT operations.
- **Security:** Azure Security Center integrates with Microsoft Defender for Endpoint and other security solutions, providing comprehensive threat protection across your entire environment.

This deep integration with the Microsoft ecosystem is a major draw for organizations already using Microsoft technologies. By choosing Azure, you can leverage your existing investments and expertise to accelerate your cloud adoption journey. The familiar tools, seamless migration paths, and unified management experience make Azure a natural extension of your Microsoft environment.

Hybrid Cloud Capabilities

Microsoft Azure recognizes that not every organization is ready or able to move all their workloads to the public cloud. That's why Azure has invested heavily in developing a robust portfolio of hybrid cloud solutions, giving you the flexibility to choose the best environment for each workload while maintaining a consistent management experience.

Azure Stack: Extending Azure On-Premises

Azure Stack is a family of products that brings the power of Azure services to your own data center. It enables you to run Azure-consistent services on-premises, allowing you to:

- **Modernize legacy applications:** You can modernize older applications by running them on Azure Stack, taking advantage of cloud-native technologies and development tools.
- **Address data sovereignty concerns:** By keeping sensitive data on-premises, you can meet regulatory and compliance requirements that mandate data residency.
- **Operate in disconnected environments:** Azure Stack can be deployed in environments with limited or no internet connectivity, making it ideal for remote locations or industries with strict security requirements.

- **Consistent experience:** Azure Stack provides a consistent experience with Azure public cloud, using the same tools, APIs, and portals. This simplifies management and enables seamless movement of workloads between on-premises and cloud environments.

Azure Arc: Simplifying Hybrid Management

Azure Arc is a hybrid cloud management platform that extends Azure's control plane to resources running on any infrastructure, including on-premises servers, virtual machines in other clouds, and even edge devices. With Azure Arc, you can:

- **Centralized management:** Manage all your resources from a single Azure portal, regardless of where they are running.
- **Unified governance and security:** Apply consistent policies and security controls across your entire hybrid environment.
- **Use Azure services anywhere:** Deploy Azure services like Azure Monitor and Azure Policy to on-premises and multi-cloud environments.

The Power of Choice

Azure's hybrid cloud capabilities give you the freedom to choose the right environment for each workload based on your specific needs and constraints. You can leverage the scalability and agility of the public cloud for some applications while keeping sensitive data or legacy systems on-premises. Azure Stack and Azure Arc provide the tools and flexibility to create a unified hybrid environment that meets your unique requirements.

By embracing a hybrid cloud strategy with Azure, you can unlock the full potential of both cloud and on-premises infrastructure, while minimizing disruption and maximizing efficiency.

Pricing and Support Options

Microsoft Azure's pricing model is designed to be flexible, offering options that cater to different usage patterns and budgetary needs. In addition, Azure provides comprehensive cost management tools and various support levels to ensure you get the most out of your cloud investment.

Flexible Pricing Options

Azure offers three primary pricing models for its services:

- **Pay-As-You-Go:** This model offers the most flexibility, allowing you to pay only for the resources you consume. You're billed per second of usage, with no upfront costs or termination fees. This is ideal for workloads with variable usage patterns or for testing and development environments.
- **Reserved Instances:** If you have predictable usage patterns, you can reserve resources in advance for one or three years and receive a significant discount compared to pay-as-you-go prices. Reserved instances are a great way to save costs on resources that you know you'll need for an extended period.
- **Spot Instances:** For workloads that can tolerate interruptions, spot instances offer a deeply discounted price on unused compute capacity. While spot instances can be evicted with short notice, they are a cost-effective option for batch processing, big data analytics, and other fault-tolerant workloads.

Azure Cost Management

Azure Cost Management is a suite of tools that helps you track, analyze, and optimize your cloud spending. It provides:

- **Cost analysis:** Get detailed breakdowns of your Azure costs by resource, service, and time period.
- **Budgeting and forecasting:** Set budgets for your Azure spending and get forecasts to anticipate future costs.
- **Recommendations:** Azure Advisor provides recommendations for optimizing your resource usage and saving costs.

By using Azure Cost Management, you can gain visibility into your cloud spending, identify areas for optimization, and proactively manage your budget.

Azure Support

Azure offers different levels of support to meet the needs of various customers:

- **Basic Support:** Included with your Azure subscription, provides access to billing and subscription management support.
- **Developer Support:** Designed for developers and IT professionals, offers technical support for Azure services.
- **Standard Support:** Provides 24/7 access to technical support and faster response times.
- **Professional Direct Support:** Offers the fastest response times and access to technical account managers for personalized support.
- **Enterprise Support:** Includes all the features of Professional Direct Support, plus proactive services like architectural guidance and operational health reviews.

The level of support you choose depends on your specific needs and budget. Microsoft also offers a robust online community and extensive documentation to help you troubleshoot issues and learn about Azure services.

By understanding Azure's flexible pricing models, utilizing the cost management tools, and choosing the right level of support, you can effectively manage your cloud costs and ensure a smooth and successful Azure experience.

Chapter Summary

In this chapter, we explored the compelling reasons to choose Microsoft Azure as your cloud platform. We highlighted Azure's vast array of services, encompassing compute, storage, databases, networking, analytics, AI, IoT, and more, making it suitable for a wide range of workloads and scenarios.

We discussed Azure's impressive global reach, with data centers in more regions than any other provider, ensuring improved performance, low latency, and high availability for users worldwide. We also touched upon Availability Zones, which provide additional fault tolerance and resilience within each region.

Security was a key focus, with emphasis on Azure's robust security measures, multi-layered defense-in-depth strategy, and comprehensive compliance certifications. We also mentioned specific security features like Azure Security Center, Azure Firewall, and Azure Key Vault.

We highlighted the seamless integration between Azure and the broader Microsoft ecosystem, explaining how this simplifies migration, management, and collaboration for organizations already using Microsoft technologies like Windows Server, Active Directory, and Office 365.

Lastly, we explored Azure's robust hybrid cloud capabilities, including Azure Stack for running Azure services on-premises and Azure Arc for extending Azure management to any infrastructure. We discussed the flexible pricing options available, such as pay-as-you-go, reserved instances, and spot instances, along with the cost management tools and various support levels offered by Azure. By understanding these key advantages, you can see why Azure stands out as a leading cloud platform. In the next chapter, we'll dive into the core concepts of Azure, laying the foundation for your journey to mastering this powerful and versatile cloud environment.

Azure Core Concepts

Outline

- Azure Subscriptions
- Azure Resource Groups
- Azure Regions and Availability Zones
- Azure Resources
- Azure Resource Manager
- Chapter Summary

Azure Subscriptions

In Azure, a **subscription** acts as your personal space within the cloud. It's a logical container that helps you organize and manage all the resources you create and use in Azure. Think of it like a virtual folder for your cloud resources.

Each subscription is associated with a billing account, meaning you'll receive a bill for all the Azure services you consume under that subscription. It also acts as a boundary for resource access and management. You can control who has access to the resources in your subscription and what they can do with them.

Types of Azure Subscriptions

Azure offers several types of subscriptions to meet different needs and budgets:

- **Free Trial:** This is a great way to get started with Azure and explore its capabilities. It provides you with free credits to try out various Azure services for a limited time.
- **Pay-As-You-Go:** This is the most flexible option, as you only pay for the resources you use. It's ideal for workloads with variable usage patterns or for individuals and small businesses who don't want to commit to a long-term contract.
- **Student:** If you're a student, you can get free access to Azure resources and services through the Azure for Students program.
- **Enterprise Agreement:** This is designed for large organizations with significant cloud needs. It offers discounted rates and additional benefits like dedicated support and customized billing options.

How Subscriptions are Used

Subscriptions can be used in various ways to organize your Azure resources:

- **Individual projects:** If you're working on a specific project, you can create a dedicated subscription for it. This helps you track the costs associated with that project and manage its resources separately.
- **Organizational departments:** Larger organizations might create separate subscriptions for different departments, such as marketing, finance, or IT. This allows each department to manage its own resources and budgets.
- **Development and production environments:** You can create separate subscriptions for development, testing, and production environments. This helps you isolate resources and prevent accidental changes or disruptions to your production systems.

Key Takeaways

Subscriptions are a fundamental concept in Azure. They help you organize, manage, and track your cloud resources effectively. By understanding the different types of subscriptions available and how they can be used, you can choose the right option for your needs and take full advantage of Azure's capabilities.

Azure Resource Groups

Think of resource groups as containers for your Azure resources. Just as you might organize files into folders on your computer, Azure resource groups help you organize your cloud resources into logical collections. These groups not only bring order to your Azure environment but also simplify resource management.

What are Resource Groups?

In Azure, a **resource group** is a logical container that holds related resources for an Azure solution. This means you can group resources like virtual machines, storage accounts, databases, and web apps that work together to support a specific application or service.

Lifecycle Management Made Easy

One of the key benefits of resource groups is that they make it easier to manage the lifecycle of your resources. When you group resources together, you can:

- **Deploy:** Deploy all the resources needed for a new application or service in one go, ensuring they are configured to work together seamlessly.
- **Update:** Update multiple resources simultaneously, streamlining the process of applying changes or upgrades.
- **Delete:** Delete all the resources associated with a specific application or service when it's no longer needed, freeing up resources and reducing costs.

This simplifies resource management and reduces the risk of errors, as you don't have to manage each resource individually.

Organizing Your Resources

You can use resource groups to organize your resources in several ways, depending on your needs and preferences:

- **By application:** Create a separate resource group for each application or service you deploy in Azure. This helps you track the resources associated with each application and manage them as a unit.
- **By environment:** Create separate resource groups for development, testing, and production environments. This isolates resources and helps you avoid accidental changes or disruptions to your production systems.
- **By department:** Create separate resource groups for different departments within your organization. This allows each department to manage its own resources and budgets independently.

Naming Conventions and Best Practices

To make the most of resource groups, it's important to follow some best practices:

- **Use meaningful names:** Choose names that clearly reflect the purpose of the resource group. For example, "Web App - Production" or "Marketing Department Resources."
- **Use a consistent naming convention:** Establish a standard naming convention for your resource groups to make it easier to identify and manage them.

- **Avoid too many or too few resource groups:** Finding the right balance is key. Too many resource groups can lead to management overhead, while too few can make it difficult to isolate and manage resources effectively.
- **Consider resource limits:** Each resource group has limits on the number of resources it can contain. Be mindful of these limits when organizing your resources.

By following these guidelines, you can create a well-organized and efficient Azure environment that's easier to manage and scale.

Azure Regions and Availability Zones

Azure's vast global infrastructure is organized into distinct geographic areas called regions. Understanding these regions and their sub-divisions, Availability Zones, is crucial for optimizing performance, ensuring resilience, and complying with data regulations.

Azure Regions: Your Cloud's Neighborhood

An Azure region is a geographical area containing one or more datacenters. These regions are strategically distributed across the globe, allowing you to deploy your resources closer to your users. Each region operates independently and offers a range of services, but not all Azure services are available in every region.

Region Pairs: A Safety Net for Your Data

Many Azure regions are paired with another region within the same geographic area (usually hundreds of miles apart). This pairing creates redundancy, as each region serves as a backup for the other. If one region experiences an outage, Azure can automatically replicate your data and applications to the paired region, ensuring continued availability and minimizing downtime. This concept is known as **geo-redundancy.**

Availability Zones: Adding Another Layer of Resilience

Within each Azure region, you might find **Availability Zones (AZs)**. These are physically separate locations within the same region, each with its own independent power, cooling, and networking infrastructure. AZs offer an additional layer of protection against localized failures like power outages, natural disasters, or network issues.

By deploying your resources across multiple AZs, you can achieve even higher availability than with region pairs alone. Azure services that support AZs can be configured to replicate data and automatically failover to a different zone if one becomes unavailable.

Choosing the Right Region

Selecting the optimal region for your Azure resources involves considering several factors:

- **Proximity to Users:** Deploying resources in a region closer to your users reduces network latency and improves application performance.
- **Data Residency:** Some regulations mandate that data be stored in specific geographic locations. Choose a region that complies with these requirements.
- **Service Availability:** Not all Azure services are available in every region. Check the availability of the services you need before choosing a region.
- **Cost:** Pricing for Azure services can vary slightly across regions. Consider cost implications alongside other factors.

Example:

If you're building a website targeting users in India, you might choose the "Central India" region to minimize latency for those users. However, if you also need to comply with European data protection regulations, you might deploy resources in the "West Europe" region to store and process data related to European users.

By understanding Azure regions and Availability Zones, you can make informed decisions about where to deploy your resources, optimizing performance, ensuring resilience, and complying with regulatory requirements.

Azure Resources

When you build solutions in Azure, you work with various components known as **Azure resources**. These are the fundamental building blocks that make up your cloud infrastructure and applications. Think of them as the individual ingredients you use to create a delicious meal. Each resource serves a specific purpose and can be combined with others to create complex and powerful solutions.

What are Azure Resources?

An Azure resource is a manageable item available through Azure. Examples include:

- **Virtual Machines (VMs):** These are virtualized computers that you can use to run applications and workloads in the cloud.
- **Storage Accounts:** These provide scalable storage options for your data, such as blobs (for unstructured data), files (for shared file systems), and disks (for virtual machine storage).
- **Databases:** Azure offers various database services, including relational databases like Azure SQL Database and NoSQL databases like Cosmos DB, to store and manage your application data.
- **Web Apps:** These simplify the deployment and management of web applications, providing features like automatic scaling and high availability.
- **Network Resources:** These include virtual networks, load balancers, and VPN gateways, allowing you to create and manage your network infrastructure in the cloud.

Resource Management

Azure resources are created within resource groups, which help you organize and manage them as a unit. You can manage your resources through various tools:

- **Azure Portal:** A web-based interface for visually managing your resources.
- **Azure CLI:** A command-line interface for managing resources using scripts and automation.
- **Azure PowerShell:** A scripting language for managing resources in a PowerShell environment.
- **Azure Resource Manager (ARM) Templates:** These are JSON files that define your infrastructure as code, enabling consistent and repeatable deployments.
- **REST APIs:** Programmatic interfaces for managing resources from your applications.

The choice of management tool depends on your preference and the level of automation you require.

Building Solutions with Azure Resources

Azure offers a vast array of resources, each designed to address specific needs. By combining these resources, you can build a wide range of cloud-based solutions, such as:

- **Websites and web applications:** Use VMs, Web Apps, and storage accounts to build scalable and reliable web solutions.
- **Mobile apps:** Leverage Azure App Service, Azure Functions, and storage accounts to build backend services for your mobile applications.

- **Data analytics solutions:** Use Azure Data Lake, Azure Synapse Analytics, and Azure Machine Learning to store, process, and analyze large datasets.
- **IoT solutions:** Connect and manage IoT devices using Azure IoT Hub and build real-time dashboards using Azure Stream Analytics.
- **AI-powered applications:** Integrate Azure Cognitive Services to add intelligent capabilities like image recognition, natural language processing, and translation to your applications.

As you progress through this book, you'll learn more about the various types of Azure resources available and how to use them to build your own cloud solutions.

Azure Resource Manager

Behind the scenes of Azure's seamless resource management lies the Azure Resource Manager (ARM). Think of it as the brain of Azure, orchestrating the creation, deployment, and management of all your resources. Let's explore what ARM is and how it leverages templates to revolutionize infrastructure management.

Azure Resource Manager: The Orchestrator

Azure Resource Manager is the deployment and management service for Azure resources. It enables you to work with resources as a group, rather than individually. When you deploy, update, or delete a resource in Azure, you interact with ARM. It handles the underlying coordination, ensuring that your resources are created in the correct order and dependencies are managed appropriately.

ARM Templates: Infrastructure as Code

ARM utilizes templates to define your Azure infrastructure as code. An ARM template is a JSON (JavaScript Object Notation) file that describes the resources you want to deploy, along with their properties and dependencies. This template acts as a blueprint for your Azure solution, allowing you to define your entire infrastructure in a single, declarative file.

By using ARM templates, you can treat your infrastructure like code. This means you can version control your templates, collaborate with others, and automate deployments. Instead of manually clicking through the Azure portal to create resources, you can define everything in a template and deploy it with a single command.

Benefits of ARM Templates

ARM templates offer several significant benefits:

- **Consistent and Repeatable Deployments:** Templates ensure that your infrastructure is deployed consistently every time, reducing the risk of human error and configuration drift.
- **Version Control:** You can track changes to your templates using version control systems like Git, making it easier to roll back to previous versions if needed.
- **Automation:** You can automate deployments using tools like Azure DevOps or GitHub Actions, saving time and effort.
- **Simplified Management:** By managing your infrastructure as code, you can easily update and maintain your Azure resources.

Examples of ARM Templates in Action

ARM templates can be used to deploy a wide range of Azure solutions, from simple web apps to complex multi-tier architectures. Here are a few examples:

- **Deploying a virtual machine with a network interface:** An ARM template can define the virtual machine, network interface, and associated resources like virtual networks and public IP addresses.
- **Creating a web app with a database:** You can use a template to deploy a web app along with a database, ensuring that the database connection strings are configured correctly.
- **Building a multi-tier application:** For more complex applications, you can use ARM templates to deploy multiple virtual machines, load balancers, and databases, orchestrating the deployment in the correct order.

By leveraging ARM templates, you can streamline your Azure deployments, improve consistency, and embrace a more efficient and automated approach to infrastructure management.

Chapter Summary

This chapter introduced you to several fundamental concepts that underpin how Azure organizes and manages resources. We began with **Azure subscriptions**, the logical containers that tie resources together for billing and access management. We then discussed **resource groups**, which provide a way to logically group resources that share a common lifecycle for easier deployment, updates, and deletion.

Next, we explored the geographical distribution of Azure, starting with **regions**, the physical locations where Azure data centers reside. We highlighted the concept of **region pairs** for redundancy and disaster recovery. We also delved into **Availability Zones**, distinct physical locations within a region that offer additional resilience against localized failures. Choosing the right region and Availability Zone involves balancing factors like proximity to users, data residency requirements, and service availability.

Finally, we defined **Azure resources** as the individual building blocks of your cloud solutions, from virtual machines to databases to web apps. We explained how resources are created within resource groups and can be managed through the Azure portal, command-line interfaces, or APIs. We wrapped up by introducing **Azure Resource Manager (ARM)**, the service that orchestrates resource deployment and management. ARM templates, which define your infrastructure as code, offer benefits like consistency, version control, automation, and simplified management.

Understanding these core concepts lays a solid foundation for your journey into the world of Azure. As you progress, you'll see how these concepts come into play as you create, manage, and scale your Azure solutions. The next chapter will guide you through the Azure Portal, the primary interface for interacting with Azure resources.

The Azure Portal – Your Gateway to Azure

Outline

- Introduction to the Azure Portal
- Key Features and Functionality
- Navigating the Portal Interface
- Accessing and Managing Resources
- Customizing Your Portal Experience
- Tips and Tricks for Using the Portal
- Chapter Summary

Introduction to the Azure Portal

Welcome to your command center for navigating the vast landscape of Microsoft Azure. The Azure Portal is a web-based user interface designed to be your one-stop shop for everything Azure. Just as you might use a control panel to manage your car's settings, the Azure Portal lets you oversee and interact with all your cloud resources in one place.

Your Central Hub for Azure

Imagine the Azure Portal as your personal dashboard into the cloud. It provides a user-friendly and intuitive way to access and manage your Azure subscriptions, create and configure resources, monitor the health and performance of your services, and explore the vast array of tools and services available.

Think of it as your mission control center for your cloud infrastructure. From here, you can launch new virtual machines, set up storage accounts, deploy web apps, configure networking, analyze data, and much more. It's your central hub for navigating the entire Azure ecosystem.

Key Benefits of the Azure Portal

- **Ease of Use:** The portal is designed to be user-friendly, even for those new to cloud computing. It provides a graphical interface with intuitive controls, wizards, and helpful documentation to guide you through tasks.
- **Comprehensive Management:** You can manage all aspects of your Azure resources from the portal, including provisioning, configuration, monitoring, and troubleshooting. This centralized approach simplifies management and reduces the need for multiple tools.
- **Customization:** The portal is highly customizable, allowing you to tailor it to your specific needs and preferences. You can create custom dashboards, add favorite resources, and personalize settings to optimize your experience.
- **Always Up-to-Date:** Microsoft continuously updates the Azure Portal with new features and improvements. This ensures that you have access to the latest capabilities and security enhancements.

In the following sections, we'll take a closer look at the Azure Portal's key features, navigation, and how to effectively use it to manage your Azure resources. By the end of this chapter, you'll be comfortable navigating the portal and using it to unleash the full power of Azure.

Key Features and Functionality

The Azure Portal is packed with features to streamline your cloud management experience. Let's explore some of its key functionalities:

Dashboard: Your Azure at a Glance

Upon logging in, you're greeted by the Azure Portal Dashboard. This customizable overview is your snapshot of your Azure environment. It offers:

- **Quick Access:** Easily access recently used resources, services, and favorites.
- **Service Health:** Get real-time updates on the health of Azure services in your region.
- **Resource Usage:** Monitor key metrics like CPU usage, network traffic, and storage consumption for your resources.
- **Personalized Widgets:** Add widgets to display information relevant to your role or tasks.
- **Customization:** Arrange widgets and layouts to suit your preferences.

Search Bar: Your Navigator

The search bar is your gateway to quickly finding anything within the Azure Portal. Whether you're looking for a specific resource, service, or documentation, simply start typing in the search bar, and Azure will suggest relevant results. It's a powerful tool for navigating the vast Azure ecosystem efficiently.

Resource Creation: Your Building Blocks

The Azure Portal simplifies the process of creating and configuring resources. Each service offers a streamlined interface with intuitive steps for provisioning and configuring your resources. You'll find helpful tooltips, documentation links, and validation checks to guide you through the process. For instance, creating a virtual machine involves selecting the operating system, size, storage options, and networking settings, all within a user-friendly wizard.

Monitoring and Alerts: Your Watchful Eye

Monitoring the health and performance of your Azure resources is crucial. The Azure Portal provides built-in monitoring tools that let you:

- **Track Metrics:** Monitor key performance indicators like CPU utilization, memory usage, and network traffic.
- **Set Alerts:** Configure alerts to notify you when specific conditions are met, such as high CPU usage or low disk space.
- **Analyze Logs:** View detailed logs to diagnose and troubleshoot issues.
- **Visualize Data:** Create custom dashboards to display real-time metrics and trends.

With these tools, you can proactively identify and resolve problems before they impact your users.

Cost Management: Your Budget Guardian

The Azure Portal offers a suite of cost management tools to help you track and optimize your cloud spending. You can:

- **Analyze Costs:** Get detailed breakdowns of your Azure costs by resource, service, and time period.
- **Set Budgets:** Create budgets and receive alerts when you approach or exceed your spending limits.
- **Forecast Costs:** Estimate your future costs based on your current usage patterns.
- **Get Recommendations:** Azure Advisor provides personalized recommendations for optimizing your resources and reducing costs.

By using these tools, you can gain visibility into your cloud spending, identify areas for cost savings, and make informed decisions about your Azure resources.

Conclusion

The Azure Portal is a powerful and versatile tool for managing your Azure resources. Its intuitive interface, comprehensive features, and customization options make it an indispensable tool for anyone working with Azure. As you continue your journey with Azure, you'll discover even more ways to leverage the portal to streamline your cloud management and unlock the full potential of the cloud.

Navigating the Portal Interface

To effectively use the Azure Portal, you'll need to get familiar with its interface. It's designed to be intuitive and user-friendly, with clear navigation and access to all the tools you need. Let's take a tour of the key elements:

The Menu: Your Azure Roadmap

On the left-hand side of the portal, you'll find the **Menu**. It's your roadmap to all the different Azure services and resources. The menu is divided into categories like:

- **Create a resource:** This section allows you to quickly create new resources like virtual machines, web apps, or databases.
- **Azure services:** Here you'll find a list of all the Azure services, organized into categories like Compute, Networking, Storage, and more.
- **Favorites:** This is where you can pin your most frequently used services or resources for quick access.
- **Resource groups:** This section provides access to your resource groups, which are collections of related resources.
- **Recent resources:** Quickly access resources that you've recently used.
- **Help + support:** Find documentation, troubleshooting guides, and community support here.

You can expand or collapse the menu categories to navigate through the hierarchy. The search bar at the top of the menu lets you quickly search for specific services or resources.

The Toolbar: Your Control Center

At the top of the Azure Portal, you'll find the **Toolbar**. It gives you quick access to essential functions and settings:

- **Subscription filter:** Switch between different Azure subscriptions you have access to.
- **Directory + subscription filter:** Switch between different Azure Active Directory tenants and subscriptions.
- **Cloud Shell:** Open the Azure Cloud Shell, a browser-based command-line interface for managing Azure resources.
- **Notifications:** View notifications about service health, alerts, and other important updates.
- **Settings:** Customize your Azure Portal experience, such as the theme, language, and default view.
- **Help:** Access help resources and documentation.
- **Your account:** Manage your Azure account settings and profile.

Breadcrumbs: Your Trail of Navigation

As you navigate through the Azure Portal, you'll notice **breadcrumbs** at the top of the page. These act like a trail of your navigation, showing you the path you've taken to reach your current location. You can click on any of the breadcrumbs to quickly jump back to a previous section. This feature is especially helpful when you're exploring complex hierarchies of resources or services.

Conclusion

By familiarizing yourself with the menu, toolbar, and breadcrumbs, you'll be able to navigate the Azure Portal with ease. This knowledge will empower you to quickly find and manage your Azure resources, explore new services, and make the most of your cloud experience.

Accessing and Managing Resources

Once you're familiar with the Azure Portal's interface, it's time to dive into accessing and managing your resources. The portal makes it easy to locate, monitor, and control the various components that make up your Azure environment.

Finding Resources

There are two primary ways to find resources in the Azure Portal:

1. **Search Bar:** The quickest way to find a resource is to use the search bar at the top of the portal. Simply start typing the name of the resource or a relevant keyword, and the portal will automatically suggest matching results. You can also filter your search by resource type, location, or subscription.
2. **Menu:** If you prefer browsing, use the menu on the left-hand side of the portal. Expand the relevant service category (e.g., Compute, Networking, Storage) and then select the resource type you're looking for (e.g., Virtual Machines, Virtual Networks, Storage Accounts). The portal will display a list of all the resources of that type within your selected subscription.

Resource Overview

When you click on a resource in the search results or the resource list, you'll be taken to the resource overview page. This page provides a wealth of information about the resource, including:

- **Resource Name:** The name you assigned to the resource when you created it.
- **Resource Type:** The type of resource, such as Virtual Machine, Storage Account, or Web App.
- **Subscription:** The Azure subscription the resource belongs to.
- **Resource Group:** The resource group the resource is associated with.
- **Location:** The Azure region where the resource is deployed.
- **Status:** The current status of the resource (e.g., Running, Stopped, Provisioning).
- **Essential Properties:** Key properties of the resource, such as its IP address, size, or configuration settings.

The resource overview page also has a menu on the left-hand side that provides access to various options for managing the resource. These options vary depending on the type of resource, but generally include settings, monitoring, activity logs, access control, and more.

Resource Actions

The Azure Portal makes it easy to perform common actions on your resources:

- **Start/Stop/Restart:** For virtual machines and some other types of resources, you can start, stop, or restart them directly from the overview page. This is useful for managing the availability and cost of your resources.
- **Scale:** For resources that support scaling, you can increase or decrease their capacity to meet demand. This might involve adding more virtual machines to a web app during peak traffic periods or increasing the storage capacity of a database.
- **Delete:** When a resource is no longer needed, you can delete it to free up resources and avoid unnecessary costs.
- **Other Actions:** Depending on the resource type, you might have access to other actions like backup, restore, resize, and update.

To perform an action on a resource, simply select the desired action from the menu or the overview page. The portal will guide you through the necessary steps and provide feedback on the progress and outcome of the action.

Tips for Managing Resources

Here are a few tips to help you manage your Azure resources effectively:

- **Use tags:** Tags are key-value pairs that you can assign to resources to categorize them and make them easier to find and manage.
- **Set up alerts:** Configure alerts to notify you when specific conditions are met, such as high CPU usage or low disk space. This allows you to proactively address potential issues.
- **Automate tasks:** Use Azure Automation or Azure Logic Apps to automate repetitive tasks like starting and stopping virtual machines or backing up data.
- **Monitor costs:** Regularly review your Azure cost management reports to track your spending and identify areas for optimization.

By mastering the tools and techniques for accessing and managing your Azure resources, you'll be well-equipped to build and maintain a successful cloud environment.

Customizing Your Portal Experience

The Azure Portal isn't just a static interface; it's designed to be flexible and adaptable to your individual needs and preferences. By customizing the portal, you can create a more personalized and efficient experience that aligns with your workflow and priorities.

Dashboards: Tailored Views of Your Azure World

The Azure Portal offers the ability to create custom dashboards. These are like personalized control panels that display the information and metrics most relevant to you. You can:

- **Choose from Pre-built Templates:** Azure provides several pre-built templates for common scenarios, such as monitoring a web app or managing virtual machines.
- **Start from Scratch:** Create a blank dashboard and add the widgets you want.
- **Add Widgets:** Widgets are the building blocks of dashboards. They display various types of information, such as charts, graphs, maps, lists, and tiles. You can add widgets for specific resources, services, or metrics.
- **Arrange and Resize:** Drag and drop widgets to arrange them on your dashboard. Resize them to fit your layout preferences.
- **Save and Share:** Save your custom dashboards and share them with colleagues who might find them useful.

Favorites: Quick Access to Your Go-To Resources

If you have resources that you use frequently, you can add them to your **Favorites** list for quick access. This saves you the hassle of navigating through the menu or searching for the resource every time.

To add a resource to your favorites:

1. Go to the resource's overview page.
2. Click the star icon next to the resource name.

Your favorited resources will then appear in the Favorites section of the menu for easy access.

Settings: Personalize Your Portal

The Azure Portal offers various settings that you can customize to create a more personalized experience:

- **Theme:** Choose between light and dark themes to suit your visual preferences.
- **Language:** Select your preferred language for the portal interface.
- **Default View:** Choose whether you want the portal to open to the Home page or a specific dashboard.
- **Notifications:** Control the types of notifications you receive and how they are delivered.

To access these settings, click on the **Settings** icon in the top-right corner of the portal.

Additional Customization Tips

- **Pin Tiles:** You can pin specific tiles to the dashboard for quick access to important actions or information.
- **Customize Dashboards for Different Roles:** Create separate dashboards for different roles or tasks. For example, a system administrator might create a dashboard focused on infrastructure health, while a developer might create one focused on application monitoring.
- **Explore the Marketplace:** The Azure Marketplace offers a wide variety of third-party tools and extensions that can further enhance your portal experience.

By taking the time to personalize the Azure Portal, you can create a workspace that's tailored to your unique needs and preferences. This can lead to increased productivity, faster decision-making, and a more enjoyable overall experience in the cloud.

Tips and Tricks for Using the Portal

To truly master the Azure Portal and maximize your productivity, try incorporating these handy tips and tricks:

Keyboard Shortcuts: Navigate with Speed

The Azure Portal offers a variety of keyboard shortcuts to help you navigate faster and perform actions more efficiently. Here are some of the most useful ones:

- **G + /:** Open the search bar.
- **G + .:** Navigate to the command bar at the top of a resource page.
- **G + N:** Create a new resource.
- **G + A:** Go to All resources.
- **G + D:** Go to the Dashboard.
- **G + R:** Go to Resource groups.
- **G + B:** Go to All services.

You can find a complete list of keyboard shortcuts in the Azure Portal documentation: https://learn.microsoft.com/en-us/azure/azure-portal/azure-portal-keyboard-shortcuts

Azure Cloud Shell: Your Command-Line Companion

The Azure Cloud Shell is a browser-based command-line interface that gives you the power of Azure CLI or Azure PowerShell right within the portal. This means you can run commands and scripts directly from your browser without having to install any software on your local machine.

To access the Cloud Shell, click on the >_ icon in the top toolbar of the portal. You can then choose between Bash (for Azure CLI) or PowerShell environments. The Cloud Shell comes pre-configured with Azure tools and utilities, making it easy to manage your resources from the command line.

Help and Support: Get Assistance When You Need It

The Azure Portal provides several resources to help you get assistance when you encounter issues or have questions:

- **Documentation:** Most pages in the portal have a "Documentation" link that takes you to the relevant Azure documentation for that service or feature.
- **Help + support:** This section of the menu provides access to various support options, including troubleshooting guides, community forums, and support tickets.
- **? icon:** Look for the question mark icon (?) throughout the portal. Clicking on it will usually open a contextual help pane with relevant information.

Remember, the Azure Portal is constantly evolving, so don't hesitate to explore and discover new features and shortcuts to improve your workflow.

By incorporating these tips and tricks into your Azure Portal usage, you'll be able to navigate the portal more efficiently, manage resources with ease, and get the most out of your cloud experience.

Chapter Summary

This chapter has served as your introduction to the Azure Portal, your central command center for managing all things Azure. We explored the portal's key features, including the dashboard for quick overviews, the powerful search bar for finding resources, the user-friendly interface for creating and configuring resources, the built-in monitoring tools, and the comprehensive cost management capabilities.

We also took a guided tour of the portal interface, covering the navigation menu, toolbar options, and the helpful breadcrumbs for tracking your location within the portal. We provided detailed instructions on accessing and managing resources, from finding them using the search bar or menu to performing common actions like start/stop, scaling, and deleting.

We emphasized the importance of customizing the Azure Portal to fit your individual needs, from creating personalized dashboards to adding frequently used resources to your favorites. We also shared tips and tricks to enhance your experience, such as using keyboard shortcuts, leveraging the Azure Cloud Shell for command-line access, and utilizing the built-in help and support resources.

With this newfound knowledge of the Azure Portal, you're well-prepared to embark on your journey of creating and managing resources in the cloud. As we move into the next section of this book, you'll put these skills into practice by creating your first Azure account and diving deeper into the portal's capabilities.

Section 2:
Getting Started with Azure

Creating Your First Azure Account

Outline

- Types of Azure Accounts
- Choosing the Right Account for You
- Signing Up for an Azure Account
- Activating Benefits and Free Credits (if applicable)
- Verifying Your Identity
- Exploring the Azure Portal
- Chapter Summary

Types of Azure Accounts

Azure offers a variety of account options to suit different users, from those who are just starting their cloud journey to large enterprises with complex requirements. Let's break down the main types of Azure accounts:

Free Trial

The Azure Free Trial is your gateway to the cloud. It's designed for new users who want to explore Azure's vast array of services without any upfront costs. With a free trial, you get:

- **Free Credits:** You'll receive a certain amount of credits that you can use to experiment with different Azure services. This gives you hands-on experience without spending any money.
- **Limited-Time Access:** The free trial typically lasts for a month, giving you ample time to explore and learn.
- **Selected Services:** Not all Azure services are available in the free trial. You'll have access to a selection of popular services to get you started.

The free trial is an excellent option for beginners who want to dip their toes into the world of Azure and get a feel for its capabilities. It allows you to try out different services, learn how to create and manage resources, and build a solid foundation in Azure before deciding on a paid subscription.

Pay-As-You-Go

Pay-As-You-Go is Azure's most flexible pricing model. With this option, you pay only for the resources you actually consume. There are no upfront costs or termination fees, and you can scale your resources up or down as needed. This makes it ideal for:

- **Variable Workloads:** If your cloud usage fluctuates, Pay-As-You-Go lets you adapt your spending accordingly.
- **Short-Term Projects:** You can quickly spin up resources for a specific project and shut them down when finished, paying only for the duration of use.

- **Cost Control:** Pay-As-You-Go gives you fine-grained control over your spending, allowing you to set budgets and alerts to avoid unexpected charges.

While it offers flexibility, Pay-As-You-Go can become costly if you have consistently high usage. In such cases, reserved instances (discussed in Chapter 2) may be a more cost-effective option.

Azure for Students

If you're a student enrolled in an accredited academic institution, you can take advantage of the Azure for Students program. This program provides you with:

- **Free Access to Azure Services:** You get free credits to use on a wide range of Azure services.
- **No Credit Card Required:** Unlike the free trial, you don't need to provide a credit card to sign up for Azure for Students.
- **Learning Resources:** The program includes access to learning resources and tutorials to help you get started with Azure.

Azure for Students is a great way for aspiring cloud professionals to gain hands-on experience with Azure and build their skills without any financial burden.

Enterprise Agreement

The Enterprise Agreement is a specialized offering designed for large organizations with significant cloud needs. It provides:

- **Discounted Rates:** Organizations that commit to a certain level of spending with Azure can receive discounted rates on services.
- **Customized Billing Options:** Enterprise Agreements offer flexible billing options tailored to the organization's specific requirements.
- **Dedicated Support:** Organizations with Enterprise Agreements have access to dedicated support teams and additional resources.

This option is best suited for large enterprises that have a well-defined cloud strategy and are looking for a long-term partnership with Microsoft Azure.

Choosing the Right Account for You

Selecting the ideal Azure account is a crucial first step in your cloud journey. Your choice will depend on several factors, including your budget, the scope of your projects, and the specific features you require.

Here's a breakdown of the best account types for different scenarios:

- **For Beginners and Experimentation:** If you're new to Azure and want to get a hands-on feel for its capabilities, the **Free Trial** is the perfect starting point. It provides you with free credits to explore various services without any financial commitment. This allows you to experiment, learn the ropes, and decide if Azure is the right fit for you.
- **For Small Projects and Individual Use:** If you have a small project or personal use case, the **Pay-As-You-Go** option offers the most flexibility. You only pay for what you use, so it's ideal if you anticipate low or intermittent usage.
- **For Students:** If you're a student, the **Azure for Students** program is a fantastic opportunity to learn and experiment with Azure without cost. It provides free access to a wide range of Azure services, perfect for coursework, personal projects, or building your cloud skills.
- **For Large Organizations and Enterprise Needs:** For larger organizations with predictable usage patterns and complex requirements, an **Enterprise Agreement** might be the most suitable option.

It offers discounted rates, customized billing options, and dedicated support, making it a valuable choice for long-term, large-scale cloud deployments.

Consider These Factors When Choosing

- **Budget:** Determine your budget for cloud services. The Free Trial and Azure for Students options are excellent for those with limited or no budget, while Pay-As-You-Go allows for greater flexibility and cost control.
- **Project Scope:** Consider the size and complexity of your projects. If you have simple projects or want to experiment, the Free Trial is a good starting point. For larger, ongoing projects, Pay-As-You-Go or an Enterprise Agreement may be more suitable.
- **Features:** Identify the specific Azure services and features you need. Not all services are available in the Free Trial, so if you have specific requirements, Pay-As-You-Go or an Enterprise Agreement may be necessary to access the full range of Azure's offerings.
- **Long-Term Needs:** Think about your long-term cloud strategy. If you plan to use Azure extensively in the future, investing in a Pay-As-You-Go or Enterprise Agreement may be a more cost-effective option in the long run.

Starting Your Azure Journey

No matter which account type you choose, creating an Azure account is the first step to unlocking the power of cloud computing. In the following sections, we'll guide you through the process of signing up for an Azure account and getting started with the Azure Portal.

Remember, the best way to learn Azure is by doing. So don't hesitate to experiment and explore different services to discover how Azure can empower your projects and accelerate your cloud journey.

Signing Up for an Azure Account

Getting started with Azure is simple and straightforward. Just follow these steps to create your first Azure account:

1. **Navigate to the Azure Website:**
   Open your web browser and go to the Azure website: https://azure.microsoft.com/free/. This will take you to the page where you can start your free trial.
2. **Choose Your Account Type:**
   Click on the "Start free" button. You'll be presented with options to sign in with an existing Microsoft account or create a new one. If you don't have a Microsoft account, you'll need to create one to proceed.
3. **Enter Personal Information:**
   You'll be asked to provide your name, email address, phone number, and country/region. Make sure to enter accurate information, as this will be used for verification and communication purposes.
4. **Verify Your Phone Number and Email Address:**
   Azure will send a verification code to your phone number and email address. Enter these codes to verify your contact information. This step is essential to ensure the security of your account and prevent unauthorized access.
5. **Provide Billing Information (If Applicable):**
   If you're signing up for a Pay-As-You-Go account, you'll be asked to provide your billing information, including your credit card details. This information is used for billing purposes and to verify your identity. If you're opting for the Free Trial, you usually won't need to provide billing information initially, but you might be asked for it later if you choose to upgrade to a paid subscription.
6. **Agree to the Terms and Conditions:**
   Carefully review the Azure terms and conditions, privacy statement, and offer details. If you agree to the terms, check the box and click on the "Sign up" button.

7. **Welcome to Azure!:**
   Congratulations! You've successfully created your Azure account. You'll be redirected to the Azure Portal, where you can start exploring and creating resources in the cloud.

Important Notes:

- The exact steps and information required may vary slightly depending on your location and the specific Azure offer you choose.
- Make sure to read the instructions carefully and provide accurate information to avoid any delays or issues with your account activation.
- If you encounter any problems during the sign-up process, Azure provides helpful resources and support channels to assist you.

Now that you have your Azure account, it's time to dive into the exciting world of cloud computing!

Activating Benefits and Free Credits (if applicable)

Congratulations on creating your Azure account! If you've opted for the Free Trial or Azure for Students program, you have access to valuable benefits and free credits to kickstart your cloud exploration. Here's how to activate them:

Free Trial Activation

1. **Log into the Azure Portal:** After signing up, you'll automatically be directed to the Azure Portal. If not, simply visit the Azure website and log in with your credentials.
2. **Check Your Credits:** In the Azure Portal, you should see a notification about your free trial credits. You can also view your credit balance in the "Cost Management + Billing" section.
3. **Start Exploring:** You can immediately start using your credits to try out various Azure services. Azure provides a helpful "Get started" guide to help you explore the most popular services.

Azure for Students Activation

1. **Verify Your Eligibility:** If you haven't already, you'll need to verify your student status through the Azure for Students portal. This typically involves providing your academic email address or other proof of enrollment.
2. **Activate Your Credits:** Once your eligibility is confirmed, you'll receive an email with instructions on how to activate your $100 Azure credit. Simply follow the link in the email and complete the activation process.
3. **Start Learning and Building:** With your credits activated, you're ready to explore Azure's vast array of services and start building your cloud skills.

Important Notes:

- **Expiration:** Free trial credits typically expire after a specific period (e.g., 30 days). Make sure to use them before they expire.
- **Usage:** Free credits can be used for most Azure services, but some exclusions may apply. Refer to the offer details for more information.
- **Upgrade:** If you exhaust your free credits or want to continue using Azure beyond the trial period, you can easily upgrade to a Pay-As-You-Go subscription.

Remember, the Azure Free Trial and Azure for Students program provide a fantastic opportunity to learn and experiment with Azure without incurring any costs. Take advantage of these offers to gain hands-on experience and build a strong foundation in cloud computing.

Verifying Your Identity

Verifying your identity is a crucial step in the Azure account creation process. It serves several important purposes:

- **Fraud Prevention:** Identity verification helps to prevent fraudulent activity and protect your financial information. It ensures that the person creating the account is the legitimate owner of the payment method and reduces the risk of unauthorized charges.
- **Account Security:** Verifying your identity adds an extra layer of security to your Azure account. It makes it more difficult for unauthorized individuals to gain access to your resources and data.
- **Compliance:** In some cases, identity verification is required to comply with regulatory requirements, particularly for accounts used by businesses or organizations.

Verification Process

The verification process typically involves one of the following methods:

- **Credit Card:** You'll be asked to provide your credit card information. A small temporary charge may be placed on your card, which is usually reversed within a few days. This charge helps to verify that the card is valid and that you have access to it.
- **Phone Number:** You'll receive a text message or phone call with a verification code. Entering this code confirms that you have access to the phone number associated with the account.

In some cases, Azure may require additional verification steps, such as providing a government-issued ID or confirming your address. This is usually only necessary for certain account types or for accounts that exhibit suspicious activity.

Why is Verification Important?

By verifying your identity, you help protect your Azure account and prevent unauthorized use. It's a small but important step in ensuring the security of your cloud resources and data.

If you have any concerns about providing your personal information, rest assured that Microsoft takes privacy and security seriously. Azure adheres to strict data protection standards and employs robust security measures to safeguard your information.

Exploring the Azure Portal

Welcome to the Azure Portal, your gateway to the cloud! Now that your account is up and running, let's take a brief tour to get you acquainted with this powerful interface.

Logging In

1. Open your web browser and navigate to the Azure Portal website: https://portal.azure.com/
2. Enter the email address associated with your Azure account and click "Next."
3. Enter your password and click "Sign in."

Your First Look: The Dashboard

The first thing you'll see after logging in is the Azure Dashboard. This is your personalized overview of your Azure environment. It's a central hub where you can:

- **View Recent Resources:** Quickly access resources you've recently worked on.
- **Monitor Service Health:** Get real-time updates on the status of Azure services.
- **Track Resource Usage:** Monitor the usage of your Azure resources.

- **Customize Widgets:** Add or remove widgets to display information relevant to you.

Finding Your Way Around: The Menu and Search Bar

On the left-hand side of the portal, you'll find the menu. It's your navigation bar for exploring Azure services and resources. Here you can:

- **Create a resource:** Quickly create new resources like virtual machines, storage accounts, or web apps.
- **Browse Azure services:** Explore the full range of Azure services organized by category (Compute, Networking, Storage, etc.).
- **Access your resource groups:** See all your resource groups and the resources they contain.
- **Manage your account:** View billing information, update your profile, and manage subscriptions.

At the top of the portal is the search bar. It's a powerful tool for quickly finding any resource, service, or documentation within Azure. Simply start typing, and the portal will suggest relevant results.

Take a Tour and Get Familiar

The best way to learn the Azure Portal is by exploring it yourself. Here are a few things you can do to get started:

- **Click Around:** Click on different sections of the menu and explore the various options.
- **Search for Resources:** Use the search bar to find specific resources or services.
- **Create a Resource:** Try creating a simple resource like a storage account to get a feel for the process.
- **Read the Documentation:** Azure has extensive documentation that can help you understand the portal and its features.

Ready for More?

Now that you've had a brief introduction to the Azure Portal, you're ready to dive deeper into managing your Azure resources. In the next chapter, we'll guide you through navigating the portal in more detail and creating your first Azure resources.

Chapter Summary

This chapter has equipped you with the essential knowledge to embark on your Azure journey. We covered the diverse types of Azure accounts available, from the Free Trial for beginners to the Enterprise Agreement for large organizations, guiding you in choosing the one that best suits your needs. You now understand the importance of verifying your identity to enhance account security and prevent fraud.

Finally, we provided a guided tour of the Azure Portal, your central command center for managing your Azure resources. We pointed out key areas like the dashboard, search bar, and menu, encouraging you to explore the portal's interface and become familiar with its basic functionalities.

With your Azure account set up and a basic understanding of the portal, you're ready to take the next step. In the following chapters, we'll delve deeper into navigating the portal, creating your first resources, and exploring the vast array of services Azure has to offer. Get ready to harness the power of the cloud and unleash your creativity with Azure!

Navigating the Azure Portal

Outline

- Accessing the Azure Portal
- Exploring the Dashboard
- Using the Search Functionality
- Understanding the Left-Hand Navigation Menu
- Working with Resource Groups
- Exploring the Top Menu Bar
- Customizing the Portal
- Chapter Summary

Accessing the Azure Portal

Accessing your Azure Portal is the first step towards managing your cloud resources. It's a simple process that you'll quickly become familiar with. Let's walk through it:

1. **Open Your Web Browser:** Launch your preferred web browser (Google Chrome, Mozilla Firefox, Microsoft Edge, etc.).
2. **Navigate to the Azure Portal:** Enter the following URL in your browser's address bar: https://portal.azure.com/
3. **Sign In with Your Microsoft Account:** You'll be directed to the Azure Portal login page. Enter the email address associated with your Azure account (the one you used to create the account) and click "Next."
4. **Enter Your Password:** On the next screen, enter your Microsoft account password and click "Sign in." If you've enabled two-factor authentication, you'll be prompted to provide a verification code.
5. **Welcome to Your Azure Portal:** Upon successful login, you'll be greeted by the Azure Portal dashboard, your personalized command center for managing your cloud resources.

Important Note: If you don't have a Microsoft account, you can easily create one for free by clicking on the "Create one!" link on the login page.

Exploring the Dashboard

Welcome to your Azure Dashboard – your personalized command center! Think of it as your home base within the Azure Portal, providing you with a bird's-eye view of your cloud environment and quick access to essential information and tools.

Your Azure Overview

The dashboard offers a comprehensive overview of your Azure resources and services. It's designed to give you a snapshot of what's happening in your Azure world, allowing you to quickly assess the health and performance of your applications and infrastructure.

Key Sections of the Dashboard

- **Recent Resources:** This section displays a list of resources you've recently accessed, making it easy to jump back to your ongoing projects.
- **Service Health:** Keep an eye on this section for real-time updates on the health of Azure services in your region. It alerts you to any potential issues or planned maintenance that might affect your resources.

- **Resource Providers:** View the status of resource providers, which are the services responsible for managing specific types of Azure resources. This helps you understand if any issues are related to the underlying resource providers.
- **Marketplace:** Explore the Azure Marketplace, where you can find a vast collection of pre-built applications, solutions, and services that you can deploy to your Azure environment.
- **Quickstart Center:** New to Azure? The Quickstart Center offers tutorials and guides to help you get started with various Azure services and features.
- **Cost Management:** This section provides a quick overview of your Azure spending, allowing you to track your costs and identify potential areas for optimization.

Customization: Making It Your Own

One of the great things about the Azure dashboard is that you can customize it to fit your specific needs and preferences. You have the flexibility to:

- **Add and Remove Tiles:** You can add tiles for specific resources, services, or metrics that are important to you. You can also remove tiles that you don't need.
- **Rearrange Tiles:** Drag and drop tiles to arrange them in the order that works best for you.
- **Change Tile Sizes:** You can resize tiles to make them larger or smaller, depending on how much information you want to see.
- **Create Multiple Dashboards:** You can create multiple dashboards for different purposes, such as a dashboard for each project or team, or a dashboard for specific types of resources.
- **Share Dashboards:** You can share your custom dashboards with other members of your team to provide them with the same view of your Azure environment.

Your Personalized Command Center

By customizing your dashboard, you can create a personalized view that gives you immediate access to the most relevant information and tools for your work. Whether you're a developer, IT administrator, or business analyst, you can tailor the dashboard to meet your specific needs.

In the next section, we'll dive deeper into the powerful search functionality of the Azure Portal, which allows you to quickly find any resource, service, or documentation within Azure.

Using the Search Functionality

One of the most powerful tools in the Azure Portal is the search bar. Located prominently at the top of the page, it acts as your gateway to quickly finding anything you need within the vast Azure ecosystem. Whether you're hunting for a specific resource, service, or piece of documentation, the search bar is your go-to tool.

How to Use the Search Bar

Using the search bar is incredibly simple:

1. **Click or Type:** You can either click on the search bar to activate it or simply start typing to initiate a search.
2. **Enter Your Search Term:** Type in the name of the resource, service, or keyword you're looking for. As you type, Azure will dynamically suggest potential matches based on your input.
3. **Review and Select:** A list of matching results will appear below the search bar. You can then click on the desired result to navigate directly to it.

Refining Your Search with Filters

To narrow down your search and find exactly what you need, you can use the filters available in the search results pane. These filters allow you to:

- **Filter by Resource Type:** Select specific resource types like virtual machines, storage accounts, or web apps to filter the results accordingly.
- **Filter by Location:** Choose a specific Azure region to see resources deployed in that location.
- **Filter by Subscription:** Limit the search results to a specific Azure subscription.

By combining keywords and filters, you can quickly pinpoint the exact resource or service you're looking for.

Tips for Effective Searching

Here are some tips to get the most out of the search bar:

- **Be Specific:** The more specific your search term, the more accurate your results will be. Instead of searching for "VM," try searching for "my-web-server-vm" if you know the name of the virtual machine you're looking for.
- **Use Quotes for Exact Matches:** Enclose your search term in quotes (e.g., "web app service") if you want to find exact matches.
- **Use Wildcards:** Use the asterisk (*) wildcard to search for partial matches. For example, searching for "web app *" will return results for all resources that start with "web app."
- **Combine Keywords:** Use multiple keywords to refine your search. For example, searching for "virtual machine Linux East US" will return results for Linux virtual machines deployed in the East US region.

Beyond Resources and Services

The search bar isn't just for finding resources and services. You can also use it to search for:

- **Documentation:** Find articles, tutorials, and quickstarts in the Azure documentation.
- **Marketplace items:** Discover applications, solutions, and services available in the Azure Marketplace.
- **Learning resources:** Find training courses and modules to expand your Azure knowledge.

Your Gateway to Azure

The search bar is a powerful and versatile tool that makes navigating the Azure Portal a breeze. By mastering its features and using it effectively, you can quickly find the resources, services, and information you need to succeed in your cloud journey.

Understanding the Left-Hand Navigation Menu

The left-hand navigation menu is your compass in the Azure Portal. It's a structured guide to the entire Azure ecosystem, providing a clear path to all the resources, services, and tools you need. Let's break down the key sections of the menu:

1. **Create a resource:**
    - This is your starting point for creating new resources in Azure.
    - It offers quick links to popular resources like virtual machines, web apps, storage accounts, and databases.
    - You can also search for specific resources by name or category.
2. **Azure services:**
    - This section provides a comprehensive list of all available Azure services.

- The services are organized into categories like Compute, Networking, Storage, Databases, AI + Machine Learning, and more.
- You can expand each category to see the specific services available within it.
- This is where you'll find the building blocks for creating your cloud solutions.
3. **Favorites:**
    - Pin your most frequently used resources and services here for easy access.
    - This saves you the hassle of searching for them every time.
    - You can customize your favorites list by adding or removing items.
4. **Resource groups:**
    - This section lists all the resource groups you've created.
    - Resource groups are logical containers for organizing related resources.
    - You can click on a resource group to view and manage the resources it contains.
5. **Recent resources:**
    - This section displays a list of resources you've recently accessed.
    - It's a convenient way to quickly return to resources you're working on.
6. **Help + support:**
    - This section provides access to Azure support resources.
    - You can find documentation, troubleshooting guides, community forums, and support tickets here.

Navigating the Menu

To navigate the menu, you can:

- **Click on a category or subcategory:** This will expand the section to reveal its contents.
- **Click on a resource or service:** This will take you to the overview page for that resource or service.
- **Use the search bar:** If you know the name of the resource or service you're looking for, you can use the search bar at the top of the menu to quickly find it.

Additional Tips

- **Pin the menu:** You can pin the menu open so it doesn't collapse when you navigate to other pages. This can be helpful if you frequently use the menu.
- **Customize the menu:** You can rearrange the order of items in the menu and hide items you don't use.
- **Use the "All services" view:** If you want to see a complete list of all Azure services, click on the "All services" option in the menu.

The left-hand navigation menu is a powerful tool for navigating the Azure Portal. By mastering its features, you can quickly find the resources and services you need to build and manage your cloud solutions.

Working with Resource Groups

As you start creating resources in Azure, you'll quickly realize the need for organization. That's where resource groups come in. They're like folders for your cloud resources, allowing you to group them together based on their purpose or relationship. This not only keeps your Azure environment tidy but also simplifies management and deployment tasks.

What are Resource Groups?

In Azure, a resource group is a logical container that holds related resources for a particular solution or application. For example, you might create a resource group for a web app and include the associated virtual machine, storage account, and database within that group. By grouping these resources together, you can manage them as a unit, making it easier to deploy, update, and delete them together.

Benefits of Using Resource Groups

Resource groups offer several key advantages:

- **Simplified Management:** Instead of managing individual resources separately, you can manage them collectively as a group. This saves time and effort, especially when dealing with complex applications with multiple resources.
- **Streamlined Deployment:** You can deploy all the resources in a resource group in one go using a single template or script. This ensures that all the resources are configured correctly and deployed in the right order.
- **Cost Tracking:** Resource groups allow you to track the costs associated with specific applications or solutions. This helps you monitor your spending and identify areas for optimization.
- **Access Control:** You can assign access policies to resource groups, allowing you to control who can access and manage the resources within each group.

Creating Resource Groups in the Azure Portal

Creating a resource group in the Azure Portal is a simple process:

1. **Navigate to Resource Groups:** In the left-hand navigation menu, click on "Resource groups."
2. **Click "Create":** Click the "Create" button at the top of the resource group list.
3. **Fill in the Details:** Provide the following information:
    - **Subscription:** Choose the Azure subscription you want to create the resource group in.
    - **Resource Group Name:** Enter a unique and descriptive name for your resource group.
    - **Region:** Select the Azure region where you want to deploy your resources. This should ideally be close to your users or where your data needs to reside.
4. **Click "Review + create"**: Review the information you've entered and click "Create" to create your resource group.

Viewing and Managing Resource Groups

You can view and manage your resource groups in the Azure Portal:

1. **Go to Resource Groups:** In the left-hand navigation menu, click on "Resource groups."
2. **Select a Resource Group:** Click on the resource group you want to view or manage.
3. **View Details:** The overview page displays information about the resource group, such as its name, location, and the resources it contains.
4. **Manage Resources:** You can add, remove, or modify resources within the resource group.
5. **Delete Resource Group:** If you no longer need the resource group, you can delete it, which will also delete all the resources within it.

Tips for Organizing Resource Groups

- **Use Descriptive Names:** Choose names that clearly reflect the purpose of the resource group (e.g., "Web App - Production" or "Marketing Department Resources").
- **Follow a Naming Convention:** Establish a standard naming convention for your resource groups to make them easier to identify and manage.
- **Don't Overuse Resource Groups:** Creating too many resource groups can lead to management overhead. Try to find a balance between grouping related resources and keeping the number of groups manageable.
- **Consider Resource Limits:** Each resource group has limits on the number of resources it can contain. Keep this in mind when organizing your resources.

By mastering resource groups, you'll be well on your way to efficiently organizing and managing your Azure environment.

Exploring the Top Menu Bar

The top menu bar of the Azure Portal is your control panel for managing your Azure experience. It houses a range of essential tools and settings that allow you to personalize the portal, access help resources, and quickly switch between accounts and environments. Let's delve into each of these options:

1. **Subscription filter:**
   - If you manage multiple Azure subscriptions (perhaps for different projects or clients), this dropdown menu lets you easily switch between them.
   - Selecting a subscription filters the resources and services displayed in the portal to only those associated with that specific subscription.
2. **Directory + subscription filter:**
   - For organizations using Azure Active Directory (Azure AD), this dropdown menu lets you switch between different Azure AD tenants (your organization's instance of Azure AD) and their associated subscriptions.
   - This is useful for users who have access to multiple Azure AD tenants, such as consultants or administrators who manage Azure environments for different clients.
3. **Cloud Shell:**
   - This button launches the Azure Cloud Shell, a browser-based command-line interface (CLI) that allows you to interact with Azure resources using either Bash (for Azure CLI) or PowerShell.
   - Cloud Shell provides a convenient way to run scripts, automate tasks, and manage your Azure resources from the comfort of your web browser.
4. **Notifications:**
   - The bell icon in the top menu bar indicates notifications. These can include:
     - Service health alerts: Notifications about service outages, planned maintenance, or other issues affecting Azure services.
     - Resource health alerts: Notifications about the health and performance of your Azure resources, such as high CPU usage or low disk space.
     - Security alerts: Notifications about potential security threats or vulnerabilities in your Azure environment.
     - Billing alerts: Notifications about your Azure usage and spending.
5. **Settings:**
   - The gear icon opens the portal settings menu, where you can personalize your Azure Portal experience. Here, you can:
     - Change the theme (light or dark mode).
     - Choose your preferred language.
     - Set your default view (Home or a specific dashboard).
     - Manage notifications.
     - Configure accessibility options.
6. **Help:**
   - This question mark icon opens a help pane that provides access to:
     - Azure documentation: Find detailed information about Azure services, features, and APIs.
     - Troubleshooting guides: Get help resolving common issues and errors.
     - Microsoft Q&A: Ask questions and get answers from the Azure community.
     - Support tickets: Create a support request if you need assistance from Microsoft.
7. **Your account:**
   - Clicking on your profile icon reveals a menu where you can:
     - View your account profile and settings.
     - Switch directories.
     - Sign out of the Azure Portal.

By mastering these top menu bar options, you'll be able to efficiently navigate, customize, and get the most out of your Azure Portal experience.

Customizing the Portal

The Azure Portal isn't just a one-size-fits-all interface; it's a dynamic workspace that you can tailor to your specific needs and preferences. By taking advantage of the customization options, you can create a personalized experience that enhances your productivity and makes your cloud management tasks more efficient.

Dashboards: Your Personalized Command Center

Think of dashboards as your personal control panels within the Azure Portal. They provide at-a-glance views of the information and metrics that are most important to you.

Creating a Custom Dashboard:

1. Click the "Dashboard" button on the top menu bar.
2. Select "+ New dashboard."
3. Give your dashboard a name and description.
4. Click "Create."
5. You'll now see an empty dashboard. To populate it, click the "Add tile" button.
6. You can choose from a wide range of tiles, such as:
   - **Metrics:** Display graphs and charts for CPU usage, network traffic, storage consumption, and more.
   - **Resource lists:** Show a list of specific resources, such as virtual machines or web apps.
   - **Markdown:** Add text, images, or links to customize your dashboard.
7. Arrange and resize the tiles to create your desired layout.
8. Save your dashboard when you're finished.

Favorites: Quick Access to Your Essentials

Do you have certain resources that you frequently access? Adding them to your **Favorites** list is a great way to save time and avoid navigating through the menu every time.

Adding Resources to Favorites:

1. Find the resource you want to add to your favorites.
2. Click the star icon next to the resource name.

The favorited resource will now appear in the "Favorites" section of the left-hand menu, making it just a click away.

Settings: Tailor Your Portal Experience

The Azure Portal offers several settings that you can customize to personalize your experience:

- **Theme:** Choose between light and dark modes to suit your visual preferences.
- **Language:** Select your preferred language for the portal interface.
- **Default View:** Decide whether you want the portal to open to the Home page or a specific dashboard.
- **Notifications:** Manage the types of notifications you receive and how they are delivered.

To access the settings, click on the gear icon in the top-right corner of the portal.

Experiment and Explore!

We encourage you to experiment with different customization options to find the perfect combination that suits your individual preferences and workflows. By personalizing the Azure Portal, you can create a more efficient and enjoyable cloud management experience.

Chapter Summary

This chapter has guided you through navigating the Azure Portal, your control center for managing Azure resources. We began by showing you how to access the portal and explored the dashboard, your personalized overview of your Azure environment. We then delved into the search bar, a powerful tool for quickly finding resources, services, and documentation within the portal.

Next, we explored the left-hand navigation menu, your roadmap to the various sections and features of Azure. You learned how to create new resources, browse Azure services, manage resource groups, access recent resources, and find help and support. We then delved into the specifics of creating and managing resource groups, emphasizing their role in organizing and streamlining your Azure resources.

Moving to the top menu bar, we covered essential options like switching between subscriptions, accessing the Azure Cloud Shell, managing notifications, customizing settings, and finding help. We also discussed how to personalize your Azure Portal experience by creating custom dashboards, adding favorites, and adjusting settings like the theme and language.

By now, you should have a solid understanding of how to navigate the Azure Portal and tailor it to your preferences. With this foundation, you're well-equipped to dive deeper into Azure and start creating and managing your cloud resources. The next chapter will introduce you to the Azure Marketplace, where you can discover and deploy a wide range of applications and services to enhance your Azure environment.

Azure Marketplace: Explore and Deploy Services

Outline

- What is the Azure Marketplace?
- Navigating the Marketplace
- Searching for Solutions
- Deploying from the Marketplace
- Managing Marketplace Solutions
- Tips for Using the Marketplace
- Chapter Summary

What is the Azure Marketplace?

Think of the Azure Marketplace as a bustling online bazaar filled with a vast array of software tools and services, all ready to be deployed in your Azure cloud environment. It's a one-stop shop where you can discover, evaluate, and deploy solutions from both Microsoft and a multitude of third-party vendors.

A Treasure Trove of Solutions

The Azure Marketplace offers a comprehensive catalog of pre-configured solutions, encompassing:

- **Virtual Machine Images:** Ready-to-use images for popular operating systems and applications, making it easy to launch virtual machines in Azure.
- **Solution Templates:** Pre-built templates for deploying complex solutions, such as multi-tier applications or development environments, saving you time and effort.
- **SaaS Applications:** Software as a Service applications that you can subscribe to and use directly from the cloud, eliminating the need for installation and maintenance.
- **Developer Tools:** Development tools and frameworks for building cloud-native applications, accelerating your development process.
- **Consulting and Managed Services:** Professional services from experienced partners to help you with your cloud projects, from migration to optimization.

Microsoft and Third-Party Offerings

The Azure Marketplace features solutions from both Microsoft and a wide range of trusted third-party vendors. You can find solutions from leading software companies like Oracle, Red Hat, Barracuda, and many others. This diversity ensures that you can find the right solutions for your specific needs, whether you're looking for enterprise-grade software or niche applications.

Simplify Your Cloud Journey

The Azure Marketplace simplifies the process of deploying and managing cloud solutions. You can easily browse through the catalog, filter by categories and keywords, read reviews, and compare different offerings. Once you've found the right solution, you can deploy it with just a few clicks, without having to worry about complex configuration or setup.

Azure Marketplace also provides tools for managing your deployed solutions, such as monitoring their performance, updating their settings, and scaling them as needed. This streamlines your cloud management and allows you to focus on your core business objectives.

In the next sections of this chapter, we'll guide you through navigating the Azure Marketplace, searching for solutions, and deploying them to your Azure environment. Get ready to discover a world of possibilities for enhancing your cloud capabilities!

Navigating the Marketplace

The Azure Marketplace isn't just a catalog; it's a carefully organized storefront designed to help you quickly find the perfect solutions for your needs. Let's take a guided tour of its key sections:

Accessing the Marketplace

There are two main ways to enter the Azure Marketplace:

1. **Left-Hand Menu:** In the Azure Portal's left-hand navigation menu, look for the "Create a resource" section. Within this section, you'll find a link to the Azure Marketplace.
2. **Dashboard:** The Azure Portal dashboard often features a tile or widget that links directly to the Marketplace. This can be a quick way to access it, especially if you've customized your dashboard to prioritize Marketplace access.

Marketplace Sections: Your Guide to Discovery

Once inside the Marketplace, you'll discover a well-structured layout that makes it easy to explore and find the right solutions:

1. **Popular Solutions:** This section showcases a curated collection of popular and trending solutions across various categories. It's a great place to start if you're looking for ideas or want to see what other Azure users are deploying.
2. **Categories:** This is where the Marketplace truly shines in terms of organization. Solutions are categorized by their primary function, such as:
    - **Compute:** Virtual machine images, container solutions, and more.
    - **Networking:** Virtual network appliances, firewalls, load balancers, and other networking tools.
    - **Storage:** Backup solutions, disaster recovery tools, and additional storage options.
    - **Databases:** Relational, NoSQL, and in-memory databases to suit your data needs.
    - **Web:** Web applications, content management systems (CMS), and e-commerce platforms.
    - **Analytics and IoT:** Big data solutions, data visualization tools, and IoT device management platforms.
    - **AI + Machine Learning:** Pre-built AI services, machine learning frameworks, and tools for building custom models.
3. This categorization allows you to quickly narrow down your search to the specific type of solution you're looking for.
4. **Industries:** For those seeking industry-specific solutions, the Marketplace offers a section that highlights solutions tailored to particular sectors, such as:
    - **Healthcare:** Electronic health record (EHR) systems, telemedicine platforms, and medical imaging solutions.
    - **Finance:** Financial management software, fraud detection tools, and risk management platforms.
    - **Retail:** E-commerce platforms, point-of-sale (POS) systems, and inventory management tools.
    - **Manufacturing:** Supply chain management solutions, predictive maintenance tools, and industrial automation software.
5. This section is invaluable if you need solutions that cater to the unique needs and compliance requirements of your industry.

Additional Features:

In addition to these main sections, the Azure Marketplace also offers:

- **Featured Solutions:** A rotating selection of new and innovative solutions highlighted by Microsoft.
- **Publisher Profiles:** Learn more about the publishers of the solutions, their offerings, and their support options.
- **Pricing and Plans:** View the pricing details for each solution, including free trials, pay-as-you-go options, and fixed-price plans.

By navigating these sections of the Azure Marketplace, you'll be able to efficiently discover and evaluate solutions that can help you achieve your business goals in the cloud.

Searching for Solutions

The Azure Marketplace offers an extensive collection of solutions, but finding the right one for your needs doesn't have to be overwhelming. The powerful search functionality within the Marketplace makes it easy to pinpoint the perfect fit.

Using the Search Bar

The search bar is located at the top of the Marketplace page. Simply start typing your query, and the Marketplace will automatically suggest relevant results as you type.

Search Filters: Narrowing Down Your Options

To further refine your search, utilize the various search filters available:

- **Keyword Search:** Use specific keywords or phrases related to the solution you're looking for. For example, if you need a content management system (CMS), you could search for "CMS" or "WordPress."
- **Category:** Select the relevant category to narrow down your search. Categories include Compute, Networking, Storage, Databases, Web, and more.
- **Industry:** If you're looking for a solution specific to your industry, such as healthcare or finance, filter by industry to see relevant options.
- **Deployment Model:** Choose between Infrastructure as a Service (IaaS) or Software as a Service (SaaS) solutions.
- **Publisher:** Search for solutions from specific publishers, such as Microsoft, Oracle, or Red Hat.
- **Pricing Model:** Filter by free trials, bring-your-own-license (BYOL), or pay-as-you-go options.
- **Operating System:** If you're looking for a virtual machine image, you can filter by operating system, such as Windows or Linux.

Tips for Effective Searching

Here are some tips to help you construct effective search queries:

- **Be Specific:** Use precise keywords that describe the functionality or features you're looking for. Instead of searching for "database," try "NoSQL database" or "document database."
- **Use Multiple Keywords:** Combine keywords to narrow down your results. For example, search for "web application firewall" instead of just "firewall."
- **Experiment with Filters:** Don't be afraid to try different filter combinations to explore the full range of available solutions.
- **Read Solution Descriptions:** Pay attention to the solution descriptions to ensure they meet your specific requirements.

- **Check Reviews and Ratings:** See what other users are saying about the solution by reading reviews and checking ratings.

Additional Search Tips:

- **Saved Searches:** If you find yourself performing similar searches frequently, you can save your search criteria for quick access later.
- **Browse by Category:** If you're not sure what you're looking for, browse through the different categories to get ideas and discover new solutions.
- **Use the "New" Filter:** To see the latest additions to the Marketplace, filter by "New."

By mastering the search functionality in the Azure Marketplace, you can quickly and easily find the solutions that best fit your needs, accelerating your cloud journey and empowering you to achieve your goals.

Deploying from the Marketplace

The Azure Marketplace not only helps you find the right solutions but also simplifies their deployment. Here's a step-by-step guide to get you started:

1. **Selecting a Solution:**
   - After you've found a solution that interests you, click on its tile in the Marketplace to open its details page.
   - On this page, you'll find a comprehensive overview of the solution, including its features, benefits, pricing details, and user reviews.
   - Carefully review this information to ensure the solution aligns with your requirements and budget.
2. **Reviewing Details and Terms:**
   - Click on the "Plans + Pricing" tab to explore the different pricing options available for the solution. Some solutions offer free trials, while others may have pay-as-you-go or subscription-based pricing.
   - Click on the "Legal" tab to review the solution's terms and conditions, including the end-user license agreement (EULA) and any other relevant legal documents.
3. **Configuring Settings:**
   - Click the "Create" button to begin the deployment process.
   - You'll be presented with a configuration page where you can customize the solution's settings based on your needs. This may include:
     - **Basics:** Choosing a subscription, resource group, and region for deployment.
     - **Virtual Machine Size (if applicable):** Selecting the appropriate size and specifications for your virtual machine.
     - **Settings:** Configuring other options like authentication, network settings, and storage options.
4. **Creating or Selecting a Resource Group:**
   - A resource group is a logical container for organizing related Azure resources.
   - If you don't have an existing resource group, you can create a new one by clicking "Create new" and entering a name.
   - If you have existing resource groups, select the appropriate one from the dropdown list.
5. **Review and Deploy:**
   - Review the deployment summary, which provides an overview of the resources that will be created and their associated costs.
   - If you're satisfied with the configuration, click "Create" to initiate the deployment process.

Monitoring Deployment Progress:

- The Azure Portal will display the deployment status. You can monitor the progress of the deployment and view any notifications or error messages.
- Once the deployment is complete, you'll receive a confirmation message. You can then access your deployed solution and start using it.

Additional Notes:

- **Deployment Time:** The deployment time can vary depending on the complexity of the solution and the resources being provisioned. Some deployments may take only a few minutes, while others may take longer.
- **Notifications:** Azure will notify you via email or the portal's notification center when the deployment is complete or if any issues arise.
- **Post-Deployment Configuration:** Some solutions may require additional configuration after deployment. Refer to the solution's documentation for any specific post-deployment steps.

By following these steps, you can easily deploy a wide range of applications, solutions, and services from the Azure Marketplace, accelerating your cloud adoption and empowering you to leverage the full potential of Azure.

Managing Marketplace Solutions

After successfully deploying a solution from the Azure Marketplace, the journey doesn't end there. The Azure Portal provides comprehensive tools for managing your deployed solutions, ensuring optimal performance and control over your resources.

Locating Deployed Solutions

1. **Resource Groups:** Navigate to the resource group where you deployed the solution. Remember, resource groups are logical containers that help you organize related resources.
2. **Resources List:** Within the resource group, you'll find a list of all the resources associated with the deployed solution. This might include virtual machines, databases, web apps, or other components depending on the nature of the solution.

Viewing Solution Status

1. **Overview Page:** Click on the solution's name to access its overview page. This page provides a summary of the solution's status, including its health, availability, and key metrics.
2. **Monitoring Tools:** Explore the monitoring section for detailed insights into the solution's performance, such as resource utilization, response times, and error rates.
3. **Activity Log:** The activity log records all operations performed on the solution, allowing you to track changes, troubleshoot issues, and identify potential security risks.

Updating Solution Settings

1. **Configuration Blade:** Navigate to the configuration blade or settings section of the solution.
2. **Modify Settings:** Make the necessary changes to the solution's configuration, such as scaling resources, adjusting security settings, or modifying network settings.
3. **Save Changes:** Apply your changes to update the solution's configuration.

Monitoring Performance

1. **Azure Monitor:** Utilize Azure Monitor to collect and analyze performance data from your deployed solution. You can create custom dashboards, set alerts, and gain insights into how the solution is performing.

2. **Application Insights (if applicable):** If the solution is a web application, you can use Application Insights to monitor its performance, availability, and usage patterns.
3. **Performance Testing:** Consider conducting performance tests to assess the solution's responsiveness and scalability under different loads.

Uninstalling a Solution

If you no longer need the deployed solution, you can easily uninstall it:

1. **Delete Resource Group:** The simplest way to uninstall a solution is to delete the resource group it's deployed to. This will remove all the associated resources, including the solution itself.
2. **Delete Individual Resources:** If you only want to remove specific resources, you can delete them individually from the resource group.

Important Considerations:

- **Backup:** Before uninstalling a solution, make sure to back up any critical data associated with it.
- **Dependencies:** Be aware of any dependencies that other resources or applications might have on the solution you're uninstalling.
- **Marketplace Terms:** Review the solution's marketplace terms to understand any potential implications or costs associated with uninstalling it.

By effectively managing your deployed marketplace solutions, you can ensure that they continue to meet your needs, operate optimally, and contribute to your overall cloud success.

Tips for Using the Marketplace

The Azure Marketplace is a powerful tool, but like any tool, it's most effective when used strategically. Here are some tips to help you get the most out of your Marketplace experience:

1. **Read Reviews and Ratings:** Before you deploy any solution, take the time to read the reviews and ratings from other Azure users. This can give you valuable insights into the solution's performance, ease of use, and overall value. Pay attention to both positive and negative feedback to get a well-rounded perspective.
2. **Take Advantage of Free Trials:** Many solutions in the Marketplace offer free trials, allowing you to test them out in your own environment before committing to a purchase. This is a great way to evaluate whether a solution meets your specific needs and integrates well with your existing systems.
3. **Check for Support Options:** When choosing a solution, consider the level of support offered by the provider. Look for solutions that come with comprehensive documentation, community forums, or even dedicated support channels. This can be invaluable if you encounter issues or have questions during deployment or usage.
4. **Compare Pricing and Plans:** Carefully evaluate the pricing options for each solution. Some solutions offer pay-as-you-go pricing, while others may require a monthly or annual subscription. Compare the different plans and choose the one that aligns with your budget and usage patterns.
5. **Stay Up-to-Date with New Offerings:** The Azure Marketplace is constantly evolving, with new solutions being added regularly. Make it a habit to check back frequently to see if there are any new offerings that might be relevant to your needs. You can also sign up for email notifications to get alerts about new solutions and updates.
6. **Consider Consulting Services:** If you're unsure which solution is right for you, or if you need help with deployment and configuration, consider leveraging the consulting services offered by Microsoft partners. These partners can provide expert guidance and support to ensure a successful implementation of your chosen solution.

7. **Experiment and Explore:** Don't be afraid to experiment with different solutions and try out new things. The Azure Marketplace is a playground for innovation, and you might discover hidden gems that can significantly benefit your business.

By following these tips, you can make the most of the Azure Marketplace and unlock its full potential for your organization. Remember, the Marketplace is more than just a catalog; it's a gateway to a vast ecosystem of solutions that can help you achieve your cloud goals.

Chapter Summary

This chapter introduced you to the Azure Marketplace, your gateway to a vast world of cloud solutions. We explored what the Marketplace is and how it simplifies the process of deploying and managing applications, services, and solutions in your Azure environment.

We guided you through navigating the Marketplace, highlighting its key sections like Popular Solutions, Categories, and Industries, to help you easily find the right offerings for your needs. We then dove into the search functionality, demonstrating how to use keywords, filters, and tips for crafting effective searches to discover the perfect solutions.

Next, we provided a detailed, step-by-step guide on deploying solutions from the Marketplace, covering everything from selecting a solution to configuring settings and managing the deployment process. Finally, we discussed how to manage your deployed solutions within the Azure Portal, including viewing their status, updating settings, monitoring performance, and uninstalling them if needed.

We concluded by offering valuable tips for maximizing your Marketplace experience, such as reading reviews, trying free trials, checking support options, comparing pricing, and staying up-to-date with new offerings. By following these guidelines, you can confidently explore the Marketplace, discover innovative solutions, and leverage them to enhance your Azure capabilities.

Armed with this knowledge, you're now ready to embark on the next phase of your Azure journey. The following section will delve into the Azure Compute Services that power your applications and workloads.

Section 3:
Azure Compute Services

Virtual Machines (VMs): Your Virtual Servers in the Cloud

Outline

- What Are Virtual Machines?
- Why Use Virtual Machines in Azure?
- Types of Azure Virtual Machines
- Creating Your First Virtual Machine
- Managing Virtual Machines
- Best Practices for Virtual Machines
- Tips and Tricks
- Chapter Summary

What Are Virtual Machines?

Imagine having a single, powerful computer, but instead of running just one operating system (like Windows or Linux), you could have multiple, each running independently as if it were on its own dedicated machine. That's the magic of virtual machines (VMs).

VMs: The Software Illusion

A virtual machine is essentially a software emulation of a physical computer system. It consists of a virtual central processing unit (CPU), memory, storage, and network interface, all running within the environment of a physical host machine.

This creates isolated environments, each with its own operating system and applications, running on a single physical server. Each VM operates independently of the others, as if it were a separate physical machine. This means you can run different operating systems (e.g., Windows and Linux) or different versions of the same operating system on the same hardware.

Key Components of a Virtual Machine

- **Hypervisor:** The hypervisor is a layer of software that sits between the virtual machines and the physical hardware. It's responsible for managing the allocation of resources to each VM, ensuring isolation, and translating instructions from the virtual machines to the underlying hardware.
- **Guest Operating System:** Each VM runs its own guest operating system, which is the operating system that the user interacts with. This can be any supported operating system, such as Windows, Linux, or macOS.
- **Virtual Hardware:** Each VM has its own virtual hardware, including a virtual CPU, memory, storage, and network interface. These virtual devices are emulated by the hypervisor and provide the resources needed for the guest operating system and applications to run.

Benefits of Virtual Machines

Virtual machines offer a number of benefits that make them a popular choice for businesses and individuals alike:

- **Isolation:** Each VM runs in its own isolated environment, protecting it from other VMs on the same host. This means that if one VM crashes or becomes infected with malware, it won't affect the other VMs.
- **Portability:** VMs can be easily moved between different physical hosts or even different cloud environments. This makes it easy to migrate workloads or create backups.
- **Resource Efficiency:** By running multiple VMs on a single physical server, you can maximize the utilization of your hardware resources. This can lead to significant cost savings compared to running separate physical servers for each workload.
- **Flexibility:** You have the flexibility to choose the operating system and software that best suit your needs for each VM.
- **Snapshotting:** You can create snapshots of VMs, which are point-in-time backups of the VM's state. This allows you to easily revert to a previous state if something goes wrong.

Virtual machines have become an indispensable tool in modern IT infrastructure, providing a versatile and efficient way to run multiple workloads on a single physical server.

Why Use Virtual Machines in Azure?

Virtual Machines (VMs) in Azure bring a whole new dimension to cloud computing, offering a powerful and versatile solution for hosting your applications and workloads. Let's delve into the compelling reasons why you should consider utilizing Azure Virtual Machines:

1. Unmatched Scalability

Azure VMs provide exceptional scalability, allowing you to effortlessly adjust resources to match your evolving needs. Whether you need to handle sudden traffic spikes or accommodate steady growth, you can easily scale your VMs up or down in minutes. This on-demand scalability ensures that your applications can handle any workload, while you only pay for the resources you actually use.

2. Flexibility to Choose Your Path

Azure offers an extensive range of VM sizes and configurations to perfectly match your workload requirements. You can choose from various options for CPU, memory, storage, and networking capabilities, tailoring your VM to your specific needs. This flexibility empowers you to optimize performance and cost for each application, ensuring you get the most out of your Azure investment.

3. Unrivaled Customizability

Azure VMs give you the freedom to install and configure your preferred operating systems and software. Whether you're running Windows, Linux, or even custom applications, you have complete control over the environment within your VMs. This allows you to create a familiar and optimized environment for your applications, ensuring compatibility and ease of management.

4. Seamless Integration with Azure Services

Azure VMs are not isolated islands. They seamlessly integrate with a vast array of other Azure services, creating a powerful ecosystem for building and running applications. You can easily connect your VMs to Azure storage services for scalable data storage, leverage Azure networking services for secure and reliable communication, and integrate with Azure databases to power your applications.

5. Streamlined Management

Azure provides multiple ways to manage your virtual machines, giving you the flexibility to choose the method that best suits your workflow:

- **Azure Portal:** The intuitive web-based interface allows you to create, configure, and manage your VMs visually.
- **Azure CLI and PowerShell:** These command-line interfaces provide a powerful way to automate and script VM management tasks.
- **Azure Resource Manager (ARM) Templates:** Define your infrastructure as code, allowing you to deploy and manage your VMs in a declarative and repeatable manner.

With these comprehensive management options, you can easily control your VMs, monitor their performance, and ensure they are running optimally.

By embracing Azure Virtual Machines, you gain a scalable, flexible, and customizable platform for running your applications and workloads in the cloud. Whether you're a small startup or a large enterprise, Azure VMs can empower you to achieve your business goals and unlock the full potential of cloud computing.

Types of Azure Virtual Machines

Azure offers a wide variety of virtual machine (VM) types, each tailored to specific workload requirements. Choosing the right VM type is crucial for optimizing performance and cost-efficiency. Let's explore the different categories:

General Purpose

These VMs offer a balanced combination of CPU and memory, making them suitable for a wide range of workloads:

- **Ideal for:** Testing and development environments, small to medium databases, low to medium traffic web servers, and applications that don't require specialized resources.
- **Examples:** The D-series and the newer Dav4, Dasv4 VM series are popular choices for general-purpose workloads.

Compute Optimized

These VMs boast a high CPU-to-memory ratio, making them perfect for tasks that demand raw processing power:

- **Ideal for:** Medium traffic web servers, network appliances, batch processes, application servers, and other compute-intensive applications.
- **Examples:** The F-series and the newer Fav4, Fasv4 VM series are designed for compute-optimized workloads.

Memory Optimized

With a high memory-to-CPU ratio, these VMs excel at handling large datasets and memory-intensive operations:

- **Ideal for:** Relational database servers, medium to large caches, in-memory analytics, and other applications that require substantial memory resources.
- **Examples:** The E-series and the newer Eav4, Easv4 VM series are optimized for memory-intensive workloads.

Storage Optimized

These VMs are engineered for high disk throughput and IOPS (input/output operations per second), making them ideal for data-heavy applications:

- **Ideal for:** Big data processing, SQL and NoSQL databases, data warehousing, and other workloads that require fast and reliable storage access.
- **Examples:** The Lsv2-series VMs are specifically designed for storage-optimized scenarios.

GPU Optimized

These specialized VMs are equipped with powerful GPUs (graphics processing units) to accelerate graphics-intensive workloads:

- **Ideal for:** Artificial intelligence (AI), machine learning, deep learning, high-performance computing (HPC), rendering, visualization, and gaming.
- **Examples:** The N-series and the newer NVv4, NVads A10 v5 VM series offer a range of GPU options to meet diverse needs.

Choosing the Right VM Type

Selecting the most suitable VM type depends on the specific requirements of your workload. Consider the following factors:

- **CPU:** How much processing power do you need?
- **Memory:** How much memory does your application require?
- **Storage:** What type and amount of storage do you need (e.g., high-performance SSDs or large HDDs)?
- **Networking:** What network bandwidth and performance do you require?
- **Budget:** What is your budget for running the VM?

Azure provides detailed documentation on each VM series, including their specifications, pricing, and recommended use cases. You can also use the Azure pricing calculator to estimate the cost of different VM types based on your anticipated usage.

By carefully evaluating your workload requirements and selecting the right VM type, you can optimize performance, minimize costs, and ensure a smooth and efficient experience running your applications in Azure.

Creating Your First Virtual Machine

Creating a virtual machine (VM) in Azure is a straightforward process that can be accomplished through the Azure Portal. Let's walk through the steps, ensuring you understand each decision along the way:

1. **Navigate to Virtual Machines:**
    - Open the Azure Portal (https://portal.azure.com/).
    - In the search bar at the top, type "Virtual Machines" and select it from the results.
    - Alternatively, click "Create a resource" in the left menu, then select "Compute," and finally, "Virtual Machine."
2. **Choose an Image:**
    - The first step is to choose the operating system (OS) for your VM. Azure offers a vast selection of images from the Marketplace, including:
        - Windows Server
        - Various Linux distributions (Ubuntu, CentOS, Debian, etc.)
        - Specialized images for applications like SQL Server or SAP
    - Select the image that matches your application requirements and preferences.
    - For this example, let's choose "Ubuntu Server 22.04 LTS - Gen2."

3. **Select a VM Size:**
   - Next, you'll need to choose the size of your VM. Azure offers a wide range of VM sizes, each with different combinations of CPU, memory, storage, and networking capabilities.
   - Consider your workload requirements when choosing a size. For a simple development or test environment, a smaller VM might suffice. For production workloads, you may need a larger VM with more resources.
   - Azure provides a handy tool to estimate the cost of different VM sizes based on your expected usage.
4. **Configure Networking and Storage:**
   - Networking:
     - You'll need to connect your VM to a virtual network. If you don't have one, you can create a new one during this step.
     - Specify the subnet within the virtual network where your VM will reside.
     - Choose whether to assign a public IP address to the VM. This will allow you to access the VM over the internet.
   - Storage:
     - Select the type and size of the disk for your VM's operating system and data. Azure offers standard HDDs, standard SSDs, and premium SSDs with varying performance levels.
     - You can also choose to attach additional data disks if needed.
5. **Set Up Authentication:**
   - Authentication is crucial for securing access to your VM. You have two main options:
     - **SSH Public Key:** This is the more secure option, especially for Linux VMs. You'll need to generate an SSH key pair and provide the public key during VM creation.
     - **Password:** You can also set a username and password for the VM. However, using strong passwords and enabling multi-factor authentication (MFA) is highly recommended for security.
6. **Deploy the VM:**
   - Review all the settings you've configured. If everything looks correct, click the "Review + create" button.
   - Azure will validate your settings and, if there are no errors, you can click "Create" to start the deployment process.
   - The deployment may take a few minutes. You can track its progress in the Azure Portal.

After Deployment:

Once the VM is deployed, you can access it through the Azure Portal or using Remote Desktop (RDP for Windows) or SSH (for Linux). You'll then be able to install software, configure settings, and start using your virtual machine in the cloud.

Managing Virtual Machines

Once your virtual machine (VM) is up and running in Azure, you have a variety of tools and options to manage its operation, performance, and security. Let's explore some key aspects of VM management:

Starting, Stopping, and Restarting VMs

Controlling your VM's power state is straightforward:

1. **Azure Portal:**
   - Navigate to your VM's overview page.
   - In the top menu bar, you'll find buttons for "Start," "Stop," and "Restart."
   - Click the appropriate button to perform the desired action.
2. **Azure CLI:**

- Use the `az vm start`, `az vm stop`, or `az vm restart` commands, followed by the VM's name or resource ID.
3. **Azure PowerShell:**
    - Use the `Start-AzVM`, `Stop-AzVM`, or `Restart-AzVM` cmdlets, along with the VM's name or resource ID.

Note: Stopping a VM deallocates its resources, so you won't be charged for compute while it's stopped. However, you'll still be charged for storage.

Connecting to the VM

To access and interact with your VM, you can use remote connection protocols:

- **Remote Desktop Protocol (RDP):** For Windows VMs, use RDP to establish a graphical desktop connection from your local machine. You'll need the VM's public IP address or DNS name and the appropriate credentials (username and password or SSH key).
- **Secure Shell (SSH):** For Linux VMs, use SSH to establish a secure command-line connection from your local machine. You'll need the VM's public IP address or DNS name and the SSH key you specified during VM creation.

Monitoring VM Performance

Azure Monitor provides a comprehensive suite of tools for tracking and analyzing your VM's performance. You can monitor metrics like:

- **CPU utilization:** Percentage of CPU being used.
- **Memory usage:** Amount of memory being used.
- **Disk I/O:** Rate of read and write operations to the VM's disks.
- **Network traffic:** Amount of data transmitted and received by the VM.

You can view these metrics in near real-time on the VM's monitoring tab, or you can create custom dashboards and alerts to proactively detect and address performance issues.

Resizing VMs

If your workload demands change, you can easily resize your VM to a different size with more or fewer resources.

1. **Azure Portal:**
    - Go to your VM's overview page.
    - Under "Settings," click "Size."
    - Select the desired VM size and click "Resize."
2. **Azure CLI or PowerShell:**
    - Use the appropriate commands or cmdlets to update the VM size.

Creating VM Snapshots

VM snapshots capture the state of a VM at a specific point in time, including the operating system, data disks, and configuration. Snapshots provide a convenient way to create backups or revert to a previous state if needed.

1. **Azure Portal:**
    - Go to your VM's overview page.
    - Under "Operations," click "Snapshots."
    - Click "Create snapshot" and follow the instructions.
2. **Azure CLI or PowerShell:**

- Use the appropriate commands or cmdlets to create a snapshot.

With these VM management techniques at your disposal, you can effectively control and optimize your Azure virtual machines to ensure they meet your application's performance, reliability, and security requirements.

Best Practices for Virtual Machines

To get the most out of your Azure virtual machines (VMs), it's essential to follow best practices that optimize performance, ensure security, and streamline management. Let's dive into some key recommendations:

Choosing the Right VM Size

Selecting the appropriate VM size is crucial for achieving the right balance of performance and cost.

- **Right-Sizing:** Start with a smaller VM size and monitor its performance. If you notice resource constraints, you can easily resize the VM to a larger size. This allows you to scale up or down based on actual usage rather than over-provisioning resources from the start.
- **Azure Advisor:** Leverage Azure Advisor, a personalized cloud consultant, to get recommendations on right-sizing your VMs based on usage patterns.
- **Consider Bursting:** If your workload experiences occasional spikes in demand, you can use Azure's auto-scaling feature to automatically add or remove VMs to handle the fluctuating load.

Using Managed Disks

Azure Managed Disks are a storage option that simplifies disk management and offers several advantages:

- **Automated Management:** Azure handles disk storage allocation, management, and backups, reducing your administrative overhead.
- **Better Reliability:** Managed Disks are highly durable and available, replicating your data across multiple storage nodes for protection against hardware failures.
- **Improved Performance:** Premium SSD Managed Disks offer high performance and low latency, ideal for demanding workloads.

Implementing Backup and Disaster Recovery

Protecting your data and ensuring business continuity are essential in the cloud. Azure provides robust backup and disaster recovery solutions for your VMs:

- **Azure Backup:** Create regular backups of your VMs to protect against data loss due to accidental deletion, corruption, or ransomware attacks.
- **Azure Site Recovery:** Replicate your VMs to a secondary region, allowing you to quickly failover in case of a disaster or outage in the primary region.

By implementing these solutions, you can safeguard your data and ensure that your applications can quickly recover from unexpected events.

Securing Your VMs

Virtual machine security is a top priority. Implement these security best practices to protect your VMs from unauthorized access and threats:

- **Strong Passwords:** Use strong passwords and change them regularly. Enable multi-factor authentication (MFA) for added security.

- **Network Security Groups (NSGs):** Use NSGs to filter network traffic to and from your VMs. This allows you to control which ports are open and restrict access to only authorized sources.
- **Just-in-Time (JIT) VM Access:** Use JIT VM access to lock down inbound traffic to your VMs and open ports only when needed for specific connections.
- **Patch Management:** Regularly apply security updates and patches to your VM's operating system and software to protect against vulnerabilities.
- **Azure Security Center:** Leverage Azure Security Center to monitor your VMs for security threats, vulnerabilities, and misconfigurations.

By adopting these best practices, you can create a secure and resilient virtual machine environment in Azure, ensuring the optimal performance and protection of your applications and data. Remember, security is an ongoing process, so regularly review and update your security measures to stay ahead of evolving threats.

Tips and Tricks

Beyond the essential management tasks, there are many tips and tricks you can employ to further optimize your Azure Virtual Machine (VM) experience:

Auto-Shutdown: Saving Money While Idle

Running VMs around the clock can quickly rack up costs, especially for development or testing environments that aren't continuously needed. Azure's **auto-shutdown** feature allows you to schedule your VMs to automatically shut down when not in use. This helps you avoid unnecessary expenses while ensuring your VMs are available when you need them.

You can configure auto-shutdown directly within the VM settings in the Azure Portal or through Azure Automation for more advanced scheduling scenarios.

Extensions: Expanding VM Capabilities

Azure VM extensions are small applications that add extra functionality to your virtual machines. These extensions can be easily installed and managed from the Azure Portal or through command-line tools.

Some popular extensions include:

- **Custom Script Extension:** Run your own scripts on the VM for tasks like installing software or configuring settings.
- **Monitoring Agent:** Install the Azure Monitor agent to collect performance data from the VM and send it to Azure Monitor for analysis and alerting.
- **Antimalware:** Protect your VM from malware and viruses with various security solutions available as extensions.
- **Backup:** Integrate your VM with Azure Backup to create automated backups for data protection.

By exploring and utilizing extensions, you can customize your VMs to suit your specific needs and streamline your operations.

Azure CLI and PowerShell: Automate for Efficiency

The Azure Command-Line Interface (CLI) and Azure PowerShell are powerful tools for automating VM management tasks. By writing scripts and commands, you can automate repetitive tasks like:

- **Provisioning:** Create and configure VMs automatically.
- **Scaling:** Automatically scale VMs up or down based on performance metrics or schedules.
- **Backup and Recovery:** Schedule backups and automate disaster recovery processes.
- **Patch Management:** Automate the installation of updates and patches to keep your VMs secure.

By automating these tasks, you can save time, reduce errors, and improve the efficiency of your Azure VM management.

Community Resources: Tap into a Wealth of Knowledge

The Azure community is a vibrant and supportive network of users, experts, and enthusiasts who are always willing to help. Here are some resources you can leverage:

- **Microsoft Documentation:** Azure's comprehensive documentation provides in-depth guides, tutorials, and references on all aspects of VM management.
- **Microsoft Q&A:** The Microsoft Q&A platform is a great place to ask questions and get answers from the Azure community.
- **Blogs and Forums:** Many online communities and forums are dedicated to Azure, where you can find discussions, tips, and tricks for working with VMs.

By tapping into these resources, you can quickly find solutions to your questions, learn from the experiences of others, and stay up-to-date with the latest Azure developments.

By incorporating these tips and tricks into your Azure VM management practices, you'll be well on your way to becoming an Azure expert.

Chapter Summary

This chapter delved into the world of virtual machines (VMs) in Azure, a fundamental building block for running various workloads in the cloud. We began by defining what a virtual machine is: a software emulation of a physical computer that allows you to run multiple operating systems and applications on a single physical server. We explored the benefits of VMs, highlighting their isolation, portability, and resource efficiency.

Next, we discussed why Azure is a compelling platform for running VMs, focusing on its scalability, flexibility, customizability, integration capabilities, and streamlined management tools. We then categorized the various types of Azure VMs, including General Purpose, Compute Optimized, Memory Optimized, Storage Optimized, and GPU Optimized, each catering to different workload requirements.

You learned how to create your first virtual machine in Azure, starting with choosing an image and selecting the right VM size. We guided you through configuring networking and storage, setting up authentication, and deploying your VM.

Finally, we explored essential aspects of VM management, including starting, stopping, and restarting VMs, connecting to them using RDP or SSH, monitoring their performance with Azure Monitor, resizing them as needed, and creating snapshots for backup and recovery. We wrapped up by sharing best practices for optimizing VM performance and security, emphasizing the importance of right-sizing, using managed disks, implementing backup and disaster recovery strategies, and securing your VMs with strong passwords, network security groups, and regular updates. We also offered additional tips and tricks for automating VM management and leveraging community resources.

With this comprehensive understanding of Azure virtual machines, you're well-equipped to harness their power for your applications and workloads. In the next chapter, we'll shift our focus to App Services, another popular compute option in Azure that simplifies the process of building and hosting web applications.

App Services: Building and Hosting Web Applications

Outline

- What are App Services?
- Why Use App Services?
- Types of App Services
- Key Features and Benefits
- Creating a Web App
- Deploying Your Application
- Managing and Scaling Web Apps
- Tips and Best Practices
- Chapter Summary

What are App Services?

Imagine you're building a house. You could spend countless hours laying the foundation, constructing walls, installing plumbing, and wiring electricity. Or, you could hire a contractor who takes care of all that for you, allowing you to focus on interior design and making the house your own.

Azure App Service is that contractor for your web applications. It's a fully managed platform that handles the underlying infrastructure, letting you concentrate on building and enhancing your application's features and functionality.

The PaaS Powerhouse

App Service is classified as a Platform as a Service (PaaS) offering. This means Microsoft Azure takes on the responsibility of managing the underlying infrastructure, including:

- **Servers:** You don't have to worry about provisioning or maintaining servers. Azure handles patching, security updates, and ensures the servers are always up-to-date.
- **Operating Systems:** Azure takes care of operating system updates and patches, so you don't have to worry about managing them.
- **Scaling:** App Service automatically scales your application based on demand, ensuring optimal performance during peak traffic periods.
- **Load Balancing:** It intelligently distributes incoming traffic across multiple instances of your application, enhancing availability and responsiveness.
- **Security:** Azure applies security patches and updates to the underlying platform, helping you protect your application from vulnerabilities.

Build and Deploy with Ease

With App Service, you can build web applications and APIs using your preferred programming languages and frameworks, such as .NET, Java, Node.js, Python, PHP, and Ruby. You can then easily deploy your code directly from popular source control repositories like GitHub, Bitbucket, or Azure DevOps.

Beyond Just Web Apps

While its name might suggest it's only for web applications, App Service is versatile. It also supports:

- **Mobile app backends:** Create powerful backends for your mobile apps with features like authentication, push notifications, and data synchronization.
- **API apps:** Design, develop, and publish APIs that can be consumed by other applications and services.
- **WebJobs:** Run background tasks and scheduled jobs to automate various processes.

A Simplified Web Development Experience

In essence, Azure App Service streamlines web development by taking care of the infrastructure heavy lifting. This allows you to:

- **Focus on Your Code:** Spend your time writing code and building features, not managing servers.
- **Accelerate Development:** Quickly deploy your applications without worrying about setting up complex infrastructure.
- **Ensure High Availability:** Let Azure handle scaling and load balancing to ensure your application is always available.
- **Strengthen Security:** Rely on Azure's robust security measures to protect your application from threats.

Azure App Service empowers you to build, deploy, and scale web applications and APIs with ease and confidence. In the next sections, we'll delve into the different types of App Services and guide you through creating and deploying your first web app in Azure.

Why Use App Services?

App Services bring a host of compelling benefits to the table, making them an attractive option for hosting web applications and APIs on Azure:

1. Simplified Development and Deployment

App Service abstracts away the complexities of infrastructure management, allowing developers to focus on what they do best – writing code. You don't have to worry about provisioning servers, installing operating systems, or configuring network settings. Azure takes care of all the underlying infrastructure, including security patching and maintenance, freeing you up to focus on building innovative applications.

2. Effortless Scalability

With App Service, scaling your application is a breeze. You can easily scale up or down based on your traffic demands, ensuring optimal performance and cost-efficiency. Azure provides various scaling options, including manual scaling, automatic scaling based on metrics like CPU usage or request count, and even scheduled scaling for predictable traffic patterns.

3. High Availability and Reliability

App Service is designed to ensure your applications are always available to your users. It provides built-in redundancy and load balancing, automatically distributing traffic across multiple instances of your app. This not only improves performance but also ensures that your app can handle spikes in traffic and remain accessible even if individual instances fail.

4. Robust Security

Azure takes security seriously, and App Service is no exception. It inherits the robust security features of the Azure platform, including network security groups, web application firewalls, and built-in DDoS protection. You can also integrate with Azure Active Directory for authentication and authorization, and Azure Key Vault for managing secrets and certificates.

5. Seamless Integration

App Service integrates seamlessly with other Azure services, making it easy to build powerful and scalable solutions. You can connect your web app to Azure databases like SQL Database or Cosmos DB, use Azure Storage for file storage, and leverage Azure Functions for serverless computing tasks. This integration streamlines your development process and allows you to build end-to-end solutions entirely within Azure.

6. Cost-Effective

App Service offers a pay-as-you-go pricing model, meaning you only pay for the resources you actually consume. You can choose from various pricing tiers based on your performance and feature requirements, ensuring that you get the best value for your money. Additionally, the ability to scale resources dynamically helps you optimize your costs by only paying for what you need.

A Winning Combination

The combination of simplified development, effortless scalability, high availability, robust security, seamless integration, and cost-effectiveness makes Azure App Service a compelling choice for hosting your web applications and APIs. By offloading the infrastructure management to Azure, you can focus on building innovative and user-friendly applications that delight your customers and drive your business forward.

Types of App Services

Azure App Service isn't just a one-trick pony. It's a versatile platform that caters to different types of applications and workloads. Let's explore the main types of App Services:

Web Apps: Your Home for Web Applications

Think of Web Apps as the bread and butter of App Service. They're designed to host and run your websites and web applications, whether you're building a simple blog, a complex e-commerce platform, or a scalable API. Web Apps support a wide array of programming languages and frameworks, including .NET, Java, Node.js, Python, PHP, and Ruby. You can easily deploy your code from various sources, including Git repositories, FTP, and Zip files.

Mobile Apps: Empowering Your Mobile Experiences

Mobile Apps are specifically designed to support the backend of your mobile applications. They provide a platform for building and hosting the server-side components of your mobile apps, such as:

- **Authentication:** User authentication and authorization
- **Data storage:** Cloud storage for user data
- **Push notifications:** Sending notifications to mobile devices
- **Offline synchronization:** Enabling data synchronization when devices are offline

With Mobile Apps, you can create engaging and feature-rich mobile experiences without having to build and maintain your own backend infrastructure.

API Apps: Simplifying API Management

API Apps are tailored for creating and managing APIs (Application Programming Interfaces). They provide a platform for hosting your APIs, managing access, monitoring usage, and scaling them as needed. API Apps support various API protocols, including REST, SOAP, and WebSocket. You can also use them to expose legacy systems or databases as APIs, making them accessible to modern applications.

WebJobs: Your Background Workhorses

WebJobs are background tasks or scheduled jobs that you can run alongside your web apps or API apps. They are perfect for performing long-running tasks, processing data in the background, or automating scheduled operations. WebJobs can be triggered by various events, such as a timer, a queue message, or a file upload. They can be written in a variety of programming languages and can leverage the power of Azure's infrastructure for scalable execution.

Choosing the Right App Service Type

The type of App Service you choose will depend on the nature of your application or workload:

- **Web Apps:** Ideal for hosting websites, web applications, and RESTful APIs.
- **Mobile Apps:** Best suited for creating backends for mobile applications.
- **API Apps:** Perfect for building and managing APIs, including exposing legacy systems as APIs.
- **WebJobs:** Great for running background tasks and scheduled jobs.

By understanding the different types of App Services, you can choose the right tool for the job, enabling you to build and deploy a wide range of applications in Azure quickly and efficiently.

Key Features and Benefits

Azure App Service offers a wide range of features designed to streamline web application development and deployment. These features not only empower you to build high-quality apps but also ensure they run smoothly, scale effortlessly, and remain secure. Let's delve into some of the key highlights:

Diverse Language and Framework Support

App Service embraces a polyglot approach, allowing you to build your applications using the technology stack you're most comfortable with. Whether you're a .NET aficionado, a Java enthusiast, or prefer the flexibility of Node.js, Python, PHP, or Ruby, App Service has got you covered. This flexibility allows you to leverage your existing skills and knowledge, while also exploring new technologies as needed.

Continuous Deployment: Your Code, Seamlessly Deployed

Gone are the days of manually deploying code updates. App Service seamlessly integrates with popular code repositories like GitHub, Bitbucket, and Azure DevOps, enabling you to set up continuous integration and deployment (CI/CD) pipelines. This means that whenever you push code changes to your repository, App Service automatically builds, tests, and deploys your application, saving you time and effort while ensuring your code is always up-to-date.

Auto-Scaling: Handle Any Traffic Load

With App Service's auto-scaling feature, you can ensure your application can gracefully handle traffic spikes without manual intervention. You can configure auto-scaling rules based on various metrics, such as CPU usage, memory consumption, or request count. When the defined thresholds are met, App Service automatically adds or removes instances of your app to maintain optimal performance.

Custom Domains and SSL Certificates: Your Brand, Securely

App Service makes it easy to enhance your brand's online presence. You can map your custom domain to your web app, giving it a professional and memorable URL. Additionally, you can secure your website with SSL certificates, encrypting traffic and protecting your users' data.

WebJobs and Deployment Slots: Enhance and Test with Confidence

WebJobs empowers you to run background tasks and scheduled jobs alongside your web app. These jobs can perform various functions like processing data, sending emails, or performing maintenance tasks. Deployment slots, on the other hand, allow you to create staging environments for testing new code and features before deploying them to production. This ensures a smooth transition and minimizes the risk of errors or downtime.

Beyond the Basics

App Service offers a wealth of additional features, including:

- **Security:** Built-in authentication and authorization, IP restrictions, and integration with Azure security services like Web Application Firewall (WAF).
- **Monitoring:** Integration with Azure Monitor for detailed logging, metrics, and alerts.
- **Backup and Restore:** Automated backups and point-in-time restore capabilities.
- **Customizable Settings:** Extensive configuration options for tailoring your app's runtime environment.
- **Global Availability:** Ability to deploy your app in multiple regions for better performance and redundancy.

With its rich feature set and developer-friendly environment, Azure App Service provides a comprehensive platform for building and hosting modern web applications and APIs.

Creating a Web App

Now that you understand the power of Azure App Services, let's dive into the practical steps of creating your first web app using the Azure Portal. Don't worry if you're a beginner – Azure makes this process surprisingly easy.

1. **Navigate to App Services:**
    - Open the Azure Portal (https://portal.azure.com/).
    - In the search bar at the top, type "App Services" and select it from the results.
    - Alternatively, click "Create a resource" in the left menu, then select "Web" and finally "Web App."
2. **Select a Runtime Stack:**
    - Here's where you choose the technology stack your web app will be built upon. Azure offers a wide variety:
        - **.NET:** For C# and ASP.NET applications
        - **Java:** For Java-based applications (Spring, Tomcat, etc.)
        - **Node.js:** For JavaScript-based applications (Express, etc.)
        - **Python:** For Python applications (Flask, Django, etc.)
        - **PHP:** For PHP applications (WordPress, etc.)
        - **Ruby:** For Ruby applications (Ruby on Rails, etc.)
    - Choose the stack you're most familiar with or the one that best suits your project.
    - For this example, let's select "Node.js."
3. **Choose a Pricing Tier and Region:**
    - Azure offers several pricing tiers for App Services, ranging from free and shared options for development and testing to premium plans with dedicated resources for production workloads. Select a tier based on your needs and budget.
    - Next, choose the Azure region where you want your web app to be hosted. Consider factors like proximity to your users and any data residency requirements.
    - For this example, we'll use a basic tier in the "East US" region.
4. **Create or Link a Resource Group:**

- As we learned in Chapter 3, resource groups help organize your Azure resources. You can create a new resource group or use an existing one. If you're just starting out, create a new one with a descriptive name.
   - Give your resource group a meaningful name that reflects its purpose (e.g., "MyWebApp-ResourceGroup").
5. **Specify App Name and Deployment Method:**
   - **App Name:** Choose a unique name for your web app. This will be part of the URL for your web app (e.g., `<your-app-name>.azurewebsites.net`).
   - **Publish:** Select how you want to deploy your code. You can choose between:
     - **Code:** Deploy code directly from a repository (like GitHub or Azure DevOps).
     - **Docker Container:** Deploy a containerized version of your application.
     - **Other options:** Azure also supports deployment from a ZIP file or FTP.
   - For now, let's select "Code" and we'll cover deployment methods later.
6. **Review and Create:**
   - Review your configuration settings. Azure will show you an estimated monthly cost based on your chosen tier.
   - If everything looks good, click "Create." Azure will then create your web app and its associated resources.

Congratulations!

You've successfully created your first web app in Azure App Service. You'll receive a notification when the deployment is complete. You can now access your web app's URL and start building out your application!

Deploying Your Application

Now that your Web App is created, it's time to breathe life into it by deploying your application code. Azure App Service offers a variety of deployment methods to cater to different workflows and preferences.

1. Azure Portal's Built-in Deployment Tools

For a simple and beginner-friendly deployment experience, the Azure Portal provides built-in deployment tools:

- **Deployment Center:** This centralized hub guides you through the deployment process step-by-step. It integrates with various source code repositories like GitHub, Bitbucket, and Azure Repos. You can also deploy from a local Git repository or a ZIP file.
- **Visual Studio Integration:** If you're using Visual Studio as your development environment, you can publish your web app directly to Azure App Service from within the IDE. This seamless integration simplifies the deployment workflow for developers.

2. Continuous Deployment with Azure DevOps or GitHub Actions

For more advanced scenarios, consider continuous deployment (CD) pipelines using Azure DevOps or GitHub Actions. These tools automate the build, test, and deployment process, ensuring your application is always up-to-date with the latest code changes.

- **Azure DevOps:** Microsoft's comprehensive DevOps platform provides a robust pipeline system for building, testing, and deploying applications. You can create custom pipelines tailored to your project's specific requirements.
- **GitHub Actions:** If your code is hosted on GitHub, you can leverage GitHub Actions to automate your workflows. GitHub Actions offers a flexible and customizable way to build and deploy your web apps.

3. Manual Deployment Options

If you prefer a more hands-on approach or need to deploy your code quickly, Azure App Service supports several manual deployment options:

- **FTP/S (File Transfer Protocol/Secure):** Upload your application files directly to your web app using FTP or the more secure FTPS protocol.
- **Web Deploy:** A Microsoft technology that enables seamless deployment of web applications to IIS servers, including Azure App Service.
- **Zip Deploy:** Package your application code into a ZIP file and upload it to App Service. This is a simple and convenient way to deploy smaller applications.

Choosing the Right Deployment Method

The best deployment method for you depends on your specific requirements and workflow:

- **Ease of Use:** If you're a beginner or prefer a simple deployment process, the Azure Portal's built-in tools are a good option.
- **Automation:** If you want to automate your deployment process and ensure continuous delivery, Azure DevOps or GitHub Actions are the way to go.
- **Flexibility:** If you need more control over the deployment process or have specific requirements, manual deployment options like FTP, Web Deploy, or Zip Deploy might be more suitable.

Remember, regardless of the deployment method you choose, Azure App Service provides a reliable and scalable platform for hosting your web applications and APIs.

Managing and Scaling Web Apps

Once your web app is up and running on Azure App Service, the next step is to ensure its optimal performance, security, and availability. App Service provides a comprehensive set of tools for managing, monitoring, and scaling your web applications to meet the demands of your users and your business.

Monitoring App Performance and Logs

Keeping a close eye on your web app's performance is crucial for identifying bottlenecks, troubleshooting issues, and ensuring a smooth user experience. App Service offers several monitoring features:

- **Application Insights:** This powerful monitoring tool provides deep insights into your application's performance, availability, and usage patterns. It can track metrics like response times, failure rates, and dependency calls. You can also use it to identify performance bottlenecks, diagnose issues, and trace transactions across your application.
- **Metrics:** Azure Monitor provides a rich set of metrics that you can use to track your web app's performance, such as CPU usage, memory consumption, and request rates. You can create custom dashboards and alerts based on these metrics to get notified of potential issues.
- **Logs:** App Service generates detailed logs that capture information about requests, errors, and application behavior. You can access these logs through the Azure Portal or use tools like Azure Monitor Logs to analyze and visualize them.

Configuring Custom Domains and SSL Certificates

To enhance your brand identity and secure your web app, you can map it to a custom domain and enable SSL encryption.

- **Custom Domains:** Instead of using the default `<your-app-name>.azurewebsites.net` URL, you can use a custom domain that reflects your brand (e.g., `www.yourcompany.com`). Azure App Service makes it easy to map your custom domain to your web app using CNAME or A records.
- **SSL Certificates:** Secure Sockets Layer (SSL) certificates encrypt the communication between your web app and its users, ensuring data privacy and security. You can purchase and bind SSL certificates to your web app directly from the Azure Portal or use your own certificates.

Scaling Up or Down

Scaling your web app is essential to handle fluctuations in traffic and ensure optimal performance. App Service offers several scaling options:

- **Manual Scaling:** You can manually increase or decrease the number of instances (servers) running your web app. This is useful for predictable traffic patterns or when you know you need more resources for a specific event.
- **Auto-scaling:** Azure App Service can automatically scale your app based on metrics like CPU usage, memory consumption, or request count. You can set scaling rules to define when and how much to scale.
- **Pricing Tier Scaling:** You can upgrade or downgrade your App Service plan to a different pricing tier, which provides different levels of resources and features.

Deployment Slots: Testing and Staging Made Easy

Deployment slots are staging environments that allow you to test new features or code updates without affecting your production application. You can deploy your changes to a staging slot, test them thoroughly, and then swap the staging slot with the production slot when you're ready. This eliminates downtime and minimizes the risk of introducing errors into your live environment.

By utilizing these management and scaling features, you can ensure that your Azure web apps run smoothly, perform optimally, and deliver a great experience to your users.

Tips and Best Practices

Building and hosting web applications with App Service is just the beginning. To truly harness its power and ensure your applications run smoothly, securely, and efficiently, here are some essential tips and best practices:

Optimize Performance: Speed and Responsiveness Matter

- **Caching:** Implement caching mechanisms to store frequently accessed data or pages, reducing the need to generate them dynamically each time. Azure offers several caching options, including in-memory caching (Azure Cache for Redis) and content caching (Azure CDN).
- **Content Delivery Networks (CDNs):** Distribute your content across servers worldwide using Azure CDN. This reduces latency for users in different locations and improves overall website speed.
- **Compression:** Enable gzip compression for text-based content like HTML, CSS, and JavaScript. This reduces the size of files transferred over the network, leading to faster load times.
- **Bundling and Minification:** Bundle and minify your JavaScript and CSS files to reduce the number of requests and file sizes, improving page load speeds.
- **Database Optimization:** Optimize your database queries and indexes for faster data retrieval.

Secure Your Apps: Protect Against Threats

- **Authentication and Authorization:** Implement robust authentication mechanisms to verify user identities and authorization to control access to sensitive resources.

- **Input Validation:** Always validate user input to prevent common security vulnerabilities like SQL injection and cross-site scripting (XSS) attacks.
- **Web Application Firewall (WAF):** Consider using Azure's Web Application Firewall to protect your web apps from common attacks and vulnerabilities.
- **Regularly Update Dependencies:** Keep your application frameworks, libraries, and dependencies up-to-date to address security vulnerabilities.
- **Enable HTTPS:** Secure your website with HTTPS to encrypt traffic and protect data transmission.

Monitor Your Apps: Stay Informed and Proactive

- **Azure Monitor:** Use Azure Monitor to collect and analyze metrics, logs, and events from your web apps. Create custom dashboards and alerts to proactively detect and address issues.
- **Application Insights:** Gain deep insights into your application's performance, availability, and usage patterns with Application Insights. It helps you diagnose issues, optimize code, and improve user experience.

Backup and Restore: Be Prepared for the Unexpected

- **Regular Backups:** Set up regular backups of your web app code and data. Azure App Service provides built-in backup functionality, or you can use Azure Backup for more comprehensive protection.
- **Disaster Recovery:** Configure disaster recovery options like geo-redundant storage or deploying your app to multiple regions to ensure business continuity in case of an outage.

Additional Best Practices

- **Use Deployment Slots:** Leverage deployment slots for testing and staging new code before deploying it to production.
- **Optimize Images:** Compress and optimize images to reduce page load times.
- **Enable Caching Headers:** Set appropriate caching headers to instruct browsers to cache static content, reducing server requests.
- **Monitor Resource Utilization:** Keep an eye on your resource utilization (CPU, memory, disk space) to ensure your app has enough resources to perform optimally.

By following these best practices, you can build and host secure, high-performing web applications with Azure App Service. Remember, continuous optimization is key, so regularly monitor your apps, apply updates, and adapt your strategies to changing needs.

Chapter Summary

This chapter has illuminated the world of Azure App Services, demonstrating how they empower you to build, deploy, and scale web applications and APIs with ease. You learned that App Service is a fully managed platform that handles infrastructure concerns like scaling, patching, and load balancing, freeing you to focus on creating your application's core functionality.

We explored the different types of App Services: Web Apps for hosting websites and web applications, Mobile Apps for powering mobile backends, API Apps for creating and managing APIs, and WebJobs for running background tasks. You gained insight into the diverse programming languages and frameworks supported by App Service, emphasizing its flexibility to accommodate your technology stack.

We highlighted the key features and benefits of App Service, such as its support for continuous deployment, auto-scaling, custom domains, SSL certificates, and deployment slots. These features collectively empower you to build robust, secure, and highly available applications.

Furthermore, we walked you through creating your first web app using the Azure Portal. You learned how to choose a runtime stack, pricing tier, and region, and configure essential settings like app name and deployment method.

The chapter concluded by explaining the various ways to deploy your application to App Service, from using the built-in deployment tools in the Azure Portal to leveraging continuous deployment pipelines with Azure DevOps or GitHub Actions. We also discussed manual deployment options like FTP, Web Deploy, and Zip deploy.

Lastly, we provided essential tips and best practices for managing and scaling your web apps, emphasizing performance optimization, security measures, monitoring techniques, and backup/disaster recovery strategies.

With this comprehensive understanding of Azure App Services, you are now equipped with the knowledge to create, deploy, and manage your own web applications in the cloud. As we move forward, we will delve into other Azure compute services, starting with Azure Functions, which offer a powerful serverless computing model for event-driven applications.

Azure Functions: Serverless Computing Made Easy

Outline

- What is Serverless Computing?
- Introduction to Azure Functions
- Why Use Azure Functions?
- Anatomy of an Azure Function
- Triggers and Bindings
- Developing and Deploying Azure Functions
- Monitoring and Scaling Azure Functions
- Tips and Best Practices
- Chapter Summary

What is Serverless Computing?

Imagine you're hosting a dinner party. Traditionally, you'd need to buy or rent a venue, set up tables and chairs, prepare the food, and handle all the logistics. Serverless computing is like having a catering service that takes care of everything. You simply tell them how many guests are coming and what dishes you want, and they handle the rest. You don't need to worry about renting a kitchen, buying groceries, or hiring staff.

That's the essence of serverless computing: a cloud computing model where you can run code without managing the underlying infrastructure. With serverless, you focus solely on writing your application code, and the cloud provider handles everything else, from provisioning servers and managing their operating systems to scaling resources based on demand.

Key Characteristics of Serverless Computing

- **No Infrastructure Management:** The most significant advantage of serverless is that you don't have to worry about servers. You don't need to provision, configure, maintain, or patch them. The cloud provider takes care of all the infrastructure-related tasks, allowing you to focus entirely on your application logic.
- **Event-Driven Execution:** Serverless functions (or "functions" for short) are triggered by events, such as HTTP requests, database changes, or messages in a queue. This means they only run when needed, making them highly efficient for event-based workloads.
- **Automatic Scaling:** Serverless platforms automatically scale your functions based on demand. If your application experiences a sudden surge in traffic, the platform will spin up more instances of your function to handle the load. Conversely, if traffic is low, the platform will scale down to save resources.
- **Pay-per-Execution:** With serverless, you only pay for the actual execution time of your functions. You're not charged for idle time or unused resources. This can result in significant cost savings, especially for applications with unpredictable or sporadic usage patterns.

Real-World Examples

Let's look at a couple of real-world scenarios where serverless computing shines:

- **Image Processing:** You have a website where users can upload images. You can use a serverless function to automatically resize, optimize, and watermark these images whenever they are uploaded.

- **Chatbots:** A serverless function can power a chatbot that responds to customer queries in real time. The function can scale seamlessly to handle thousands of concurrent conversations.

In a Nutshell

Serverless computing is a game-changer for developers. It allows you to build and run applications without the hassle of managing infrastructure. This model is highly scalable, cost-effective, and well-suited for event-driven workloads. Whether you're building a simple web application or a complex enterprise solution, serverless computing can simplify your development process and help you focus on what truly matters – delivering innovative and valuable applications to your users.

Introduction to Azure Functions

Azure Functions is your gateway to the world of serverless computing on the Azure platform. It's a cloud service that allows you to run small pieces of code, called "functions," without managing the underlying infrastructure.

Event-Driven Power

The magic of Azure Functions lies in its **event-driven** nature. Instead of constantly running, your functions are triggered into action by specific events. These events can be almost anything, including:

- **HTTP requests:** When a user visits a website or triggers a webhook.
- **Timer events:** On a scheduled basis, such as every hour or every day.
- **Queue messages:** When a new message is added to an Azure Storage Queue.
- **Blob storage events:** When a new or updated file is added to Azure Blob Storage.
- **Cosmos DB changes:** When data is added, modified, or deleted in a Cosmos DB database.
- **And many more:** Azure Functions integrates with a wide range of Azure services and external systems, allowing you to trigger functions based on various events.

Coding Your Way: Multiple Languages Supported

You're not confined to a single programming language when working with Azure Functions. You can write your functions in a variety of popular languages, including:

- **C#:** Microsoft's object-oriented language, often used with the .NET framework.
- **JavaScript:** A versatile scripting language commonly used for web development.
- **Python:** A popular high-level language known for its simplicity and readability.
- **Java:** A widely-used object-oriented language suitable for enterprise applications.
- **PowerShell:** Microsoft's automation and scripting language, ideal for administrative tasks.
- **Custom Handlers:** Azure Functions even allows you to run functions written in other languages using custom handlers.

This flexibility means you can leverage your existing skills and preferences when building serverless applications in Azure.

A Simple Analogy

Think of Azure Functions as a team of specialized agents. Each agent (function) is trained to handle a specific task (event). When a trigger occurs (like receiving an HTTP request), the appropriate agent is called into action to complete the task. The agents are highly efficient, only working when needed, and they can scale up or down automatically based on the workload.

In essence, Azure Functions is a powerful and versatile tool for building event-driven applications in the cloud. Its serverless nature, event-driven execution, and multi-language support make it an ideal choice for a wide range of scenarios, from simple automations to complex enterprise workflows.

Why Use Azure Functions?

Azure Functions offers a compelling alternative to traditional web applications and virtual machines, especially for certain types of workloads and development scenarios. Here are some of the key advantages that make Azure Functions an attractive choice:

1. No Infrastructure Management

The biggest advantage of Azure Functions is the freedom from infrastructure management. You don't need to worry about provisioning or managing servers, operating systems, or any other underlying infrastructure. Azure takes care of all that, allowing you to focus solely on writing your code. This significantly reduces operational overhead and allows you to focus on delivering value to your users.

2. Event-Driven Architecture

Azure Functions are event-driven, meaning they execute in response to specific events or triggers. This makes them ideal for a variety of scenarios, such as:

- **Processing data in real-time:** Respond to events like incoming data streams, file uploads, or database changes.
- **Automating tasks:** Trigger functions on a schedule or based on specific events to automate repetitive tasks.
- **Building lightweight APIs:** Create APIs that are triggered by HTTP requests.

By only executing when needed, Azure Functions are highly efficient and cost-effective, as you only pay for the actual execution time.

3. Automatic Scaling

Azure Functions automatically scale based on demand. When your application experiences increased traffic or workload, Azure dynamically allocates resources to handle the load. This ensures that your functions can handle any traffic volume without requiring you to manually provision or manage additional resources. This scalability allows you to focus on building your application without worrying about capacity planning or performance bottlenecks.

4. Pay-per-Execution Pricing

Azure Functions follow a pay-per-execution pricing model, where you are charged only for the time your functions run. There are no upfront costs or charges for idle time. This makes Azure Functions a cost-effective option, especially for workloads with unpredictable or sporadic usage patterns.

5. Seamless Integration with Azure Services

Azure Functions seamlessly integrate with a wide range of Azure services, including:

- **Azure Storage:** Connect to Blob Storage, Queue Storage, and Table Storage for storing and retrieving data.
- **Azure Cosmos DB:** Interact with your Cosmos DB databases to perform operations like reading, writing, and querying data.
- **Azure Event Hubs:** Receive and process events from Azure Event Hubs, a highly scalable event ingestion service.

- **Azure Logic Apps:** Integrate your functions with Logic Apps to build complex workflows and orchestrate processes across different Azure services.

This rich integration capability allows you to build powerful and scalable applications that leverage the full spectrum of Azure services.

6. Variety of Triggers and Bindings

Azure Functions offer a wide array of triggers and bindings, making it easy to connect your functions to various event sources and data sinks. Triggers define the events that cause your functions to run, while bindings provide a declarative way to integrate your functions with other services and data. This simplifies the process of building event-driven applications and reduces the amount of boilerplate code you need to write.

By leveraging these advantages, Azure Functions can empower you to build efficient, scalable, and cost-effective applications in the cloud without the burden of infrastructure management. Whether you're a startup or an enterprise, Azure Functions can help you accelerate your development process and deliver innovative solutions faster.

Anatomy of an Azure Function

To understand how Azure Functions work, let's dissect their structure and explore the key components that make them tick. Think of it like taking apart a watch to see the gears that make it tell time.

Function Code: The Heart of the Matter

At the core of every Azure Function is your **function code**. This is the logic you write, defining what the function does when it's triggered. You have the flexibility to write your code in various programming languages supported by Azure Functions, such as C#, JavaScript, Python, or Java.

Your code can perform a wide range of tasks, from processing data and interacting with other services to generating responses for HTTP requests or performing complex calculations. It's the brains of your serverless operation.

Triggers: The Initiators of Action

Triggers are the events that set your functions in motion. They define what actions or conditions cause your function to execute. Azure Functions supports a variety of triggers, including:

- **HTTP Triggers:** Your function runs when it receives an HTTP request. This is commonly used to build APIs or webhooks.
- **Timer Triggers:** Your function runs on a predefined schedule, such as every hour or every day. This is useful for running scheduled tasks or background processes.
- **Queue Triggers:** Your function runs when a new message arrives in an Azure Storage Queue. This is often used for processing asynchronous tasks or integrating with other Azure services.
- **Blob Storage Triggers:** Your function runs when a new or updated file is added to Azure Blob Storage. This is handy for image processing, data analysis, or file synchronization.
- **Event Grid Triggers:** Your function runs in response to events from various Azure services or custom events. This allows you to build reactive applications that respond to changes in your environment.
- **Cosmos DB Triggers:** Your function runs when there are changes in a Cosmos DB database, enabling real-time data processing and synchronization.

Bindings: Connecting the Dots

Bindings are the glue that connects your functions to other Azure services or data sources. They provide a declarative way to integrate with services like storage accounts, queues, databases, and event hubs. Bindings streamline the process of reading and writing data, eliminating the need to write boilerplate code for handling connections and data serialization.

Azure Functions supports input and output bindings. Input bindings provide data to your function, while output bindings send data from your function to other services or destinations. This allows you to easily interact with other Azure services without writing complex integration code.

Function App: The Container

A **function app** is a container for one or more functions that share the same hosting plan, runtime, and resources. Think of it as a project folder where you organize your functions. You can deploy, manage, and scale your functions as a unit within the function app.

Each function app has its own unique name, which is part of the function's URL (e.g., `https://myfunctionapp.azurewebsites.net/api/myfunction`). You can have multiple function apps within your Azure subscription, each serving different purposes or applications.

The Big Picture

By understanding the anatomy of an Azure Function - the function code, triggers, bindings, and function app - you'll be well-equipped to start building your own serverless applications. In the following sections, we'll delve deeper into triggers and bindings, explore the development and deployment process, and provide tips and best practices for maximizing the power and efficiency of Azure Functions.

Triggers and Bindings

Triggers and bindings are two fundamental concepts in Azure Functions that work together to streamline the process of building event-driven applications. They act as the bridge between your function code and external events and data sources, enabling your functions to respond to triggers and interact with various Azure services seamlessly.

Triggers: The Catalysts of Action

A trigger is the event that kicks off your Azure Function's execution. It defines what kind of event or condition causes your function to run. Azure Functions support a wide variety of triggers, including:

- **HTTP Triggers:** Your function is executed when it receives an HTTP request, such as a GET, POST, PUT, or DELETE request. This is commonly used to build serverless APIs or webhooks.
- **Timer Triggers:** Your function is executed on a pre-defined schedule, like every hour or every day. This is perfect for automating scheduled tasks, such as sending reminder emails or cleaning up data.
- **Queue Triggers:** Your function is triggered whenever a new message is added to an Azure Storage Queue. This is often used for processing asynchronous tasks, such as image resizing or order processing.
- **Blob Storage Triggers:** Your function is executed when a new or updated file is added to Azure Blob Storage. This is useful for scenarios like image processing, data analysis, or file synchronization.
- **Cosmos DB Triggers:** Your function is triggered when there are changes (inserts, updates, or deletes) in a Cosmos DB database. This enables real-time data processing and synchronization.
- **Event Hub Triggers:** Your function is triggered when events are received from Azure Event Hubs, a highly scalable event ingestion service. This is ideal for processing large volumes of data from various sources.

Bindings: Connecting the Dots

While triggers initiate function execution, bindings are the connectors that facilitate the flow of data between your function and other Azure services or external systems. Bindings simplify the process of reading and writing data, eliminating the need for you to write boilerplate code for handling connections and data serialization.

Azure Functions supports various types of bindings, including:

- **Storage Queue Bindings:** You can use input bindings to read messages from a queue and output bindings to add messages to a queue.
- **Blob Storage Bindings:** Input bindings let you read the contents of a blob, and output bindings allow you to create or update blobs.
- **Cosmos DB Bindings:** Input bindings let you query and read documents from a Cosmos DB database, while output bindings enable you to create, update, or delete documents.
- **Table Storage Bindings:** Input and output bindings allow you to interact with Azure Table Storage, a NoSQL key-value store.
- **HTTP Bindings:** Input bindings can provide the details of the incoming HTTP request, while output bindings allow you to return an HTTP response.

Putting it All Together

Think of triggers and bindings as a dynamic duo that works in harmony. Triggers tell your functions *when* to run, while bindings tell them *what* to do with the data. By combining triggers and bindings, you can create powerful and flexible serverless applications that can respond to various events and interact with a wide range of Azure services and data sources.

Developing and Deploying Azure Functions

Azure Functions offers a flexible development experience, catering to various preferences and skill levels. You can choose from several tools and methods to create, test, and deploy your serverless functions.

1. Azure Portal: The Integrated Development Environment

For beginners or those seeking a quick and easy way to get started, the Azure Portal provides a built-in code editor and tools for developing and deploying Azure Functions directly in the browser.

- **Creation and Editing:** You can create a new function, choose a template, and write your code directly within the portal. The editor supports multiple languages and offers syntax highlighting and basic code completion features.
- **Testing:** The portal allows you to test your functions locally within the browser by providing sample inputs and viewing the output.
- **Deployment:** You can directly deploy your function code to Azure from the portal, either manually or by connecting to a source control repository like GitHub or Azure DevOps.

2. Visual Studio Code: The Developer's Powerhouse

Visual Studio Code (VS Code) is a popular code editor that offers a more robust development experience for Azure Functions. The Azure Functions extension for VS Code provides a comprehensive set of tools for:

- **Local Development:** Create, edit, and debug your functions locally on your machine. The extension provides code templates, snippets, and debugging tools to streamline development.
- **Integrated Testing:** Test your functions locally with integrated debugging and test tools.
- **Seamless Deployment:** Easily deploy your functions directly to Azure from within VS Code.

- **Remote Debugging:** Debug your functions running in Azure directly from VS Code.

3. Other Tools and IDEs

If you prefer a different development environment, several other tools and IDEs support Azure Functions development, including:

- **Visual Studio:** Microsoft's flagship IDE provides a comprehensive development environment for building Azure Functions projects.
- **IntelliJ IDEA:** This popular Java IDE offers a plugin for Azure Functions development.
- **Azure Functions Core Tools:** A command-line interface (CLI) that allows you to develop and test functions locally from your terminal.

4. Deployment Options

Once your functions are ready, you have multiple options for deploying them to Azure:

- **From Code Repository:** Connect your function app to a source code repository like GitHub, Bitbucket, or Azure DevOps. Azure will then automatically deploy your code whenever you push changes to the repository.
- **ZIP Deployment:** Package your function code and dependencies into a ZIP file and upload it to Azure.
- **Container Deployment:** Package your function as a Docker container and deploy it to Azure Container Instances or Azure Kubernetes Service (AKS).
- **Azure Portal:** Manually deploy your function code through the Azure Portal's code editor.

Choosing Your Path

The best development and deployment method for you depends on your personal preferences, experience level, and project requirements. If you're a beginner or prefer a simple approach, the Azure Portal might be the easiest way to get started. For more advanced scenarios or if you need a more robust development environment, Visual Studio Code or another IDE might be a better choice.

Remember, regardless of the tools you use, Azure Functions provides a flexible and powerful platform for building event-driven applications in the cloud.

Monitoring and Scaling Azure Functions

To ensure your Azure Functions perform optimally and efficiently, it's essential to monitor their performance and understand how Azure scales them based on demand. Thankfully, Azure provides robust tools and features to help you do just that.

Monitoring Performance

Azure offers two primary tools for monitoring the performance of your functions:

1. **Azure Monitor:**
- **Metrics:** Azure Monitor collects a wide range of metrics for your functions, including executions, success rates, duration, and memory usage. You can visualize these metrics in the Azure Portal or create custom dashboards for deeper insights.
- **Logs:** Azure Functions automatically log detailed information about each function execution, including start and end times, input and output data, and any errors or exceptions. These logs can be accessed through Azure Monitor Logs, providing a valuable resource for troubleshooting and analysis.
2. **Application Insights:**

- **Distributed Tracing:** Application Insights provides distributed tracing capabilities, allowing you to track requests across multiple functions and services. This is particularly useful for understanding the performance of complex serverless applications.
- **Performance Monitoring:** Monitor response times, dependencies, and exceptions to identify performance bottlenecks and optimize your functions.
- **Custom Events and Metrics:** Collect custom events and metrics from your functions to gain deeper insights into their behavior and usage patterns.

Scaling Azure Functions

One of the major advantages of Azure Functions is their ability to scale automatically based on demand. When your functions experience increased load, Azure dynamically allocates resources to handle the additional requests. This ensures that your applications remain responsive and performant even during traffic spikes.

Azure Functions scale out by adding more instances of your function app. The number of instances is determined by factors like the number of incoming requests, queue length, and CPU usage. Azure's scaling algorithm continuously monitors these metrics and adjusts the number of instances as needed.

Manual Scaling Options

While Azure Functions typically handle scaling automatically, you also have the option to configure scaling settings manually. This gives you more fine-grained control over how your functions scale in response to demand.

- **Consumption Plan:** In the Consumption plan, scaling is fully automatic, and you don't have any control over the number of instances.
- **Premium Plan:** The Premium plan gives you more control over scaling, allowing you to configure minimum and maximum instance counts, as well as warm-up instances to reduce cold start delays.
- **Dedicated (App Service) Plan:** If you're running your functions in an App Service Plan, you can leverage the scaling features of App Service to manually or automatically scale your functions.

Best Practices for Scaling

To optimize the scaling of your Azure Functions, consider the following best practices:

- **Monitor Function Performance:** Regularly monitor your function's performance metrics and logs to understand how it's performing under different loads.
- **Adjust Scaling Settings:** If you notice performance issues or bottlenecks, consider adjusting the scaling settings in your function app's hosting plan.
- **Optimize Code:** Ensure your function code is efficient and well-optimized to minimize execution time and resource usage.
- **Utilize Durable Functions:** For long-running or stateful workflows, consider using Durable Functions, which provide built-in state management and orchestration capabilities.

By monitoring your Azure Functions and understanding the scaling mechanisms, you can ensure that your applications can handle any workload and deliver a seamless user experience.

Tips and Best Practices

As you embark on your Azure Functions development journey, keep these practical tips and best practices in mind to create efficient, scalable, and cost-effective serverless applications:

Keep Functions Small and Focused

Think of your functions as individual building blocks. Each function should ideally perform a single, well-defined task. This modular approach promotes reusability, improves code maintainability, and simplifies testing. By breaking down complex tasks into smaller functions, you can isolate problems more easily and update individual components without affecting the entire application.

Optimize Performance

Performance is key in any application, and Azure Functions are no exception. Here are some tips to optimize the performance of your functions:

- **Asynchronous Patterns:** Use asynchronous programming patterns (async/await in C#, Promises in JavaScript) to avoid blocking operations and improve the responsiveness of your functions.
- **Avoid Long-Running Operations:** Azure Functions are designed for short-lived executions. If you have long-running tasks, consider breaking them down into smaller steps or using Durable Functions for orchestration.
- **Caching:** Cache data or responses to avoid redundant calculations and improve response times.
- **Code Optimization:** Profile your code to identify performance bottlenecks and optimize your algorithms and data structures.

Leverage Bindings

Bindings are a powerful feature of Azure Functions that simplifies integration with other Azure services and data sources. By using bindings, you can avoid writing boilerplate code for connecting to services and handling data serialization. This not only makes your code cleaner and more concise but also reduces the risk of errors. Explore the various input and output bindings available for Azure Storage, Cosmos DB, Event Hubs, and other services to streamline your integrations.

Monitor and Log

Monitoring and logging are essential for understanding how your functions are performing and identifying potential issues.

- **Azure Monitor:** Use Azure Monitor to collect metrics and logs from your functions. This can help you track execution times, error rates, and resource usage.
- **Application Insights:** Leverage Application Insights to gain deeper insights into your application's performance, dependencies, and user behavior.
- **Structured Logging:** Use a structured logging framework like Serilog or NLog to capture rich information about your function's execution in a format that's easy to analyze.

By actively monitoring and logging, you can proactively detect and resolve issues before they impact your users.

Cost Optimization

While Azure Functions are generally cost-effective, it's still important to be mindful of your spending. Here are some tips to optimize your Azure Functions costs:

- **Understand the Billing Model:** Azure Functions are billed based on the number of executions, execution time, and memory consumed. Familiarize yourself with the pricing details to estimate your costs.
- **Choose the Right Plan:** Azure Functions offer different hosting plans with varying features and pricing. Choose the plan that best suits your needs and budget.
- **Reserved Instances:** If you have predictable usage patterns, consider using reserved instances to get a discount on your compute costs.

- **Optimize Cold Starts:** Azure Functions may experience cold starts, where the function instance needs to be initialized before it can execute. This can lead to increased latency for the first request. To minimize cold starts, consider using pre-warmed instances or the Premium plan.

By following these best practices and tips, you can harness the full power of Azure Functions to build efficient, scalable, and cost-effective serverless applications.

Chapter Summary

This chapter has illuminated the world of Azure Functions, a powerful serverless computing service that can revolutionize how you build and deploy applications in the cloud. We started by exploring the concept of serverless computing, emphasizing its key benefit of eliminating the need for infrastructure management. You learned how serverless functions execute on-demand, scale automatically, and are billed based on actual usage, making them a cost-effective and efficient choice for many scenarios.

Next, we introduced Azure Functions as Microsoft's serverless offering, highlighting its event-driven architecture and support for multiple programming languages. We then delved into the anatomy of an Azure Function, examining its key components:

- **Function Code:** The core logic that defines the actions your function performs.
- **Triggers:** The events that initiate the execution of your function, such as HTTP requests or queue messages.
- **Bindings:** The declarative way to connect your function to other Azure services or data sources, simplifying integration and data exchange.
- **Function App:** The container that houses one or more related functions, sharing the same hosting plan and resources.

We discussed the various types of triggers available in Azure Functions, such as HTTP triggers, timer triggers, queue triggers, blob storage triggers, Cosmos DB triggers, and event hub triggers. We also explained different types of input and output bindings for integrating with Azure Storage, Cosmos DB, and other services.

You gained an overview of the development and deployment process for Azure Functions, learning about different tools like the Azure Portal, Visual Studio Code, and other IDEs. We also discussed various deployment options, including deploying from code repositories or using ZIP files.

Finally, we explored how to monitor and scale Azure Functions using Azure Monitor and Application Insights, ensuring optimal performance and reliability. We provided tips and best practices for designing efficient functions, optimizing performance, leveraging bindings, monitoring, and managing costs.

With this knowledge, you're now equipped to explore the world of serverless computing with Azure Functions. You can start building event-driven applications, automating tasks, and creating scalable APIs without the hassle of managing infrastructure. In the next chapter, we'll move on to Azure Kubernetes Service (AKS), another powerful compute service in Azure that's designed for orchestrating containerized applications at scale.

Azure Kubernetes Service (AKS): Orchestrating Containers at Scale

Outline

- What are Containers?
- What is Kubernetes?
- Introduction to Azure Kubernetes Service (AKS)
- Why Use AKS?
- Key Features of AKS
- Creating an AKS Cluster
- Deploying Applications to AKS
- Managing and Scaling AKS Clusters
- Tips and Best Practices
- Chapter Summary

What Are Containers?

Imagine you're packing for a trip. You wouldn't just throw all your clothes, toiletries, and gadgets into a suitcase haphazardly. Instead, you'd neatly organize them into separate compartments or bags. This makes it easier to find what you need, ensures that items don't get damaged, and allows you to efficiently pack and unpack your suitcase.

Containers are like those compartments for your applications. They are a lightweight and portable way to package and run software. Each container encapsulates everything an application needs to run:

- **Code:** The application's source code and any associated files.
- **Runtime:** The language runtime or interpreter needed to execute the code (e.g., Python, Node.js, Java).
- **Dependencies:** Libraries, frameworks, and other software components that the application relies on.
- **System Tools:** Essential system tools and libraries, such as a shell or package manager.

Containers: A Self-Contained Universe

By bundling all these components together, containers create a self-contained environment for your application. This means that your application will run consistently across different environments, whether it's your local development machine, a testing server, or a production environment in the cloud. You don't have to worry about missing dependencies or conflicting libraries – everything your application needs is neatly packaged within the container.

Benefits of Containers

Containers offer several key benefits that make them a popular choice for modern software development and deployment:

- **Portability:** Containers are highly portable. They can run on any system that has a container runtime installed, regardless of the underlying operating system or infrastructure. This allows you to easily move your applications between different environments without having to worry about compatibility issues.

- **Isolation:** Each container runs in its own isolated environment, separate from other containers and the host operating system. This isolation prevents conflicts between applications and ensures that each application has its own dedicated resources.
- **Efficiency:** Containers are lightweight and consume fewer resources than virtual machines. They share the host operating system's kernel, which means they don't need to boot up a full operating system for each container. This allows you to run more containers on the same hardware, increasing efficiency and reducing costs.
- **Scalability:** Containers are designed to be easily scalable. You can quickly create new instances of a container to handle increased demand, and you can just as easily shut down containers when they're no longer needed. This makes containers ideal for building scalable and resilient applications.

The Container Revolution

Containers have revolutionized the way software is developed and deployed. They offer a consistent, portable, and efficient way to package and run applications, making it easier to build, test, deploy, and manage complex software systems. In the next section, we'll explore Kubernetes, a powerful platform for orchestrating containerized applications at scale.

What is Kubernetes?

As we explored in the previous section, containers are a fantastic way to package and run applications. But what if you have hundreds or even thousands of containers running simultaneously? How do you manage them efficiently, ensure they're running smoothly, and scale them as needed?

That's where Kubernetes comes in. Kubernetes (often abbreviated as K8s) is an open-source platform designed specifically for orchestrating containerized applications at scale. Think of it as the conductor of an orchestra, where each musician (container) plays a specific instrument (service), and the conductor (Kubernetes) ensures that they all work together harmoniously to create beautiful music (your application).

The Container Conductor

Kubernetes automates the deployment, scaling, and management of containerized applications. Here's how it orchestrates this complex process:

- **Container Orchestration:** Kubernetes ensures that the right number of containers are running to meet demand. It automatically starts new containers when needed and shuts them down when they're no longer required. This ensures that your application can handle varying levels of traffic without manual intervention.
- **Self-Healing:** Kubernetes constantly monitors the health of your containers. If a container fails, Kubernetes automatically restarts or replaces it to keep your application running smoothly. This self-healing capability helps you maintain high availability and minimize downtime.
- **Service Discovery:** Kubernetes automatically assigns IP addresses and DNS names to containers, making them discoverable within the cluster. This allows containers to communicate with each other seamlessly, even as they are scaled up or down.
- **Load Balancing:** Kubernetes distributes incoming traffic across multiple containers to ensure high availability and scalability. It also provides features like session affinity and health checks to ensure that traffic is routed to healthy containers.
- **Storage Orchestration:** Kubernetes can manage the persistent storage of data used by containers. It allows you to mount storage volumes from various sources, such as Azure Disk Storage or Azure Files, to your containers, ensuring that your data is preserved even if a container is restarted or replaced.

The Kubernetes Advantage

Kubernetes has become the de facto standard for container orchestration due to its numerous benefits:

- **Scalability:** Kubernetes makes it easy to scale your applications up or down to meet demand.
- **Portability:** Kubernetes can run on various infrastructure providers, including on-premises servers, public clouds (like Azure), and hybrid environments.
- **Extensibility:** Kubernetes is highly extensible, with a vast ecosystem of plugins and tools that allow you to customize and extend its functionality.
- **Large Community:** Kubernetes has a large and active community of users and contributors, which ensures continuous development, support, and innovation.

In the next section, we'll introduce you to Azure Kubernetes Service (AKS), a managed Kubernetes offering on Azure that simplifies the deployment and management of Kubernetes clusters.

Introduction to Azure Kubernetes Service (AKS)

While Kubernetes is a powerful tool for orchestrating containers, setting up and managing a Kubernetes cluster can be a complex and time-consuming task. That's where Azure Kubernetes Service (AKS) comes to the rescue. AKS is a managed Kubernetes service on Azure that simplifies the deployment, management, and scaling of containerized applications, allowing you to focus on your applications rather than the underlying infrastructure.

AKS: Your Kubernetes Autopilot

Think of AKS as your Kubernetes autopilot. It takes care of the heavy lifting of managing a Kubernetes cluster, freeing you from many of the operational burdens. With AKS, Azure handles tasks like:

- **Cluster Management:** AKS automatically provisions and scales the underlying infrastructure that powers your Kubernetes cluster. This includes virtual machines, networking, and storage. You simply specify the desired cluster size and configuration, and AKS takes care of the rest.
- **Control Plane Management:** The Kubernetes control plane is the brains of the cluster, responsible for managing workloads, scheduling containers, and maintaining the desired state. AKS manages the control plane for you, ensuring it's highly available, secure, and up-to-date.
- **Node Management:** The worker nodes in your AKS cluster are where your containers actually run. AKS automatically manages the worker nodes, including provisioning, scaling, and patching. You can easily add or remove nodes as your workload demands change.
- **Upgrades and Patching:** Kubernetes is a rapidly evolving platform, with new features and security updates released regularly. AKS takes care of upgrading and patching your Kubernetes environment, ensuring that you're always running the latest and most secure version.

The AKS Advantage

AKS offers several key advantages over self-managed Kubernetes clusters:

- **Simplified Management:** AKS eliminates the complexity of managing a Kubernetes cluster, freeing you up to focus on developing and deploying your applications.
- **Reduced Operational Overhead:** Azure handles many of the operational tasks associated with Kubernetes, such as provisioning, scaling, and maintenance.
- **Increased Reliability:** AKS ensures high availability for your Kubernetes cluster by automatically replicating the control plane and providing features like automatic node repair and self-healing.
- **Enhanced Security:** AKS integrates with Azure Active Directory (AAD) for authentication and authorization, and it supports network policies for isolating workloads and protecting sensitive data.
- **Cost-Effectiveness:** With its pay-as-you-go pricing model, AKS allows you to pay only for the resources you use, making it a cost-effective option for running containerized applications.

By leveraging the power of AKS, you can harness the benefits of Kubernetes without the operational overhead. This allows you to focus on building and scaling your applications, while Azure takes care of the underlying infrastructure and ensures a reliable, secure, and cost-effective environment.

Why Use AKS?

While Kubernetes offers immense power and flexibility for managing containerized applications, it can also be complex to set up and maintain. Azure Kubernetes Service (AKS) steps in to address this challenge, providing a managed Kubernetes environment that simplifies operations and unlocks a range of benefits. Let's delve into why AKS might be the perfect fit for your cloud-native applications:

1. Simplified Kubernetes Management

AKS takes the complexity out of Kubernetes. Azure handles the operational overhead of managing the underlying infrastructure, including the control plane, worker nodes, and networking components. This means you don't need to worry about tasks like provisioning servers, configuring the Kubernetes control plane, or managing upgrades and patches. Instead, you can focus your time and resources on developing and deploying your applications.

2. Effortless Scalability

With AKS, scaling your containerized applications becomes a breeze. You can easily scale up or down the number of nodes in your cluster based on demand, ensuring optimal resource utilization and performance. AKS supports both manual and automatic scaling, allowing you to adapt to varying workloads and traffic patterns.

3. High Availability and Reliability

AKS is designed to provide a highly available and resilient environment for your applications. Azure automatically replicates the Kubernetes control plane across multiple nodes, ensuring that your cluster remains operational even if individual nodes fail. AKS also offers features like automatic node repair and self-healing, which help maintain application uptime and minimize downtime.

4. Seamless Integration with Azure Services

AKS seamlessly integrates with a wide range of Azure services, providing a comprehensive ecosystem for building and running cloud-native applications. Here are some notable integrations:

- **Azure Container Registry (ACR):** Store and manage your container images in ACR and easily deploy them to your AKS cluster.
- **Azure Monitor:** Collect and analyze logs and metrics from your AKS cluster and applications to gain insights into their health and performance.
- **Azure Active Directory (AAD):** Integrate with AAD to control access to your AKS cluster and resources with role-based access control (RBAC).
- **Azure DevOps:** Streamline your continuous integration and continuous delivery (CI/CD) pipelines for deploying applications to AKS.
- **Azure Load Balancer:** Distribute traffic across your application pods for high availability and scalability.

5. Robust Security

AKS inherits Azure's robust security features, ensuring that your containerized applications and data are protected from threats. This includes:

- **Network Security:** Azure provides network security groups (NSGs) and virtual network (VNet) integration to control inbound and outbound traffic to your AKS cluster.
- **Identity and Access Management:** Integrate with Azure AD to manage user access and permissions, ensuring that only authorized personnel can access your cluster resources.
- **Azure Policy:** Apply policy definitions to your AKS cluster to enforce security and compliance standards.
- **Azure Defender for Kubernetes:** This security solution provides threat protection, vulnerability scanning, and runtime protection for your container workloads.

6. Cost-Effectiveness

AKS follows a pay-as-you-go pricing model, so you only pay for the virtual machines and other resources you consume. This makes it a cost-effective option, especially compared to maintaining your own Kubernetes cluster on-premises. Additionally, AKS's autoscaling capabilities help you optimize costs by automatically adjusting resources based on demand.

By choosing AKS, you're not just getting a Kubernetes platform; you're getting a fully managed service that simplifies operations, enhances reliability and security, and seamlessly integrates with the broader Azure ecosystem. This makes it an excellent choice for organizations of all sizes that want to leverage the power of Kubernetes for their containerized applications.

Key Features of AKS

Azure Kubernetes Service (AKS) is packed with features that simplify the deployment and management of Kubernetes clusters, making it an attractive option for both beginners and experienced Kubernetes users. Let's explore some of its key highlights:

Managed Kubernetes Control Plane

The Kubernetes control plane is the brains of the cluster, responsible for critical tasks like scheduling containers, managing network traffic, and storing cluster state. With AKS, you don't have to worry about setting up or maintaining this control plane yourself. Azure manages it for you, ensuring high availability, security, and automatic updates. This frees you from the operational burden of managing the control plane and allows you to focus on your applications.

Automatic Upgrades

Keeping your Kubernetes environment up-to-date is crucial for security and stability. AKS simplifies this process by automatically applying updates and security patches to the Kubernetes control plane and node components. You can also configure automatic upgrades for your applications, ensuring that they are always running on the latest versions.

Serverless Kubernetes with ACI Integration

Azure Container Instances (ACI) is a serverless container service that allows you to run containers on-demand without having to provision or manage any infrastructure. AKS integrates seamlessly with ACI, allowing you to run serverless containers alongside your regular Kubernetes pods. This gives you the flexibility to choose the right compute model for each workload, whether it's a long-running application or a short-lived task.

Virtual Nodes: Dynamic Scaling with ACI

AKS virtual nodes take serverless computing to the next level. With virtual nodes, you can dynamically scale your AKS cluster using Azure Container Instances (ACI) to handle sudden bursts of traffic or high-demand workloads. This allows you to scale your cluster rapidly and efficiently, without having to wait for new nodes to be provisioned.

Role-Based Access Control (RBAC)

Security is a top priority in any Kubernetes environment. AKS integrates with Azure Active Directory (AAD) to provide role-based access control (RBAC). This allows you to define granular permissions for users and groups, ensuring that only authorized personnel can access your cluster and its resources.

Azure DevOps Integration

Azure DevOps provides a comprehensive set of tools for building, testing, and deploying applications. AKS integrates seamlessly with Azure DevOps, allowing you to create CI/CD pipelines that automate the process of building, testing, and deploying containerized applications to your AKS cluster. This streamlined workflow accelerates your development process and ensures that your applications are always up-to-date.

Azure Monitor Integration

Monitoring the health and performance of your AKS cluster and applications is crucial for ensuring their smooth operation. AKS integrates with Azure Monitor, providing you with a centralized view of logs, metrics, and alerts from your cluster. You can create custom dashboards and alerts to proactively identify and address issues before they impact your users.

By leveraging these key features, AKS empowers you to build, deploy, and manage scalable and reliable containerized applications in Azure with ease and confidence. Whether you're a beginner or a seasoned Kubernetes expert, AKS provides a managed platform that simplifies the complexities of Kubernetes and accelerates your cloud-native journey.

Creating an AKS Cluster

Let's walk through the steps of creating your first Azure Kubernetes Service (AKS) cluster using the user-friendly Azure Portal interface.

1. **Choosing a Resource Group and Region:**

   - Open the Azure Portal (https://portal.azure.com/).
   - In the search bar, type "Kubernetes Services" and select it from the results.
   - Click "Create" to start the AKS cluster creation process.
   - On the "Basics" tab, choose your subscription (if you have multiple).
   - **Resource group:** Select an existing resource group or create a new one by clicking "Create new." Give it a descriptive name, such as "myAKSCluster-rg."
   - **Region:** Select the region closest to your users or where your data needs to reside. Consider factors like service availability and compliance requirements. For this example, we'll use "East US."
   - **Kubernetes version:** Choose the desired Kubernetes version. AKS offers several supported versions, with the default usually being a good starting point.
   - **Availability zones:** For higher availability, you can choose to distribute your cluster nodes across multiple Availability Zones within the region. We'll skip this for now and leave it at "None."

2. **Specifying the Kubernetes Version and Node Size:**

   - **Node size:** Select the virtual machine size for your cluster's worker nodes. This determines the resources (CPU, memory, storage) available to your containers. Choose a size that aligns with your workload requirements and budget. Start with a smaller size and scale up later if needed.

- **Node count:** Specify the initial number of nodes you want in your cluster. You can scale this up or down later. For our example, we'll start with 1 node.

3. **Configuring Networking and Authentication:**

- **Networking:**
    - **Network configuration:** Choose between "Kubenet" (basic networking) or "Azure CNI" (advanced networking with more features). We'll select "Kubenet" for simplicity.
- **Authentication:**
    - **Authentication method:** Choose between "Service principal" (recommended for production environments) or "System-assigned managed identity." For our example, we'll use "System-assigned managed identity."
    - You can customize other options like network policies and Azure Policy if needed, but we'll keep the defaults for now.

4. **Deploying the AKS Cluster:**

- **Tags (Optional):** Add tags to your cluster for better organization and cost tracking.
- **Review + create:** Carefully review your configuration. Azure will show you an estimated cost based on your selections.
- **Create:** Click "Create" to start the deployment process.

Monitoring Deployment Progress:

- The deployment process may take several minutes. You can track its progress on the deployment page.
- Once the deployment is complete, you'll see a notification and you can access your AKS cluster from the Azure Portal.

Congratulations! You've successfully created your first AKS cluster. You're now ready to start deploying and managing containerized applications on Azure.

Deploying Applications to AKS

Once your AKS cluster is up and running, the exciting part begins: deploying your containerized applications. Azure offers multiple avenues for achieving this, each catering to different levels of expertise and automation preferences. Let's explore these methods:

Using kubectl: The Command-Line Powerhouse

`kubectl` is the command-line tool that empowers you to interact with and manage your Kubernetes cluster. It's your Swiss Army knife for deploying and managing applications on AKS. Here's a simplified example of how to deploy an application using `kubectl`:

1. **Create a Deployment:** A Deployment describes the desired state of your application, including the number of replicas (pods) to run and the container image to use. You'll define this in a YAML file and apply it using `kubectl apply -f <your-deployment-file>.yaml`
2. **Expose the Deployment:** If your application needs to be accessible from outside the cluster, you'll create a Service to expose it. This can be done with another YAML file and the command `kubectl apply -f <your-service-file>.yaml`.

While powerful, `kubectl` requires a deeper understanding of Kubernetes concepts and commands.

Using Helm: The Package Manager for Kubernetes

For more complex applications, Helm simplifies the deployment process. Helm is a package manager for Kubernetes that allows you to define, install, and upgrade even the most intricate applications using reusable packages called Helm charts.

1. **Find a Chart:** Helm has a vast repository of pre-built charts for popular applications. You can search for a chart using the `helm search` command.
2. **Install the Chart:** Once you've found the chart you need, you can install it using `helm install <chart-name>`. Helm will automatically fetch the necessary container images and deploy the application to your cluster.

Helm makes it easy to manage the complex dependencies and configurations of large applications, making your deployment process smoother and more reliable.

Using Azure DevOps or GitHub Actions: Automation for the Win

For a truly streamlined and efficient approach, consider leveraging Azure DevOps or GitHub Actions to automate your application deployments. These platforms provide CI/CD (Continuous Integration/Continuous Deployment) capabilities, allowing you to automatically build, test, and deploy your applications whenever you push changes to your code repository.

With a CI/CD pipeline, you can:

- **Automatically build and test your application code.**
- **Package your application into container images.**
- **Push the container images to Azure Container Registry.**
- **Deploy the updated images to your AKS cluster.**

This automation not only saves you time and effort but also ensures that your applications are always up-to-date and running on the latest code.

Choosing Your Deployment Strategy

The best deployment strategy for you depends on your specific needs and level of expertise. If you're just starting out with Kubernetes, the Azure Portal or Helm might be easier options. However, if you're looking for maximum automation and efficiency, investing in a CI/CD pipeline is worth the effort.

No matter which method you choose, Azure Kubernetes Service provides a robust and scalable platform for deploying and managing your containerized applications. With its diverse tooling options, you can find the perfect workflow that fits your development style and project requirements.

Managing and Scaling AKS Clusters

Once your AKS cluster is up and running, effectively managing and scaling it is crucial for ensuring your applications perform optimally and efficiently. Azure provides various tools and features to simplify these tasks, allowing you to focus on delivering value to your users.

Scaling the Cluster: Adapting to Demand

As your applications grow and traffic fluctuates, you'll need to adjust the capacity of your AKS cluster to match the demand. Scaling in AKS involves adding or removing nodes (virtual machines) in your cluster. There are two primary ways to scale:

- **Manual Scaling:** You can manually add or remove nodes through the Azure Portal, Azure CLI, or PowerShell. This is suitable for predictable scaling needs or when you want to have full control over the scaling process.

- **Cluster Autoscaler:** For dynamic and automatic scaling, AKS integrates with the Kubernetes Cluster Autoscaler. This feature monitors the resource usage of your pods (containers) and automatically adds or removes nodes to meet demand. You can configure the autoscaler to scale within a specified range and based on certain metrics like CPU utilization or memory usage.

Upgrading the Cluster: Stay Up-to-Date

Kubernetes is a rapidly evolving platform, so staying current with the latest version is crucial for security, performance, and new features. AKS simplifies the upgrade process by providing automated upgrades for the Kubernetes control plane and node components. You can also manually trigger upgrades through the Azure Portal, Azure CLI, or PowerShell.

Regularly upgrading your cluster ensures you benefit from the latest Kubernetes enhancements and security patches.

Monitoring the Cluster: Keeping a Watchful Eye

Monitoring the health and performance of your AKS cluster is essential for identifying and troubleshooting issues, optimizing resource utilization, and ensuring a smooth user experience. Azure Monitor integrates seamlessly with AKS, providing a comprehensive suite of monitoring tools:

- **Metrics:** Collect and analyze metrics like CPU usage, memory usage, network traffic, and pod health to understand the performance of your cluster and applications.
- **Logs:** Gather logs from your Kubernetes components, pods, and containers to troubleshoot issues and gain insights into your applications.
- **Alerts:** Set up alerts based on specific metrics or log events to get notified of potential problems.
- **Azure Monitor for Containers:** This specialized monitoring solution provides deeper insights into your containerized workloads, including container logs, health checks, and live data.

Managing Access and Security: Safeguarding Your Cluster

Ensuring the security of your AKS cluster is paramount. Azure offers several features to help you protect your cluster and applications:

- **Role-Based Access Control (RBAC):** Define granular permissions for users and groups, allowing you to control who can access your cluster and what actions they can perform.
- **Network Policies:** Isolate pods within your cluster and control traffic between them, reducing the risk of unauthorized access.
- **Azure Private Link:** Privately connect your AKS cluster to other Azure services, enhancing security by preventing data from being exposed to the public internet.
- **Azure Policy:** Apply policy definitions to your AKS cluster to enforce security and compliance standards.
- **Azure Defender for Kubernetes:** This security solution provides threat protection, vulnerability scanning, and runtime protection for your container workloads.

By following these best practices and leveraging the tools provided by AKS, you can confidently manage and scale your Kubernetes clusters, ensuring they are reliable, secure, and performant.

Tips and Best Practices

As you delve deeper into the world of Azure Kubernetes Service (AKS), consider these practical tips and best practices to streamline your workflows, enhance security, and ensure optimal performance for your containerized applications.

1. **Embrace Helm Charts: Simplify Complex Deployments**

Helm is your best friend when it comes to deploying and managing complex applications on Kubernetes. Helm charts are packages that define, install, and upgrade even the most intricate applications, consisting of multiple Kubernetes resources, configurations, and dependencies. By leveraging pre-built Helm charts or creating your own, you can simplify the deployment process, promote reusability, and ensure consistent configurations across environments.

2. **Monitor Your Cluster: Stay Informed and Proactive**

Azure Monitor is your window into the health and performance of your AKS cluster. Utilize its capabilities to collect and analyze logs and metrics from your Kubernetes components, pods, and containers. Create custom dashboards and alerts to proactively detect and address issues. Azure Monitor for Containers provides additional insights into container-specific metrics and events.

3. **Secure Your Cluster: Defense in Depth**

Security is paramount in a Kubernetes environment. Implement these best practices to safeguard your AKS cluster:

- **Role-Based Access Control (RBAC):** Define granular permissions for users and groups, restricting access to only necessary resources and actions.
- **Network Policies:** Isolate pods and control traffic flow within your cluster to minimize the attack surface.
- **Private Cluster:** Consider creating a private cluster, where the Kubernetes API server is not exposed to the public internet, adding an extra layer of security.
- **Image Scanning:** Regularly scan your container images for vulnerabilities using tools like Azure Container Registry's built-in scanning capabilities.

4. **Keep Your Cluster Up-to-Date: Don't Fall Behind**

Kubernetes is a rapidly evolving ecosystem, with new features and security updates released frequently. It's crucial to keep your AKS cluster up-to-date to take advantage of these improvements and protect against vulnerabilities. AKS simplifies upgrades by providing automated upgrade channels for the control plane and nodes. Plan and test your upgrades carefully to minimize disruptions.

5. **Automate with Azure DevOps or GitHub Actions: Embrace the DevOps Culture**

Embrace the DevOps philosophy by automating your deployment and management workflows. Utilize Azure DevOps or GitHub Actions to create CI/CD pipelines that automatically build, test, and deploy your applications to AKS. This not only saves you time and effort but also ensures consistent and reliable deployments.

Additional Tips:

- **Resource Quotas:** Use resource quotas to limit resource consumption per namespace, ensuring fair allocation across teams and projects.
- **Pod Disruption Budgets:** Define pod disruption budgets to protect your applications from unexpected disruptions during cluster operations like upgrades or scaling.
- **Affinity and Anti-Affinity:** Use node affinity and anti-affinity rules to control where your pods are scheduled, ensuring they run on the most suitable nodes for optimal performance and resource utilization.

By following these tips and best practices, you can create a well-managed, secure, and high-performing AKS environment that empowers you to run your containerized applications with confidence. Remember, the world of Kubernetes is constantly evolving, so stay curious, keep learning, and adapt your practices as needed to maximize the value of AKS for your organization.

Chapter Summary

This chapter introduced you to the powerful world of container orchestration with Azure Kubernetes Service (AKS). We began by establishing the foundation with containers, explaining how they encapsulate applications and their dependencies for seamless portability and isolation. We then introduced Kubernetes, the open-source platform that automates the deployment, scaling, and management of containerized applications, acting as a conductor for your container orchestra.

We delved into Azure Kubernetes Service (AKS), highlighting its role as a managed Kubernetes offering that simplifies the complexities of Kubernetes management. You learned about the key advantages of AKS, including simplified management, scalability, high availability, seamless integration with other Azure services, robust security, and cost-effectiveness.

We explored the key features of AKS, from its managed control plane and automatic upgrades to its serverless capabilities and integration with Azure DevOps for streamlined CI/CD. You gained insights into creating an AKS cluster, deploying applications using tools like `kubectl` and Helm, and managing and scaling your clusters to meet your evolving needs.

Finally, we provided a collection of tips and best practices for working with AKS, such as using Helm charts, monitoring your cluster with Azure Monitor, implementing security measures, keeping your cluster up-to-date, and automating deployments with Azure DevOps or GitHub Actions.

Armed with this knowledge, you're now prepared to embark on your journey with AKS, leveraging its power and flexibility to deploy and manage scalable, reliable, and secure containerized applications in the cloud. As we move forward, in the next section we will explore Azure storage services, the backbone of data management in the cloud.

Section 4:
Azure Storage Services

Azure Blob Storage: Storing Unstructured Data

Outline

- Introduction to Unstructured Data
- What is Azure Blob Storage?
- Types of Blobs
- Understanding Blob Storage Structure
- Blob Storage Tiers
- Key Features of Azure Blob Storage
- Creating a Storage Account and Container
- Uploading and Managing Blobs
- Accessing Blobs
- Best Practices for Blob Storage
- Chapter Summary

Introduction to Unstructured Data

In today's digital age, we are generating an unprecedented amount of data. This data comes in various forms, and not all of it fits neatly into traditional, organized structures. This brings us to the concept of **unstructured data**.

What is Unstructured Data?

Unstructured data is information that does not follow a predefined data model or schema. It lacks a specific format or organization, making it difficult to analyze and process using traditional database tools. Unstructured data can be text-heavy, such as emails, social media posts, or documents, or it can be multimedia content like images, videos, or audio files.

Examples of Unstructured Data

Unstructured data is everywhere, encompassing a vast array of content types, including:

- **Textual Data:** Emails, word processing documents, social media posts, website content, customer reviews, news articles, and even books like this one!
- **Multimedia Data:** Images, videos, audio files, presentations, and medical imaging (like X-rays and MRIs).
- **Log Files:** System and application logs generated by servers, devices, and software.
- **Sensor Data:** Data collected from sensors in IoT devices, industrial equipment, or environmental monitoring systems.
- **Social Media Data:** Posts, comments, likes, shares, and other interactions on social media platforms.

Challenges of Managing Unstructured Data

Managing unstructured data can be challenging due to its inherent lack of structure and organization. Some of the key challenges include:

- **Volume:** Unstructured data often comes in large volumes, making it difficult to store, process, and analyze.
- **Variety:** Unstructured data encompasses a wide variety of formats, making it difficult to standardize and analyze with traditional tools.
- **Velocity:** Unstructured data is often generated at a high velocity, requiring storage solutions that can handle the influx of data.
- **Value Extraction:** Extracting meaningful insights from unstructured data can be complex and time-consuming, often requiring specialized tools and techniques.

Why a Scalable and Cost-Effective Storage Solution Matters

Due to the growing volume and importance of unstructured data, it's crucial to have a scalable and cost-effective storage solution that can handle its unique characteristics. This is where cloud storage services like Azure Blob Storage come in. They offer:

- **Scalability:** Cloud storage can scale effortlessly to accommodate massive amounts of unstructured data, eliminating the need to invest in expensive hardware.
- **Durability:** Cloud providers typically replicate data across multiple locations, ensuring high durability and protection against data loss.
- **Accessibility:** Unstructured data stored in the cloud can be accessed from anywhere with an internet connection, enabling easy collaboration and data sharing.
- **Cost-Effectiveness:** Cloud storage often follows a pay-as-you-go pricing model, making it a cost-effective option, especially for storing large volumes of data that are not accessed frequently.

In the next section, we'll delve deeper into Azure Blob Storage and explore how it addresses these challenges and provides a powerful solution for storing and managing your unstructured data in the cloud.

What is Azure Blob Storage?

Azure Blob Storage is Microsoft's cloud-based answer to the challenges of storing and managing vast amounts of unstructured data. Imagine it as a massive, endlessly expandable warehouse where you can store anything from simple text files to high-definition videos, images, and even large datasets for machine learning.

Object Storage: The Foundation

At its core, Azure Blob Storage is an object storage service. Unlike traditional file systems, which organize data into a hierarchical structure of folders and files, object storage treats each piece of data as a discrete object. Each object includes the data itself, metadata (information about the data, like its name, size, and content type), and a unique identifier that allows you to retrieve it.

Optimized for Unstructured Data

Blob Storage is particularly well-suited for storing unstructured data. Its design allows for massive scalability, enabling you to store petabytes of data without worrying about capacity limitations. It's also highly durable, ensuring that your data is safeguarded against hardware failures, data corruption, or natural disasters.

Key Characteristics of Azure Blob Storage

Azure Blob Storage boasts several key characteristics that make it a powerful and versatile storage solution:

- **Scalability:** Blob Storage can effortlessly scale to accommodate massive amounts of data. You can start with a few gigabytes and scale up to petabytes as your needs grow, without having to re-architect your application or worry about capacity planning.
- **Durability:** Azure replicates your data across multiple storage nodes and data centers, ensuring high durability and protection against data loss. It offers different redundancy options to meet your specific needs.
- **Security:** Blob Storage provides various security features, including role-based access control (RBAC), encryption at rest and in transit, and network security groups (NSGs) to restrict access to your storage account.
- **Accessibility:** You can access your blobs from anywhere in the world using HTTP or HTTPS protocols. This makes it easy to integrate Blob Storage with your applications and services, regardless of their location.
- **Cost-Effectiveness:** Blob Storage offers a variety of storage tiers, allowing you to choose the most cost-effective option based on your data access patterns.

In the following sections, we'll delve deeper into the different types of blobs, how they're organized, and the steps involved in creating and managing your Blob Storage resources.

Types of Blobs

Azure Blob Storage offers three types of blobs, each designed to handle different data scenarios and access patterns. Let's explore their unique characteristics and ideal use cases:

Block Blobs: The Workhorse for Large Objects

Block blobs are the most common type of blob in Azure Storage. They are optimized for storing large amounts of text or binary data, such as images, videos, documents, or backup files.

Key Characteristics:

- **Storage Limit:** Can store up to about 190.7 TiB of data.
- **Composition:** Composed of blocks of data that can be managed individually.
- **Upload Process:** Uploads happen by dividing the data into blocks, uploading each block independently, and then committing the block list. This allows for efficient parallel uploads and resumable uploads for large files.

Use Cases:

- **Media Storage:** Storing images, videos, and audio files for websites or applications.
- **Data Archiving:** Archiving large datasets or backup files that don't need frequent access.
- **Data Analysis:** Storing raw data for analysis and processing using tools like Azure Databricks or HDInsight.

Append Blobs: Ideal for Log Files and Growing Data

Append blobs are specialized for append-only scenarios, where data is added sequentially over time. This makes them perfect for storing log files, sensor data, or any data that is constantly growing.

Key Characteristics:

- **Optimized for Append:** Highly efficient for adding new blocks of data to the end of the blob.
- **Limited Random Access:** Not ideal for frequent updates or random access operations.

Use Cases:

- **Log Storage:** Storing application or system logs that are continuously written to.

- **Sensor Data:** Collecting data from IoT devices or sensors that generate a continuous stream of data.
- **Audit Trails:** Maintaining an append-only log of events or transactions for compliance or auditing purposes.

Page Blobs: Designed for Random Access

Page blobs are optimized for random read and write operations. They are primarily used for storing virtual hard disks (VHDs) that back Azure virtual machines. However, they can also be used for other types of data that require random access, such as databases or large binary files.

Key Characteristics:

- **Random Access:** Allows you to read or write data at any offset within the blob.
- **Storage Limit:** Can store up to 8 TiB of data.
- **Composition:** Made up of fixed-size pages that can be modified individually.

Use Cases:

- **Virtual Machine Disks:** Storing VHDs for Azure VMs.
- **Database Storage:** Used for storing data files for some database systems.
- **High-Performance Computing:** Storing large binary files that require fast random access.

Choosing the Right Blob Type

Selecting the appropriate blob type depends on your specific use case and access patterns:

- **Block blobs:** Ideal for most general-purpose object storage scenarios, especially for large files.
- **Append blobs:** Best suited for append-only scenarios where data is added sequentially.
- **Page blobs:** Primarily used for VHDs and other scenarios requiring random access.

By understanding the different types of blobs and their characteristics, you can choose the most appropriate storage option for your data, optimizing performance, and cost-efficiency in Azure Blob Storage.

Understanding Blob Storage Structure

Azure Blob Storage organizes your data into a simple yet powerful hierarchical structure. Understanding this structure is key to effectively managing and accessing your blobs. Let's break down the components:

Storage Account: Your Blob Storage Realm

At the top level, you have the **Storage Account**. This is a unique namespace in Azure for your blob data. Think of it as your personal domain within Blob Storage, where you can create and manage multiple containers. Each storage account has its own access keys, which are used to authenticate requests to the storage service.

Container: Organizing Your Blobs

Within a storage account, you create **containers** to organize your blobs. A container is simply a logical grouping of blobs. You can think of it like a folder on your computer, where you group related files together.

Containers provide a way to categorize and manage your blobs, making it easier to find and access the data you need. For example, you might create a container for images, another for videos, and a third for documents.

Blob: The Individual Data Unit

A **blob** is an individual object stored within a container. It can be any type of unstructured data, such as text files, images, videos, or application data. Each blob has a unique name within its container, and it also has a URL that can be used to access it over the internet.

Blob Names and URLs

- **Blob Names:** Blob names are strings that uniquely identify a blob within its container. They must adhere to specific naming rules and can include letters, numbers, hyphens, and periods.
- **Blob URLs:** Each blob has a unique URL that can be used to access it over the internet. The URL follows a standard format:

    https://<storage-account-name>.blob.core.windows.net/<container-name>/<blob-name>

Let's break down this URL:

- `<storage-account-name>`: The name of your storage account.
- `.blob.core.windows.net`: The Blob Storage service endpoint.
- `<container-name>`: The name of the container where the blob is stored.
- `<blob-name>`: The name of the blob you want to access.

Example

Let's say you have a storage account named "mystorageaccount" and a container named "images." Within this container, you have a blob named "profile-picture.jpg." The URL for this blob would be:

https://mystorageaccount.blob.core.windows.net/images/profile-picture.jpg

By understanding the hierarchical structure of Blob Storage and how to use blob names and URLs, you can effectively manage and access your unstructured data in the cloud.

Blob Storage Tiers

Azure Blob Storage offers a tiered pricing model with different options tailored to how frequently you need to access your data. This flexibility allows you to optimize costs by selecting the appropriate tier for each type of data you store. Let's explore the three main tiers:

Hot Tier: For Data in the Fast Lane

The Hot tier is designed for data that you anticipate accessing frequently. It offers the lowest access cost but comes with higher storage costs. This tier is ideal for:

- **Active workloads:** Applications that require frequent read and write operations.
- **Data that is actively used:** Files that are regularly downloaded, updated, or processed.
- **Interactive content:** Images, videos, or other media that are served to users.

Think of the Hot tier as the express lane in a supermarket checkout. It's designed for quick transactions and frequent access.

Cool Tier: For Data Taking a Break

The Cool tier is a good fit for data that is accessed less frequently. It has lower storage costs than the Hot tier, but the cost per transaction (access cost) is higher. This tier is suitable for:

- **Short-term backups:** Data that you need to keep for a limited time, but might need to access occasionally.
- **Older media files:** Images or videos that are still relevant but not as popular as newer content.
- **Disaster recovery data:** Data that you need to store for disaster recovery purposes but rarely access under normal circumstances.

The Cool tier is like the regular checkout lane. It's a good choice for items you don't need right away but still want to have readily available.

Archive Tier: For Data in Deep Storage

The Archive tier is the most cost-effective storage option for data that is rarely accessed. However, retrieving data from the Archive tier takes longer (several hours) and incurs additional retrieval costs. This tier is best suited for:

- **Long-term archiving:** Data that you need to retain for regulatory, compliance, or historical purposes but rarely access.
- **Cold storage:** Data that you might need to access in the future but don't require immediate access.
- **Backup archives:** Older backups that you want to keep for long-term retention.

The Archive tier is like storing items in a remote warehouse. It's great for long-term storage, but accessing the items takes time and effort.

Choosing the Right Tier

Selecting the appropriate tier for your data depends on your specific use case and access patterns. Consider these factors:

- **Access Frequency:** How often will you need to access the data? Hot tier for frequent access, Cool tier for occasional access, Archive tier for rare access.
- **Data Retention:** How long do you need to keep the data? Cool tier for short-term retention (30 days minimum), Archive tier for long-term retention (180 days minimum).
- **Cost:** Hot tier is the most expensive for storage, but has the lowest access costs. Archive tier is the cheapest for storage, but has the highest access costs.

By understanding the different Blob Storage tiers and their cost implications, you can make informed decisions to optimize your storage strategy and minimize your expenses while ensuring your data is stored safely and accessible when needed.

Key Features of Azure Blob Storage

Azure Blob Storage is not just a place to dump your data; it's a powerhouse of features designed to make storing and managing your unstructured data a breeze. Let's highlight some of its key capabilities:

Scalability: Room to Grow

Whether you're dealing with gigabytes or petabytes of data, Azure Blob Storage has you covered. It offers massive scalability, allowing you to effortlessly store and manage massive amounts of data without worrying about capacity limitations. Need to store a few images for your personal blog? No problem. Need to store petabytes of medical imaging data for a healthcare organization? Blob Storage can handle it.

Durability: Data That Endures

Your data is precious, and Azure Blob Storage treats it accordingly. It replicates your data multiple times across different storage nodes and data centers, ensuring that your data remains safe even in the face of hardware failures, network outages, or even natural disasters. Azure offers various redundancy options, allowing you to choose the level of durability that best suits your needs and budget.

Security: Keeping Your Data Safe

Azure Blob Storage provides a robust set of security features to safeguard your data:

- **Authentication and Authorization:** Control access to your storage account and blobs using Azure Active Directory (AAD) or Shared Access Signatures (SAS) to grant limited permissions.
- **Encryption:** Protect your data with encryption at rest (using Azure Storage Service Encryption) and in transit (using HTTPS). You can also use customer-managed keys for additional control over encryption.
- **Network Security:** Restrict access to your storage account to specific virtual networks or IP addresses using Network Security Groups (NSGs).
- **Soft Delete:** Recover accidentally deleted blobs within a retention period.
- **Immutability Policies:** Make your blobs immutable (unchangeable) for a specified period, protecting them from accidental or malicious deletion or modification.

Accessibility: Your Data, Anywhere, Anytime

With Azure Blob Storage, your data is accessible from anywhere in the world with an internet connection. You can easily access your blobs using a variety of tools and protocols:

- **Azure Portal:** Manage your storage account and blobs through the Azure Portal's intuitive interface.
- **Azure Storage Explorer:** A desktop application for managing Blob Storage and other Azure storage services.
- **AzCopy:** A command-line utility for high-performance data transfer to and from Blob Storage.
- **REST APIs:** Interact with Blob Storage programmatically from your applications using the Azure Storage REST API.
- **Azure SDKs:** Use Azure SDKs for various programming languages (like .NET, Java, Python, and Node.js) to seamlessly integrate Blob Storage with your applications.

Data Lifecycle Management: Automate and Optimize

Azure Blob Storage allows you to automate the movement of data between different storage tiers based on your access patterns. You can define policies to automatically transition blobs from hot storage (for frequent access) to cool storage (for less frequent access) or archive storage (for rarely accessed data). This helps you optimize costs by storing data in the most cost-effective tier based on its usage.

In conclusion, Azure Blob Storage offers a comprehensive set of features that empower you to store and manage your unstructured data effectively in the cloud. Its scalability, durability, security, accessibility, and cost-effectiveness make it a compelling choice for a wide range of use cases, from simple file storage to complex data archiving and analysis scenarios.

Creating a Storage Account and Container

Now that you understand the basics of Blob Storage, let's create your first storage account and container using the Azure Portal. This step-by-step guide will walk you through the process, ensuring a smooth and successful setup.

1. Choosing a Resource Group and Storage Account Name:

- **Open the Azure Portal:** Navigate to the Azure Portal (https://portal.azure.com/).

- **Search for Storage Accounts:** Type "Storage Accounts" in the search bar at the top and select it from the results.
- **Click "Create":** Click on the "Create" button to initiate the creation process.
- **Choose Subscription:** If you have multiple subscriptions, select the one you want to use for your storage account.
- **Resource group:** Select an existing resource group or create a new one. (As discussed in Chapter 3, it's good practice to organize resources into groups.)
- **Storage account name:** Enter a unique name for your storage account. It must be between 3 and 24 characters in length and can only include lowercase letters and numbers.

2. **Selecting a Region and Performance Tier:**

- **Region:** Choose the Azure region closest to you or your users for optimal performance and to comply with any data residency requirements.
- **Performance:** Select the performance tier that matches your needs. The options are:
  - **Standard:** The default tier, suitable for most workloads.
  - **Premium:** Offers higher performance for workloads that require low latency and high throughput.

3. **Configuring Redundancy Options:**

- **Redundancy:** Choose the redundancy option that best suits your availability and durability requirements. The options are:
  - **Locally-redundant storage (LRS):** Data is replicated within a single data center for low cost but lower durability.
  - **Zone-redundant storage (ZRS):** Data is replicated across multiple availability zones within a region for higher durability.
  - **Geo-redundant storage (GRS):** Data is replicated to a secondary region for the highest level of durability.
  - **Read-access geo-redundant storage (RA-GRS):** Similar to GRS, but also provides read access to the data in the secondary region.

4. **Creating the Storage Account:**

- **Review + create:** Carefully review your selections and click "Create" to create the storage account. The deployment might take a few minutes.

5. **Creating a Container:**

- **Navigate to Storage Account:** Once the storage account is created, navigate to it from the resource list.
- **Data storage:** In the left-hand menu, under "Data storage," click "Containers."
- **Create Container:** Click "+ Container" and provide a name for your container. Note: Container names must be lowercase.
- **Set Public Access Level:** Choose the appropriate public access level for your container. Unless you have a specific reason to make it public, it's recommended to keep it private.
- **Create:** Click "Create" to create the container.

Congratulations! You now have a storage account and container ready to store your blobs. In the next section, we'll learn how to upload and manage your data within the container.

Uploading and Managing Blobs

Now that you've set up your storage account and container, let's get down to the business of actually storing your data. Azure Blob Storage provides several convenient ways to upload, manage, and interact with your blobs.

Uploading Blobs

You have three main options for uploading blobs to your container:

1. **Azure Portal:**
    - This is the simplest way for beginners to get started.
    - Navigate to your container in the Azure Portal.
    - Click the "Upload" button.
    - Select the files you want to upload and configure any desired settings (e.g., access tier, metadata).
    - Click "Upload" to start the process.
2. **Azure Storage Explorer:**
    - This is a free desktop application from Microsoft that provides a visual interface for managing Azure storage resources, including blobs.
    - Connect to your storage account, navigate to your container, and simply drag and drop files or folders to upload them.
3. **AzCopy:**
    - This is a command-line utility designed for high-performance data transfer in and out of Azure Storage.
    - It's ideal for bulk uploads or scenarios where you need to automate the upload process.
    - Use commands like `azcopy copy` to upload files or folders to your container.

Managing Blobs

Once your blobs are uploaded, you can manage them using various tools and methods:

- **Listing Blobs:** View a list of all the blobs within your container using the Azure Portal, Azure Storage Explorer, or AzCopy.
- **Downloading Blobs:** Download individual blobs or entire folders of blobs to your local machine.
- **Copying Blobs:** Copy blobs between containers or storage accounts.
- **Moving Blobs:** Move blobs between containers within the same storage account.
- **Deleting Blobs:** Delete individual blobs or entire containers.

Here's a quick overview of the commands you can use with AzCopy:

Action	AzCopy Command
List blobs	`azcopy list`
Download blobs	`azcopy download`
Copy blobs	`azcopy copy`
Delete blobs	`azcopy remove`
Sync data	`azcopy sync` (to sync between locations)

Important Considerations:

- **Blob Sizes:** Block blobs have a maximum size limit of about 4.75 TiB (tebibytes). Append blobs have a lower limit. If you need to store larger files, consider breaking them down into smaller chunks or using a different storage option like Azure Data Lake Storage.
- **Permissions:** Ensure that you have the necessary permissions to upload, download, and manage blobs in your container. You can manage permissions through Azure Active Directory (AAD) or Shared Access Signatures (SAS).
- **Networking:** Be mindful of network bandwidth and latency when uploading or downloading large blobs. If you're dealing with very large datasets, consider using AzCopy for faster transfers.

By mastering these tools and techniques, you can efficiently upload, manage, and interact with your blobs in Azure Blob Storage.

Accessing Blobs

Azure Blob Storage offers multiple methods for accessing your blobs, catering to a wide range of use cases and security requirements. Let's explore these different access options:

Public Access: Open to the World

By default, containers in Azure Blob Storage are private. However, you can configure a container or individual blobs for public access, making them accessible to anyone with the blob's URL.

Considerations:

- **Use Cases:** Public access is suitable for hosting static websites, sharing files publicly, or providing access to large datasets for public consumption.
- **Security:** Be cautious when using public access, as it can expose your data to anyone. Only use it for data that is not sensitive or confidential.

Shared Access Signatures (SAS): Temporary and Secure Access

Shared Access Signatures (SAS) provide a more secure way to grant access to your blobs. A SAS is a token that you can append to a blob's URL, granting limited access permissions to the blob for a specific period. SAS tokens can be configured with various restrictions, such as:

- **Start and expiry time:** Define the time window during which the SAS is valid.
- **Permissions:** Specify the allowed operations, such as read, write, list, or delete.
- **IP address range:** Restrict access to specific IP addresses or ranges.

Considerations:

- **Use Cases:** SAS is ideal for scenarios where you want to grant temporary or limited access to specific blobs, such as sharing a file with a client or allowing an application to upload data to a specific container.
- **Security:** SAS offers a more granular and secure way to control access to your blobs compared to public access.

Azure Storage Explorer: Your Visual Gateway

Azure Storage Explorer is a free desktop application from Microsoft that provides a convenient visual interface for managing your Azure storage resources, including blobs. With Storage Explorer, you can:

- **Browse and manage containers:** Easily create, delete, and navigate through your containers.
- **Upload, download, and delete blobs:** Drag and drop files or folders to upload or download blobs. Delete unwanted blobs with ease.
- **Edit blob properties:** View and modify blob metadata, access tiers, and other properties.

- **Generate SAS tokens:** Create SAS tokens for specific blobs or containers.

Storage Explorer is a user-friendly tool that simplifies working with Blob Storage, especially for those who prefer a visual interface over command-line tools.

Programmatic Access: Integrate with Your Applications

For more advanced scenarios or when you need to automate blob operations, you can use Azure SDKs or REST APIs to interact with Blob Storage directly from your applications.

- **Azure SDKs:** Microsoft provides SDKs for various programming languages, including .NET, Java, Python, and Node.js. These SDKs provide convenient libraries and functions for interacting with Blob Storage.
- **REST APIs:** If you're using a language that doesn't have an official Azure SDK, you can use the Azure Storage REST API to interact with Blob Storage directly. This gives you maximum flexibility, but it also requires more knowledge of HTTP requests and REST principles.

Choosing the Right Access Method

The best way to access your blobs depends on your specific needs:

- **Public Access:** For publicly accessible data or static websites.
- **SAS:** For granting temporary or restricted access to specific blobs.
- **Azure Storage Explorer:** For a visual and user-friendly way to manage blobs.
- **Programmatic Access:** For integrating Blob Storage into your applications or automating tasks.

By understanding the different access methods available, you can choose the one that best suits your requirements and ensures a secure and efficient way to access your blob data.

Best Practices for Blob Storage

While Azure Blob Storage is easy to use, adhering to best practices ensures optimal performance, cost efficiency, and maintainability of your data. Let's delve into some tips that will help you make the most of this powerful storage service:

1. Naming Conventions: Keep It Clear and Consistent

Imagine a library without a cataloging system – chaos would reign! The same principle applies to Blob Storage. Use clear and consistent naming conventions for your storage accounts, containers, and blobs. This makes it easier to identify and locate your data. For instance:

- **Storage Account:** `myappstorageaccount`
- **Container:** `images`, `logs`, `backups`
- **Blob:** `product-image-123.jpg`, `error-log-20240603.txt`

2. Directory Structure: Mimic Your Familiar Folders

Just like you organize files into folders on your computer, create a logical directory structure within your containers. This can be achieved using virtual folders (simulated using delimiters in blob names). A clear hierarchy makes it easier to manage and find your blobs. For example:

/images/products/product-image-123.jpg
/logs/application/error-log-20240603.txt
/backups/weekly/database-backup-20240527.bak

3. Metadata: Your Data's Digital ID

Blob metadata is like an ID card for your data. It's a collection of name-value pairs that you can attach to a blob to store additional information. This can include details like the author, creation date, content type, or any custom attributes relevant to your application. Metadata makes it easier to search, filter, and manage your blobs.

4. Snapshotting: The Time Machine for Your Blobs

Azure Blob Storage allows you to create snapshots of your blobs. A snapshot captures the state of a blob at a specific point in time, creating a read-only copy. This is a fantastic way to:

- **Create Backups:** Protect against accidental deletion or data corruption by having point-in-time backups.
- **Versioning:** Track changes to your blobs over time and revert to previous versions if needed.

5. Lifecycle Management: Automate for Efficiency

Data lifecycle management (DLM) is a set of policies that automate the movement of blobs between storage tiers based on rules you define. For instance, you can set a rule to automatically move blobs to the cool tier after 30 days of inactivity and to the archive tier after 90 days. This optimizes costs by storing data in the most cost-effective tier based on its access frequency.

Additional Best Practices:

- **Use the Right Tools:** Utilize the Azure Portal, Azure Storage Explorer, or AzCopy for managing your blobs, choosing the tool that best suits your workflow.
- **Monitor Storage Analytics:** Track capacity, transactions, and other metrics to understand your storage usage patterns and optimize performance.
- **Secure Your Blobs:** Utilize features like encryption, access control lists (ACLs), and Shared Access Signatures (SAS) to protect your data.
- **Plan for Disaster Recovery:** Replicate your blobs to a secondary region for added protection against regional outages.

By adhering to these best practices, you can ensure that Azure Blob Storage becomes an indispensable asset in your cloud arsenal, providing you with a scalable, reliable, and cost-effective solution for managing your unstructured data.

Chapter Summary

This chapter delved into Azure Blob Storage, Microsoft's object storage solution for the cloud. You learned that it's designed to handle massive amounts of unstructured data, including text, images, videos, and other diverse data formats.

We began by defining unstructured data and explaining why it presents unique challenges in terms of volume, variety, velocity, and value extraction. We then introduced Azure Blob Storage as a scalable, durable, secure, and accessible solution that addresses these challenges.

Next, we explored the three types of blobs available in Blob Storage:

- **Block blobs:** Optimized for storing large amounts of data that can be uploaded in blocks. Ideal for media files, backups, and data analysis.
- **Append blobs:** Optimized for append-only operations, like logging. Ideal for log files, sensor data, and audit trails.

- **Page blobs:** Optimized for random read and write operations. Primarily used for VHDs but can also be used for other types of data.

We then examined the hierarchical structure of Blob Storage, understanding the relationship between storage accounts, containers, and blobs. We also discussed the concept of blob names and URLs, which are used to uniquely identify and access blobs.

Next, we discussed the different storage tiers available in Blob Storage:

- **Hot tier:** For frequently accessed data, offering the lowest access cost but higher storage costs.
- **Cool tier:** For less frequently accessed data, balancing cost and access times.
- **Archive tier:** For rarely accessed data with the lowest storage costs but higher retrieval costs.

You learned how to choose the appropriate tier based on your data access patterns and retention requirements.

We then highlighted the key features of Blob Storage, such as scalability, durability, security, accessibility, and data lifecycle management. These features collectively make Blob Storage a powerful and versatile solution for storing and managing unstructured data in the cloud.

Finally, you walked through the process of creating a storage account and container in Azure Blob Storage using the Azure Portal. We also explored different methods for uploading and managing your blobs, including the Azure Portal, Azure Storage Explorer, and AzCopy. We discussed how to access blobs using public access, Shared Access Signatures, Azure Storage Explorer, or programmatic access.

The chapter concluded with best practices for using Blob Storage effectively, emphasizing the importance of naming conventions, directory structures, metadata, snapshotting, and lifecycle management.

By now, you should have a solid understanding of Azure Blob Storage and its various capabilities. In the next chapter, we'll shift our focus to another type of Azure storage service: Azure Files, which provides a managed file share solution in the cloud.

Azure File Storage: Shared File Systems in the Cloud

Outline

- What are File Shares?
- Why Use Azure File Storage?
- Key Features and Benefits
- Creating an Azure File Share
- Mounting File Shares
- Managing File Shares
- Security and Access Control
- Azure File Sync
- Tips and Best Practices
- Chapter Summary

What Are File Shares?

Imagine a central library where everyone can store and access books, documents, and other resources. This shared space fosters collaboration, allowing individuals to work together on projects, access information easily, and maintain a single source of truth for important documents.

In the world of computing, file shares serve a similar purpose. A file share is essentially a storage location on a network that multiple users or computers can access. It's a central repository where you can store and organize files, folders, and other data, making them available to authorized users across your network.

Purpose of File Shares

File shares have been a cornerstone of on-premises IT infrastructure for decades. They offer several key advantages:

- **Centralized Storage:** Instead of scattering files across individual computers, you can consolidate them in a central location, making them easier to manage, back up, and secure.
- **Collaboration:** File shares enable seamless collaboration among team members. Multiple users can access and work on the same files simultaneously, fostering teamwork and productivity.
- **Simplified Backup and Recovery:** Having a central repository for your files simplifies the backup and recovery process. You can easily back up the entire file share or specific folders, ensuring that your data is protected in case of hardware failure or accidental deletion.
- **Access Control:** File shares allow you to implement granular access controls, specifying which users or groups have permission to read, write, or modify files. This ensures that sensitive data is protected and only accessible to authorized personnel.

How File Shares Work

File shares typically use the Server Message Block (SMB) protocol, a standard protocol for sharing files across a network. This protocol allows clients (such as Windows, Linux, or macOS computers) to access files on the file server as if they were stored locally.

Typical Uses of File Shares

File shares are commonly used for a wide range of scenarios, including:

- **Document Sharing:** Teams can collaborate on documents, spreadsheets, presentations, and other files.
- **Application Data Storage:** Applications can store configuration files, log files, and other data on a file share.
- **Software Distribution:** Software installers or updates can be stored on a file share for easy distribution to users.
- **Home Directories:** Organizations can provide users with personal file storage space on a file share.

In the next section, we'll explore how Azure File Storage brings the power and convenience of file shares to the cloud, offering even more benefits and flexibility.

Why Use Azure File Storage?

Azure File Storage takes the concept of file shares and elevates it to the cloud, offering a powerful and flexible solution that overcomes many of the limitations of traditional on-premises file shares.

The Cloud-Powered File Share

Azure File Storage is a fully managed file share service that allows you to create file shares in the cloud. It provides a familiar interface and functionality similar to on-premises file shares, but with the added benefits of cloud computing. You can access your files from anywhere with an internet connection using standard protocols like SMB (Server Message Block) and NFS (Network File System).

Advantages Over Traditional File Shares

Let's delve into the key advantages that Azure File Storage offers over traditional file shares:

1. **Scalability:**
   - Need more storage space? No problem. Azure File Storage scales effortlessly to accommodate your growing data needs. You can start small and easily expand your capacity as your requirements change. This eliminates the need for complex capacity planning and expensive hardware upgrades.
2. **High Availability and Durability:**
   - Azure File Storage is built for reliability. It automatically replicates your data across multiple storage nodes and data centers, ensuring high availability and durability. Even if a hardware failure occurs, your data remains safe and accessible.
3. **Global Access:**
   - Unlike on-premises file shares, which are typically limited to your local network, Azure File Storage gives you global access to your files. You can access, share, and collaborate on your files from anywhere in the world with an internet connection.
4. **Seamless Integration:**
   - Azure File Storage seamlessly integrates with other Azure services, such as Azure Virtual Machines and Azure Backup. You can easily mount your Azure file shares to your VMs, use them as shared storage for your applications, or back them up to Azure for added protection.
5. **Cost-Effectiveness:**
   - Azure File Storage follows a pay-as-you-go pricing model, meaning you only pay for the storage you use. This eliminates the need for upfront capital expenses on hardware and software. You can also choose between different storage tiers (Standard and Premium) to optimize costs based on your performance and feature requirements.

Beyond the Basics

In addition to these core benefits, Azure File Storage offers several other advantages:

- **Snapshots:** Create point-in-time copies of your file shares for backup and recovery.
- **Azure File Sync:** Synchronize your on-premises file shares with Azure File Storage for a hybrid storage solution.
- **Security:** Protect your data with encryption at rest, authentication, and authorization.
- **Management:** Easily manage your file shares through the Azure Portal, PowerShell, or Azure CLI.

By leveraging Azure File Storage, you can modernize your file share infrastructure, improve collaboration, enhance data availability, and reduce costs.

Key Features and Benefits

Azure File Storage comes packed with features that make it a versatile and powerful tool for managing your files in the cloud. Let's dive into its key capabilities:

SMB Protocol Support: Familiarity in the Cloud

Azure File Storage speaks the language of your existing applications. It fully supports the Server Message Block (SMB) protocol, the industry-standard for file sharing in Windows environments. This means you can seamlessly connect to your Azure file shares from Windows, Linux, or macOS clients using the same tools and processes you're already familiar with.

NFS Protocol Support (Premium Tier): Empowering Linux Workloads

For Linux-based workloads, Azure File Storage offers NFS protocol support in its premium tier. This enables you to seamlessly mount Azure file shares to Linux virtual machines or on-premises servers, providing a native file system experience for your applications.

Azure AD Integration: Secure and Centralized Access Control

Azure Active Directory (Azure AD) integration brings enterprise-grade identity and access management to your Azure file shares. You can leverage your existing Azure AD credentials to authenticate users and control access to your files. This ensures that only authorized users can access, modify, or delete files, enhancing security and compliance.

Large File Share Support (Premium Tier): Storage Without Limits

For scenarios where you need to store massive amounts of data, the premium tier of Azure File Storage offers support for file shares up to 100 TiB in size. This immense capacity makes it suitable for large-scale data repositories, content libraries, or backup archives.

Snapshot Support: Your Safety Net

Azure File Storage provides snapshot functionality, allowing you to create point-in-time copies of your file shares. Snapshots act as a backup mechanism, enabling you to recover your files in case of accidental deletion, data corruption, or ransomware attacks. You can easily create snapshots on-demand or schedule them to run automatically.

Azure File Sync: Bridging On-Premises and Cloud

Azure File Sync is a service that enables you to seamlessly synchronize your on-premises file servers with Azure File Storage. This creates a hybrid storage solution where you can store your files in the cloud for scalability and redundancy, while keeping a local cache on your servers for fast access. Azure File Sync also offers cloud tiering, which automatically moves infrequently accessed files to the cloud, freeing up local storage space.

Additional Benefits

Azure File Storage offers several other notable features, including:

- **Encryption at Rest:** Your data is automatically encrypted using Microsoft-managed keys to protect it from unauthorized access.
- **Soft Delete:** Recover accidentally deleted files within a retention period.
- **High Performance:** Premium file shares offer high throughput and low latency for demanding workloads.
- **Easy Management:** Manage your file shares through the Azure Portal, PowerShell, or Azure CLI.

By leveraging these powerful features, Azure File Storage empowers you to build modern, scalable, and secure file share solutions in the cloud.

Creating an Azure File Share

Creating a file share in Azure is a simple process that can be done in a few clicks within the Azure Portal. Let's walk through the steps:

1. Navigate to Your Storage Account:

- Open the Azure Portal and search for "Storage accounts" in the search bar.
- Select your existing storage account from the list. If you don't have one yet, refer back to Chapter 12 for instructions on creating one.

2. Select "File Shares":

- On the storage account page, in the left-hand menu, under the "Data storage" section, click on "File shares."

3. Click "+ File share" to Create a New File Share:

- This will open a new blade (a panel within the portal) where you'll configure the settings for your file share.

4. Specify a Name and Quota:

- **Name:** Enter a name for your file share. This name will be part of the URL used to access your files (e.g., `https://<yourstorageaccountname>.file.core.windows.net/<filesharename>`).
- **Quota:** Set the quota (maximum size) for your file share. You can choose from several preset sizes or enter a custom value. Keep in mind that you can always increase the quota later if needed.

5. Configure Optional Settings (Advanced):

- **Storage Tier:** Choose between:
    - **Transaction Optimized:** Ideal for general-purpose file sharing and sync workloads.
    - **Hot:** Optimized for frequently accessed data.
    - **Cool:** Optimized for less frequently accessed data with longer retention requirements.
    - **Premium:** Optimized for high-performance applications that require low latency and high IOPS (input/output operations per second). Premium file shares also support larger file sizes (up to 100 TiB) and NFS protocol access.

- **Encryption:** Enable encryption to protect your data at rest. Azure offers both Microsoft-managed keys and customer-managed keys for encryption.

6. Click "Create":

- Review your settings to ensure they are correct.
- Click "Create" to create your file share. The deployment should take only a few moments.

That's it! You've successfully created your Azure File Share. You can now access it from your applications, virtual machines, or on-premises servers using the SMB protocol or NFS protocol (if you chose a Premium file share).

Important Note: Remember that Azure File Storage follows a pay-as-you-go pricing model, so you'll be billed based on the amount of storage you use and the number of transactions performed.

Mounting File Shares

Once you've created your Azure File Share, you'll want to access it as if it were a local drive on your computer. This process, called "mounting," allows you to seamlessly work with your Azure files using the familiar tools and interfaces of your operating system. Let's see how this works on different platforms:

Windows: Map Network Drive

1. **Open File Explorer:** Launch File Explorer (formerly known as Windows Explorer).
2. **Map Network Drive:**
   - Click on "This PC" in the left sidebar.
   - In the "Computer" ribbon menu, click on "Map network drive."
   - In the dialog that appears, choose a drive letter (e.g., "Z:") to assign to your Azure file share.
3. **Enter Path and Credentials:**

In the "Folder" field, enter the URL of your Azure file share. The URL follows this format:
`\\<storage-account-name>.file.core.windows.net\<file-share-name>`

   - Replace `<storage-account-name>` with your actual storage account name and `<file-share-name>` with the name of your file share.
   - If prompted, enter your storage account credentials (username and password or a Shared Access Signature (SAS) token) to authenticate.
4. **Connect:** Click "Finish." Your Azure file share will be mounted as a network drive with the assigned drive letter, and you can access it just like any other local drive.

Linux: Mount with `mount` Command

1. **Install cifs-utils:** Make sure the `cifs-utils` package is installed on your Linux system. You can usually install it using your distribution's package manager (e.g., `apt-get install cifs-utils` for Ubuntu or Debian).
2. **Create Mount Point:** Create a directory where you want to mount the file share. For example: `sudo mkdir /mnt/azurefileshare`
3. **Mount the File Share:** Use the `mount` command with the following syntax:

```
sudo mount -t cifs //<storage-account-name>.file.core.windows.net/<file-share-name> <mount-point> -o vers=<smb-version>,username=<storage-account-name>,password='<storage-account-key>',dir_mode=0777,file_mode=0777
```

Replace placeholders with your actual values. You can find your storage account key in the Azure Portal.

macOS: Connect to Server in Finder

1. **Open Finder:** Launch Finder on your macOS device.
2. **Connect to Server:**
   - Click "Go" in the top menu bar and select "Connect to Server."

In the dialog that appears, enter the URL of your Azure file share in the following format: smb://<storage-account-name>.file.core.windows.net/<file-share-name>

   -
3. **Authenticate:** Enter your storage account credentials (username and password or SAS token) when prompted.
4. **Access Files:** Your Azure file share will appear in Finder, and you can access its files and folders like any other network share.

Additional Notes:

- For improved performance, especially with premium file shares, consider using the `nconnect` mount option on Linux.
- Azure AD authentication is supported on Windows and Linux but not yet on macOS for file share mounts. For macOS, you'll need to use a storage account key or SAS token.

Mounting your Azure file share makes your cloud files easily accessible, enabling seamless integration between your local environment and Azure Storage.

Managing File Shares

Managing your Azure File Shares is a breeze with the intuitive tools provided in the Azure Portal. Let's explore how you can view and modify properties, create snapshots, control access, and monitor the performance of your file shares:

Viewing and Modifying Properties

1. **Navigate to Your File Share:** In the Azure Portal, go to your storage account, select "File shares," and then click on the file share you want to manage.
2. **Overview Page:** The overview page displays essential information about your file share, such as its name, storage tier, quota, and usage statistics.
3. **Properties Tab:** Click on the "Properties" tab to view and modify various settings, including:
   - **Description:** Add a description to provide additional context about the file share's purpose.
   - **Quota:** Increase or decrease the maximum size (quota) of the file share.
   - **Storage Tier:** Change the storage tier between Transaction Optimized, Hot, or Cool, depending on your access patterns and cost considerations (premium tier file shares cannot be converted to standard tiers).
   - **Encryption:** Enable or disable encryption for your file share.

Creating Snapshots: Your Safety Net

Snapshots are point-in-time copies of your file share. They provide a valuable backup and recovery mechanism, allowing you to restore your files to a previous state if needed.

1. **Snapshots Tab:** Navigate to the "Snapshots" tab on your file share's page.
2. **Create Snapshot:** Click the "Create snapshot" button.

3. **Name and Description (Optional):** Optionally, provide a name and description for your snapshot.
4. **Create:** Click "Create" to create the snapshot. This process is usually quick, but it may take longer for larger file shares.

Setting Up Access Control: Sharing with Security

Azure File Storage offers various ways to control who can access your file shares and what they can do with the files:

1. **Shared Access Signatures (SAS):** Generate SAS tokens to provide granular, time-limited access to your file shares or specific files. You can specify permissions like read, write, list, or delete.
2. **Azure Active Directory (AAD):** Integrate with Azure Active Directory to authenticate users and manage permissions using your existing identity infrastructure. This allows you to enforce fine-grained access controls based on roles and groups.
3. **Network Security Groups (NSGs):** Use NSGs to filter network traffic to and from your storage account, controlling which IP addresses or virtual networks can access your file shares.

Monitoring Usage and Performance

Azure Monitor provides valuable insights into your file share's usage and performance. You can track metrics like:

- **Storage capacity:** The amount of data stored in your file share.
- **Transactions:** The number of read, write, and other file operations.
- **Success and error rates:** The percentage of successful and failed file operations.
- **Latency:** The time it takes to complete file operations.

You can view these metrics in the Azure Portal or create custom dashboards and alerts to proactively identify and address performance issues.

Tips for Efficient Management

- **Use Azure File Sync:** Consider using Azure File Sync to centralize your file shares in Azure while maintaining local access to frequently used files.
- **Monitor Costs:** Keep track of your storage costs using Azure Cost Management tools.
- **Optimize Performance:** For high-performance workloads, consider using premium file shares, which offer higher throughput and lower latency.

By mastering these management techniques, you can ensure that your Azure File Shares are well-organized, secure, and optimized for your specific needs.

Security and Access Control

Protecting your data stored in Azure File Shares is paramount. Azure provides a robust set of tools to ensure your files are secure and only accessible to authorized individuals. Let's explore these security measures:

Shared Access Signatures (SAS): Granular and Time-Limited Access

Think of Shared Access Signatures (SAS) as temporary access passes for your Azure files. You can generate these secure tokens to grant specific permissions (read, write, list, delete) to individual files or entire file shares. Crucially, SAS tokens are time-limited, meaning you can define their validity period, ensuring that access is revoked automatically after a certain time.

To create a SAS token in the Azure Portal:

1. Navigate to your storage account and select the "File shares" section.
2. Click on the file share you want to secure.
3. Under "Settings," choose "Shared access signature."
4. Configure the desired permissions, start and expiry time, and other options.
5. Click "Generate SAS" to create the token.

You can then share the SAS URL (which includes the token) with the people who need access to your files.

Azure Active Directory (AAD) Integration: Centralized Identity Management

For organizations that already use Azure Active Directory (AAD) for identity management, integrating it with Azure File Storage provides a seamless and centralized way to control access. You can:

- **Authenticate users with their existing AAD credentials:** This eliminates the need for separate credentials for Azure File Storage.
- **Manage permissions using AAD roles and groups:** Assign permissions to users or groups based on their roles within your organization. This provides a granular and flexible way to control access.
- **Enable single sign-on (SSO):** Allow users to access Azure File Shares seamlessly using their existing AAD login credentials.

To enable AAD authentication, you'll need to configure your storage account to use AAD Domain Services or Azure AD DS authentication. This is typically done by your Azure administrator.

Network Security Groups (NSGs): Controlling Network Access

Network Security Groups (NSGs) act as a firewall for your Azure storage account. They allow you to define rules that control inbound and outbound network traffic. You can:

- **Allow or deny traffic based on source or destination IP addresses, ports, and protocols.**
- **Limit access to specific virtual networks:** This ensures that only authorized virtual networks can access your storage account and file shares.
- **Implement network security rules at the storage account level:** This protects all your Azure Storage services, including Blob Storage, File Storage, and Queue Storage.

To configure NSGs for your storage account:

1. Navigate to your storage account in the Azure Portal.
2. Under "Settings," click "Networking."
3. In the "Firewalls and virtual networks" tab, you can define your network security rules.

By combining these three security measures—SAS, AAD integration, and NSGs—you can create a multi-layered security approach that protects your Azure File Shares from unauthorized access and ensures that your data is only accessible to the right people at the right time.

Azure File Sync

Azure File Sync is a service that seamlessly blends your on-premises file servers with the power of Azure File Storage. It acts as a bridge, allowing you to centralize your organization's file shares in the cloud while maintaining the performance and familiarity of local file access. Think of it as having the best of both worlds: the scalability and durability of the cloud combined with the speed and convenience of local access.

How Azure File Sync Works

Azure File Sync transforms your on-premises Windows Servers into a fast cache of your Azure file share. When you enable Azure File Sync for a file share, a sync agent is installed on your on-premises server. This agent continuously synchronizes the files between the server and your Azure file share.

When users access files on the on-premises server, they'll experience the same performance as if the files were stored locally. However, behind the scenes, Azure File Sync ensures that the most recent versions of the files are always available in the cloud.

Benefits of Azure File Sync

Azure File Sync offers several key benefits:

- **Cloud Tiering:** With cloud tiering enabled, only your most frequently accessed files are cached on your local server. The rest of the files are tiered to the cloud, freeing up valuable local storage space. When a user requests a tiered file, Azure File Sync seamlessly recalls it from the cloud on-demand.
- **Multi-Site Access and Sync:** Azure File Sync is a perfect solution for organizations with multiple locations. You can install sync agents on servers at different sites, and they will all sync to the same Azure file share. This ensures that all your locations have access to the latest versions of files and provides a unified file sharing experience for your users.
- **Business Continuity and Disaster Recovery:** Azure File Sync provides built-in redundancy and automatic failover, ensuring high availability for your files. If your on-premises server goes down, users can still access their files from the cloud. You can also easily restore files from Azure File Storage if needed.
- **Cloud Backup:** Azure File Sync simplifies your backup strategy by automatically backing up your on-premises file shares to Azure File Storage. This eliminates the need for complex on-premises backup infrastructure and provides an offsite copy of your data for disaster recovery purposes.

When to Use Azure File Sync

Azure File Sync is an excellent choice for scenarios where you want to:

- **Centralize your file shares:** Consolidate your on-premises file shares in the cloud for easier management, scalability, and redundancy.
- **Optimize storage usage:** Free up local storage space by tiering infrequently accessed files to the cloud.
- **Provide multi-site access and sync:** Ensure all your locations have access to the latest versions of files.
- **Simplify backup and disaster recovery:** Leverage Azure File Storage's built-in redundancy and backup capabilities.

By leveraging the power of Azure File Sync, you can modernize your file share infrastructure, improve collaboration, and enhance data protection, all while enjoying the benefits of cloud scalability and flexibility.

Tips and Best Practices

To maximize the benefits of Azure File Storage and ensure smooth operation, consider these practical tips and best practices:

Performance Optimization:

- **Premium File Shares for Demanding Workloads:** If your applications require high throughput and low latency, opt for premium file shares. They are backed by high-performance SSDs and offer significantly faster performance than standard file shares.

- **Caching (Premium Tier):** Premium file shares support caching, which allows you to cache frequently accessed files locally on your on-premises servers, further improving performance.
- **Network Optimization:** Ensure your network connection to Azure is optimized for file share access. Use a fast and reliable network connection to minimize latency and maximize throughput.

Snapshotting: A Safety Net for Your Data

- **Regular Snapshots:** Create snapshots of your file shares regularly to protect your data against accidental deletion, corruption, or ransomware attacks. You can schedule automatic snapshots to simplify the process.
- **Test Restores:** Periodically test restoring files from snapshots to ensure they are working correctly and that you can recover your data in case of an emergency.
- **Snapshot Retention:** Determine the appropriate retention period for your snapshots based on your recovery point objective (RPO) and regulatory requirements.

Azure File Sync: Bridging the Gap

- **Centralized File Shares:** Use Azure File Sync to centralize your organization's file shares in Azure File Storage. This provides a single source of truth for your files, simplifies backup and disaster recovery, and enables multi-site collaboration.
- **Cloud Tiering:** Enable cloud tiering to automatically move infrequently accessed files to the cloud, freeing up local storage space on your on-premises servers.
- **Selective Sync:** You can choose which files or folders to sync, giving you granular control over which data is stored locally and in the cloud.

Security: Protect Your Valuable Assets

- **Authentication and Authorization:** Implement strong authentication and authorization mechanisms to control access to your file shares.
- **Shared Access Signatures (SAS):** Generate SAS tokens to grant limited and time-bound access to specific files or directories within your file shares.
- **Azure Active Directory (AAD) Integration:** Use AAD for centralized identity and access management, leveraging your existing user accounts and groups.
- **Network Security Groups (NSGs):** Restrict network access to your storage account using NSGs to prevent unauthorized access.
- **Encryption:** Enable encryption at rest to protect your data from unauthorized access even if the physical storage media is compromised.

Additional Tips:

- **Monitor Storage Analytics:** Regularly review your storage analytics to track your usage, identify trends, and optimize your storage costs.
- **Choose the Right Storage Tier:** Select the appropriate storage tier based on your data access patterns and budget.
- **Naming Conventions:** Use clear and consistent naming conventions for your file shares and files to make them easier to manage.
- **Azure Storage Explorer:** Use the Azure Storage Explorer to visually manage your file shares and perform various operations like uploading, downloading, and managing snapshots.

By following these best practices and utilizing the powerful features of Azure File Storage, you can create a secure, scalable, and highly available file sharing solution in the cloud.

Chapter Summary

This chapter delved into Azure File Storage, a robust cloud-based file share solution. We began by explaining the concept of file shares and their significance in traditional on-premises environments, highlighting their benefits for collaboration, data consolidation, and simplified backup.

We then introduced Azure File Storage as a fully managed cloud service that mirrors the functionality of on-premises file shares, but with the added advantages of cloud scalability, high availability, and global access. Key benefits like seamless integration with other Azure services and the cost-effective pay-as-you-go pricing model were emphasized.

Next, we explored the various features and benefits that make Azure File Storage a compelling choice. These include support for both SMB and NFS protocols, seamless integration with Azure Active Directory for robust security, support for large file shares, snapshot capabilities for backup and recovery, and Azure File Sync for creating hybrid file share solutions.

We walked you through the process of creating an Azure File Share using the Azure Portal, providing step-by-step instructions on selecting a storage account, specifying a name and quota, and configuring optional settings like storage tiers and encryption.

You also learned how to mount Azure File Shares on different operating systems, including Windows, Linux, and macOS, to access your cloud files as if they were local drives. We discussed managing file shares, including viewing and modifying properties, creating snapshots, and monitoring usage and performance.

Security was a key focus, with detailed explanations of how to secure access to your file shares using Shared Access Signatures (SAS), Azure Active Directory authentication, and Network Security Groups (NSGs). Additionally, we introduced Azure File Sync as a way to synchronize on-premises file shares with Azure for enhanced collaboration and data protection.

We concluded the chapter with practical tips and best practices for optimizing Azure File Storage usage, such as utilizing premium file shares for high-performance workloads, creating regular snapshots, leveraging Azure File Sync, and implementing robust security measures.

With this comprehensive understanding of Azure File Storage, you're now equipped to create and manage cloud-based file shares that are scalable, secure, and accessible from anywhere. As you progress through this book, you'll discover how Azure File Storage can be a valuable asset in your cloud computing arsenal, enabling you to build sophisticated and efficient solutions for your data storage needs.

Azure Table Storage: NoSQL Storage for Key-Value Data

Outline

- What is NoSQL?
- Introduction to Azure Table Storage
- Key-Value Data Model
- Understanding Table Storage Structure
- Scenarios and Use Cases
- Creating a Table
- Working with Entities
- Querying Table Storage
- Scaling and Performance
- Tips and Best Practices
- Chapter Summary

What is NoSQL?

In the world of databases, there's a fascinating evolution beyond the traditional relational model – enter NoSQL. Short for "not only SQL," NoSQL databases offer a different approach to storing and managing data, one that is better suited for the demands of modern applications.

Breaking Free from Relational Rigidity

Traditional SQL databases, also known as relational databases, organize data into tables with rows and columns, enforcing a strict schema with relationships between tables. While this model works well for structured data, it can become rigid and less efficient when dealing with large volumes of unstructured or rapidly changing data.

NoSQL databases, on the other hand, are non-relational. They don't adhere to the rigid schema of SQL databases and offer more flexible data models, such as key-value pairs, documents, graphs, or wide-column stores. This flexibility allows for easier adaptation to evolving data structures and faster development cycles.

Designed for Specific Needs

NoSQL databases are not meant to replace SQL databases entirely. Instead, they are designed to complement them, offering specialized solutions for specific use cases and data models. For example, a NoSQL database might be a better choice for:

- **Large volumes of data:** NoSQL databases excel at handling massive datasets that would be difficult to manage in a traditional SQL database.
- **Unstructured or semi-structured data:** NoSQL databases can easily store and process data that doesn't fit neatly into a tabular format, such as documents, social media posts, or sensor data.
- **High-performance applications:** NoSQL databases are often designed for high performance, offering fast read and write operations, making them suitable for real-time applications.
- **Flexible schemas:** NoSQL databases allow you to evolve your data model as your application grows and changes, without requiring complex schema migrations.

Flexibility, Scalability, and Performance

The key advantages of NoSQL databases over traditional SQL databases include:

- **Flexibility:** NoSQL databases offer flexible data models that can adapt to changing requirements, making them easier to work with for developers.
- **Scalability:** NoSQL databases can easily scale horizontally across multiple servers, accommodating large volumes of data and high traffic loads.
- **Performance:** NoSQL databases are often optimized for specific types of queries and operations, delivering fast performance for those use cases.

When to Choose NoSQL

Choosing between SQL and NoSQL depends on your specific needs. Consider factors such as:

- **Data model:** Does your data fit neatly into a relational model (SQL) or would a different model like key-value, document, or graph (NoSQL) be more appropriate?
- **Scalability requirements:** Do you expect your application to handle large volumes of data or high traffic loads? NoSQL databases are often better suited for these scenarios.
- **Performance needs:** Do you need fast read and write operations for specific types of queries? NoSQL databases can offer optimized performance for certain use cases.
- **Development flexibility:** Do you need a flexible data model that can evolve with your application? NoSQL databases provide more flexibility in this regard.

In the following sections, we'll delve into Azure Table Storage, a popular NoSQL offering from Microsoft that uses a key-value data model. You'll learn how it works, its key features, and how to use it to build scalable and efficient applications in the cloud.

Introduction to Azure Table Storage

In the world of NoSQL databases, Azure Table Storage emerges as a versatile and scalable solution for managing structured data. Think of it as a massive spreadsheet in the cloud, designed to store vast amounts of information in a simple yet efficient way.

Azure Table Storage: A NoSQL Dynamo

Azure Table Storage is a key-value store, a type of NoSQL database where data is stored as collections of key-value pairs. This model makes it incredibly easy to store and retrieve data, especially when you don't need complex relationships between data entities.

Part of the Azure Storage Family

Table Storage is a member of the Azure Storage platform, a comprehensive suite of cloud storage services offered by Microsoft. This means it integrates seamlessly with other Azure storage services like Blob Storage and Queue Storage, allowing you to build complete solutions that leverage the strengths of each service.

Key Features That Set it Apart

Azure Table Storage boasts several key features that make it a popular choice for a wide range of applications:

- **Scalability:** Table Storage is designed to scale massively, effortlessly handling petabytes of data. You can store millions of entities in a single table, and Azure automatically manages the underlying infrastructure to ensure consistent performance as your data grows.

- **High Availability:** Azure replicates your data across multiple storage nodes and data centers, providing high availability and durability. Your data remains accessible even in the face of hardware failures or network outages.
- **Cost-Effectiveness:** Table Storage is a cost-effective option, especially for storing large volumes of structured data. It follows a pay-as-you-go pricing model, meaning you only pay for the storage and transactions you use.
- **Fast Access:** Table Storage is optimized for fast access to data, making it suitable for scenarios where you need to quickly retrieve or update individual entities.
- **Flexible Schema:** Unlike traditional relational databases, Table Storage doesn't enforce a rigid schema. This means you can add or modify properties for your entities as your application evolves, without having to redesign your entire data model.
- **Integration:** Table Storage integrates seamlessly with other Azure services, such as Azure Functions, Logic Apps, and Cosmos DB. This allows you to build powerful, end-to-end solutions that leverage the full capabilities of the Azure platform.

In the following sections, we'll delve deeper into the structure of Table Storage, explore its key-value data model, and discuss how to create and work with tables and entities.

Key-Value Data Model

At the heart of Azure Table Storage is the key-value data model. This simple yet powerful model makes it easy to store and retrieve large amounts of structured data, especially when you don't need complex relationships between your data elements.

Entities: Your Data's Building Blocks

Think of each piece of data you store in Table Storage as an **entity**. An entity is similar to a row in a traditional database table, but with a key difference: there's no fixed schema. Each entity can have its own unique set of properties, allowing for greater flexibility.

Properties: Key-Value Pairs

An entity's properties are stored as **key-value pairs**. The key is a name that identifies the property, and the value is the data associated with that key. For example, a customer entity might have properties like:

- **PartitionKey:** CustomerID
- **RowKey:** OrderNumber
- **CustomerName:** "John Doe"
- **EmailAddress:** "[email address removed]"

The `PartitionKey` and `RowKey` are special properties that together form the primary key for an entity. They determine how your data is distributed and accessed within Table Storage.

Simplicity and Flexibility

The key-value data model offers several advantages:

- **Simplicity:** It's easy to understand and work with, making it ideal for developers who don't want to deal with complex schema definitions.
- **Flexibility:** You can easily add, modify, or remove properties for your entities without impacting other entities in the table. This makes it easier to adapt your data model to changing requirements.
- **Scalability:** The key-value model lends itself well to horizontal scaling, allowing you to distribute your data across multiple storage nodes for improved performance and capacity.

When to Use the Key-Value Model

The key-value data model is best suited for scenarios where:

- **Relationships between data entities are not complex:** If your data doesn't have many relationships or if the relationships are simple, the key-value model can be a good fit.
- **You need fast access to individual items:** Table Storage is optimized for quick lookups of individual entities based on their keys.
- **You have large volumes of structured data:** The key-value model can handle massive datasets efficiently, making it suitable for big data scenarios.

Examples of Key-Value Data Use Cases

Azure Table Storage is commonly used for storing:

- **User profile data:** Each user can be represented as an entity with properties like username, email, and preferences.
- **Device telemetry:** Data collected from IoT devices can be stored as entities with properties like device ID, timestamp, and sensor readings.
- **Session state:** Web applications can store user session data in Table Storage for easy retrieval and management.
- **Logs and events:** Application logs and events can be stored as entities for analysis and troubleshooting.

By understanding the key-value data model and its advantages, you can leverage the power of Azure Table Storage to build efficient and scalable applications that handle structured data with ease.

Understanding Table Storage Structure

To effectively use Azure Table Storage, it's important to understand its hierarchical structure, which is designed to organize and access data efficiently. Let's break down the key components:

Storage Account: Your Table Storage Home

Just like with Blob Storage, the **Storage Account** is the top-level container in Azure Table Storage. It acts as a unique namespace for your tables and provides a way to manage them collectively. Each storage account has its own set of access keys, which are used to authenticate requests to the Table Storage service.

Table: A Collection of Entities

Within a storage account, you create **tables** to store your data. A table is a collection of entities that share a similar structure or purpose. Think of it like a spreadsheet, where each row represents an entity and each column represents a property (key-value pair).

However, unlike a traditional spreadsheet, Azure Table Storage doesn't enforce a rigid schema. This means that each entity within a table can have its own unique set of properties, giving you the flexibility to adapt your data model as your needs evolve.

Entity: A Row of Data

An **entity** represents a single item of data within a table. It's essentially a collection of properties, which are key-value pairs that describe the entity. For example, an entity representing a customer might have properties like CustomerID, Name, Email, and Address.

PartitionKey and RowKey: The Unique Identifiers

Each entity in Azure Table Storage is uniquely identified by a combination of two keys:

- **PartitionKey:** This key determines how your data is distributed across storage nodes. Entities with the same PartitionKey are stored together, allowing for efficient querying and scaling.
- **RowKey:** This key uniquely identifies an entity within its partition.

Together, the PartitionKey and RowKey form a composite primary key that ensures every entity in the table is uniquely identifiable.

Visualizing the Structure

To illustrate, here's a simple visual representation of the Azure Table Storage structure:

```
Storage Account
 |
 ---Table 1
 |   |
 |   ---Entity 1 (PartitionKey: "A", RowKey: "1")
 |   ---Entity 2 (PartitionKey: "A", RowKey: "2")
 |   ---Entity 3 (PartitionKey: "B", RowKey: "1")
 |
 ---Table 2
     |
     ---Entity 1 (PartitionKey: "X", RowKey: "1")
     ---Entity 2 (PartitionKey: "Y", RowKey: "1")
```

In this example, the storage account contains two tables. Table 1 has three entities, two of which share the same PartitionKey ("A") but have different RowKey values. Table 2 has two entities with different PartitionKey values but the same RowKey value.

Understanding this structure is fundamental for designing efficient data models and optimizing query performance in Azure Table Storage.

Scenarios and Use Cases

Azure Table Storage's simplicity, scalability, and speed make it a valuable asset in a wide variety of scenarios. Let's explore some common use cases where its key-value data model shines:

1. Storing User Data for Web Applications

Think about all the user data a typical web application needs to manage: user profiles, preferences, settings, authentication tokens, and more. Azure Table Storage excels at storing this type of data. Each user can be represented as an entity, with properties like `UserID`, `UserName`, `Email`, and `Preferences`. This allows for quick and efficient retrieval of individual user profiles.

2. Managing Device Information for IoT Applications

The Internet of Things (IoT) generates massive amounts of data from sensors and devices. Azure Table Storage can be used to store this data, with each device represented as an entity. Properties might include `DeviceID`, `Timestamp`, `SensorData`, and `Location`. This allows you to track device status, analyze sensor data, and monitor IoT systems effectively.

3. Logging and Telemetry Data

Logs and telemetry data are often semi-structured and can grow rapidly. Table Storage is a great choice for storing this type of data due to its scalability and cost-effectiveness. You can log events, errors, or performance metrics as entities with properties like `Timestamp`, `LogLevel`, `Message`, and other relevant details.

4. Storing Application Settings and Configurations

Azure Table Storage is an excellent option for storing application settings and configurations. You can create a table to hold configuration values as entities, with properties like `SettingName` and `SettingValue`. This allows you to easily retrieve and update configuration data without having to modify your application code.

5. Building Leaderboards and High Score Tables

For gaming applications or any scenario where you need to track rankings or scores, Azure Table Storage is a perfect fit. Each entry in the leaderboard can be stored as an entity, with properties like `UserID`, `Score`, and `Timestamp`. You can then easily query the table to retrieve the top scores or rankings.

6. Additional Use Cases

Beyond these common scenarios, Azure Table Storage can be used for a variety of other purposes, including:

- **Caching:** Storing frequently accessed data in Table Storage for faster retrieval.
- **Message Queuing:** Implementing a simple messaging system using table entities as messages.
- **Data Archiving:** Storing infrequently accessed data for long-term preservation.

Choosing the Right Tool for the Job

While Azure Table Storage is versatile, it's not the best choice for every scenario. Consider these factors when deciding if it's right for you:

- **Data model:** If your data has complex relationships or requires complex joins, a relational database might be a better fit.
- **Query flexibility:** Table Storage supports limited query capabilities compared to SQL databases. If you need complex queries or ad-hoc reporting, consider other options like Azure Cosmos DB.

By understanding the strengths and limitations of Azure Table Storage, you can choose the right storage solution for your specific needs and leverage its unique capabilities to build scalable and efficient applications.

Creating a Table

Creating a table in Azure Table Storage is a straightforward process through the Azure Portal. Think of it as setting up a new spreadsheet to hold your data. Let's walk through the steps:

1. **Navigate to Your Storage Account:**
    - Open the Azure Portal (https://portal.azure.com/) and log in with your credentials.
    - In the search bar, type "Storage accounts" and select it from the results.
    - Click on the storage account where you want to create the table.
2. **Select "Tables":**
    - In the left-hand navigation menu of your storage account, under the "Data storage" section, click on "Tables."
3. **Click "+ Table" to Create a New Table:**
    - On the Tables page, you'll see a list of your existing tables (if any). Click the "+ Table" button at the top to open a new blade (a panel within the portal) for creating a table.
4. **Specify a Table Name:**

- In the "Table name" field, enter a unique and descriptive name for your table.
- Table names can contain letters, numbers, and hyphens, and they must be between 3 and 63 characters long.
- Remember that table names are case-sensitive and cannot include spaces or special characters.

5. **Click "Create":**
   - Review the table name to make sure it's correct.
   - Click the "Create" button to create your new table.

Congratulations! You've successfully created a table in Azure Table Storage. You'll see it listed on the Tables page. You can now start adding entities (data) to your table.

Important Notes:

- **Data Storage:** Azure Table Storage is a NoSQL database, so it doesn't enforce a strict schema like traditional relational databases. This means you can add entities with different sets of properties to the same table.
- **Naming Conventions:** It's a good practice to use a consistent naming convention for your tables to make them easier to identify and manage. For example, you might use a prefix like "Customer_" or "Product_" to indicate the type of data stored in the table.
- **PartitionKey and RowKey:** Each entity in a table must have a unique combination of PartitionKey and RowKey. These keys determine how your data is distributed and accessed within Table Storage. We'll discuss them in more detail in the next section.

Now that you have your table ready, you can start populating it with your data and leveraging the powerful features of Azure Table Storage to build scalable and efficient applications.

Working with Entities

Azure Table Storage empowers you to perform the fundamental CRUD operations (Create, Read, Update, Delete) on your data entities, making it a flexible and dynamic storage solution. Let's explore these operations, along with the concept of batch operations for efficient data processing.

Inserting Entities

To insert a new entity into your Azure Table, you'll need to create a new object representing the entity and populate its properties. Here's an example in C#:

```
// Create a new customer entity TableEntity customer = new
TableEntity("Customers", "Cust123") { {"FirstName", "John"}, {"LastName",
"Doe"}, {"Email", "[email address removed]"}, {"Phone", "123-456-7890"} }; //
Insert the entity into the table await tableClient.AddEntityAsync(customer);
```

In this example, we create a `TableEntity` object with the partition key "Customers" and the row key "Cust123." We then add properties for the customer's first name, last name, email, and phone number. Finally, we insert the entity into the "Customers" table using the `AddEntityAsync` method.

Retrieving Entities

You can retrieve entities from a table using point queries, range queries, or table queries. Here's an example of a point query in Python:

```
# Retrieve a specific entity entity = table_client.get_entity("Customers",
"Cust123") print(entity)
```

In this example, we retrieve the entity with the partition key "Customers" and the row key "Cust123."

Updating Entities

To update an existing entity, you can modify its properties and then call the `UpdateEntityAsync` method (C#) or the `update_entity` method (Python). Azure Table Storage supports both replacing the entire entity (replace) and merging changes with the existing entity (merge).

Deleting Entities

Deleting an entity is straightforward:

```
// Delete an entity await tableClient.DeleteEntityAsync("Customers", "Cust123");
```

In this C# example, we delete the entity with the partition key "Customers" and the row key "Cust123."

Batch Operations

When you need to perform multiple operations on entities, such as inserting, updating, or deleting a set of entities, you can use batch operations to improve efficiency. Batch operations allow you to send multiple requests in a single transaction, reducing the number of round trips to the server. Azure Table Storage supports batch operations for up to 100 entities at a time.

Code Examples

The specific code for working with entities in Azure Table Storage will vary depending on your chosen programming language and SDK. However, the general concepts and operations remain the same. Consult the Azure documentation and SDK references for your preferred language to get detailed instructions and examples.

By understanding the CRUD operations and the concept of batch operations, you can efficiently manage the data in your Azure Table Storage tables.

Querying Table Storage

Azure Table Storage provides various query options to retrieve specific data from your tables. It's important to understand these options and their syntax to efficiently fetch the information you need.

Query Types

There are three primary query types in Azure Table Storage:

1. **Point Queries:** The most efficient type of query, it retrieves a single entity by specifying both the `PartitionKey` and `RowKey`. This is akin to looking up a specific cell in a spreadsheet by its row and column coordinates.
2. **Range Queries:** These queries retrieve multiple entities within a specified range of `PartitionKey` and/or `RowKey` values. This is like selecting a range of cells in a spreadsheet.
3. **Table Queries:** These queries retrieve all entities within a table. This is similar to selecting an entire spreadsheet, and it's the least efficient type of query.

Query Syntax and Operators

Azure Table Storage uses a specific syntax for querying, with various operators to filter and sort your results.

- **Filter Operators:**
    - eq (equal)
    - ne (not equal)
    - gt (greater than)
    - ge (greater than or equal)
    - lt (less than)
    - le (less than or equal)
    - and (logical AND)
    - or (logical OR)
    - not (logical NOT)
- **Sorting:**
    - Results are automatically sorted in ascending order by PartitionKey and then by RowKey.
    - You can't sort by other properties directly.

Filtering and Sorting Results

To filter your query results, you can use the filter parameter in combination with the operators mentioned above. For example, to retrieve all entities with a specific PartitionKey value, you would use a filter like:

PartitionKey eq 'myPartitionKey'

To retrieve all entities within a specific range of RowKey values, you would use a filter like:

PartitionKey eq 'myPartitionKey' and RowKey ge 'startRowKey' and RowKey le 'endRowKey'

As mentioned earlier, sorting results by properties other than PartitionKey and RowKey isn't directly supported. However, you can work around this limitation by designing your RowKey values in a way that allows for the desired sorting. For example, if you want to sort entities by date, you can use a RowKey format like "YYYYMMDD-uniqueId."

Querying Programmatically

You can query Azure Table Storage programmatically using various Azure SDKs (like the Azure Storage SDK for .NET or the Azure Storage Client Library for Python) or by making direct REST API calls. These methods provide more flexibility and control over your queries, allowing you to construct complex filters and retrieve results in a structured format.

Considerations for Querying

- **Performance:** Point queries are the most efficient because they use the table's indexes to quickly locate the desired entity. Range queries are also relatively efficient, but table scans (retrieving all entities) can be slow for large tables.
- **Partitioning:** The choice of your PartitionKey is crucial for query performance and scalability. Entities with the same PartitionKey are stored on the same partition, and queries that filter by PartitionKey can be executed efficiently within that partition.
- **Data Modeling:** Design your table schema and entity properties carefully to optimize for your most common queries. Consider the types of queries you'll be performing most frequently and choose a PartitionKey that allows for efficient filtering.

By understanding the different query options, syntax, and operators available in Azure Table Storage, you can effectively retrieve the data you need and build applications that leverage the scalability and performance benefits of this NoSQL storage solution.

Scaling and Performance

Azure Table Storage is designed to handle massive amounts of data and scale seamlessly to meet the growing needs of your applications. Understanding its scaling mechanisms and performance optimization techniques is crucial for building efficient and responsive solutions.

Automatic Scaling: Effortless Expansion

Azure Table Storage automatically scales to accommodate your data growth. It distributes your data across multiple storage nodes, ensuring that your application can handle high volumes of traffic and requests without sacrificing performance. This means you don't need to worry about manually provisioning additional resources or re-architecting your application as your data grows.

Partitioning: The Key to Scalability

Partitioning is the secret behind Azure Table Storage's scalability. Each table is divided into multiple partitions, and each partition can store a subset of your entities. When you insert an entity into a table, Azure automatically determines which partition to store it in based on the entity's `PartitionKey`.

By partitioning your data, Azure Table Storage can distribute the load across multiple storage nodes, enabling parallel processing of requests and ensuring consistent performance even at high scale.

Optimizing Performance

While Azure Table Storage automatically scales, there are several steps you can take to further optimize its performance:

1. **Design Efficient PartitionKey and RowKey Values:**
   - The choice of `PartitionKey` is critical for performance. Entities with the same `PartitionKey` are stored together, so queries that filter by `PartitionKey` can be executed quickly within a single partition.
   - Choose a `PartitionKey` that distributes your data evenly across partitions to avoid hot spots (partitions with excessive load).
   - The RowKey uniquely identifies an entity within its partition. Design your `RowKey` values to support your common query patterns and enable efficient sorting of results.
2. **Use Batch Operations:**
   - When you need to perform multiple operations on entities (inserts, updates, deletes), use batch operations. Batching allows you to send multiple requests in a single transaction, reducing the number of round-trips to the server and improving performance significantly.
3. **Optimize Query Filters:**
   - Avoid table scans by using filters that include the `PartitionKey` value. This will limit the query to a specific partition, resulting in faster response times.
   - Use range queries to retrieve multiple entities within a specific range of `PartitionKey` and RowKey values. This is more efficient than retrieving all entities and filtering them on the client-side.
   - Avoid complex filters that require scanning large amounts of data. Instead, design your data model and queries in a way that leverages the natural indexing provided by `PartitionKey` and RowKey.
4. **Client-Side Caching:**

- If you have frequently accessed data that doesn't change often, consider implementing client-side caching to reduce the number of requests to Table Storage and improve response times.
5. **Monitor Performance:**
    - Use Azure Monitor metrics to track the performance of your Table Storage operations. Monitor metrics like average latency, throughput, and error rates to identify potential bottlenecks and optimize your application.

By following these best practices and understanding how Azure Table Storage scales and performs, you can build high-performance applications that can handle massive amounts of structured data with ease.

Tips and Best Practices

To make the most out of Azure Table Storage and ensure optimal performance, cost-efficiency, and maintainability, consider incorporating these practical tips and best practices into your development workflow:

Choose the Right Data Model

Before diving into Table Storage, take a step back and evaluate whether the key-value data model aligns with your application's requirements. While Table Storage offers simplicity and scalability, it's not the ideal solution for every scenario. If your data has complex relationships or requires frequent joins between entities, a relational database might be a more suitable choice.

Design Efficient PartitionKey and RowKey Values

The design of your `PartitionKey` and `RowKey` is critical for query performance and scalability in Azure Table Storage.

- **PartitionKey Strategy:** Choose a `PartitionKey` that distributes your data evenly across partitions to avoid hot spots (partitions with excessive load). Consider the most common query patterns in your application and select a `PartitionKey` that allows for efficient filtering and retrieval of data.
- **RowKey Strategy:** The `RowKey` uniquely identifies an entity within its partition. Design your `RowKey` values to support your query patterns and enable efficient sorting of results. Consider using a reverse chronological order or a hierarchical structure to organize your data logically.
- **Composite Keys:** You can also combine multiple attributes into your `PartitionKey` or `RowKey` to create a composite key that better reflects your data model and query requirements.

Use Batch Operations

Batch operations are a powerful way to improve the efficiency of your Table Storage interactions. Instead of sending individual requests for each operation (insert, update, delete), you can group multiple operations into a single batch request. This reduces the overhead of multiple network calls and can significantly improve performance, especially when dealing with large numbers of entities.

Monitor Performance

Regularly monitor the performance of your Table Storage operations using Azure Monitor metrics. Keep an eye on metrics like:

- **Average server latency:** The average time taken to process requests on the server-side.
- **Success E2E latency:** The average end-to-end latency, including network transit time.

- **Throttle percentage:** The percentage of requests that are being throttled due to exceeding the service's limits.
- **Available throughput (ingress and egress):** The amount of data being transferred in and out of your storage account.

By monitoring these metrics, you can identify potential performance bottlenecks, optimize your queries, and ensure that your application is performing as expected.

Consider Scalability

Azure Table Storage automatically scales to handle large volumes of data, but it's essential to understand how partitioning works to ensure optimal scalability.

- **Partitioning:** Azure distributes your data across multiple partitions based on the `PartitionKey` values. Each partition has its own scalability limits, so choosing the right `PartitionKey` strategy is crucial for ensuring your application can scale seamlessly.
- **Hot Partitions:** If a particular partition becomes a "hot spot" (receives an excessive amount of traffic), it can impact the performance of your entire table. Monitor your partition usage and consider repartitioning your data if necessary.

By following these tips and best practices, you can unlock the full potential of Azure Table Storage and build high-performance, scalable, and cost-effective applications that leverage the benefits of this NoSQL storage solution. Remember, careful planning and optimization are key to achieving success with Table Storage.

Chapter Summary

This chapter introduced Azure Table Storage, a NoSQL key-value store that provides a simple and scalable solution for managing large amounts of structured data. We first explored the concept of NoSQL databases, highlighting their flexibility and suitability for specific use cases compared to traditional relational databases.

We then delved into the core concepts of Azure Table Storage, explaining its key-value data model, where data is stored as entities (rows) with properties (key-value pairs). The flexibility of this model allows you to easily add or modify properties without the constraints of a rigid schema.

We also explored the hierarchical structure of Table Storage, consisting of storage accounts, tables, and entities, with each entity uniquely identified by its PartitionKey and RowKey.

Azure Table Storage finds applications in various scenarios, such as storing user data, managing IoT device information, logging telemetry data, storing application settings, and even building leaderboards.

You learned how to create a table in the Azure Portal, a straightforward process involving navigating to your storage account, selecting "Tables," and providing a unique table name.

We discussed the fundamental operations for working with entities: inserting, retrieving, updating, and deleting. You also gained insight into batch operations, which allow you to efficiently process multiple entities in a single transaction.

Furthermore, we explored the different ways to query data in Table Storage, including point queries, range queries, and table queries, and how to filter and sort results using the available query syntax and operators.

Lastly, we delved into the scaling and performance aspects of Table Storage, highlighting its ability to automatically scale to handle massive amounts of data. You learned about partitioning and how it helps distribute data across multiple storage nodes for improved performance. We also offered tips on optimizing performance by designing efficient PartitionKey and RowKey values, using batch operations, and monitoring Table Storage metrics with Azure Monitor.

By understanding these concepts and best practices, you're now equipped to leverage the power of Azure Table Storage for your applications that require scalable, high-performance storage of structured data. In the next chapter, we'll explore another Azure Storage service, Azure Queue Storage, which is designed for handling asynchronous messaging and workflows.

Azure Queue Storage: Asynchronous Messaging and Workflows

Outline

- What is Asynchronous Messaging?
- What is Azure Queue Storage?
- Key Concepts and Terminology
- Benefits of Using Azure Queue Storage
- Creating and Managing Queues
- Adding Messages to Queues
- Reading and Processing Messages
- Advanced Features and Scenarios
- Best Practices
- Chapter Summary

What is Asynchronous Messaging?

In the digital realm, communication between systems or components can happen in two distinct ways: synchronously or asynchronously. Let's unravel the concept of asynchronous messaging and understand why it's a valuable tool in modern application architecture.

Synchronous Communication: Real-Time Interaction

Imagine a phone call – you talk, the other person listens and responds immediately. This is an example of synchronous communication. In the software world, this translates to a client sending a request to a server and waiting for an immediate response before proceeding. While this model works well for real-time interactions, it has limitations when dealing with tasks that might take time to complete or when systems need to communicate independently.

Asynchronous Messaging: The Message in a Bottle

Asynchronous messaging, in contrast, is like sending a message in a bottle. You toss the bottle into the sea, and it eventually reaches its destination, even if you're no longer there to witness it. Similarly, in asynchronous messaging, a sender transmits a message to a queue, and the receiver can retrieve and process the message at its own convenience. This decoupling of sender and receiver offers several advantages.

How Asynchronous Messaging Works

1. **The Message:** A message is a self-contained unit of data that can be text, JSON, XML, or any other format. It typically includes information about the task to be performed or the data to be processed.
2. **The Queue:** A queue is a temporary storage location for messages. Think of it as a holding area where messages wait patiently for their turn to be processed.
3. **The Producer:** The producer is the component or system that creates and sends messages to the queue.
4. **The Consumer:** The consumer is the component or system that retrieves and processes messages from the queue.

Benefits of Asynchronous Messaging

Asynchronous messaging offers several compelling advantages:

- **Loose Coupling:** The sender and receiver are decoupled, meaning they don't need to be online simultaneously. This allows systems to evolve independently and communicate even when they are temporarily unavailable.
- **Scalability:** Message queues can handle varying volumes of messages, allowing systems to scale independently based on demand. This is particularly useful for scenarios with unpredictable or bursty traffic patterns.
- **Reliability:** Even if a receiver is temporarily down or overloaded, messages remain safely stored in the queue until the receiver is ready to process them. This ensures that messages are not lost and can be processed later.
- **Improved Responsiveness:** In synchronous communication, the sender is blocked until it receives a response. Asynchronous messaging allows the sender to continue with other tasks while the message is being processed, leading to a more responsive system.

Common Use Cases

Asynchronous messaging is used in a wide range of scenarios, including:

- **Order Processing:** An e-commerce website might use a message queue to handle order processing in the background, ensuring a smooth and responsive user experience.
- **Data Ingestion:** A data pipeline can use a message queue to buffer incoming data from various sources, allowing for smoother processing and analysis.
- **Event-Driven Architectures:** Microservices-based architectures often rely on asynchronous messaging for communication between services.

In the next section, we'll delve into Azure Queue Storage, Microsoft's fully managed cloud-based message queue service that provides a simple and scalable way to implement asynchronous messaging in your Azure applications.

What is Azure Queue Storage?

Azure Queue Storage is Microsoft's solution for managing asynchronous communication and workflows in the cloud. Imagine it as a reliable and efficient postal service for your applications. Just as a postal service stores letters until they're delivered, Queue Storage acts as a buffer, holding messages until they're ready to be processed by the intended recipient.

A Simple Yet Powerful Message Queue Service

At its core, Azure Queue Storage is a message queue service. It allows you to send and receive messages between different components of your application or even between different applications altogether. These messages can be simple text strings, JSON objects, XML documents, or any other format that suits your needs.

Queue Storage provides a simple API for adding messages to queues and retrieving them for processing. It ensures that messages are delivered reliably and in the order they were sent, making it ideal for building distributed systems that need to communicate asynchronously.

Key Features of Azure Queue Storage

Azure Queue Storage offers a range of features that make it a robust and reliable message queue service:

- **Scalability:** Queue Storage can handle large volumes of messages, scaling automatically to meet your demands. Whether you're dealing with a few messages per minute or thousands per second, Queue Storage can adapt to your needs.

- **Durability:** Your messages are stored redundantly in multiple locations, ensuring their persistence even in the face of hardware failures or data center outages. You can rest assured that your messages are safe and won't be lost.
- **Visibility Timeout:** This feature allows you to control how long a message remains invisible to other consumers after it's retrieved from the queue. This is important for ensuring that messages are processed only once and are not lost if a consumer fails to process them within a certain timeframe.
- **Message Time-to-Live (TTL):** You can set an expiration time for messages, after which they are automatically deleted from the queue. This helps prevent the accumulation of old or irrelevant messages.
- **Dead-Letter Queue (DLQ):** A dead-letter queue is a special queue that stores messages that cannot be processed successfully. This allows you to troubleshoot and reprocess failed messages later.

Use Cases for Azure Queue Storage

Azure Queue Storage is a versatile tool that can be used in a variety of scenarios:

- **Decoupling Components:** Use queues to decouple components of a distributed application, allowing them to communicate asynchronously.
- **Load Leveling:** Smooth out spikes in traffic or workload by buffering messages in a queue.
- **Task Queues:** Create task queues to process background tasks or long-running operations.
- **Workflows:** Orchestrate complex workflows by passing messages between different stages of a process.
- **Event-Driven Architectures:** Build event-driven applications that react to events by processing messages from queues.

In the next sections, we'll delve deeper into the key concepts and terminology of Azure Queue Storage, and then explore how to create, manage, and interact with queues using various tools and APIs.

Key Concepts and Terminology

Understanding the terminology of Azure Queue Storage is crucial for effectively using this service. Let's break down the key concepts and terms you'll encounter:

Queue: Your Message Inbox

In Azure Queue Storage, a **queue** is a storage location for messages. Think of it like an inbox for your applications. It can hold an unlimited number of messages, each waiting to be processed. Queues provide a reliable way to store messages and ensure they are delivered to the intended recipient.

Message: The Unit of Information

A **message** is a unit of data that you store in a queue. It can be any format, including text, JSON, XML, or binary data. The size of a message can be up to 64 KB. Messages are typically used to transmit information between different components of an application or between different applications.

Producer: The Message Sender

The **producer** is the component or application that creates and sends messages to the queue. It can be a web application, a mobile app, a background process, or any other system that needs to communicate asynchronously with another system. The producer simply adds messages to the queue and doesn't have to worry about how or when the messages are processed.

Consumer: The Message Receiver

The **consumer** is the component or application that retrieves and processes messages from the queue. It can be a worker process, a background task, or any other system that is designed to consume messages from the queue and perform the required actions. The consumer dequeues messages from the queue and processes them one at a time.

Visibility Timeout: Temporary Invisibility Cloak

When a consumer retrieves a message from the queue, the message is not immediately deleted. Instead, it becomes invisible to other consumers for a specified period, known as the **visibility timeout**. This allows the consumer to process the message without the risk of another consumer retrieving and processing the same message simultaneously. If the consumer fails to process the message within the visibility timeout, the message becomes visible again and can be retrieved by another consumer.

Message Time-to-Live (TTL): Expiration Date

Every message in a queue has a **time-to-live (TTL)**, which is the maximum time it can live in the queue before being automatically deleted. This is useful for preventing the accumulation of old or irrelevant messages in the queue. You can set the TTL for a message when you add it to the queue or configure a default TTL for the entire queue.

Summary Table

Term	Description
Queue	A storage location for messages.
Message	A unit of data stored in a queue.
Producer	The component that sends messages to a queue.
Consumer	The component that retrieves and processes messages from a queue.
Visibility Timeout	The time a message is hidden from other consumers after retrieval.
Message TTL	The maximum time a message can live in the queue.

Benefits of Using Azure Queue Storage

Azure Queue Storage is a powerful tool that brings a host of advantages to the table when building distributed and scalable applications. Let's delve into the key benefits that make it a popular choice for handling asynchronous messaging and workflows:

1. Loose Coupling: Empowering Independent Components

In a distributed system, it's often desirable to have components that can operate independently without being tightly bound to each other. Queue Storage facilitates this by enabling **loose coupling**. Producers and consumers interact with the queue, not directly with each other. This means that they can evolve independently, be written in different languages, and even be deployed in different environments.

2. Scalability: Handling the Flood of Messages

Modern applications often need to handle varying volumes of messages, from a trickle during off-peak hours to a deluge during peak times. Azure Queue Storage is built to scale. It can automatically adjust its capacity to handle the fluctuating message volume, ensuring that your application can process messages efficiently even under heavy load.

3. Reliability: Never Miss a Beat

Message delivery is critical in many applications. Azure Queue Storage guarantees that messages are not lost, even in the face of temporary failures. If a consumer fails to process a message, it will become visible again in the queue after the visibility timeout expires, allowing another consumer to pick it up. This ensures that messages are eventually processed and your application remains resilient.

4. Load Leveling: Smoothing Out the Peaks

When an application experiences sudden spikes in traffic or workload, it can become overwhelmed and unresponsive. Queue Storage acts as a buffer, absorbing these spikes by storing messages temporarily. Consumers can then process these messages at their own pace, smoothing out the load and ensuring that your application remains responsive even during peak times.

5. Message Ordering: First In, First Out (FIFO)

In many scenarios, it's crucial to maintain the order in which messages are processed. Azure Queue Storage guarantees First-In-First-Out (FIFO) message delivery. This means that messages are retrieved from the queue in the same order they were added, ensuring the correct sequence of operations in your workflows.

6. Cost-Effectiveness: Pay for What You Use

Azure Queue Storage follows a simple and transparent pricing model. You pay only for the storage you use and the number of transactions performed on the queue. This pay-as-you-go approach eliminates the need for upfront capital expenses and allows you to scale your costs based on your actual usage.

By leveraging these benefits, Azure Queue Storage empowers you to build scalable, reliable, and cost-effective applications that can handle asynchronous communication and complex workflows with ease. Whether you're building a simple message processing system or a sophisticated distributed application, Queue Storage provides a robust foundation for your messaging needs.

Creating and Managing Queues

Let's get hands-on with Azure Queue Storage! We'll guide you through creating and managing your message queues directly within the Azure Portal. This intuitive interface makes it easy to set up queues and start sending and receiving messages.

1. Navigate to Your Storage Account:

- Open the Azure Portal (https://portal.azure.com/) and log in.
- In the search bar, type "Storage accounts" and select it from the results.
- Click on the storage account where you want to create the queue.

2. Select "Queues":

- In the left-hand navigation menu of your storage account, under the "Data storage" section, click on "Queues." You'll see a list of your existing queues (if any).

3. Click "+ Queue" to Create a New Queue:

- Click the "+ Queue" button at the top of the Queues page. This opens a new blade on the right side where you'll provide the queue details.

4. **Specify a Queue Name:**

   - Enter a unique name for your queue.
   - Queue names must be lowercase, start with a letter or number, and can contain only letters, numbers, and hyphens.
   - The maximum length of a queue name is 63 characters.

5. **Configure Optional Settings (Advanced):**

   - **Message Time-to-Live (TTL):** Set the maximum time (in days) that a message can live in the queue before being automatically deleted. The default is seven days.
   - **Enable logging:** Enable logging to record details about queue operations, such as insertions, deletions, and reads. This can be helpful for debugging and monitoring.
   - **Enable versioning:** Create a new copy of a blob each time the blob is modified.

6. **Click "Create":**

   - Review your settings and click "Create" to create your new queue. The queue should appear in your list of queues within a few seconds.

Managing Queues:

Once your queue is created, you can manage it from the Queues page in the Azure Portal. You can perform the following actions:

- **View Queue Properties:** Click on the queue name to view its properties, such as message count, size, and last modified time.
- **Add Messages:** Click the "Add message" button to manually add messages to the queue.
- **Peek at Messages:** Peek at the messages in the queue without dequeuing them.
- **Delete Queue:** Delete the queue if you no longer need it.

You've now mastered the basics of creating and managing queues in Azure Queue Storage through the Azure Portal. In the next section, we'll explore how to add messages to your queues using various methods.

Adding Messages to Queues

Now that you have your queue set up, it's time to start sending messages! Azure Queue Storage offers multiple avenues for adding messages to your queues, catering to different use cases and development preferences.

1. Azure Portal: The User-Friendly Way

For simple tasks or when you're just starting out, the Azure Portal provides a convenient way to add messages directly through its interface:

1. **Navigate to Your Queue:** In the Azure Portal, go to your storage account, select "Queues," and click on the queue you want to add messages to.
2. **Add Message:** Click the "Add message" button.
3. **Enter Message Content:** In the "Message text" field, enter the content of your message. This can be a simple text string, a JSON object, an XML document, or any other data format you choose.
4. **Optional Settings:** You can also set the following optional parameters:
   - **Time to Live (TTL):** The maximum time (in seconds) that the message should remain in the queue before being automatically deleted.
   - **Visibility Timeout:** The amount of time (in seconds) that the message should remain invisible to other consumers after being dequeued.

5. **Add Message:** Click "OK" to add the message to the queue.

2. Azure Storage SDKs: Programmatic Power

For more programmatic control and automation, Azure provides Software Development Kits (SDKs) for various languages, such as .NET, Java, Python, and Node.js. These SDKs offer libraries and functions for interacting with Queue Storage, including adding messages.

Here's a C# example using the Azure.Storage.Queues package:

```
QueueClient queueClient = new QueueClient(connectionString, queueName); await
queueClient.SendMessageAsync("Hello, Azure Queue!");
```

3. REST APIs: Flexibility for Any Language

If you're using a language that doesn't have an official Azure SDK, you can use the Azure Queue Storage REST API to interact with queues. This allows you to add messages to queues from virtually any programming language or platform that can make HTTP requests.

Batching Messages: Efficiency at Scale

If you need to add a large number of messages to a queue, you can use batch operations to send multiple messages in a single request. This is more efficient than sending individual messages, as it reduces the number of network round-trips. Azure Queue Storage allows you to batch up to 20 messages in a single request.

Choosing Your Method

The best way to add messages to your Azure queues depends on your specific use case and preferences:

- **Azure Portal:** Ideal for simple tasks and for getting started.
- **Azure SDKs:** Offers a convenient and type-safe way to interact with queues programmatically.
- **REST APIs:** Provides the most flexibility and is suitable for languages without official SDKs.
- **Batching:** Use batch operations for improved efficiency when adding a large number of messages.

By understanding these different methods, you can choose the one that best suits your needs and efficiently integrate Azure Queue Storage into your applications.

Reading and Processing Messages

In the world of Azure Queue Storage, the retrieval and processing of messages by consumer applications are fundamental actions. Let's dive into how you can read and process messages from a queue using SDKs or REST APIs, while also understanding crucial concepts like visibility timeout and peeking at messages.

Retrieving Messages: SDKs vs. REST APIs

Azure provides two primary ways to interact with queues and retrieve messages:

1. **Azure Storage SDKs:**
   - **Ease of Use:** SDKs (available for various programming languages like .NET, Java, Python, Node.js, etc.) offer a convenient and idiomatic way to interact with Azure services. They abstract away the complexities of the underlying REST APIs, making it easier to write code.
   - **Type Safety and Error Handling:** SDKs provide type-safe interfaces and built-in error handling, reducing the risk of errors and making your code more robust.

- **Example (C#):**
  ```csharp
  QueueClient queueClient = new QueueClient(connectionString, queueName); QueueMessage[] messages = await queueClient.ReceiveMessagesAsync(maxMessages: 10); foreach (QueueMessage message in messages) { string messageText = message.Body.ToString(); // Process the message await queueClient.DeleteMessageAsync(message.MessageId, message.PopReceipt); }
  ```

2. **REST APIs:**
   - **Flexibility:** The Azure Storage REST API provides the most flexible way to interact with queues. You can use any programming language or tool that can make HTTP requests.
   - **Lower-Level Control:** REST APIs offer fine-grained control over your requests and responses, allowing you to customize the behavior as needed.
   - **Example (Python):**
     ```python
     from azure.storage.queue import QueueClient queue_client = QueueClient.from_connection_string(conn_str="my_connection_string", queue_name="myqueue") messages = queue_client.receive_messages() for message in messages: print(message.content) queue_client.delete_message(message)
     ```

Visibility Timeout: Preventing Concurrent Processing

When a consumer retrieves a message from the queue, the message isn't immediately deleted. Instead, it becomes invisible to other consumers for a specified duration, known as the visibility timeout. This prevents multiple consumers from processing the same message simultaneously.

The default visibility timeout is 30 seconds, but you can customize it to suit your application's needs. If the consumer fails to process the message within the timeout period, the message becomes visible again, allowing another consumer to pick it up.

Peeking at Messages: A Sneak Peek

If you want to see what messages are in the queue without actually removing them, you can use the "peek" functionality. This allows you to examine the messages without changing their visibility or affecting their position in the queue.

Deleting Messages: Completing the Cycle

Once a consumer has successfully processed a message, it should delete the message from the queue. This ensures that the message is not processed again and prevents the queue from becoming cluttered with outdated information. To delete a message, you need its unique message ID and pop receipt, which are returned when you retrieve the message.

Best Practices

- **Always Delete Messages:** Make sure your consumers delete messages after successful processing to avoid duplicate processing and keep your queue clean.
- **Handle Errors:** Implement robust error handling to deal with situations where a consumer might fail to process a message. Consider using a dead-letter queue to store messages that consistently fail.
- **Set Appropriate Visibility Timeout:** Choose a visibility timeout that gives your consumers enough time to process messages but is short enough to prevent long delays if a consumer fails.

By understanding these concepts and following best practices, you can effectively leverage Azure Queue Storage to build scalable and reliable asynchronous messaging systems.

Advanced Features and Scenarios

While Azure Queue Storage is straightforward in its core functionality, it also offers several advanced features that unlock greater flexibility and power for handling complex messaging and workflow scenarios.

Queue Leasing: Exclusive Processing Rights

Imagine you have a task that requires some time to complete, and you don't want other workers to start working on the same task simultaneously. This is where **queue leasing** comes into play.

When a message is dequeued from the queue, it's not immediately deleted. Instead, it becomes invisible to other consumers for a specified visibility timeout period. During this time, you have exclusive rights to process the message. However, if you fail to complete the processing within the visibility timeout, the message reappears in the queue, allowing another consumer to pick it up.

Queue leasing gives you the ability to extend this visibility timeout, effectively "renewing the lease" on the message and preventing other consumers from accessing it while you're still working on it. This is particularly useful for long-running tasks or tasks that require exclusive access to resources.

Message Deferral: Postpone for Later

Sometimes, you might retrieve a message from the queue but realize that you're not yet ready to process it. In such cases, you can use the **message deferral** feature to temporarily hide the message from other consumers.

By deferring a message, you essentially postpone its processing for a specified period. This is useful when you need to delay the execution of a task or when you want to re-order messages in the queue based on certain criteria.

Message Update: Modify on the Fly

Azure Queue Storage allows you to **update** the content or properties of a message that's already in the queue. This can be useful for scenarios where you need to modify the data being processed or change the metadata associated with a message. For example, you might update a message to indicate its priority or to add additional information required for processing.

Poison Queues: Handling Problematic Messages

Sometimes, messages might fail to be processed due to errors or unexpected conditions. These failed messages, often called **poison messages**, can clog up your queue and prevent other messages from being processed efficiently.

To handle poison messages, you can create a **dead-letter queue (DLQ)**. A DLQ is a separate queue where you can move messages that have failed to be processed a certain number of times. This allows you to isolate problematic messages and analyze them later to identify and fix the underlying issues.

Advanced Scenarios

By combining these advanced features, you can build sophisticated messaging and workflow solutions in Azure Queue Storage. For example, you could create a system that:

- Leases messages for exclusive processing of long-running tasks.
- Defers messages that are not yet ready to be processed.
- Updates messages with additional information as they progress through a workflow.
- Moves poison messages to a dead-letter queue for further analysis.

These advanced capabilities make Azure Queue Storage a versatile tool for building a wide range of distributed applications, from simple event-driven systems to complex business processes.

Best Practices

Azure Queue Storage is a powerful tool, but like any tool, it's most effective when used with care and consideration. Here are some best practices to help you maximize the benefits and avoid potential pitfalls:

Message Size: Keep it Compact

While Azure Queue Storage supports messages up to 64 KB in size, it's generally recommended to keep your messages as small as possible. Smaller messages translate to faster processing times and lower costs. If you need to store larger payloads, consider storing them in Blob Storage and referencing them within your queue messages.

Visibility Timeout: Strike the Right Balance

The visibility timeout is the time period during which a message is hidden from other consumers after it has been dequeued. A shorter timeout can lead to more frequent checks for new messages, potentially increasing costs. A longer timeout might delay processing if a consumer fails. Choose a visibility timeout that balances message processing time and the risk of duplicate processing.

Error Handling: Be Prepared for the Unexpected

Not every message will be processed successfully. Your consumers should be prepared to handle errors gracefully and prevent failed messages from blocking the queue. Consider implementing retry logic for transient errors and using a dead-letter queue (DLQ) to store messages that consistently fail.

Monitoring: Keep an Eye on the Pulse

Azure Monitor provides valuable insights into your queue's performance. Regularly monitor metrics like:

- **Queue Length:** This indicates the number of messages waiting to be processed. A growing queue length might signal a bottleneck in your consumer's processing capabilities.
- **Message Age:** This shows how long messages have been in the queue. Older messages might indicate processing delays or issues with your consumers.
- **Success and Error Rates:** Monitor the success and failure rates of message processing to identify potential problems with your application logic.

By monitoring these metrics, you can proactively detect and address issues before they escalate into major problems.

Security: Guard Your Data

Protecting your queue data is essential. Utilize Azure's security features to control access and safeguard your messages:

- **Shared Access Signatures (SAS):** Generate SAS tokens with limited permissions and expiry times to grant access to specific queues or operations.
- **Azure Active Directory (AAD):** Integrate with Azure AD to control access to your storage account using role-based access control (RBAC).
- **Network Security Groups (NSGs):** Restrict network access to your storage account using NSGs to prevent unauthorized access from specific IP addresses or virtual networks.

Additional Best Practices

- **Queue Naming:** Use descriptive and consistent naming conventions for your queues to make them easier to identify and manage.
- **Message Content:** Design your message content to be easily parsed and processed by your consumers. Avoid complex or nested data structures.
- **Versioning:** If your application relies on message schema, consider versioning your messages to ensure backward compatibility.
- **Batching:** For high-throughput scenarios, use batch operations to send or receive multiple messages in a single request, improving efficiency.

By adhering to these best practices, you can leverage Azure Queue Storage to build scalable, reliable, and secure messaging solutions that empower your applications to communicate and collaborate effectively in the cloud.

Chapter Summary

This chapter introduced you to Azure Queue Storage, a powerful tool for implementing asynchronous messaging and building scalable, reliable applications in the cloud. We began by explaining the concept of asynchronous messaging and its advantages over synchronous communication, emphasizing the loose coupling, scalability, and reliability it offers.

Next, we introduced Azure Queue Storage as a simple and scalable cloud-based message queue service. We highlighted its key features, including scalability to handle large message volumes, durability to ensure message persistence, visibility timeout for controlled message processing, message time-to-live (TTL) for automatic message expiration, and dead-letter queues (DLQs) for managing failed messages.

We then delved into the fundamental concepts and terminology of Azure Queue Storage, defining terms like queue, message, producer, consumer, visibility timeout, and message TTL.

You learned how to create and manage queues in Azure Queue Storage using the Azure Portal, a straightforward process that involves navigating to your storage account, selecting "Queues," and providing the necessary information for your new queue.

We also explored how to add messages to queues using the Azure Portal, Azure Storage SDKs, or REST APIs, highlighting the option to batch messages for efficiency.

You then learned how consumers can retrieve and process messages from queues using Azure Storage SDKs or REST APIs, understanding the concepts of visibility timeout and peeking messages.

Finally, we discussed advanced features like queue leasing, message deferral, and message update, which provide additional flexibility for managing complex workflows. We also touched upon poison queues and their role in handling failed message processing.

The chapter concluded with a set of best practices for using Azure Queue Storage effectively, emphasizing the importance of small message sizes, appropriate visibility timeouts, robust error handling, monitoring queue performance with Azure Monitor, and securing your queues using SAS or AAD authentication.

With this knowledge, you're now equipped to leverage Azure Queue Storage to build scalable, reliable, and efficient messaging solutions for your applications. As we move forward, we'll delve into the world of Azure networking, starting with virtual networks, which provide the foundation for building private networks in the cloud.

Section 5:
Azure Networking

Virtual Networks: Building Your Private Cloud Network

Outline

- What is a Virtual Network?
- Why Use Virtual Networks in Azure?
- Key Components of a Virtual Network
- Creating a Virtual Network
- Subnets and IP Addressing
- Network Security Groups (NSGs)
- Connecting Virtual Networks
- Tips and Best Practices
- Chapter Summary

What is a Virtual Network?

Imagine you're building a neighborhood in the cloud. You want to create a secure, private space where all your houses (Azure resources) can interact with each other while controlling access from the outside world. That's precisely what an Azure Virtual Network (VNet) allows you to do.

Your Private Cloud Neighborhood

A Virtual Network is your own private network within the vast Azure cloud environment. It provides a logical isolation of your Azure resources, allowing you to group them together and manage them as a unit. Within this private network, you can deploy and connect various Azure services like virtual machines, web applications, databases, and more.

The Importance of VNets

Virtual networks play a crucial role in Azure for several reasons:

- **Isolation and Security:** By creating a VNet, you establish a secure boundary around your resources, shielding them from unauthorized access. This isolation is essential for protecting sensitive data and applications from potential threats.
- **Traffic Control:** VNets give you granular control over traffic flow. You can define custom routing rules, set up network security groups (NSGs) to filter traffic, and implement virtual appliances like firewalls and load balancers. This allows you to create a secure and optimized network topology for your applications.
- **Private IP Addressing:** Within a VNet, you can assign private IP addresses to your Azure resources. This means your resources are not directly accessible from the public internet, adding another layer of security.

- **Connectivity:** VNets can be connected to your on-premises network using VPN gateways or ExpressRoute, enabling you to create a hybrid cloud environment where resources can communicate seamlessly between the cloud and your data center.

Building Your Virtual Infrastructure

Think of a VNet as a blank canvas where you can design and build your own network infrastructure in the cloud. You can create subnets to segment your network, deploy virtual machines to run your applications, set up load balancers to distribute traffic, and configure network security groups to protect your resources.

By mastering virtual networks, you gain the ability to build secure, scalable, and flexible network architectures in Azure, tailored to the specific needs of your applications and workloads. In the next sections, we'll dive deeper into the key components of virtual networks and guide you through the process of creating and configuring your own private cloud network in Azure.

Why Use Virtual Networks in Azure?

Virtual Networks (VNets) are foundational building blocks in Azure that unlock a wealth of benefits for your cloud infrastructure. They offer a range of advantages that enhance security, control, connectivity, and integration, making them indispensable for most Azure deployments. Let's delve deeper into why you should leverage VNets in your Azure environment:

1. **Isolation and Security: Shielding Your Resources**
   - **Private Network Space:** Think of a VNet as a secure perimeter around your Azure resources. It acts as a private network space within Azure, isolating your resources from other networks and the public internet.
   - **Network Segmentation:** You can further divide your VNet into subnets, creating logical boundaries to isolate different workloads or application tiers.
   - **Security Rules:** VNets allow you to implement network security groups (NSGs) that act as a firewall, filtering inbound and outbound traffic to control access to your resources.
2. **Traffic Control: Directing the Flow**
   - **Custom Routing:** VNets empower you to define custom routing rules, allowing you to precisely control how traffic flows within your VNet and between VNets.
   - **Network Appliances:** You can deploy virtual network appliances like firewalls, intrusion detection systems, and network virtual appliances (NVAs) to enhance security and control traffic flow.
   - **Load Balancing:** Integrate with Azure Load Balancer to distribute traffic across multiple instances of your applications, ensuring high availability and scalability.
3. **Private IP Addressing: Staying Hidden**
   - **Private IP Space:** By default, resources within a VNet are assigned private IP addresses. This means they are not directly accessible from the public internet, adding a layer of obscurity and protection.
   - **NAT Gateways:** If you need outbound internet connectivity for your VMs, you can use a Network Address Translation (NAT) gateway to translate private IP addresses to public IP addresses.
4. **Connectivity: Bridging the Gap**
   - **Hybrid Cloud:** Connect your VNets to your on-premises network using VPN gateways or ExpressRoute. This enables you to create a hybrid cloud environment where resources in the cloud and on-premises can communicate securely.
   - **VNet Peering:** Connect VNets within the same Azure region or across different regions to enable seamless communication between resources.
   - **Global VNet Peering:** Connect VNets across regions globally, providing low-latency and private connectivity for your distributed applications.
5. **Integration with Azure Services:**
   - **Service Endpoints:** Privately access Azure services like Azure Storage or Azure SQL Database from your VNet, without exposing traffic to the public internet.

- **Private Link:** Establish private connections to Azure PaaS services, ensuring that your data stays within the Microsoft backbone network.
- **Azure Firewall:** Integrate with Azure Firewall to centrally manage network security policies and protect your VNet from threats.

By leveraging virtual networks in Azure, you can create a secure, flexible, and efficient network infrastructure that aligns with your specific business requirements. Whether you're building a simple website or a complex enterprise application, VNets provide the foundation for a reliable and scalable cloud environment.

Key Components of a Virtual Network

A virtual network (VNet) is a complex yet organized entity composed of various components that work together to create your private network space in Azure. Understanding these components is essential for designing and managing a VNet that meets your needs. Let's break down the key building blocks:

Address Space: The Foundation of Your Network

The address space defines the range of IP addresses that can be used within your VNet. You specify this range using Classless Inter-Domain Routing (CIDR) notation (e.g., 10.0.0.0/16). The size of your address space determines how many resources you can deploy within the VNet. Careful planning of the address space is crucial, as you don't want to run out of IP addresses as your VNet grows.

Subnets: Dividing and Conquering

Subnets are smaller segments of your VNet's address space. They provide a way to logically group resources within your VNet and apply specific network policies or security rules to each group. For example, you could create separate subnets for your web servers, application servers, and databases. Subnets also play a role in routing traffic within the VNet.

Network Interface (NIC): The Resource's Connection

A network interface (NIC) is a virtual network adapter that you attach to a virtual machine (VM) or other Azure resource. The NIC provides the resource with a private IP address from the VNet's address space, enabling it to communicate with other resources within the VNet and, if configured, with resources outside the VNet.

Virtual Network Gateway: Your Bridge to the Outside World

A virtual network gateway acts as a bridge between your VNet and other networks, such as your on-premises network or another Azure VNet. It provides secure connectivity options like:

- **VPN Gateway:** Enables site-to-site VPN connections between your VNet and on-premises network using the IPsec protocol.
- **ExpressRoute Gateway:** Connects your on-premises network to Azure using a private, dedicated connection for higher bandwidth and reliability.

Network Security Group (NSG): Your Virtual Firewall

A network security group (NSG) is a set of security rules that filter network traffic to and from resources in a subnet. These rules allow or deny traffic based on criteria like source and destination IP addresses, ports, and protocols. NSGs are essential for protecting your resources from unauthorized access and securing your network.

Route Table: Directing Traffic

A route table is a set of rules that determines how network traffic is routed within a VNet. Each subnet within a VNet is associated with a route table, which specifies the next hop for traffic destined for different destinations. You can define custom routes to direct traffic to specific network appliances, virtual network gateways, or the internet.

Putting it All Together

These components work together to form the backbone of your virtual network in Azure. By understanding their roles and how they interact, you can design a network architecture that meets your specific requirements for security, isolation, traffic control, and connectivity. In the following sections, we'll guide you through creating your own virtual network and configuring these components to build a secure and efficient network infrastructure in the cloud.

Creating a Virtual Network

Now that we understand the components and benefits of virtual networks (VNets), let's walk through the process of creating one in Azure using the Azure Portal.

1. **Choosing a Resource Group and VNet Name:**

   - **Open the Azure Portal:** Navigate to the Azure portal (https://portal.azure.com/).
   - **Search for Virtual Networks:** In the search bar at the top, type "Virtual networks" and select it from the results.
   - **Click "Create":** Click on the "Create" button to initiate the VNet creation process.
   - **Basics Tab:**
     - **Subscription:** Choose the Azure subscription you want to create the VNet in (if you have multiple).
     - **Resource group:** Select an existing resource group or create a new one by clicking "Create new." Give it a descriptive name, such as "myVNet-rg."
     - **Name:** Enter a unique name for your VNet (e.g., "myVNet").
     - **Region:** Select the Azure region where you want to deploy your VNet. Choose a region close to your users or your on-premises network for optimal performance.

2. **Defining the Address Space (IP Addresses Tab):**

   - **IPv4 address space:** Enter the range of IP addresses that will be used within your VNet. This range should not overlap with any other existing networks. You'll specify the range using CIDR notation (e.g., `10.0.0.0/16`).
   - **Subnet name:** Enter a name for your first subnet (e.g., "default").
   - **Subnet address range:** Define the IP address range for the subnet within the overall address space of your VNet (e.g., `10.0.0.0/24`).

3. **Adding More Subnets (Optional):**

   - If you need to create additional subnets, click on "Add subnet."
   - Repeat the process of entering a subnet name and address range for each additional subnet.

4. **Creating the VNet (Review + create tab):**

   - **Review:** Double-check all the information you've entered to ensure accuracy.
   - **Create:** Click the "Create" button to start the VNet creation process. The deployment will take a few minutes.

After Deployment:

Once the deployment is complete, you'll see a notification in the portal. You can then navigate to your newly created VNet in the "Virtual networks" section of the portal.

Key Points to Remember:

- **Plan Your Address Space Carefully:** Ensure that your address space is large enough to accommodate all the resources you plan to deploy within the VNet. You can add more address spaces later, but it's easier to plan ahead.
- **Start with a Default Subnet:** It's good practice to create a default subnet to catch any traffic that doesn't match a more specific subnet route.
- **Consider Security:** Think about how you'll secure your VNet. You can use network security groups (NSGs) to control traffic flow and protect your resources.

Congratulations! You've successfully created your first virtual network in Azure. Now you have a private network space where you can deploy and manage your Azure resources. In the next section, we'll dive deeper into subnets and IP addressing.

Subnets and IP Addressing

Imagine your virtual network (VNet) as a large plot of land. You wouldn't build all your houses (Azure resources) randomly across this land, would you? You'd divide it into smaller lots, each with its own purpose and boundaries. Subnets within a VNet function similarly, creating smaller, logical groupings of IP addresses to organize and manage your resources effectively.

What are Subnets?

A subnet is a range of IP addresses within your VNet's address space. It acts as a smaller network within your larger network, allowing you to segment your resources and apply specific network policies to each subnet. For example, you could create a subnet for your web servers, another for your database servers, and a third for your internal application servers.

Why Subnets Matter

Subnets provide several key benefits:

- **Resource Organization:** They help you organize your resources logically, making your VNet easier to manage and troubleshoot.
- **Security:** You can apply network security groups (NSGs) to subnets, controlling traffic flow between subnets and the internet. This allows you to isolate sensitive resources and implement granular security policies.
- **Network Optimization:** Subnets can help you optimize network traffic by routing specific types of traffic to designated subnets.
- **Role Assignment:** You can assign different roles and permissions to different subnets, ensuring that only authorized users and applications can access specific resources.

Subnet Planning: Key Considerations

When designing your VNet, careful subnet planning is essential. Consider the following factors:

- **Number of Subnets:** Determine how many subnets you need based on your application architecture and security requirements. Start with a few essential subnets and add more as needed.
- **Subnet Sizes:** Each subnet has its own IP address range. Choose subnet sizes that can accommodate the maximum number of resources you expect to deploy in each subnet. Azure reserves five IP addresses in each subnet for internal use, so make sure to account for that.

- **Subnet Purpose:** Give each subnet a descriptive name that reflects its purpose (e.g., "web-subnet," "database-subnet").
- **Network Security Groups (NSGs):** Plan your NSG rules in advance to control traffic flow between subnets and the internet.
- **Future Growth:** Leave room for future growth in your subnet design. It's easier to add subnets later than to reconfigure existing ones.

Example Subnet Configuration

Let's say your VNet has an address space of 10.0.0.0/16. You could divide it into the following subnets:

Subnet Name	Address Range	Purpose
web-subnet	10.0.1.0/24	Web servers
app-subnet	10.0.2.0/24	Application servers
db-subnet	10.0.3.0/24	Database servers
management-subnet	10.0.4.0/24	Management and jumpbox

Summary

By understanding the concept of subnets and applying these best practices for subnet planning, you can create a well-organized, secure, and scalable virtual network in Azure that supports the growth and evolution of your applications.

Network Security Groups (NSGs)

In the physical world, we use firewalls to control access to our homes and businesses. In the cloud, Azure offers a similar mechanism called Network Security Groups (NSGs) to protect your virtual networks and the resources within them.

NSGs: The Gatekeepers of Your Virtual Network

An NSG is like a virtual firewall that filters network traffic to and from Azure resources within a subnet. It acts as a gatekeeper, allowing or denying traffic based on a set of security rules that you define. These rules are based on several factors:

- **Source:** The origin of the traffic, such as a specific IP address, a range of IP addresses, or an entire virtual network.
- **Destination:** The target of the traffic, which could be a specific VM, a subnet, or a service endpoint.
- **Port:** The network port used by the traffic (e.g., port 80 for HTTP, port 443 for HTTPS).
- **Protocol:** The network protocol used by the traffic (e.g., TCP, UDP, ICMP).

By creating and configuring NSG rules, you can precisely control which traffic is allowed or denied access to your resources.

Creating NSG Rules: Building Your Defense

Creating NSG rules is a straightforward process in the Azure Portal:

1. **Navigate to Your Network Security Group:** Go to your virtual network (VNet) in the Azure Portal, select "Network security groups," and click on the NSG you want to edit.
2. **Add a New Rule:** Click on "Add" to create a new inbound or outbound security rule.
3. **Define Rule Properties:**

- **Source:** Specify the source of the traffic (e.g., specific IP address, IP range, or service tag like "AzureLoadBalancer").
- **Destination:** Choose the destination of the traffic (e.g., a specific VM, a subnet, or a service tag like "VirtualNetwork").
- **Port:** Select the port or port range to which the rule applies. You can use predefined service tags like "HTTP" or "HTTPS" or specify a custom port range.
- **Protocol:** Choose the protocol (TCP, UDP, ICMP, or Any).
- **Action:** Select whether to "Allow" or "Deny" the traffic.
- **Priority:** Assign a priority to the rule. Rules are processed in priority order, with lower numbers having higher priority.

4. **Save the Rule:** Click "Add" to save the new rule.

Common NSG Rules for Securing Azure Resources

Here are some common NSG rules used to secure Azure resources:

- **Allow RDP/SSH:** Allow incoming traffic on port 3389 (RDP) or port 22 (SSH) from specific IP addresses or ranges for remote administration.
- **Allow HTTP/HTTPS:** Allow incoming traffic on port 80 (HTTP) or port 443 (HTTPS) for web applications.
- **Restrict Access to Database Servers:** Deny all incoming traffic except from specific IP addresses or virtual networks that need to access your database servers.
- **Block Outbound Traffic:** Deny all outbound traffic except for specific ports or destinations, preventing unauthorized data exfiltration.

Best Practices for NSGs

- **Default Rules:** Azure automatically creates default rules for each NSG. These rules allow all outbound traffic and deny all inbound traffic. Be sure to customize these rules based on your specific security requirements.
- **Priority:** Pay careful attention to the priority of your rules. Rules with lower priority numbers are processed first, so ensure your rules are ordered correctly to achieve the desired filtering behavior.
- **Granularity:** Create NSGs for specific subnets or even individual network interfaces to implement fine-grained security controls.
- **Regular Review:** Regularly review your NSG rules to ensure they are still relevant and effective.

By understanding and applying network security groups effectively, you can create a secure and robust network environment for your Azure resources, protecting them from unauthorized access and potential threats.

Connecting Virtual Networks

Azure Virtual Networks (VNets) are powerful on their own, but their true potential shines when you connect them to other networks, whether it's another VNet in Azure or your on-premises network. Azure provides three primary mechanisms for connecting VNets, each with its own advantages and use cases.

1. VNet Peering: The Neighborhood Connection

Imagine two neighboring houses sharing a fence gate, allowing residents to move freely between them. VNet peering is similar. It creates a low-latency, high-bandwidth connection between two VNets within the same Azure region. Once peered, the VNets behave as if they are part of the same network, allowing resources within each VNet to communicate directly using their private IP addresses.

Key Benefits of VNet Peering:

- **Low Latency:** Traffic between peered VNets stays within the Azure backbone network, minimizing latency and ensuring fast communication.
- **High Bandwidth:** The connection between peered VNets can support high bandwidth, suitable for transferring large amounts of data.
- **No Public IP Addresses:** Communication between peered VNets occurs over private IP addresses, enhancing security.
- **Simple Configuration:** VNet peering is relatively easy to set up and manage through the Azure Portal.

2. VPN Gateways: The Secure Tunnel

Think of a VPN gateway as a secure tunnel that connects your VNet to your on-premises network over the public internet. It uses the industry-standard IPsec (Internet Protocol Security) protocol to encrypt traffic, ensuring secure communication between your on-premises resources and your Azure resources.

Key Benefits of VPN Gateways:

- **Secure Connectivity:** VPN gateways provide a secure way to connect your on-premises network to Azure over the internet.
- **Cross-Premises Connectivity:** Allows your on-premises applications and users to access resources in Azure, and vice versa.
- **Hybrid Cloud:** VPN gateways enable you to create a hybrid cloud environment, where you can seamlessly integrate your on-premises resources with Azure services.

3. ExpressRoute: The Private Highway

ExpressRoute takes connectivity to the next level by providing a private, dedicated connection between your on-premises network and Azure. Unlike VPN gateways, which rely on the public internet, ExpressRoute connections go through a private network provider, ensuring higher reliability, lower latency, and predictable performance.

Key Benefits of ExpressRoute:

- **High Bandwidth:** ExpressRoute connections offer higher bandwidth than VPN gateways, making them suitable for large-scale data transfer.
- **Low Latency:** By bypassing the public internet, ExpressRoute provides a more consistent and predictable network latency.
- **Reliability:** ExpressRoute connections are typically more reliable than internet-based VPN connections.
- **Security:** ExpressRoute connections are private and isolated from the public internet, enhancing security.

Choosing the Right Connection Option

The optimal choice for connecting your virtual networks depends on your specific requirements and budget:

- **VNet Peering:** Ideal for connecting VNets within the same Azure region for low-latency, high-bandwidth communication.
- **VPN Gateway:** A good choice for securely connecting your VNet to your on-premises network over the public internet, especially for smaller workloads or budget-conscious scenarios.
- **ExpressRoute:** Best suited for large-scale, mission-critical workloads that require high bandwidth, low latency, and reliable connectivity between your on-premises network and Azure.

By understanding these different connection options, you can choose the best approach to seamlessly integrate your virtual networks and create a robust and flexible network architecture in Azure.

Tips and Best Practices

Creating and managing virtual networks in Azure doesn't have to be overwhelming. By following these best practices and tips, you can streamline your workflow, optimize network performance, and ensure the security of your cloud resources.

1. IP Address Planning: Laying the Groundwork

Proper IP address planning is fundamental to a well-functioning VNet.

- **Choose the Right Address Space:** Select an address space (e.g., 10.0.0.0/16) that is large enough to accommodate your current and future needs. Azure allows you to add more address spaces later, but careful planning upfront can save you headaches down the road.
- **Subnet Allocation:** Divide your address space into subnets based on your workload requirements and security considerations. Consider factors like the number of resources in each subnet, the types of traffic they will handle, and the desired level of isolation.
- **IP Address Reuse:** If you have multiple VNets, avoid overlapping IP address ranges to prevent conflicts and routing issues.

2. Network Security: Guarding the Gates

Security is paramount in any network environment, and Azure VNets are no exception. Here are some essential security measures:

- **Network Security Groups (NSGs):** Deploy NSGs to filter network traffic at the subnet or network interface level. Define rules that allow or deny traffic based on source, destination, port, and protocol.
- **Service Endpoints:** Use service endpoints to secure traffic between your VNet and Azure services like Azure Storage or Azure SQL Database.
- **Azure Firewall:** Consider implementing Azure Firewall for centralized network security management and advanced threat protection.
- **Web Application Firewall (WAF):** If you're hosting web applications, use a WAF to protect against common web attacks like SQL injection and cross-site scripting.
- **Bastion Hosts:** Use bastion hosts to provide secure jump servers for managing your VMs without exposing them directly to the internet.

3. Monitoring: Keeping a Watchful Eye

Regularly monitor the health and performance of your VNets to detect and troubleshoot issues promptly. Utilize the following tools:

- **Azure Network Watcher:** This service provides tools for monitoring, diagnosing, and gaining insights into your network traffic. You can capture network packets, analyze traffic flows, and troubleshoot connectivity issues.
- **Azure Monitor for Networks:** This feature of Azure Monitor provides detailed metrics and logs for your network resources, allowing you to track performance and identify anomalies.
- **Azure Advisor:** This personalized cloud consultant can provide recommendations for improving the performance and security of your VNets.

4. Automation: Streamlining Operations

Embrace infrastructure as code (IaC) practices to automate the deployment and management of your VNets. Azure Resource Manager (ARM) templates allow you to define your network infrastructure in a declarative format. This simplifies deployments, ensures consistency across environments, and enables you to easily track changes and roll back if needed.

Additional Tips:

- **Naming Conventions:** Use clear and consistent naming conventions for your VNets, subnets, and other network resources to make them easier to identify and manage.
- **Documentation:** Keep thorough documentation of your network configuration, including IP address ranges, subnet assignments, and security rules.
- **Testing:** Regularly test your network connectivity and security to ensure everything is functioning as expected.
- **Azure Updates:** Stay informed about Azure updates and new features that can enhance your VNet capabilities.

By implementing these best practices and tips, you can create and manage virtual networks in Azure that are secure, efficient, and scalable, providing a solid foundation for your cloud applications and services.

Chapter Summary

This chapter has laid the groundwork for understanding virtual networks (VNets) in Azure, a cornerstone of building secure and scalable cloud infrastructure. We started by defining a VNet as your private network space within Azure, where you can deploy and manage your resources with enhanced security and control.

The key advantages of using VNets were outlined, emphasizing their role in isolation, security, traffic control, private IP addressing, and connectivity. You learned how VNets enable you to segment your network, implement custom routing rules, connect to on-premises networks, and integrate with various Azure services.

We then broke down the essential components that make up a VNet, including:

- **Address space:** The range of IP addresses available for resources within the VNet.
- **Subnets:** Smaller divisions of the address space used for logical grouping and applying network policies.
- **Network interface (NIC):** The virtual network adapter that connects a VM or other resource to the VNet.
- **Virtual network gateway:** The service that facilitates secure connections to other networks.
- **Network security group (NSG):** The virtual firewall that filters traffic to and from resources.
- **Route table:** The set of rules that determines how traffic is routed within the VNet.

You were guided through the step-by-step process of creating a VNet using the Azure Portal, starting with choosing a resource group and VNet name, then defining the address space and adding subnets. We delved deeper into the concept of subnets and IP addressing, emphasizing the importance of proper planning for resource isolation and network security.

The concept of Network Security Groups (NSGs) was explained in detail, highlighting their role as a virtual firewall and how to create rules to control traffic based on source, destination, port, and protocol. We provided examples of common NSG rules used for securing Azure resources.

Finally, we explored the different ways to connect VNets, including VNet peering for low-latency communication between VNets within the same region, VPN gateways for secure connections to on-premises networks, and ExpressRoute for high-bandwidth, private connections.

By understanding these concepts and best practices, you're now equipped with the knowledge to design and manage your own virtual networks in Azure. As we move forward, we'll explore more advanced networking topics like load balancers and application gateways, empowering you to build complex and scalable network architectures in the cloud.

Load Balancers: Distributing Traffic for High Availability

Outline

- What is Load Balancing?
- Benefits of Load Balancing
- Types of Load Balancers in Azure
    - Azure Load Balancer
    - Azure Application Gateway
    - Azure Traffic Manager
- Choosing the Right Load Balancer
- Creating an Azure Load Balancer
- Configuring Load Balancing Rules
- Health Probes and Monitoring
- Tips and Best Practices
- Chapter Summary

What is Load Balancing?

Imagine a busy intersection with cars streaming in from all directions. Without a traffic cop, the intersection would quickly become a chaotic mess, with some lanes overloaded while others remain underutilized. A traffic cop's role is to direct vehicles to different lanes, ensuring smooth and efficient traffic flow.

Load balancing, in the world of networking, functions much like that traffic cop. It's a technique used to distribute incoming network traffic evenly across a group of servers or other resources. By spreading the workload, load balancing prevents any single server from becoming overwhelmed, ensuring optimal performance, responsiveness, and reliability for your applications and services.

How Load Balancing Works

A load balancer acts as an intermediary between clients and servers. When a client sends a request to your application, the load balancer intercepts the request and decides which server in the backend pool should handle it. This decision is based on various factors, such as:

- **Server load:** The load balancer monitors the utilization of each server in the backend pool and directs traffic to the server with the lowest load.
- **Round-robin algorithm:** The load balancer might simply distribute requests sequentially across the servers in a round-robin fashion.
- **Session persistence:** In some cases, the load balancer might maintain session persistence, ensuring that subsequent requests from the same client are directed to the same server to maintain session state.
- **Geographic location:** If your application is deployed across multiple regions, the load balancer might direct traffic to the server closest to the client to minimize latency.

Benefits of Load Balancing

Load balancing offers a multitude of benefits for your applications and services:

- **High Availability:** By distributing traffic across multiple servers, load balancing ensures that your application remains available even if one server fails. If a server becomes unresponsive, the load balancer automatically detects the failure and redirects traffic to healthy servers.
- **Scalability:** As your application traffic grows, you can easily add more servers to the backend pool and the load balancer will automatically include them in the traffic distribution. This allows you to scale your application horizontally without having to make significant changes to your infrastructure.
- **Performance Optimization:** Load balancing ensures that no single server is overloaded, preventing performance bottlenecks and ensuring optimal response times for your users.
- **Resource Utilization:** By distributing the workload evenly, load balancing maximizes the utilization of your servers, allowing you to get the most out of your hardware investment.
- **Security:** Load balancers can act as reverse proxies, hiding your backend servers from the public internet and providing an additional layer of security.

In the following sections, we'll explore the different types of load balancers available in Azure and how to use them to build highly available and scalable applications.

Benefits of Load Balancing

Load balancers are indispensable tools in modern cloud architectures, offering a multitude of benefits that can significantly enhance the performance, reliability, and security of your applications and services. Let's dive into the key advantages of utilizing load balancers in Azure:

1. High Availability: Your Application's Lifeline

In the digital age, downtime is not an option. Load balancers play a pivotal role in ensuring the high availability of your applications. By distributing incoming traffic across multiple instances of your application, load balancers prevent any single instance from becoming overwhelmed. This means that even if one instance fails or becomes overloaded, the load balancer seamlessly redirects traffic to other healthy instances, ensuring your application remains accessible and responsive to users.

2. Scalability: Growing with Grace

As your application gains popularity and traffic increases, load balancers make it easy to scale horizontally. You can simply add more instances of your application to the backend pool, and the load balancer will automatically distribute traffic across all available instances. This allows you to handle increased traffic loads without having to redesign your application or invest in expensive hardware upgrades.

3. Performance Optimization: Speed and Efficiency

Load balancers not only distribute traffic but also optimize its flow. They ensure that each server in the backend pool receives a balanced workload, preventing any single server from becoming a bottleneck. This results in improved response times, faster page loads, and an overall smoother user experience.

4. Fault Tolerance: Adapting to Failures

In a distributed environment, failures are inevitable. Load balancers add a layer of fault tolerance by continuously monitoring the health of backend instances. If an instance becomes unhealthy, the load balancer automatically detects the failure and stops directing traffic to it, ensuring that users are not impacted by the outage. Once the instance recovers, the load balancer seamlessly brings it back into rotation.

5. Security: Shielding Your Backend

Load balancers can also act as reverse proxies, meaning they sit in front of your backend servers and handle incoming requests. This protects your backend servers from direct exposure to the internet, reducing the risk of attacks and vulnerabilities. You can also configure security rules on the load balancer to filter traffic and prevent unauthorized access.

Additional Benefits

In addition to these core benefits, load balancers in Azure offer additional advantages like:

- **Cost Savings:** By optimizing resource utilization and preventing overprovisioning, load balancers can help you save on your cloud infrastructure costs.
- **Global Traffic Management:** Azure Traffic Manager, a DNS-based load balancer, can distribute traffic across different Azure regions, optimizing for performance and availability based on user location.
- **SSL Offloading:** Application Gateway, a web traffic load balancer, can offload SSL/TLS termination, freeing up your backend servers to focus on application logic.
- **Session Persistence:** Load balancers can maintain session affinity, ensuring that requests from the same client are directed to the same backend server, improving user experience and maintaining session state.

By leveraging load balancers in Azure, you can build highly available, scalable, and secure applications that can handle the demands of modern workloads and deliver a seamless experience to your users.

Types of Load Balancers in Azure

Azure offers several load balancer options, each designed to address specific traffic distribution needs and operating at different layers of the network stack. Let's start by understanding the foundational Azure Load Balancer.

Azure Load Balancer

Azure Load Balancer is the workhorse of load balancing in Azure, operating at the transport layer (Layer 4) of the Open Systems Interconnection (OSI) model. This means it works with protocols like TCP (Transmission Control Protocol) and UDP (User Datagram Protocol), the workhorses of internet communication.

How It Works

Azure Load Balancer functions as a single point of contact for incoming traffic. It receives traffic on its frontend IP address and distributes it to backend pool instances based on configured rules. The rules you set define how the traffic is distributed, often using algorithms like round-robin (taking turns) or least connections (choosing the least busy server).

Key Use Cases

Azure Load Balancer excels at handling scenarios where you need to distribute traffic for:

- **Virtual Machines (VMs):** Balance traffic across multiple VMs running your applications. This ensures high availability and scalability for your applications, as the load balancer automatically distributes traffic to the available VMs.
- **Virtual Machine Scale Sets (VMSS):** Distribute traffic across identical VMs in a VMSS. This allows you to easily scale your applications up or down based on demand.
- **On-Premises Servers:** Extend load balancing to your on-premises servers, integrating them with your Azure resources. This is useful in hybrid scenarios where you have both cloud and on-premises components.

Types of Azure Load Balancers

Azure Load Balancer offers two SKUs (Stock Keeping Units):

- **Basic Load Balancer:** Provides essential load balancing capabilities at a lower cost, suitable for smaller workloads and simple scenarios.
- **Standard Load Balancer:** Offers advanced features like high availability across zones, outbound connections, and support for IPv6. It's designed for production workloads and enterprise applications.

Considerations

Azure Load Balancer is a powerful tool for distributing TCP and UDP traffic. However, it does not inspect or modify the contents of the traffic. If you need more sophisticated routing based on application layer (Layer 7) information like HTTP headers or URL paths, you should consider Azure Application Gateway, which we'll discuss in the next section.

Azure Application Gateway

While Azure Load Balancer excels at handling general network traffic, Azure Application Gateway steps in as the specialized load balancer for web traffic. It operates at the application layer (Layer 7) of the OSI model, giving it a deeper understanding of the HTTP/HTTPS traffic it manages. This enables it to perform advanced routing and traffic management based on application-level criteria.

Understanding Application Layer (Layer 7) Load Balancing

Unlike Layer 4 load balancers, which only see IP addresses and ports, Application Gateway can inspect the actual content of HTTP requests. This means it can make intelligent routing decisions based on:

- **URL Path:** Route traffic to different backend pools based on the URL path (e.g., /images to image servers, /api to API servers).
- **HTTP Headers:** Route traffic based on specific HTTP headers, such as the "Host" header for multi-site hosting.
- **Cookie Values:** Route traffic based on cookies to maintain session affinity.

Key Use Cases

Azure Application Gateway is tailor-made for the following scenarios:

- **Web Applications:** Deliver high-performance and secure web applications by distributing traffic, optimizing routing, and providing advanced features like SSL termination and web application firewall (WAF).
- **Microservices:** Route traffic to different microservices based on URL paths or headers, creating a flexible and scalable microservices architecture.
- **APIs:** Expose and manage APIs securely, with features like API throttling, rate limiting, and authentication.
- **Content Management Systems (CMS):** Optimize the delivery of CMS platforms like WordPress or Drupal by caching content and routing traffic to the appropriate servers.

Additional Features

In addition to its advanced routing capabilities, Azure Application Gateway offers several other features that make it a comprehensive solution for web traffic management:

- **SSL/TLS Termination:** Offload the processing of SSL/TLS encryption from your web servers, improving performance and reducing the load on your backend resources.

- **Web Application Firewall (WAF):** Protect your web applications from common web attacks like SQL injection, cross-site scripting (XSS), and distributed denial-of-service (DDoS) attacks.
- **WebSocket Support:** Handle real-time communication protocols like WebSocket for applications like chat, gaming, and collaborative tools.
- **Integration with Azure services:** Seamlessly integrate with other Azure services like Azure Monitor for monitoring and logging, Azure Key Vault for certificate management, and Azure Active Directory for authentication and authorization.

Choosing Azure Application Gateway

If you're looking for a powerful and versatile load balancer for your web applications and APIs, Azure Application Gateway is a great choice. Its ability to intelligently route traffic based on application-specific criteria, along with its robust security and performance features, make it a valuable asset for building modern web architectures.

Azure Traffic Manager

Imagine you have a website that serves users worldwide. How do you ensure that users in different countries get the fastest and most reliable access to your website? Azure Traffic Manager is your answer.

Azure Traffic Manager operates at the DNS (Domain Name System) level, which is the backbone of how the internet routes traffic. When a user types your website's address into their browser, their DNS resolver sends a request to Traffic Manager. Traffic Manager then determines the best endpoint (which could be a website hosted in a specific Azure region, an external endpoint, or even another Traffic Manager profile) to send the user to. This all happens in the blink of an eye, ensuring a smooth and seamless user experience.

How It Works: DNS-Based Routing

Traffic Manager uses various routing methods to decide which endpoint to direct traffic to. The most common methods include:

- **Performance Routing:** This method directs users to the endpoint with the lowest latency (response time) from their location. This is ideal for ensuring the fastest possible response times for your global audience.
- **Geographic Routing:** This method directs users to specific endpoints based on their geographic location. This is useful for complying with data sovereignty requirements or providing localized content.
- **Priority Routing:** This method allows you to prioritize traffic to a specific endpoint. This is useful for scenarios where you have a primary endpoint and want to direct traffic to secondary endpoints only if the primary endpoint is unavailable.
- **Weighted Routing:** This method distributes traffic across multiple endpoints based on weighted values. You can assign higher weights to endpoints that you want to receive more traffic. This is useful for A/B testing or gradually rolling out new versions of your application.
- **Subnet Routing:** This method allows you to direct traffic based on the IP address range (subnet) of the user. This is helpful for internal applications that are accessed from specific networks.

Key Use Cases

Azure Traffic Manager is a valuable tool for a variety of scenarios:

- **Global Load Balancing:** Distribute traffic across multiple Azure regions to improve performance and availability.
- **Geo-Redundancy and Disaster Recovery:** Direct traffic to a backup region in case of an outage in the primary region.
- **Multi-Site Hosting:** Route traffic to different websites based on the user's location or other criteria.

- **A/B Testing:** Gradually roll out new features or versions of your application to a subset of users.
- **Geographic Compliance:** Comply with data sovereignty regulations by directing traffic to endpoints in specific geographic locations.

Choosing Azure Traffic Manager

If you have a globally distributed application or service and need to ensure optimal performance, high availability, and geographic compliance, Azure Traffic Manager is a powerful and flexible solution. By leveraging its DNS-based routing capabilities, you can create a seamless and optimized user experience for your global audience.

Choosing the Right Load Balancer

Azure offers a variety of load balancers, each with its own strengths and ideal use cases. Selecting the right one for your scenario is crucial for optimizing performance, ensuring reliability, and managing costs effectively. Here's a guide to help you make an informed decision:

1. Type of Traffic: Layer 4 vs. Layer 7

The first factor to consider is the type of network traffic your application handles:

- **Azure Load Balancer:** This is your go-to choice for general TCP or UDP traffic. It's perfect for balancing traffic for virtual machines, virtual machine scale sets, and on-premises servers. It operates at Layer 4, so it doesn't inspect the contents of the traffic, making it suitable for various protocols and applications.
- **Azure Application Gateway:** If your application primarily deals with HTTP or HTTPS web traffic, Application Gateway is the way to go. It operates at Layer 7 (the application layer), allowing it to understand and route traffic based on HTTP headers, cookies, and URL paths. This is essential for advanced scenarios like cookie-based session affinity, URL path-based routing, and SSL offloading.

2. Routing Complexity: Basic vs. Advanced

Consider the level of routing complexity you require:

- **Azure Load Balancer:** This is best suited for simple scenarios where you need to distribute traffic evenly across backend servers. It doesn't offer advanced routing features like URL-based routing or cookie-based affinity.
- **Azure Application Gateway:** If you need more sophisticated routing capabilities based on application-level criteria, Application Gateway is the answer. It can route traffic based on URL paths, HTTP headers, and other application-specific parameters.

3. Global Traffic Management: Regional vs. Global

Think about whether you need to distribute traffic across multiple Azure regions:

- **Azure Load Balancer:** This operates within a single region and is not suitable for global traffic management.
- **Azure Traffic Manager:** If your application is deployed in multiple regions and you need to distribute traffic globally, Azure Traffic Manager is the ideal choice. It uses DNS-based routing to direct traffic to the optimal endpoint based on factors like geographic location or performance.

Decision Matrix

Feature	Azure Load Balancer	Azure Application Gateway	Azure Traffic Manager
Traffic Type	TCP/UDP	HTTP/HTTPS	DNS
OSI Layer	Layer 4	Layer 7	Global
Routing Complexity	Basic	Advanced	Global
Multi-Region Support	No	No	Yes
Typical Use Cases	VMs, VMSS, On-Premises	Web Apps, APIs, Microservices	Global Load Balancing

Choosing Wisely

By understanding the capabilities and limitations of each load balancer, you can make an informed decision and select the one that best aligns with your specific needs. Remember, you can also combine different load balancers to create a comprehensive solution that addresses various traffic management scenarios.

Creating an Azure Load Balancer

Let's walk through the steps of creating a load balancer within the Azure Portal, allowing you to efficiently distribute traffic and bolster the availability of your applications.

1. Selecting a Resource Group and Load Balancer Name:

- **Open the Azure Portal:** Navigate to the Azure portal (https://portal.azure.com/).
- **Search for Load Balancers:** In the search bar at the top, type "Load balancers" and select it from the results.
- **Click "Create":** Click on the "Create" button to initiate the load balancer creation process.
- **Basics Tab:**
    - **Subscription:** Choose the Azure subscription you want to create the load balancer in (if you have multiple).
    - **Resource group:** Select an existing resource group or create a new one by clicking "Create new." Give it a descriptive name, like "myLoadBalancer-rg."
    - **Name:** Enter a unique name for your load balancer (e.g., "myLoadBalancer").
    - **Region:** Select the Azure region where you want to deploy your load balancer. This should ideally be the same region where your backend resources (virtual machines, virtual machine scale sets, etc.) are located.

2. Choosing a Type and SKU:

- **Type:**
    - **Public:** If you want your load balancer to be accessible from the public internet, choose "Public."
    - **Internal:** If you want your load balancer to be accessible only within your virtual network, choose "Internal."
- **SKU:**
    - **Basic:** This SKU offers essential load balancing features at a lower cost, suitable for smaller workloads and simple scenarios.
    - **Standard:** This SKU offers advanced features like high availability across zones, outbound connections, and support for IPv6. It's designed for production workloads and enterprise applications.

3. **Configuring Frontend IP Configuration:**

- **Frontend IP address:**
    - For a **public** load balancer, you can choose to create a new public IP address or use an existing one. If you choose to create a new one, you can specify its name and IP address type (static or dynamic).
    - For an **internal** load balancer, you'll need to specify an existing private IP address from your virtual network's address space.

4. **Configuring Backend Pools:**

- **Backend pools:** A backend pool is a group of resources that will receive traffic from the load balancer.
    - Click "Add a backend pool" to create a new pool.
    - Give your backend pool a name (e.g., "myBackendPool").
    - Choose the type of backend resources:
        - **Virtual machine:** Select individual virtual machines.
        - **Virtual machine scale set:** Select a scale set of identical virtual machines.
        - **IP address:** Enter the IP addresses of the resources you want to include in the pool.
- **Health probes:** Configure health probes to monitor the health of your backend pool instances. These probes periodically check the responsiveness of your resources to ensure that the load balancer only directs traffic to healthy instances. We'll delve into health probes in more detail later.
- **Load balancing rules:** Load balancing rules define how incoming traffic is distributed across the backend pool instances. We'll cover these rules in the next section.

Once you've completed these steps, review your configuration and click "Create" to deploy your load balancer. Azure will then provision the necessary resources and configure your load balancer according to your settings.

Configuring Load Balancing Rules

Load balancing rules are the heart of an Azure Load Balancer. They define the precise way incoming traffic is distributed across the resources in your backend pool. By configuring these rules strategically, you can ensure that your applications are highly available, responsive, and can efficiently handle varying workloads.

What Load Balancing Rules Do

At their core, load balancing rules establish a mapping between the load balancer's frontend IP address and port and the backend pool instances' IP addresses and ports. This mapping determines which backend instance receives each incoming request based on specific criteria.

A typical load balancing rule consists of:

- **Frontend IP Configuration:** The public IP address and port that the load balancer listens on.
- **Backend Pool:** The group of virtual machines or instances that will receive traffic from the load balancer.
- **Protocol and Port:** The protocol (TCP or UDP) and port number that the rule applies to. For example, a rule might be for TCP traffic on port 80 (HTTP).
- **Health Probe:** (Optional) A health probe to monitor the health of backend instances and ensure that only healthy instances receive traffic. We'll discuss health probes in more detail later.
- **Session Persistence (Optional):** A mechanism for maintaining session affinity, where requests from the same client are directed to the same backend instance for a certain period. This is often used for applications that rely on session state, such as shopping carts or login sessions.

Distribution Modes: How Traffic is Balanced

Azure Load Balancer offers several distribution modes (also known as load balancing algorithms) that determine how incoming traffic is spread across the backend pool:

- **Round Robin:** The simplest and most common mode. Requests are distributed sequentially across the backend instances in a round-robin fashion.
- **Least Connections:** This mode directs new connections to the backend instance with the fewest active connections. This can be useful when backend instances have different processing capabilities.
- **Source IP Affinity (Session Persistence):** This mode ensures that requests from the same client IP address are consistently sent to the same backend instance. This is important for maintaining session state in certain applications.

Creating a Load Balancing Rule in the Azure Portal

1. **Navigate to Your Load Balancer:** In the Azure Portal, go to your load balancer and select "Load balancing rules" under "Settings."
2. **Add a New Rule:** Click on the "Add" button to create a new load balancing rule.
3. **Configure Rule Properties:**
   - **Name:** Give your rule a descriptive name.
   - **Frontend IP Address:** Choose the frontend IP configuration (public IP address) that the rule will apply to.
   - **Protocol:** Select the protocol (TCP or UDP).
   - **Port:** Enter the port number that the load balancer will listen on for this rule.
   - **Backend Pool:** Select the backend pool that you want to distribute traffic to.
   - **Backend Port:** Enter the port number that the backend instances will listen on.
   - **Health Probe:** (Optional) Select the health probe you want to use to monitor the health of the backend instances.
   - **Session Persistence:** (Optional) If you need session persistence, choose the desired method (e.g., Client IP or Client IP and protocol).
4. **Save the Rule:** Click "Add" to save your new load balancing rule.

Managing Load Balancing Rules

You can modify existing rules or add new ones as your application requirements change. Be sure to monitor the performance of your load balancer and backend pool to ensure optimal resource utilization and responsiveness.

Health Probes and Monitoring

Load balancers are designed to distribute traffic, but how do they know which backend instances are healthy and capable of handling requests? That's where health probes come in. They act as the load balancer's health inspectors, continuously monitoring the responsiveness and availability of your backend resources.

The Role of Health Probes

Health probes are simple tests that the load balancer periodically performs on each backend instance. They check if the instance is alive and responding to requests. If an instance fails the health probe a certain number of times, the load balancer considers it unhealthy and removes it from rotation, ensuring that traffic is only directed to healthy and responsive instances. This automatic failover mechanism helps maintain the high availability of your application.

How Health Probes Work

Health probes are configured with specific parameters:

- **Protocol:** The protocol used to send the probe request (e.g., HTTP, HTTPS, TCP).
- **Port:** The port number that the probe will target on the backend instance.
- **Path (for HTTP/HTTPS):** The specific URL path that the probe will request (e.g., `/health`).
- **Interval:** How often the probe is sent (e.g., every 5 seconds).
- **Unhealthy Threshold:** The number of consecutive probe failures required before the instance is considered unhealthy.

The load balancer sends a probe request to the backend instance according to the configured interval. If the instance responds successfully (e.g., with an HTTP 200 OK status code), the instance is considered healthy. If the instance fails to respond or returns an error response, the probe fails. Once the number of consecutive probe failures exceeds the unhealthy threshold, the load balancer removes the instance from rotation.

Configuring Health Probes in Azure Load Balancers

In Azure Load Balancers, you can configure health probes as part of the load balancer configuration. Here's how:

1. **Navigate to Your Load Balancer:** Go to your load balancer in the Azure Portal.
2. **Health Probes:** Under "Settings," select "Health probes."
3. **Add:** Click "+ Add" to create a new health probe.
4. **Configure Probe:**
   - **Name:** Provide a descriptive name.
   - **Protocol:** Select the protocol (HTTP, HTTPS, or TCP).
   - **Port:** Enter the port number.
   - **Path (for HTTP/HTTPS):** Specify the URL path if using HTTP or HTTPS.
   - **Interval:** Set the probe interval.
   - **Unhealthy threshold:** Set the number of consecutive failures.
5. **Save:** Click "Add" to save the health probe.

Types of Health Probes

Azure Load Balancer supports the following types of health probes:

- **HTTP/HTTPS probes:** These probes send an HTTP or HTTPS request to a specified URL path on the backend instance. The probe succeeds if the instance returns an HTTP status code in the 200-399 range.
- **TCP probes:** These probes establish a TCP connection to a specified port on the backend instance. The probe succeeds if the connection can be established.

Best Practices for Health Probes

- **Choose the Right Protocol:** Use HTTP/HTTPS probes for web applications and TCP probes for other types of applications.
- **Select an Appropriate Interval:** The probe interval should be short enough to detect failures quickly, but not so frequent that it overwhelms the backend instance.
- **Set a Reasonable Unhealthy Threshold:** The unhealthy threshold should be high enough to avoid false positives but low enough to quickly remove failing instances.
- **Monitor Probe Results:** Regularly monitor the health probe results to ensure your backend instances are healthy and responding to requests.

By configuring and monitoring health probes, you can ensure that your Azure Load Balancer always directs traffic to healthy instances, maximizing the availability and reliability of your applications.

Tips and Best Practices

Using load balancers effectively requires thoughtful planning and configuration. Follow these best practices to optimize performance, ensure high availability, and maintain a secure environment for your applications:

High Availability: Redundancy is Key

- **Multiple Instances:** Always deploy multiple instances of your application behind the load balancer. This creates redundancy, so if one instance fails, the others can continue handling traffic.
- **Availability Zones:** Distribute your backend instances across multiple Availability Zones within a region. This protects against localized failures like data center outages or hardware malfunctions.
- **Cross-Region Deployment:** For mission-critical applications, consider deploying your application in multiple Azure regions and use Azure Traffic Manager to distribute traffic globally, ensuring high availability even in the face of regional outages.

Autoscaling: Adapt to Demand

- **Virtual Machine Scale Sets (VMSS):** Integrate your load balancer with VMSS to automatically scale the number of backend instances based on demand. This ensures that your application can handle traffic spikes without manual intervention.
- **Autoscale Rules:** Define scaling rules based on metrics like CPU usage, memory usage, or request count. Set thresholds for scaling up or down based on your application's performance requirements.
- **Scheduled Scaling:** For predictable traffic patterns, you can schedule scaling operations to proactively add or remove instances at specific times.

Monitoring: Keep a Watchful Eye

- **Azure Monitor:** Use Azure Monitor to collect and analyze metrics, logs, and events from your load balancer and backend instances. This will help you identify performance bottlenecks, troubleshoot issues, and optimize your application.
- **Custom Alerts:** Set up custom alerts based on specific metrics or events to get notified of potential problems before they impact your users.
- **Network Watcher:** Utilize Azure Network Watcher to monitor the health and connectivity of your load balancer and backend instances. You can use features like connection troubleshoot and packet capture to diagnose network issues.

Security: Defense in Depth

- **Network Security Groups (NSGs):** Apply NSGs to your load balancer and backend subnets to restrict traffic to only authorized sources and ports.
- **Web Application Firewall (WAF):** If you're using Azure Application Gateway, enable the WAF to protect your web applications from common vulnerabilities and attacks like SQL injection, cross-site scripting (XSS), and DDoS attacks.
- **Azure DDoS Protection:** Consider enabling Azure DDoS Protection for your public IP addresses to protect against volumetric and protocol attacks.
- **Least Privilege Principle:** Follow the principle of least privilege by granting backend instances only the permissions they need to function. Avoid exposing them directly to the internet if possible.

Additional Best Practices

- **Load Balancer SKU:** Choose the appropriate SKU (Basic or Standard) based on your feature and performance requirements. The Standard SKU offers more advanced features like high availability across zones and outbound connections.
- **Health Probe Configuration:** Carefully configure your health probes to ensure that your load balancer accurately detects unhealthy instances and removes them from rotation.
- **Session Persistence:** If your application requires session affinity (e.g., for maintaining shopping carts or login sessions), configure the load balancer to use the appropriate session persistence method.
- **Load Testing:** Regularly perform load testing on your application to understand its behavior under different traffic loads and identify potential bottlenecks.

By adhering to these best practices and incorporating load balancing into your Azure architecture, you can create highly available, scalable, and secure applications that deliver a superior user experience.

Chapter Summary

This chapter delved into the vital concept of load balancing in Azure, a technique that distributes network traffic across multiple servers or resources to ensure optimal performance, high availability, and reliability for your applications.

We began by defining load balancing and illustrating its importance using the analogy of a traffic cop managing traffic flow at a busy intersection. You learned how load balancers act as intermediaries between clients and servers, directing requests to the most appropriate backend instance based on factors like server load, algorithms, session persistence, and geographic location.

The chapter then explored the key benefits of load balancing in Azure:

- **High Availability:** Ensuring your applications remain accessible even if individual servers fail.
- **Scalability:** Easily handling increased traffic by adding more resources behind the load balancer.
- **Performance Optimization:** Distributing workload evenly to prevent bottlenecks and improve response times.
- **Fault Tolerance:** Automatically detecting and routing traffic away from unhealthy instances.
- **Security:** Acting as a reverse proxy to protect backend servers and implementing security measures.

Next, we discussed the three main types of load balancers available in Azure:

- **Azure Load Balancer:** Operating at the transport layer (Layer 4) for basic TCP/UDP traffic distribution.
- **Azure Application Gateway:** Operating at the application layer (Layer 7) for more advanced routing based on HTTP/HTTPS traffic.
- **Azure Traffic Manager:** A DNS-based load balancer for global traffic management across different Azure regions.

You gained insights into choosing the right load balancer based on your specific requirements, considering factors like traffic type, routing complexity, and global reach.

Finally, we provided a step-by-step guide on how to create an Azure Load Balancer using the Azure Portal, explaining the key configurations involved, such as selecting a resource group, choosing a type and SKU, and setting up frontend IP addresses and backend pools.

The chapter concluded with practical tips and best practices for effectively utilizing load balancers, emphasizing the importance of high availability, autoscaling, monitoring, and security measures.

Azure DNS: Managing Domain Names and Resolutions

Outline

- What is DNS?
- Why Use Azure DNS?
- DNS Zones and Record Types
- Creating a DNS Zone
- Managing DNS Records
- Private DNS Zones
- Azure DNS Features and Benefits
- Tips and Best Practices
- Chapter Summary

What is DNS?

Imagine trying to remember the phone number of every single person you know. It would be a daunting task! That's where a phonebook comes in handy. It allows you to easily find a person's phone number by looking up their name.

The Domain Name System (DNS) functions much like a phonebook for the internet. It's a global system that translates human-readable domain names (like www.example.com) into machine-readable IP addresses (like 192.0.2.1). This translation is essential because computers use IP addresses to identify and communicate with each other over the internet.

How DNS Works: A Behind-the-Scenes Look

1. **The Query:** When you enter a domain name into your web browser, your computer sends a query to a DNS resolver (usually provided by your internet service provider or ISP).
2. **Recursive Search:** The DNS resolver then starts a recursive search, contacting various DNS servers in a hierarchical manner until it finds the authoritative name server for the domain you're looking for.
3. **The Answer:** The authoritative name server responds with the IP address associated with the domain name.
4. **Caching:** The DNS resolver stores the IP address in its cache for a certain period (determined by the Time-to-Live or TTL value in the DNS record). This means that future requests for the same domain name can be resolved faster without having to repeat the entire DNS lookup process.
5. **Connection:** With the IP address in hand, your computer can now establish a connection with the web server hosting the website and retrieve the requested content.

DNS: The Backbone of the Internet

DNS is a critical component of the internet's infrastructure. It's what allows us to use memorable and easy-to-use domain names instead of having to remember long strings of numbers (IP addresses). Without DNS, the internet as we know it would not be possible.

Beyond Websites: More Than Meets the Eye

DNS isn't just used for websites. It's also used for email routing (MX records), domain ownership verification (TXT records), and other essential internet services.

In a Nutshell

DNS is the invisible force that translates domain names into IP addresses, enabling us to navigate the internet with ease. It's a complex yet efficient system that plays a vital role in the smooth functioning of the internet as a whole.

Why Use Azure DNS?

Azure DNS isn't just another DNS provider; it's a robust and feature-rich service that leverages the power and global reach of Azure to deliver exceptional reliability, security, and performance for your domain name management. Here's why you should consider entrusting your DNS to Azure:

1. Reliability and Performance: Built on a Rock-Solid Foundation

Azure DNS is built on Microsoft's global network infrastructure, which means your DNS queries are resolved quickly and reliably from anywhere in the world. Azure's vast network of data centers ensures high availability and redundancy, minimizing the risk of downtime for your DNS records.

2. Security: Protecting Your Domain

DNS security is a critical concern in today's internet landscape. Azure DNS offers robust security features to safeguard your domains and DNS records:

- **DNSSEC (Domain Name System Security Extensions):** This technology adds an extra layer of security by digitally signing your DNS records, ensuring that the responses are authentic and have not been tampered with. This protects against attacks like DNS spoofing and cache poisoning.
- **Role-Based Access Control (RBAC):** Control access to your DNS zones and records using granular permissions, ensuring that only authorized personnel can make changes to your DNS configuration.
- **Azure DDoS Protection:** Azure DNS benefits from Azure's built-in DDoS protection, shielding your domains from volumetric and protocol attacks.

3. Scalability: Handling Growth with Ease

Whether you have a small website or a large enterprise application, Azure DNS can easily scale to handle your needs. It's designed to handle millions of DNS queries per second, ensuring that your domain names are always resolvable, even during traffic spikes. As your application grows, Azure DNS scales with you, providing consistent and reliable DNS resolution.

4. Seamless Integration: A Unified Azure Experience

Azure DNS integrates seamlessly with other Azure services, making it a natural choice for organizations that are already invested in the Azure ecosystem. You can manage your DNS zones and records alongside your other Azure resources, such as virtual machines, web apps, and storage accounts, using the familiar Azure Portal or command-line tools. This centralized management approach simplifies your workflow and reduces the complexity of managing multiple systems.

5. Ease of Use: Intuitive Management

The Azure Portal provides an intuitive and user-friendly interface for managing your DNS zones and records. You can easily create new zones, add and edit DNS records, and monitor the health of your DNS infrastructure. Azure also offers comprehensive documentation and support to help you get the most out of Azure DNS.

The Azure DNS Advantage

By choosing Azure DNS, you're not just getting a DNS service; you're getting a comprehensive solution that offers reliability, security, scalability, integration, and ease of use. It's a powerful tool that can help you build and manage your online presence with confidence.

DNS Zones and Record Types

Think of the Domain Name System (DNS) as a vast library of information. To organize this information, DNS uses a hierarchical structure with domains and subdomains. At the heart of this structure are DNS zones, which contain individual records that provide specific details about the domain or subdomain.

DNS Zones: Organizing Your DNS Records

A DNS zone is a distinct part of the DNS namespace that is managed by a specific organization or administrator. It essentially acts as a container for all the DNS records associated with a particular domain. For example, the DNS zone for "example.com" would contain all the DNS records for that domain, such as the records for www.example.com, mail.example.com, or any subdomains.

DNS zones provide a way to delegate control of a portion of the DNS namespace to a specific entity. The owner of a DNS zone has the authority to manage the DNS records within that zone.

DNS Record Types: The Information Units

Within a DNS zone, you'll find various types of DNS records. Each record type serves a specific purpose and provides different information about the domain or subdomain. Here are some common types:

- **A Records (Address Records):** The most fundamental type of DNS record, A records map a domain name or subdomain to an IPv4 address. This is how your web browser knows where to find a website when you enter its address.
- **AAAA Records (IPv6 Address Records):** Similar to A records, AAAA records map a domain name or subdomain to an IPv6 address. This is the newer version of the internet protocol that provides a much larger address space.
- **CNAME Records (Canonical Name Records):** These records create aliases for your domain names. For example, you could create a CNAME record so that blog.example.com points to the same IP address as www.example.com.
- **MX Records (Mail Exchange Records):** These records specify the mail servers responsible for receiving email for a domain. When you send an email to [email address removed], the sender's mail server uses the MX records to find the correct mail server for the domain.
- **TXT Records (Text Records):** These records allow you to store arbitrary text information in DNS. They are often used for:
    - **Domain Verification:** Proving you own the domain when setting up email services or other tools.
    - **Email Security:** Implementing Sender Policy Framework (SPF) records, which help prevent email spoofing.
    - **Other Configurations:** Storing various types of information, such as DKIM (DomainKeys Identified Mail) records for email authentication or DMARC (Domain-based Message Authentication, Reporting, and Conformance) records for email security reporting.

Understanding the different types of DNS records and how they are used is essential for effectively managing your domain names and ensuring that your websites, email, and other services are accessible and secure.

Creating a DNS Zone

Setting up a DNS zone in Azure is the first step to managing your domain's DNS records in the cloud. The Azure Portal makes this process intuitive and user-friendly. Let's walk through the steps:

1. **Navigating to Azure DNS:**

   - **Open the Azure Portal:** Log into your Azure account at https://portal.azure.com/.
   - **Search for DNS zones:** In the search bar at the top of the portal, type "DNS zones" and select it from the results.

2. **Clicking "+ Create DNS zone":**

   - On the DNS zones page, click the blue "+ Create DNS zone" button at the top left.

3. **Entering the Zone Name:**

   - **Subscription:** Choose the Azure subscription where you want to create the DNS zone (if you have multiple).
   - **Resource group:** Select an existing resource group or create a new one. This is where your DNS zone will be organized along with other related resources.
   - **Name:** Enter the name of the DNS zone you want to create. This is typically your domain name (e.g., "example.com"). Note that you can only create a zone for a domain you own or control.

4. **Additional Settings (Optional):**

   - **Review + create:** Carefully review your choices. Azure will show you a validation checkmark if everything is in order.
   - **Tags:** You can add tags to your DNS zone to help organize and categorize your resources.

5. **Clicking "Create":**

   - Once you've reviewed your settings, click the "Create" button. Azure will start the process of creating your DNS zone. This usually takes a few minutes.

After Creation:

After the DNS zone is created, you'll be taken to the zone's overview page. Here you'll find the name servers assigned to your zone. You'll need to update the name servers at your domain registrar to point to these Azure DNS name servers for the changes to take effect.

Important Considerations:

- **Domain Ownership:** You can only create DNS zones for domains that you own or control. Before creating a zone, ensure you have access to the domain registrar where the domain is registered.
- **Propagation Time:** After updating your name servers at your domain registrar, it may take some time for the changes to propagate across the internet. This typically takes a few hours but can sometimes take up to 48 hours.

With your new DNS zone in place, you're now ready to start adding and managing DNS records to control how traffic is routed to your domain.

Managing DNS Records

Now that you've created your DNS zone, it's time to populate it with records. DNS records hold the vital information that translates your domain name into actionable instructions for devices on the internet. Let's delve into how you can manage these records within the Azure Portal:

Adding Records: Building Your Domain's Map

1. **Access Your DNS Zone:**
   - In the Azure Portal, navigate to your DNS zone.
2. **Add Record Set:**
   - Click the "+ Record set" button at the top.
3. **Select Record Type:**
   - Choose the type of record you want to create. Common options include:
     - **A Record:** Maps a domain or subdomain to an IPv4 address (e.g., your web server's address).
     - **AAAA Record:** Similar to A records, but for IPv6 addresses.
     - **CNAME Record:** Creates an alias for one domain name to point to another (e.g., www to point to your main domain).
     - **MX Record:** Specifies the mail server(s) responsible for handling email for your domain.
     - **TXT Record:** Used for various purposes, such as email authentication or domain verification.
4. **Enter Record Details:**
   - Depending on the record type, fill in the required fields. This typically includes:
     - **Name:** The subdomain or hostname (e.g., "www" or "mail"). Leave this blank for the root domain.
     - **TTL:** The time-to-live, which controls how long DNS resolvers cache the record before checking for updates.
     - **Value:** The target IP address, domain name, or text data, depending on the record type.
5. **Save Record Set:**
   - Click "OK" or "Save" to create the new record.

Editing Records: Keeping Information Current

1. **Select the Record:**
   - In your DNS zone, click on the record you want to edit.
2. **Edit Properties:**
   - Modify the relevant fields, such as the value or TTL.
3. **Save Changes:**
   - Click "Save" to apply your changes.

Deleting Records: Removing Obsolete Entries

1. **Select the Record:**
   - In your DNS zone, click on the record you want to delete.
   - Click the "Delete" button (usually a trash can icon).
2. **Confirm Deletion:**
   - A confirmation prompt will appear. Click "Yes" to delete the record.

Importing and Exporting Records: Bulk Management

1. **Import:**
   - Click "Import" (often a download arrow icon) and provide a file containing your DNS records in zone file format.
   - This is helpful for migrating DNS records from another provider or restoring from a backup.
2. **Export:**
   - Click "Export" (often an upload arrow icon) to download a zone file containing all your DNS records.
   - This provides a backup of your DNS configuration and can be used to migrate to another DNS provider.

Remember:

- **Propagation Time:** Changes to DNS records may take some time to propagate across the internet due to caching.
- **Test Changes:** Before deleting or modifying records, ensure you understand their purpose to avoid service interruptions.

By mastering these record management techniques in Azure DNS, you gain full control over your domain's configuration, ensuring smooth and reliable resolution for your users.

Private DNS Zones

Imagine you have a company directory that lists the names and phone extensions of all your employees. This directory is only accessible within your company's network, ensuring privacy and security. Private DNS zones in Azure operate in a similar way, but instead of names and phone numbers, they manage domain names and IP addresses within your virtual network (VNet).

What are Private DNS Zones?

A private DNS zone is a DNS zone that is hosted and resolved within a virtual network. This means that the records within the zone are only accessible to resources within the VNet, such as virtual machines, web apps, or other Azure services.

Think of it as an internal phonebook for your cloud resources. Instead of using public IP addresses, you can assign custom domain names to your resources (e.g., `appserver.internal.contoso.com`) and use private DNS to resolve those names to their corresponding IP addresses.

Why Use Private DNS Zones?

Private DNS zones offer several advantages over using public DNS for internal name resolution:

- **Improved Security:** By keeping your internal DNS records private, you prevent them from being exposed to the public internet. This reduces the risk of DNS hijacking or other attacks that could compromise your resources.
- **Simplified Name Resolution:** Private DNS zones make it easier to manage and maintain name resolution for your internal resources. You can use meaningful and consistent names for your resources, making them easier to identify and remember.
- **Customizable:** You have full control over the DNS records within your private zone. You can add, edit, and delete records as needed to match your specific requirements.
- **Split-Horizon DNS:** You can use private DNS zones in conjunction with public DNS zones to create a split-horizon DNS configuration. This allows you to have different DNS records for internal and external users, which can be useful for security and compliance reasons.

Use Cases for Private DNS Zones

Private DNS zones are ideal for scenarios where you want to:

- **Resolve names for internal resources:** Use private DNS to give your virtual machines, databases, and other Azure resources human-readable names that are only accessible within your VNet.
- **Implement name resolution for custom applications:** If you're building custom applications that run on Azure, you can use private DNS zones to provide name resolution for your application components.
- **Secure your DNS data:** By keeping your internal DNS records private, you can reduce the risk of unauthorized access and protect your environment from DNS-related attacks.

Creating and Managing Private DNS Zones

Azure makes it easy to create and manage private DNS zones through the Azure Portal or using command-line tools like Azure CLI or PowerShell. The process is similar to creating a public DNS zone, but you'll specify the virtual network where the zone should be accessible.

By leveraging private DNS zones in Azure, you can create a more secure and manageable environment for your internal applications and resources.

Azure DNS Features and Benefits

Azure DNS stands out among DNS providers due to its rich feature set and seamless integration with the Azure ecosystem. Let's recap the key features and benefits that make it a compelling choice for managing your domain names and DNS records:

Anycast Networking: Speed and Reliability

Azure DNS leverages Anycast networking, a routing technique that directs DNS queries to the nearest available DNS server. This ensures that your users receive the fastest possible response times, regardless of their location. Additionally, Anycast networking enhances the reliability of your DNS resolution by providing redundancy and failover in case of server outages.

Alias Records: Dynamic Updates Made Easy

Alias records are a unique feature of Azure DNS that simplifies DNS management for Azure resources. They act as pointers to Azure resources like Public IP addresses, Traffic Manager profiles, or Content Delivery Network (CDN) endpoints. The key advantage of alias records is that they automatically update if the underlying IP address of the resource changes, ensuring your DNS records remain accurate without manual intervention.

Health Checks: Proactive Monitoring

Azure DNS offers health checks that allow you to monitor the health and availability of your DNS records and their associated endpoints. You can configure health checks to periodically probe your endpoints and trigger alerts if they become unresponsive. This proactive monitoring helps you detect and address issues quickly, ensuring the availability and reliability of your DNS resolution.

Traffic Manager Integration: Global Traffic Routing

Azure Traffic Manager is a DNS-based traffic routing service that allows you to distribute traffic across multiple Azure regions based on different criteria like performance, geographic location, or weighted distribution. By integrating Azure DNS with Traffic Manager, you can seamlessly direct user traffic to the optimal endpoint for their location and network conditions.

Private DNS Zones: Internal Name Resolution

Private DNS zones provide name resolution for resources within your virtual network (VNet). They allow you to assign custom domain names to your internal resources and resolve them privately within your VNet without exposing them to the public internet. This enhances security and simplifies name resolution for your internal applications.

The Azure DNS Advantage

With its combination of reliability, performance, security, scalability, integration, and ease of use, Azure DNS is a powerful tool for managing your domain names and DNS records. Whether you're a small business or a large enterprise, Azure DNS provides a comprehensive solution that can help you optimize your DNS infrastructure and ensure a smooth and secure experience for your users.

Tips and Best Practices

Managing DNS in Azure can be seamless and efficient with a bit of strategic planning and adherence to best practices. Here are some tips to help you get the most out of Azure DNS:

Naming Conventions: Clarity and Consistency

- **Clear and Descriptive Names:** Choose names for your DNS zones and records that clearly reflect their purpose. For example, use "www" for your website's main record and "mail" for your email server's MX record.
- **Consistent Naming Scheme:** Establish a consistent naming convention across your DNS zones and records. This makes it easier to manage and understand your DNS configuration, especially as your environment grows.

Record TTL: Balancing Speed and Updatability

- **Time-to-Live (TTL):** The TTL value of a DNS record determines how long the record is cached by DNS resolvers before they request a fresh copy.
- **Shorter TTL for Frequent Changes:** If you expect your DNS records to change frequently, use shorter TTL values (e.g., 60 seconds). This ensures that changes propagate quickly, but it also means more frequent DNS queries.
- **Longer TTL for Static Records:** If your DNS records rarely change, use longer TTL values (e.g., 1 hour or more). This reduces DNS query traffic, but it also means that changes may take longer to propagate.

Health Checks: Ensure Availability

- **Monitor Critical Endpoints:** For critical DNS records (e.g., those for your website or email server), configure health checks. Azure DNS will periodically check the health of the associated endpoint and automatically update the record if it becomes unhealthy. This helps ensure high availability for your services.
- **Choose the Right Protocol:** Azure DNS supports HTTP, HTTPS, and TCP health checks. Choose the appropriate protocol based on the type of endpoint you're monitoring.
- **Set Appropriate Intervals and Thresholds:** Configure the health check interval (how often to check) and the unhealthy threshold (how many failures before considering the endpoint unhealthy) based on your application's requirements.

DNSSEC: Elevate Your Security

- **DNS Security Extensions (DNSSEC):** Enable DNSSEC for your DNS zones to add an extra layer of security. DNSSEC uses digital signatures to authenticate DNS responses, preventing attackers from tampering with or forging your DNS records.
- **Zone Signing:** Sign your DNS zones with DNSSEC to ensure the integrity of your DNS data.
- **Key Management:** Properly manage your DNSSEC keys, including regular key rotation, to maintain security.

Documentation: Your DNS Roadmap

- **Detailed Records:** Maintain detailed documentation of your DNS configuration, including zone names, record types, values, TTLs, and any associated health checks. This will be invaluable for troubleshooting issues and ensuring the smooth operation of your DNS infrastructure.

- **Change Tracking:** Track all changes made to your DNS records, including who made the change, when it was made, and the reason for the change. This helps with auditing and troubleshooting.
- **Regular Reviews:** Periodically review your DNS configuration to ensure it's up-to-date and aligned with your current needs.

By following these best practices, you can effectively manage your DNS infrastructure in Azure, ensuring optimal performance, security, and reliability for your domains and their associated services.

Chapter Summary

This chapter has illuminated the fundamental concepts and practical usage of Azure DNS, Microsoft's cloud-based Domain Name System service. We began by explaining DNS, the internet's phonebook, and how it translates human-readable domain names into machine-readable IP addresses.

Next, we outlined the compelling reasons to choose Azure DNS, emphasizing its reliability, performance, security, scalability, integration with other Azure services, and user-friendly interface. We then delved into the structure of DNS, highlighting the concept of DNS zones as containers for DNS records and describing the various record types, including A, AAAA, CNAME, MX, and TXT records, and their roles in directing traffic and enabling different services.

You learned how to create a DNS zone in the Azure Portal, a simple process that involves providing the zone name and selecting a resource group and subscription. We then provided detailed instructions on managing DNS records, including adding new records, editing existing ones, deleting unwanted records, and importing or exporting records in bulk.

The chapter also introduced the concept of private DNS zones, which offer secure and simplified name resolution for internal resources within your virtual network. We highlighted the benefits of private DNS zones, such as improved security and customizable name resolution.

Finally, we summarized the key features and benefits of Azure DNS, including Anycast networking for fast and reliable resolution, alias records for dynamic updates, health checks for proactive monitoring, Traffic Manager integration for global traffic routing, and private DNS zones for internal name resolution.

We concluded by offering practical tips and best practices for effectively managing DNS in Azure, emphasizing the importance of clear naming conventions, appropriate record TTL values, health checks, DNSSEC for enhanced security, and thorough documentation.

By mastering Azure DNS, you're now equipped to manage your domain names and DNS records effectively, ensuring seamless and secure access to your websites, applications, and other online services. In the next chapter, we'll shift our focus to another crucial aspect of Azure networking: Content Delivery Networks (CDNs), which are designed to optimize the delivery of your content to users worldwide.

Content Delivery Network (CDN): Optimizing Content Delivery

Outline

- What is a Content Delivery Network (CDN)?
- Why Use a CDN?
- How CDNs Work
- Azure Content Delivery Network
- Key Features of Azure CDN
- Creating and Configuring an Azure CDN Endpoint
- Customizing Azure CDN Behavior
- Integrating Azure CDN with Your Web Applications
- Monitoring and Optimizing Azure CDN Performance
- Best Practices and Tips
- Chapter Summary

What is a Content Delivery Network (CDN)?

Imagine you're ordering a product online. If the product is shipped from a warehouse thousands of miles away, it will naturally take longer to arrive at your doorstep than if it were shipped from a warehouse nearby. Content Delivery Networks (CDNs) apply this same principle to the digital world, making your website's content "closer" to your users, resulting in faster load times and a better user experience.

A Network of Content Hubs

At its core, a CDN is a geographically distributed network of servers, often called edge servers or Points of Presence (PoPs). These servers are strategically located around the world, closer to where your users are.

Instead of serving all your website's content from a single origin server, a CDN caches (stores copies of) your content on these edge servers. When a user requests a web page or other content from your website, the CDN directs the request to the nearest edge server, which then delivers the cached content to the user.

Analogy: The Warehouse Network

Think of a CDN as a network of warehouses storing goods. If you have a single warehouse located in New York, and you have customers all over the country, it will take a long time for them to receive their orders. However, if you have multiple warehouses located closer to your customers, the delivery time will be significantly reduced.

Similarly, a CDN with multiple edge servers around the world can dramatically reduce the distance that content needs to travel, resulting in faster delivery and happier users.

Benefits of CDNs

CDNs offer a host of benefits, including:

- **Improved Website Performance:** By serving content from the closest edge server, CDNs reduce latency (the time it takes for data to travel between the server and the user's device). This leads to faster page load times, especially for users located far from your origin server.

- **Reduced Bandwidth Costs:** Since CDNs cache content, they offload traffic from your origin server. This reduces the amount of data transferred from your origin server, lowering your bandwidth costs.
- **Increased Content Availability and Redundancy:** If one edge server goes down, the CDN can automatically route traffic to another available server, ensuring that your content remains accessible.
- **Enhanced Security:** Many CDNs offer security features like DDoS protection and web application firewalls (WAFs) to help protect your website from malicious attacks.
- **Improved SEO:** Faster page load times and improved user experience can contribute to better search engine rankings.

In the next sections, we'll delve into Azure CDN, Microsoft's content delivery network service, and explore how to use it to optimize the delivery of your website's content.

Why Use a CDN?

Content Delivery Networks (CDNs) are a game-changer for websites and applications that aim to deliver content quickly, reliably, and securely to a global audience. Let's explore the compelling reasons why you should consider incorporating a CDN into your infrastructure:

1. Turbocharged Performance: Faster Page Loads

The most obvious and immediate benefit of using a CDN is a significant boost in website performance. By caching your content on edge servers that are strategically located closer to your users, CDNs dramatically reduce the distance that data needs to travel. This means:

- **Faster Page Load Times:** Websites load faster, as users don't have to wait for content to be fetched from a distant origin server.
- **Reduced Latency:** The time it takes for data to travel between the server and the user's device (latency) is minimized, leading to a more responsive and interactive experience.
- **Improved User Experience:** Faster websites lead to happier users, increased engagement, and higher conversion rates.

2. Reduced Bandwidth Costs: Savings That Add Up

Hosting a website or application can quickly become expensive, especially when you're dealing with high traffic volumes and large files like images or videos. CDNs help you save on bandwidth costs in several ways:

- **Reduced Traffic to Origin Server:** CDNs cache content on their edge servers, which means fewer requests are sent to your origin server. This reduces the amount of data transferred from your origin, lowering your bandwidth consumption.
- **Compression:** Many CDNs automatically compress your files before delivering them to users, further reducing data transfer and bandwidth costs.
- **Optimized Routing:** CDNs intelligently route traffic to the most optimal edge server based on factors like network conditions and server load, minimizing data transfer and improving efficiency.

3. Increased Scalability: Handle Traffic Spikes with Ease

During peak traffic periods, your origin server can become overwhelmed, leading to slowdowns or even outages. CDNs alleviate this problem by distributing the load across their network of edge servers. This means that your website can handle even the most demanding traffic spikes without sacrificing performance.

4. Security: A Shield Against Threats

CDNs often come with built-in security features that can help protect your website from malicious attacks:

- **DDoS Protection:** CDNs can absorb and mitigate Distributed Denial of Service (DDoS) attacks, preventing your website from being overwhelmed by malicious traffic.
- **Web Application Firewall (WAF):** Some CDNs offer WAFs to protect your website from common web attacks like SQL injection and cross-site scripting (XSS).
- **HTTPS Encryption:** CDNs can offload SSL/TLS encryption, freeing up your origin server's resources and ensuring secure data transmission.

5. Improved SEO: A Boost in Rankings

Search engines like Google consider website speed and performance as important factors in their ranking algorithms. By improving your website's load times and user experience, CDNs can indirectly contribute to better search engine rankings, leading to increased organic traffic and visibility.

In Summary:

CDNs offer a compelling combination of performance, reliability, cost savings, and security benefits. Whether you're running a small blog or a large e-commerce platform, a CDN can significantly enhance your website's performance and deliver a superior user experience.

How CDNs Work

Behind the scenes, CDNs orchestrate a complex yet efficient process to deliver your website's content to users with blazing speed and unwavering reliability. Let's take a closer look at the steps involved in this content delivery journey:

1. **Content Origin: Your Home Base**
   At the heart of every CDN is the **content origin**, which is the primary server where your website's content resides. This could be a web server, an Azure Storage account, or any other storage location that houses your website's files (HTML, CSS, JavaScript, images, videos, etc.).
2. **CDN Edge Servers: The Distribution Network**
   Surrounding the content origin is a vast network of **CDN edge servers (PoPs)**. These servers are strategically located around the world, closer to your users, in data centers or internet exchange points. They act as caching points for your content, storing copies of your website's files to reduce the distance they need to travel to reach users.
3. **DNS Resolution: Finding the Closest Server**
   When a user enters your website's URL in their browser, a DNS (Domain Name System) lookup occurs. Instead of resolving to the IP address of your origin server, the DNS directs the request to the nearest CDN edge server. This decision is based on factors like the user's geographic location and the health and capacity of the edge servers.
4. **Cache Hit/Miss: Serving from the Cache or Fetching Fresh**
   Once the request reaches the edge server, the CDN checks its cache to see if it has a copy of the requested content.
   - **Cache Hit:** If the content is found in the cache (a cache hit), the edge server immediately serves it to the user. This is the fastest way to deliver content, as it doesn't require any communication with the origin server.
   - **Cache Miss:** If the content is not found in the cache (a cache miss), the edge server requests the content from the origin server, caches it for future requests, and then delivers it to the user.
5. **Content Delivery: Optimized for Speed and Reliability**
   The CDN optimizes the delivery of your content in several ways:
   - **Closest Server:** Content is served from the geographically closest edge server, reducing latency and improving response times.

- **Load Balancing:** If one edge server is overloaded, the CDN can automatically route traffic to another server with more capacity.
- **Connection Optimization:** CDNs often use techniques like TCP optimization and persistent connections to speed up data transfer.
- **Compression and Minification:** Many CDNs compress and minify your files to reduce their size and improve download speeds.

In a Nutshell

By distributing your content across a global network of edge servers and optimizing the delivery path, CDNs significantly improve website performance, reduce latency, and enhance the user experience. They also provide scalability, reliability, and security benefits, making them a valuable asset for any website or application that serves a global audience.

Azure Content Delivery Network (CDN)

When it comes to delivering content to a global audience, speed and reliability are paramount. Azure Content Delivery Network (CDN) is Microsoft's solution to this challenge. It's a high-performance, globally distributed network that turbocharges your website and application performance by caching your content at edge locations closer to your users.

Azure CDN: More Than Just Speed

Think of Azure CDN as your website's personal trainer. It not only helps your content reach users faster but also offers a wide array of features to enhance your website's overall performance, security, and scalability.

- **Global Reach:** Azure CDN has a vast network of edge servers strategically placed around the world. This ensures that your content is delivered from the server closest to the user, regardless of their location, minimizing latency and maximizing speed.
- **Performance Optimization:** Azure CDN employs various techniques to optimize content delivery, including caching, compression, and request routing. This results in faster page load times, reduced bandwidth consumption, and a smoother user experience.
- **Security:** Azure CDN provides robust security features like DDoS protection, custom domain HTTPS, and web application firewall (WAF) integration to safeguard your content and protect your website from malicious attacks.
- **Integration with Azure Services:** Azure CDN seamlessly integrates with other Azure services like Azure Storage, Web Apps, and Cloud Services, making it easy to incorporate into your existing Azure infrastructure.
- **Customizable Rules:** You have granular control over how Azure CDN caches and delivers your content. You can define custom rules to cache specific file types, set expiration times, and manipulate headers.

Types of Azure CDN

Azure offers different CDN options to cater to various needs:

- **Azure CDN from Microsoft:** Microsoft's own CDN offering, providing a basic set of features for general-purpose content delivery.
- **Azure CDN from Verizon:** A premium offering with advanced features like real-time analytics, rules engine, and custom domain support.
- **Azure CDN from Akamai:** Another premium offering known for its extensive global network and advanced security features.

Choosing the Right Azure CDN

The best Azure CDN for you will depend on your specific requirements and budget. If you're just starting out, the Azure CDN from Microsoft might be sufficient. However, if you need advanced features or have demanding performance or security needs, consider the premium offerings from Verizon or Akamai.

In the next sections, we'll delve deeper into the key features of Azure CDN, guide you through creating and configuring your CDN endpoints, and explore how to integrate CDN with your web applications. Get ready to supercharge your content delivery and give your users the blazing-fast experience they deserve!

Key Features of Azure CDN

Azure CDN is more than just a network of servers; it's a comprehensive content delivery platform packed with features designed to optimize the delivery of your web content. Let's explore some of its key capabilities:

1. Global Reach: Bringing Your Content Closer to Everyone

Azure CDN boasts a vast network of edge servers strategically distributed across the globe. This global footprint ensures that your content is always served from the server closest to your users, regardless of their location. Whether your users are in North America, Europe, Asia, or anywhere else, Azure CDN can significantly reduce latency and deliver your content with blazing speed.

2. Performance Optimization: Speed and Efficiency

Azure CDN employs a variety of techniques to optimize the delivery of your content, ensuring a fast and smooth user experience:

- **Caching:** Caching is the process of storing copies of your content on edge servers. When a user requests your content, the CDN can serve it directly from the cache instead of fetching it from your origin server. This significantly reduces latency and improves response times.
- **Compression:** Azure CDN automatically compresses your content before delivering it to users, reducing file sizes and further improving page load speeds.
- **Request Routing:** Azure CDN intelligently routes user requests to the optimal edge server based on factors like network conditions, server load, and geographic location. This ensures that users are always connected to the fastest and most reliable server.
- **Protocol Optimization:** Azure CDN supports modern protocols like HTTP/2 and Brotli compression, further enhancing the speed and efficiency of content delivery.

3. Security: Shielding Your Content

Security is a top priority for any web application, and Azure CDN offers a range of features to protect your content and your users:

- **DDoS Protection:** Distributed Denial of Service (DDoS) attacks can cripple your website by flooding it with traffic. Azure CDN provides built-in DDoS protection to mitigate these attacks and keep your site online.
- **Custom Domain HTTPS:** You can secure your content with HTTPS using custom domain names, ensuring that traffic between your users and the CDN is encrypted.
- **Web Application Firewall (WAF):** Azure CDN integrates with Azure's Web Application Firewall, which protects your web applications from common vulnerabilities and attacks like SQL injection and cross-site scripting (XSS).

4. Integration with Azure Services: A Seamless Fit

Azure CDN seamlessly integrates with other Azure services, making it easy to incorporate into your existing Azure infrastructure. You can use it to accelerate the delivery of content from:

- **Azure Storage:** Static websites, images, videos, and other files stored in Azure Blob Storage or Azure File Storage.
- **Azure Web Apps:** Dynamic web applications hosted on Azure App Service.
- **Azure Cloud Services:** Legacy cloud services running on Azure.

This integration simplifies the process of setting up and managing your CDN configuration, as you can manage all your Azure resources from a central location.

5. Customizable Rules: Tailor Your Delivery

Azure CDN gives you granular control over how your content is cached and delivered. You can define custom rules to:

- **Cache specific file types or paths:** You can choose which types of content to cache (e.g., images, videos, HTML files) and which to exclude from caching.
- **Set cache expiration times:** Define how long cached content should be stored on edge servers before it's refreshed from the origin.
- **Modify request and response headers:** Add or remove headers to control caching behavior, set security policies, or customize responses for specific scenarios.

With this level of customization, you can fine-tune Azure CDN to perfectly match your content delivery requirements.

Creating and Configuring an Azure CDN Endpoint

Let's walk through the steps of creating and configuring an Azure CDN endpoint using the Azure Portal. By the end of this process, you'll have a powerful tool to speed up your content delivery and enhance user experiences.

1. Selecting a CDN Profile:

- **Open the Azure Portal:** Navigate to the Azure portal (https://portal.azure.com/).
- **Search for CDN Profiles:** In the search bar at the top, type "CDN profiles" and select it from the results.
- **Click "Create":** Click on the "Create" button to initiate the CDN profile creation process.
- **Choose Provider and Tier:**
    - **Profile name:** Provide a unique name for your CDN profile (e.g., "myCDNProfile").
    - **Subscription:** Select the Azure subscription where you want to create the CDN profile (if you have multiple).
    - **Resource group:** Select an existing resource group or create a new one.
    - **Pricing tier:** Choose the pricing tier that suits your needs and budget. Consider factors like features, performance, and support when making your selection.
    - **CDN Provider:** Choose the provider you want to use for your CDN. Azure offers options from Microsoft, Verizon, and Akamai.

2. Creating the CDN Profile:

- **Review + create:** Carefully review your selections and click "Create" to create the CDN profile. The deployment might take a few minutes.

3. Creating the CDN Endpoint:

- **Open CDN Profile:** Once the CDN profile is created, navigate to it from the resource list.
- **Endpoints:** In the left-hand menu, under "Settings," click "Endpoints."
- **Add Endpoint:** Click the "+ Endpoint" button.
- **Name:** Enter a unique name for your CDN endpoint (e.g., "myEndpoint").

- **Origin type:** Choose the type of origin server that will provide the content for your CDN:
    - **Storage:** For content stored in Azure Blob Storage or Azure File Storage.
    - **Web App:** For content hosted on Azure App Service.
    - **Cloud Service:** For content hosted on Azure Cloud Services.
    - **Custom origin:** For content hosted on an external server.
- **Origin hostname:** Enter the hostname or IP address of your origin server.
- **Origin path (optional):** If you want to cache only a specific path within your origin server, enter it here.
- **Origin host header (optional):** Enter the host header you want Azure CDN to send with each request to the origin.
- **Protocol and origin port:** Choose the protocol (HTTP or HTTPS) and port that your origin server uses.
- **Optimized for:** Select the type of content you want to optimize delivery for. This will determine the default optimization settings applied by Azure CDN.

4. **Configuring Optimization Settings:**

- **Caching Rules:**
    - Navigate to the "Caching rules" section and create rules to define how long different types of content should be cached on the edge servers.
    - You can create custom rules based on file extensions, query strings, or HTTP headers.
- **Compression:**
    - Enable compression to reduce the size of files transferred over the network. Azure CDN supports both Gzip and Brotli compression.

5. **Create the CDN Endpoint:**

- **Review + create:** Review your configuration settings and click "Create" to create your CDN endpoint.

Once your CDN endpoint is created, Azure CDN will automatically start caching your content on its edge servers. You can monitor the progress and status of your endpoint in the Azure Portal.

To ensure seamless integration with your website or application, you'll also need to update your DNS settings to point to your CDN endpoint's hostname. We'll cover this in a later section.

Customizing Azure CDN Behavior

While Azure CDN comes with sensible defaults, you'll often want to fine-tune its behavior to match your specific requirements. This is where the powerful Rules Engine comes in, allowing you to define custom rules that control how Azure CDN caches, processes, and delivers your content.

The Rules Engine: Your CDN Policy Maker

Think of the Rules Engine as the brain behind your CDN's decision-making. It evaluates incoming requests against a set of predefined rules and takes appropriate actions based on those rules. This allows you to:

- **Customize Caching Behavior:** Control how long different types of content are cached on the edge servers, optimizing for freshness or performance.
- **Modify Request/Response Headers:** Add, remove, or modify headers to influence caching behavior, security policies, or other aspects of content delivery.
- **URL Rewriting:** Modify URLs on the fly to redirect traffic, optimize paths, or perform A/B testing.
- **Geo-Filtering:** Restrict or customize content delivery based on the geographic location of the user.
- **Device Detection:** Tailor content delivery based on the type of device accessing your website.

- **And More:** The Rules Engine offers a wide range of capabilities to customize the behavior of your Azure CDN.

Types of Rules

Azure CDN Rules Engine supports three main types of rules:

1. **Caching Rules:**
   - **Purpose:** Control how long content is cached on edge servers.
   - **Example:** Cache images for 7 days, cache HTML pages for 1 hour, don't cache dynamic content.
2. **Origin Rules:**
   - **Purpose:** Configure how Azure CDN interacts with your origin server.
   - **Example:** Specify origin timeouts, enable compression for specific file types, or override origin host headers.
3. **Delivery Rules:**
   - **Purpose:** Customize how content is delivered to users.
   - **Example:** Set response headers to control browser caching behavior, rewrite URLs for SEO optimization, or add security headers like HSTS (HTTP Strict Transport Security).

Creating and Managing Rules

You can create and manage rules within the Azure Portal:

1. **Navigate to Your CDN Endpoint:** Go to your CDN profile and select the endpoint you want to configure.
2. **Rules Engine:** Under "Settings," select "Rules engine."
3. **Add Rule:** Click the "Add rule" button to create a new rule.
4. **Configure Rule:**
   - **Name:** Give your rule a descriptive name.
   - **Match Condition:** Specify the condition that triggers the rule (e.g., URL path, file extension, HTTP header).
   - **Action:** Choose the action to perform when the condition is met (e.g., cache, modify headers, redirect).
   - **Order:** Set the order in which the rules are processed. Rules with lower numbers have higher priority.
5. **Save Rule:** Click "Add" to save the rule.

Tips for Using Rules Engine:

- **Start Simple:** Begin with basic caching and origin rules before experimenting with more advanced features.
- **Test Thoroughly:** Test your rules in a staging environment before applying them to production.
- **Use Built-in Features:** Azure CDN offers many pre-built features that can be enabled through the Rules Engine, such as compression and query string caching. Explore these before creating custom rules.
- **Monitor and Optimize:** Use Azure Monitor to track the impact of your rules on CDN performance and make adjustments as needed.

By mastering the Azure CDN Rules Engine, you gain the power to fine-tune your content delivery to match your specific requirements. This flexibility enables you to optimize performance, enhance security, and deliver a personalized experience to your users.

Integrating Azure CDN with Your Web Applications

Once you've created and configured your Azure CDN endpoint, it's time to connect it to your web applications. This integration ensures that your web content is served from the CDN's edge servers, delivering faster loading times and improved performance for your users. Let's explore the key steps involved:

Updating DNS Records: Pointing the Way

The Domain Name System (DNS) acts as the internet's address book, translating domain names into IP addresses. To route traffic to your CDN endpoint, you'll need to update your DNS records at your domain registrar (the company where you registered your domain).

1. **Obtain CDN Endpoint Hostname:** In the Azure Portal, navigate to your CDN endpoint and note down its hostname. This typically follows the format `<endpointname>.azureedge.net`.
2. **Update DNS Records:** Log in to your domain registrar's control panel and locate the DNS settings for your domain. You'll need to create or modify the following records:
   - **CNAME Record:** Create a CNAME record for your website's hostname (e.g., www) that points to your CDN endpoint hostname.
   - **A Record (Optional):** If you want to support root domain access (e.g., `example.com` without the "www"), create an A record that points to the CDN endpoint's IP address.
3. **Propagation Time:** DNS changes can take some time to propagate across the internet. Be patient, as it may take several hours or even a day for the changes to take full effect.

Configuring Web Server Settings: Optimization at the Source

To maximize the benefits of your CDN, ensure that your origin server (the server where your website files are hosted) is properly configured:

- **Enable Compression:** Enable Gzip or Brotli compression on your web server to reduce the size of files transferred over the network.
- **Set Caching Headers:** Configure cache control headers to instruct browsers and the CDN to cache static content like images, CSS, and JavaScript files for longer durations. This reduces the number of requests sent to your origin server and improves page load times.

Using Azure CDN Libraries and SDKs: Programmatic Integration

Azure provides SDKs (Software Development Kits) for various programming languages, such as .NET, Java, Python, and Node.js. These SDKs offer libraries and functions for interacting with Azure CDN programmatically. You can use them to:

- **Purge Content:** Clear the CDN cache for specific files or paths if you need to update your content quickly.
- **Manage Custom Domains:** Programmatically add or remove custom domains from your CDN endpoints.
- **Configure Rules Engine:** Create and manage custom rules using the SDKs to fine-tune CDN behavior.
- **Monitor CDN Performance:** Access metrics and logs programmatically to track CDN performance and troubleshoot issues.

By utilizing the available SDKs, you can automate CDN management tasks and integrate CDN functionality directly into your applications.

Integration with Azure Services: A Seamless Ecosystem

Azure CDN seamlessly integrates with other Azure services, making it easy to use it with your existing cloud infrastructure. For example, you can:

- **Use Azure Storage as an Origin:** Store your website's static content in Azure Blob Storage and use it as the origin for your CDN endpoint.
- **Host Your Web App on Azure App Service:** Azure CDN integrates easily with Web Apps, allowing you to accelerate content delivery for your dynamic web applications.
- **Secure Your Content with Azure Front Door:** For advanced scenarios, you can combine Azure CDN with Azure Front Door to create a global routing and acceleration solution that optimizes for performance, reliability, and security.

By integrating Azure CDN with your web applications and other Azure services, you can create a powerful and efficient content delivery solution that enhances user experience and reduces your infrastructure costs.

Monitoring and Optimizing Azure CDN Performance

A well-performing CDN is essential for delivering a fast and smooth user experience. Azure CDN provides robust monitoring and optimization tools to help you track performance, identify bottlenecks, and fine-tune your configuration for optimal results. Let's delve into how you can monitor and enhance your CDN's performance:

Monitoring Azure CDN Performance: Key Metrics to Track

Azure CDN offers a wealth of metrics that you can use to gauge the performance of your CDN endpoint. Here are some of the most important ones:

- **Cache Hit Ratio:** This metric indicates the percentage of requests that are served directly from the CDN cache, without having to fetch content from the origin server. A higher cache hit ratio generally means better performance and lower bandwidth costs.
- **Bandwidth Usage:** This metric shows the amount of data transferred from the CDN to users. Monitoring bandwidth usage can help you track your data transfer costs and identify potential areas for optimization.
- **Latency:** This measures the time it takes for a request to reach the CDN and for the content to be delivered to the user. Lower latency means faster load times for your users.
- **Errors:** Monitor the number of errors encountered during content delivery, such as 404 errors (not found) or 500 errors (internal server error). This can help you identify issues with your origin server or CDN configuration.
- **Requests per Second (RPS):** Track the number of requests processed by the CDN per second. This metric helps you understand your traffic patterns and assess the load on your CDN.

You can access these metrics through the Azure Portal, Azure Monitor, or by using the Azure CDN REST API.

Optimizing Azure CDN Performance: Fine-Tuning for Speed

Once you understand your CDN's performance metrics, you can start optimizing its behavior. Here are some strategies:

- **Caching Rules:**
  - **Optimize Cache Duration:** Set appropriate cache expiration times for different types of content. Static content like images and videos can often be cached for longer durations than dynamic content.
  - **Utilize Query String Caching:** If your content varies based on query strings, you can configure Azure CDN to cache different versions of your content based on specific query parameters.

- **Geo-Filtering:** If you have different versions of your content for different regions, you can use geo-filtering rules to cache and deliver the appropriate content based on the user's location.
- **Compression:**
    - **Enable Compression:** Make sure compression is enabled for all compressible content types (e.g., text, HTML, CSS, JavaScript). Azure CDN supports both Gzip and Brotli compression.
    - **Optimize Compression Settings:** Adjust the compression level to balance file size reduction and CPU usage on the edge servers.
- **Origin Server Optimization:**
    - **Enable Keep-Alive:** Keep-Alive connections allow multiple requests to be sent over a single TCP connection, reducing overhead and improving performance.
    - **Tune Origin Timeouts:** Adjust the timeout values for connections between the CDN and your origin server to account for slow responses or network latency.
- **Advanced Features:**
    - **Azure CDN Premium Features:** Consider using features like rules engine, real-time analytics, and custom domain HTTPS to further customize and optimize your CDN behavior.
    - **HTTP/2:** Enable HTTP/2 support to improve page load times by allowing multiple requests and responses over a single connection.

Continuous Optimization: An Ongoing Process

CDN optimization is an ongoing process. As your website or application evolves and traffic patterns change, you'll need to adjust your CDN configuration to ensure optimal performance.

By regularly monitoring your CDN metrics, experimenting with different optimization settings, and staying up-to-date with Azure CDN's latest features, you can deliver a fast, reliable, and secure content experience to your users worldwide.

Best Practices and Tips

While Azure CDN is relatively easy to set up, optimizing it for peak performance and efficiency requires understanding and applying key best practices. Let's explore some tips to make your CDN work smarter for you:

1. Cache Static Content: Unleash the Power of the Edge

Static content like images, videos, CSS stylesheets, and JavaScript files are ideal candidates for caching. By storing these assets on the CDN's edge servers, you significantly reduce the load on your origin server and deliver content much faster to users.

Key points to consider:

- **Cacheable Content Types:** Most web browsers are designed to cache certain file types automatically. However, you can fine-tune the caching behavior using the CDN's rules engine to specify cache durations for specific file types or paths.
- **Cache Expiration:** Set appropriate cache expiration times for your static content. Consider factors like how frequently you update your content and how critical it is for users to see the latest versions.

2. Purge Cache: Keeping Content Fresh

When you update your website's content, you want your users to see the latest version as quickly as possible. This is where cache purging comes in. Purging the cache instructs the CDN to remove stale content from its edge servers and fetch fresh copies from your origin server.

How to Purge: You can purge the cache for specific files or paths through the Azure Portal or programmatically using the Azure CDN REST API or SDKs.

3. Utilize Custom Domains: Brand Recognition and SEO

By default, Azure CDN assigns a generic hostname to your endpoint (e.g., `<endpointname>.azureedge.net`). However, you can enhance your brand identity and improve search engine optimization (SEO) by mapping your own custom domain to the CDN endpoint. This allows you to serve your content from a recognizable and memorable URL.

4. Enable HTTPS: Security First

Securing your website with HTTPS is essential for protecting user data and building trust. Azure CDN makes it easy to enable HTTPS for your custom domains, ensuring that all traffic between your users and the CDN is encrypted. This helps protect against man-in-the-middle attacks and ensures the privacy of sensitive information.

5. Monitor Performance: Stay Vigilant

Regularly monitoring your CDN's performance is crucial for identifying potential issues and optimizing its configuration. Azure Monitor provides comprehensive metrics and logs that you can use to track:

- **Cache hit ratio:** The percentage of requests served from the cache.
- **Bandwidth usage:** The amount of data transferred from the CDN.
- **Latency:** The time it takes for content to be delivered to users.
- **Errors:** The number of errors encountered during content delivery.

By keeping a close watch on these metrics, you can proactively identify bottlenecks, optimize caching rules, and adjust your CDN settings to maximize performance.

Additional Tips:

- **Utilize Pre-fetching:** If you have predictable user navigation patterns, you can enable pre-fetching to cache content before users request it, further improving page load times.
- **Optimize Image Sizes:** Compress and optimize your images to reduce their size without sacrificing quality. This can significantly improve page load times, especially on mobile devices.
- **Leverage Rules Engine:** Use the Azure CDN Rules Engine to create custom rules for caching, origin behavior, and content delivery. This allows you to tailor your CDN's behavior to your specific needs.
- **Test Different Configurations:** Experiment with different caching rules, compression settings, and other optimizations to find the best configuration for your website or application.

By applying these best practices and tips, you can harness the full power of Azure CDN to deliver your content with blazing speed, unwavering reliability, and robust security. This will not only enhance the user experience but also contribute to better search engine rankings and increased user engagement.

Chapter Summary

This chapter illuminated the world of Content Delivery Networks (CDNs) and their crucial role in optimizing content delivery for modern web applications. You learned that a CDN is a geographically distributed network of servers that cache content closer to users, dramatically improving website performance, reducing latency, and enhancing user experience.

We explored the key benefits of using a CDN, which include:

- **Improved Performance:** Faster page load times and reduced latency.
- **Reduced Bandwidth Costs:** Offloading traffic from the origin server and minimizing data transfer.
- **Increased Scalability:** Handling high traffic loads and sudden spikes with ease.
- **Security:** Protecting against threats like DDoS attacks and providing features like web application firewalls.
- **Improved SEO:** Contributing to better search engine rankings through enhanced speed and user experience.

We then delved into how CDNs work, examining the five-step process of content origin, CDN edge servers, DNS resolution, cache hit/miss, and optimized content delivery. This understanding of the underlying mechanisms empowers you to make informed decisions about CDN configuration and optimization.

The chapter introduced you to Azure Content Delivery Network (Azure CDN), Microsoft's powerful CDN offering. We highlighted its key features, such as:

- **Global Reach:** A vast network of edge servers for fast content delivery worldwide.
- **Performance Optimization:** Techniques like caching, compression, and request routing to enhance speed and efficiency.
- **Security:** Features like DDoS protection, custom domain HTTPS, and WAF integration.
- **Integration with Azure Services:** Seamless integration with Azure Storage, Web Apps, and Cloud Services.
- **Customizable Rules:** Granular control over caching and delivery behavior through the Rules Engine.

You were then guided through the step-by-step process of creating and configuring an Azure CDN endpoint, covering the selection of a CDN profile, pricing tier, origin server, and optimization settings. We also discussed how to customize Azure CDN behavior using the Rules Engine to define caching rules, origin rules, and delivery rules.

Finally, we explored how to integrate Azure CDN with your web applications by updating DNS records, configuring web server settings, and using Azure CDN libraries and SDKs for programmatic access. We emphasized the importance of monitoring CDN performance and optimizing settings based on metrics like cache hit ratio, bandwidth usage, and latency.

Armed with this knowledge, you can now leverage Azure CDN to supercharge your website or application's performance, improve user experience, and reduce costs. Remember, the best way to master Azure CDN is to experiment with its features, monitor performance, and continuously optimize your configuration based on your specific requirements.

Section 6:
Azure Databases

Azure SQL Database: Relational Database in the Cloud

Outline

- Relational Databases: A Quick Refresher
- Introducing Azure SQL Database
- Why Choose Azure SQL Database?
- Deployment Models: Single Database vs. Elastic Pool vs. Managed Instance
- Key Features of Azure SQL Database
- Creating an Azure SQL Database
- Connecting to Your Azure SQL Database
- Migrating Databases to Azure SQL Database
- Managing and Scaling Azure SQL Databases
- Security Best Practices for Azure SQL Database
- Tips and Tricks
- Chapter Summary

Relational Databases: A Quick Refresher

Before we dive into Azure SQL Database, let's take a moment to refresh our understanding of relational databases, the foundation upon which Azure SQL Database is built.

The Building Blocks: Tables, Rows, and Columns

At its core, a relational database organizes data into **tables**. Think of a table as a spreadsheet, where each row represents a single record (like a customer or a product), and each column represents an attribute of that record (like a customer's name or a product's price).

- **Tables:** Each table has a name and a set of columns.
- **Rows:** Each row represents a unique record within the table.
- **Columns:** Each column defines a specific attribute of the data, such as a customer's name, email address, or phone number.

Keys and Relationships: Connecting the Dots

Relational databases use keys to establish relationships between tables. These keys allow you to connect related data across multiple tables.

- **Primary Key:** A primary key is a column (or combination of columns) that uniquely identifies each row in a table. For example, a `CustomerID` column might be the primary key for a "Customers" table.

- **Foreign Key:** A foreign key is a column in one table that references the primary key of another table. This establishes a link between the two tables, allowing you to create relationships between data.

SQL: The Language of Relational Databases

Structured Query Language (SQL) is the standard language used to interact with relational databases. You use SQL to perform various operations on your data, such as:

- **Querying:** Retrieve specific data from tables based on certain conditions (e.g., "Select all customers from California").
- **Inserting:** Add new records to a table.
- **Updating:** Modify existing records in a table.
- **Deleting:** Remove records from a table.

SQL provides a powerful and flexible way to manage and manipulate your data in a relational database.

Benefits of Relational Databases

Relational databases offer several advantages that make them a popular choice for many applications:

- **Data Integrity:** Relational databases enforce data integrity through constraints like primary keys, foreign keys, and data types. This ensures that your data is consistent and accurate.
- **Relationships:** You can easily model relationships between different data entities, allowing you to represent complex business logic.
- **ACID Compliance:** Relational databases adhere to ACID (Atomicity, Consistency, Isolation, Durability) properties, ensuring that transactions are processed reliably and data remains consistent even in the event of failures.
- **Structured Query Language (SQL):** SQL is a powerful and standardized language for querying and manipulating data in relational databases.
- **Mature Technology:** Relational databases have been around for decades, and a vast ecosystem of tools, libraries, and resources is available to support their use.

Choosing the Right Database

While relational databases are powerful and versatile, they are not the best fit for every scenario. Consider these factors when deciding whether to use a relational database:

- **Structured Data:** If your data fits well into a tabular format with predefined relationships, a relational database is a good choice.
- **Complex Queries:** If your application requires complex queries that involve joining multiple tables, a relational database can handle this well.
- **Data Integrity:** If data consistency and accuracy are critical, a relational database's integrity constraints can be beneficial.
- **Scalability:** If you need to scale your database horizontally across multiple servers, relational databases might present challenges compared to NoSQL databases.

By understanding the fundamentals of relational databases, you'll be better prepared to leverage the power of Azure SQL Database, a fully managed relational database service that brings the benefits of SQL Server to the cloud.

Introducing Azure SQL Database

Imagine the power and reliability of Microsoft SQL Server, but without the hassle of managing and maintaining the underlying infrastructure. That's the essence of Azure SQL Database. It's a fully managed relational database service offered by Microsoft Azure, bringing the familiar SQL Server engine to the cloud.

Your Database, Minus the Hardware Headaches

Azure SQL Database eliminates the need for you to manage hardware, install software, or worry about patching and updates. Microsoft takes care of all the underlying infrastructure and maintenance tasks, allowing you to focus on building and scaling your applications.

The Familiarity of SQL Server in the Cloud

If you're already familiar with SQL Server, you'll feel right at home with Azure SQL Database. It shares the same SQL Server engine, ensuring compatibility with your existing applications and queries. This simplifies the migration of on-premises SQL Server databases to the cloud, minimizing the learning curve and potential disruptions.

Key Features That Make It Shine

Azure SQL Database is packed with features that make it a compelling choice for modern cloud applications:

- **Built-in High Availability:** Your database is automatically replicated and protected from failures, ensuring high availability and minimal downtime.
- **Scalability:** Easily scale your database resources up or down to meet the demands of your application. Azure SQL Database offers various service tiers and compute sizes to fit your needs.
- **Security:** Leverage Azure's robust security features to protect your database data, including encryption at rest and in transit, network security groups, and threat detection.
- **Automatic Backups:** Azure SQL Database automatically creates backups of your data, ensuring you can recover from unexpected events or errors.
- **Global Reach:** Deploy your database in different Azure regions around the world for better performance and redundancy.
- **Performance:** Azure SQL Database is optimized for performance, offering features like intelligent query processing and automatic tuning to ensure your queries run efficiently.
- **Cost-Effectiveness:** Choose from various pricing tiers to match your budget and usage patterns. Azure SQL Database follows a pay-as-you-go model, so you only pay for the resources you use.

Your Reliable Partner in the Cloud

Azure SQL Database is more than just a database service. It's a reliable partner in the cloud that simplifies database management, empowers you to scale your applications effortlessly, and provides peace of mind with built-in security and high availability. Whether you're a startup building your first application or a large enterprise migrating complex workloads to the cloud, Azure SQL Database offers a scalable, secure, and cost-effective solution for your database needs.

Why Choose Azure SQL Database?

Azure SQL Database is a powerful and versatile cloud-based relational database service that offers numerous advantages over traditional on-premises SQL Server deployments. Let's explore the compelling reasons why you should consider migrating your SQL Server workloads to Azure SQL Database:

1. Fully Managed: Let Azure Handle the Heavy Lifting

Say goodbye to the headaches of managing database infrastructure! Azure SQL Database is a fully managed service, meaning Microsoft takes care of the following tasks for you:

- **Patching and Updates:** Azure automatically applies security patches and updates to the SQL Server engine, ensuring your database is always up-to-date and protected against vulnerabilities.
- **Backups:** Azure SQL Database automatically creates backups of your data, protecting you from data loss due to accidental deletion, corruption, or disasters.
- **High Availability:** Azure SQL Database ensures high availability by automatically replicating your data to multiple replicas. In case of a failure, your database will automatically failover to a healthy replica, minimizing downtime.

By offloading these maintenance tasks to Azure, you can free up your IT staff to focus on more strategic initiatives that add value to your business.

2. Scalability: Adapt to Your Needs with Ease

As your application grows and your data needs change, Azure SQL Database allows you to easily scale your resources up or down to meet demand. You can adjust the compute power and storage capacity of your database without any downtime, ensuring that your application can handle any workload.

3. High Availability: Keep Your Data Accessible

Azure SQL Database provides built-in high availability, ensuring that your database is always accessible and resilient to failures. This is achieved through automatic failover to a replica database if the primary database becomes unavailable. Azure also provides features like geo-replication, allowing you to replicate your database to another region for disaster recovery and read scalability.

4. Security: Protecting Your Valuable Data

Azure SQL Database inherits the robust security features of the Azure platform, including:

- **Encryption at Rest:** Your data is encrypted by default using Transparent Data Encryption (TDE). You can also use customer-managed keys for additional control over encryption.
- **Encryption in Transit:** Data transmitted between your application and the database is encrypted using SSL/TLS.
- **Network Security:** You can restrict access to your database using virtual networks, firewall rules, and private endpoints.
- **Threat Detection:** Azure SQL Database Advanced Threat Protection can detect and alert you to potential security threats, such as SQL injection attacks or anomalous data access patterns.

5. Global Reach: Serve Users Worldwide

Azure SQL Database allows you to deploy your database in various regions around the world. This lets you choose the location that best suits your needs, ensuring optimal performance for users in different geographical locations. You can also replicate your database across regions for redundancy and disaster recovery.

6. Cost-Effectiveness: Pay for What You Use

Azure SQL Database offers a variety of pricing tiers and purchase models to suit your budget and usage patterns. You can choose between:

- **vCore-based purchasing model:** Gives you more granular control over compute and storage resources, allowing you to optimize costs based on your workload requirements.
- **DTU-based purchasing model:** A simplified model where resources are bundled into Database Transaction Units (DTUs), making it easier to estimate costs.

Azure SQL Database also offers reserved instances and Azure Hybrid Benefit, which can help you save on costs further.

By migrating to Azure SQL Database, you can streamline your database management, improve performance and scalability, enhance security, and reduce costs. Whether you're a small business or a large enterprise, Azure SQL Database can provide a reliable and cost-effective solution for your relational database needs.

Deployment Models: Single Database vs. Elastic Pool vs. Managed Instance

Azure SQL Database offers three distinct deployment models, each designed to cater to different needs and scenarios. Understanding these models and their trade-offs will help you make an informed decision when choosing the best fit for your database workloads.

Single Database: Simple and Predictable

Think of a single database as a standalone house. It has its own resources (compute, storage, memory) and operates independently. This model is best suited for:

- **Smaller applications:** Applications that don't require a large number of databases or complex features.
- **Predictable workloads:** Applications with consistent usage patterns, making it easier to estimate resource needs.

Key Points:

- **Isolation:** Each database has its own resources and is isolated from other databases.
- **Simplified Management:** Easy to manage and monitor.
- **Predictable Pricing:** Costs are based on the selected service tier and compute size.

Elastic Pool: Shared Resources for Cost Optimization

Imagine an elastic pool as an apartment complex with shared amenities. Multiple databases share a pool of resources (CPU, memory, storage), allowing them to scale dynamically based on demand. This model is perfect for:

- **Multiple databases with varying workloads:** If you have several databases with unpredictable or fluctuating usage patterns, an elastic pool can help you save costs by pooling resources and ensuring that unused resources from one database are available to others.
- **SaaS applications:** Software-as-a-Service (SaaS) providers often use elastic pools to host multiple customer databases, allowing them to scale resources based on customer demand.

Key Points:

- **Shared Resources:** Databases within the pool share resources, allowing for cost optimization.
- **Dynamic Scaling:** Databases can scale automatically within the pool based on their individual needs.
- **Cost-Effective:** Generally more cost-effective than managing multiple single databases.

Managed Instance: SQL Server in the Cloud

A Managed Instance is a fully managed instance of SQL Server in the cloud. It provides near 100% compatibility with on-premises SQL Server, making it the easiest path for migrating complex applications to the cloud.

- **Ideal for:** Complex applications, large databases, or applications that require features not available in single databases or elastic pools.

- **Examples:** Applications that rely on SQL Server Agent, cross-database queries, or complex instance-level configurations.

Key Points:

- **Near 100% Compatibility:** Provides the closest experience to an on-premises SQL Server environment.
- **Instance-Level Features:** Supports instance-level features like SQL Agent jobs, linked servers, and CLR assemblies.
- **VNet Integration:** Can be deployed in your own virtual network for enhanced security and control.

Comparison Table

Feature	Single Database	Elastic Pool	Managed Instance
Isolation	High	Medium	High
Scalability	Manual	Automatic (within pool)	Manual
Pricing Model	Predictable	Shared (based on pool)	Predictable (vCore-based)
Compatibility with SQL Server	Partial (most features)	Partial (most features)	Near 100%
Ideal Use Cases	Smaller apps, predictable workloads	Multiple databases, varying workloads	Complex apps, high compatibility needs

By understanding the nuances of these deployment models, you can select the right one for your specific needs, ensuring that your Azure SQL Database solution is optimized for performance, scalability, and cost-effectiveness.

Key Features of Azure SQL Database

Azure SQL Database is not just a cloud-hosted version of SQL Server. It's a comprehensive database service that comes packed with powerful features designed to optimize performance, enhance security, and simplify management. Let's explore some of the standout features that make Azure SQL Database a compelling choice:

Intelligent Performance: Your Database's Personal Tuner

- **Automatic Tuning:** Azure SQL Database continuously monitors your workload and automatically tunes your database for optimal performance. It analyzes query patterns, identifies bottlenecks, and recommends index optimizations and other performance improvements.
- **Query Performance Insights:** This feature provides deep visibility into your query performance, helping you identify slow-running queries and optimize them for faster execution.
- **Intelligent Insights:** Get proactive recommendations for improving performance based on usage patterns and potential issues.

Advanced Threat Protection: Your Database's Security Guard

- **Threat Detection:** Azure SQL Database Advanced Threat Protection (ATP) detects and alerts you to potential security threats to your database in real time. It can identify anomalies like SQL injection attacks, data exfiltration attempts, and unusual login patterns.
- **Vulnerability Assessment:** This feature regularly scans your database for security vulnerabilities and provides recommendations for remediation.

- **Auditing:** Azure SQL Database logs all database activity, providing a detailed audit trail that can be used for security investigations and compliance.

Geo-Replication: Peace of Mind with Data Redundancy

- **Active Geo-Replication:** Replicate your database to multiple Azure regions around the world. This ensures high availability and data redundancy, protecting your data from regional outages and providing read scalability.
- **Automatic Failover Groups:** Easily configure automatic failover to a secondary replica in another region in case of a disaster or outage.

Azure Hybrid Benefit: Save on Licensing Costs

- **Bring Your Own License:** If you already have SQL Server licenses with Software Assurance, you can reuse them with Azure SQL Database. This can significantly reduce your licensing costs compared to purchasing new licenses for Azure.

Integration with Azure Services: Building Powerful Solutions

Azure SQL Database seamlessly integrates with other Azure services, enabling you to build comprehensive and scalable solutions. Some key integrations include:

- **Azure Functions:** Trigger serverless functions based on database events, such as new data insertions or updates.
- **Azure Logic Apps:** Create workflows that automate business processes and integrate with your database.
- **Azure Virtual Machines:** Host your applications on Azure VMs and connect them to Azure SQL Database for data storage and retrieval.

These are just a few of the many features and benefits that Azure SQL Database offers. By leveraging these capabilities, you can build high-performance, secure, and reliable database solutions in the cloud without the hassle of managing infrastructure.

Creating an Azure SQL Database

Ready to get your data organized in the cloud? Let's walk through creating your Azure SQL Database using the Azure Portal. This will be your home for storing, managing, and querying structured data, leveraging the power and flexibility of the cloud.

1. **Choosing Subscription, Resource Group, and Database Name:**

- **Open the Azure Portal:** Navigate to the Azure portal (https://portal.azure.com/) and log in.
- **Search for SQL databases:** In the search bar at the top, type "SQL databases" and select it from the results.
- **Click "Create":** Click the "Create" button to begin the creation process.
- **Basics Tab:**
    - **Subscription:** Choose the Azure subscription where you want to create the database.
    - **Resource group:** Select an existing resource group or create a new one. (As discussed in Chapter 3, it's good practice to organize resources into groups.)
    - **Database name:** Enter a unique name for your database (e.g., "salesdb" or "inventorydb").
    - **Server:** Choose to create a new server or use an existing one. If you're creating a new server, you'll need to provide a unique server name, admin login, and password.

2. **Selecting a Deployment Model:**

- **Workload Type:**

- **Choose "Single database" for a single, isolated database instance.** This is suitable for most applications and offers various service tiers and purchase models.
- **Choose "Elastic pool" to pool resources across multiple databases.** This is a cost-effective option for databases with unpredictable or varying usage patterns.
- **Choose "Managed Instance" for the highest compatibility with on-premises SQL Server.** This is ideal for complex applications with specific SQL Server features or configurations.

3. **Configuring Compute and Storage Resources:**

- **Compute + storage:** This section lets you configure the performance and capacity of your database.
    - **For single databases, you can choose the service tier (Basic, Standard, or Premium) and compute size (DTUs or vCores).** Higher tiers and sizes offer better performance and features but come at a higher cost.
    - **For elastic pools, you'll configure the pool size and the maximum DTUs or vCores per database.**
    - **For managed instances, you'll select the instance size (vCores) and storage type (General Purpose or Business Critical).**
- **Storage:** Specify the maximum storage size for your database. This can be increased later if needed.

4. **Setting Up Network Connectivity and Security:**

- **Networking:**
    - **Connectivity method:** Choose how you want to connect to your database. The options include:
        - **Public endpoint:** Allows connections from any internet-connected device.
        - **Private endpoint:** Allows connections only from within your virtual network.
    - **Redirect connections to the public endpoint:** This is a legacy option for backward compatibility. It's recommended to use private endpoints for enhanced security.
- **Additional Settings (Optional):**
    - **Data source:** You can choose to create a blank database or select a sample database.
    - **Collation:** Specify the collation for your database (e.g., SQL_Latin1_General_CP1_CI_AS).
    - **Advanced settings:** Customize additional settings like zone redundancy and backup retention period.
- **Review + create:** Carefully review your configuration choices.
- **Create:** Click the "Create" button to deploy your Azure SQL Database.

Once deployment is complete, you'll receive a notification, and you can then connect to your database using your preferred tools or methods. Congratulations on creating your first Azure SQL Database!

Connecting to Your Azure SQL Database

Accessing your Azure SQL Database is a breeze, thanks to the variety of tools and methods available. Whether you prefer a graphical interface, code-based interactions, or command-line tools, Azure has you covered.

1. SQL Server Management Studio (SSMS): The Familiar Friend

If you've worked with SQL Server on-premises, you're likely acquainted with SQL Server Management Studio (SSMS). The good news is that SSMS can also connect to your Azure SQL Database. This provides a familiar and intuitive way to manage your database, including querying data, designing tables, and executing administrative tasks.

Connecting with SSMS:

1. **Obtain Connection Details:** In the Azure Portal, navigate to your SQL database and note the **server name**, **database name**, and **login credentials** (either SQL authentication or Azure Active Directory).
2. **Open SSMS:** Launch SSMS on your local machine.
3. **Connect to Server:**
   - Click "Connect" -> "Database Engine…"
   - In the "Server name" field, enter your Azure SQL Database server name (usually in the format `<your_server_name>.database.windows.net`).
   - Choose the appropriate authentication method and enter your credentials.
   - Click "Connect."

2. Azure Data Studio: The Cross-Platform Companion

Azure Data Studio is a modern, cross-platform database tool that works with SQL Server, Azure SQL Database, and PostgreSQL. It offers a streamlined interface and intelligent code editing features.

Connecting with Azure Data Studio:

1. **Obtain Connection Details:** Same as with SSMS.
2. **Open Azure Data Studio:** Launch Azure Data Studio.
3. **Add Connection:** Click on the "Add Connection" button.
4. **Enter Connection Details:** Fill in the server name, database name, authentication method, and credentials.
5. **Connect:** Click "Connect" to establish the connection.

3. Programming Languages and Libraries: Coding Your Way

For programmatic access, Azure provides SDKs (Software Development Kits) for various languages, allowing you to interact with your database directly from your applications.

- **.NET (C#):** Use the `Microsoft.Data.SqlClient` namespace to establish a connection and execute SQL commands.
- **Java:** Use the `Microsoft JDBC Driver for SQL Server` to connect to and work with Azure SQL Database.
- **Python:** Use the `pyodbc` library to connect to and query your database.

4. Command-Line Tools: Efficient and Scriptable

For administrators or those comfortable with command-line interfaces, Azure offers:

- **sqlcmd:** A command-line utility for connecting to and querying SQL Server and Azure SQL Database.
- **Invoke-SqlCmd (PowerShell):** A PowerShell cmdlet that provides similar functionality to sqlcmd.

Example (sqlcmd):

```
sqlcmd -S <your_server_name>.database.windows.net -U <your_user_name> -P <your_password> -d <your_database_name> -Q "SELECT * FROM Customers"
```

This command connects to your Azure SQL Database and executes a simple SELECT query to retrieve all rows from the "Customers" table.

Choosing Your Connection Method

The best way to connect to your Azure SQL Database depends on your role, preferences, and specific use case.

- **SSMS:** Ideal for database administrators and developers who need a graphical interface for managing and querying databases.
- **Azure Data Studio:** A good option for developers who prefer a lightweight, cross-platform tool with intelligent code editing features.
- **Programming Languages and Libraries:** Essential for building applications that interact with your database programmatically.
- **Command-Line Tools:** Useful for automation, scripting, and quick ad-hoc queries.

Migrating Databases to Azure SQL Database

Migrating your databases to Azure SQL Database doesn't have to be a daunting task. Azure offers several tools and strategies to make the process as smooth and efficient as possible, ensuring minimal disruption to your applications and data.

Azure Database Migration Service (DMS): Your Migration Assistant

If you're looking for a simplified and fully managed migration experience, Azure Database Migration Service (DMS) is your go-to tool. DMS handles the heavy lifting of migrating your databases from various sources to Azure SQL Database. It supports migrations from:

- SQL Server on-premises
- SQL Server on Azure VMs
- MySQL
- PostgreSQL
- Oracle

DMS provides a guided workflow that assesses your source database, recommends the optimal target database settings in Azure, and then orchestrates the migration process, including schema and data transfer. It also offers features like minimal downtime migration and ongoing data replication to ensure a smooth transition.

BACPAC/DACPAC Import/Export: Packing and Unpacking Your Database

BACPAC and DACPAC files are essentially archive formats for SQL Server databases.

- **BACPAC (Backup Package):** Contains both the schema (table definitions, views, stored procedures) and the data of your database.
- **DACPAC (Data-Tier Application Package):** Contains only the schema of your database, without the data.

You can export your on-premises SQL Server database as a BACPAC or DACPAC file and then import it into Azure SQL Database. This method is relatively simple and can be done through the Azure Portal or using command-line tools like `sqlpackage.exe`.

SQL Server Migration Assistant (SSMA): Assessing and Migrating

SSMA is a free tool from Microsoft that helps you assess and migrate your on-premises SQL Server or Azure SQL Managed Instance databases to Azure SQL Database. It automates the conversion of your database schema and objects, minimizing manual effort. SSMA also provides a detailed assessment report that highlights potential compatibility issues and suggests fixes before you migrate.

Choosing Your Migration Strategy

The best migration strategy for you depends on several factors:

- **Source and Target:** What type of database are you migrating from, and what is your target Azure SQL Database deployment model (single database, elastic pool, or managed instance)?
- **Database Size and Complexity:** How large is your database, and how complex is its schema? Larger and more complex databases might require more sophisticated migration tools.
- **Downtime Tolerance:** Can your application tolerate downtime during the migration? Some migration methods allow for minimal downtime or even zero downtime migrations.
- **Budget:** What is your budget for the migration? DMS is a fully managed service that might incur additional costs, while BACPAC/DACPAC and SSMA are free tools.

Migration Best Practices

Regardless of the method you choose, follow these best practices for a smooth and successful migration:

- **Assess:** Before migrating, thoroughly assess your database for compatibility issues and potential challenges.
- **Test:** Thoroughly test your application in a staging environment after the migration to ensure everything works as expected.
- **Monitor:** Monitor your database performance after the migration and optimize it if needed.
- **Back up:** Always create a backup of your on-premises database before starting the migration process.

By understanding the different migration options and following these best practices, you can confidently and efficiently migrate your databases to Azure SQL Database, unlocking the benefits of cloud scalability, performance, and reliability for your applications.

Managing and Scaling Azure SQL Databases

Once your Azure SQL Database is set up, effective management is crucial for ensuring optimal performance, reliability, and cost-efficiency. Azure provides a suite of tools and features to monitor, scale, and protect your database.

Monitoring Performance: Keeping a Pulse on Your Database

Azure Monitor is your window into the health and performance of your Azure SQL Database. It collects and analyzes various metrics that provide valuable insights into how your database is performing.

Key Metrics to Monitor:

- **CPU utilization:** The percentage of CPU resources being used by your database. High CPU utilization may indicate the need to scale up your compute resources.
- **Memory usage:** The amount of memory being used by your database.
- **Storage utilization:** The amount of storage space consumed by your data and log files.
- **Query performance:** The duration of individual queries and overall query throughput. Monitor this to identify slow queries that may need optimization.
- **Deadlocks:** Occurrences of deadlocks, which can block transactions and impact performance.

Tools and Techniques:

- **Azure Portal:** The Azure Portal provides built-in charts and graphs to visualize these metrics.
- **Query Performance Insights:** This tool offers a deeper analysis of query performance, helping you identify the most resource-intensive queries and optimize them.
- **Azure Monitor Logs:** Collect and analyze detailed logs from your database to diagnose issues and troubleshoot errors.

- **Metrics Alerts:** Set up alerts to notify you when specific performance thresholds are exceeded, allowing you to proactively address potential issues.

Scaling Resources: Expanding or Shrinking as Needed

Azure SQL Database offers flexible scaling options, allowing you to easily adjust your database's resources to meet your workload demands.

- **Vertical Scaling:** Scale up or down the compute size (DTUs or vCores) and storage capacity of your database. This can be done without any downtime for most scenarios.
- **Horizontal Scaling (Read Scale-Out):** For read-heavy workloads, create read-only replicas of your database in different regions. This distributes the read load and improves performance for geographically distributed users.
- **Elastic Pools:** If you have multiple databases with varying usage patterns, consider using an elastic pool to share resources between them. This allows you to optimize costs by automatically allocating resources based on the demand of individual databases.

Automated Backups: Peace of Mind with Data Protection

Azure SQL Database automatically creates full, differential, and transaction log backups of your database. These backups are stored in geo-redundant storage, ensuring that your data is protected even in the event of a regional outage. You can configure the backup retention period (up to 35 days) and choose the storage redundancy option that meets your compliance and recovery needs.

Point-in-Time Restore: Time Travel for Your Data

In case of accidental data deletion, corruption, or other errors, you can easily restore your Azure SQL Database to a specific point in time. This is done using the point-in-time restore feature, which allows you to select a specific backup to restore from. This gives you the ability to "rewind" your database to a known good state, minimizing data loss and downtime.

By understanding and utilizing these management and scaling capabilities, you can ensure that your Azure SQL Database remains performant, reliable, and secure, even as your application and data needs evolve.

Security Best Practices for Azure SQL Database

Securing your Azure SQL Database is paramount to safeguard sensitive information and ensure business continuity. Here are the best practices to fortify your database against potential threats:

1. Authentication and Authorization: The Gatekeepers of Your Data

- **Azure Active Directory (AAD) Authentication:** Leverage Azure Active Directory (AAD) for centralized identity and access management. This allows you to use your existing organizational accounts and streamline authentication for your database users.
- **Role-Based Access Control (RBAC):** Assign roles and permissions to users and groups based on their responsibilities. This granular approach ensures that users only have access to the data and operations they need, minimizing the risk of unauthorized access or accidental changes.
- **Principle of Least Privilege:** Grant users the minimum permissions necessary to perform their tasks. Avoid granting excessive privileges, as this can increase the potential impact of a security breach.

2. Network Security: Shielding Your Database

- **Virtual Networks (VNets):** Place your Azure SQL Database within a virtual network to isolate it from the public internet and control access through network security groups (NSGs) and service endpoints.
- **Firewall Rules:** Configure firewall rules to allow access only from authorized IP addresses or virtual networks. This prevents unauthorized access attempts and minimizes the risk of attacks.
- **Private Endpoints:** For enhanced security, consider using private endpoints, which provide a private IP address for your Azure SQL Database within your VNet, ensuring traffic never leaves the Microsoft backbone network.

3. Encryption: Locking Down Your Data

- **Encryption at Rest:** Ensure your data is encrypted at rest using Transparent Data Encryption (TDE). This means your data is encrypted on the disk and backup files, protecting it from unauthorized access even if the physical storage media is compromised.
- **Encryption in Transit:** Azure SQL Database enforces encryption for data in transit using SSL/TLS. Verify that your client applications are configured to use encrypted connections.

4. Advanced Threat Protection: The Early Warning System

- **Azure Defender for SQL:** Enable this security feature to get real-time threat detection alerts. It uses machine learning to identify and alert you to potential security vulnerabilities and suspicious activities, such as SQL injection attacks, anomalous data access patterns, and potential data exfiltration attempts.

Additional Security Tips

- **Regularly Update:** Keep your Azure SQL Database and client applications updated with the latest patches and security fixes.
- **Monitor Audit Logs:** Regularly review audit logs to detect any unusual or unauthorized activity.
- **Principle of Least Privilege:** Grant users only the minimum permissions necessary to perform their tasks.
- **Data Masking:** Use data masking to hide sensitive data from unauthorized users.

By following these best practices and utilizing Azure's robust security features, you can create a multi-layered defense strategy that protects your Azure SQL Database from internal and external threats, ensuring the confidentiality, integrity, and availability of your data.

Tips and Tricks

While Azure SQL Database is designed for ease of use, a few tips and tricks can help you optimize performance, save costs, and get the most out of this powerful service.

1. Query Optimization: Unleash the Speed

- **Query Performance Insights:** Regularly review Query Performance Insights in the Azure Portal to identify slow-running queries and understand their impact on performance.
- **Automatic Tuning:** Enable automatic tuning, and Azure will proactively recommend and apply performance optimizations like index creation or query rewrite suggestions. You can review and apply these recommendations selectively.
- **Manual Tuning:** For more granular control, use the Query Store to analyze query performance, identify bottlenecks, and optimize queries manually. Consider techniques like rewriting queries, adding indexes, or optimizing table structures.

2. Indexing: Your Database's Fast Track

Proper indexing is crucial for efficient query performance. Azure SQL Database provides various index types, including clustered indexes, nonclustered indexes, and columnstore indexes. Analyze your query patterns and create appropriate indexes to speed up data retrieval. However, avoid over-indexing, as too many indexes can also negatively impact performance.

3. Connection Pooling: Efficient Resource Management

Connection pooling allows your applications to reuse existing connections to the database, reducing the overhead of establishing new connections for each request. This can significantly improve application performance, especially for high-traffic applications. Most programming languages and frameworks offer built-in connection pooling libraries or extensions that you can use to easily enable this feature.

4. Geo-Replication: For Resilience and Reach

- **Disaster Recovery:** If your application requires high availability and disaster recovery, consider geo-replication. This creates a readable secondary replica of your database in another region, allowing you to quickly fail over to the replica in case of an outage in the primary region.
- **Read Scalability:** Geo-replication can also be used to improve read performance for globally distributed applications. By routing read requests to the nearest replica, you can reduce latency and provide a better user experience.

5. Azure SQL Database Managed Instance: Seamless Migration Path

If you have complex SQL Server workloads or need features that are not available in single databases or elastic pools, Azure SQL Database Managed Instance is the ideal solution. It provides near 100% compatibility with on-premises SQL Server, making it a seamless lift-and-shift migration path. Managed Instance also offers features like instance-level configurations, SQL Agent jobs, and linked servers, which are essential for complex applications.

Additional Tips

- **Use the Right Service Tier:** Choose the service tier (Basic, Standard, or Premium) and compute size (DTUs or vCores) that matches your workload requirements and budget.
- **Monitor Storage:** Keep an eye on your storage usage and scale up if needed to avoid running out of space.
- **Configure Alerts:** Set up alerts in Azure Monitor to notify you of potential performance or security issues.
- **Security:** Always prioritize security by following best practices like using strong passwords, enabling firewall rules, and restricting access to authorized users.
- **Azure Advisor:** Leverage Azure Advisor for personalized recommendations on optimizing your Azure SQL Database configuration and performance.
- **Cost Optimization:** Use tools like Azure Cost Management to track your database costs and identify potential savings.

By incorporating these tips and best practices into your Azure SQL Database strategy, you can create a high-performance, secure, and cost-effective database solution that powers your applications and drives your business forward.

Chapter Summary

This chapter introduced you to Azure SQL Database, a fully managed relational database service in the cloud. We highlighted its advantages over traditional on-premises SQL Server, emphasizing its fully managed nature, scalability, high availability, robust security, global reach, and cost-effectiveness.

We explored the three deployment models available for Azure SQL Database: Single Database, Elastic Pool, and Managed Instance. Each model caters to different needs, from smaller applications with predictable usage patterns to complex enterprise workloads requiring high compatibility with on-premises SQL Server.

You were introduced to the key features that make Azure SQL Database stand out, including:

- **Intelligent Performance:** Automatic tuning and query performance insights for optimized performance.
- **Advanced Threat Protection:** Real-time detection of security threats and vulnerabilities.
- **Geo-Replication:** Data replication across multiple regions for disaster recovery and read scalability.
- **Azure Hybrid Benefit:** Cost savings by using existing SQL Server licenses with Software Assurance.
- **Integration with Azure Services:** Seamless integration with other Azure services for building powerful solutions.

We walked you through the steps of creating an Azure SQL Database using the Azure Portal, explaining how to choose the right deployment model, configure compute and storage resources, and set up network connectivity and security.

You also learned about the various ways to connect to your Azure SQL database, including SQL Server Management Studio (SSMS), Azure Data Studio, programming languages and libraries, and command-line tools.

We discussed different migration strategies for moving your existing databases to Azure SQL Database, such as Azure Database Migration Service, BACPAC/DACPAC import/export, and SQL Server Migration Assistant (SSMA).

Finally, we provided essential tips and best practices for managing and scaling Azure SQL Databases, including monitoring performance, scaling resources, configuring automated backups, using point-in-time restore, and implementing security best practices like authentication, authorization, network security, and encryption.

With this solid understanding of Azure SQL Database, you're now equipped to leverage this powerful service to build and manage your relational databases in the cloud. In the next chapter, we'll shift our focus to another database offering: Azure Cosmos DB, a globally distributed, multi-model database service.

Azure Cosmos DB: Globally Distributed NoSQL Database

Outline

- NoSQL Databases and Global Distribution
- Introducing Azure Cosmos DB
- Why Choose Azure Cosmos DB?
- Azure Cosmos DB APIs and Data Models
- Creating a Cosmos DB Account and Database
- Working with Containers and Items
- Querying Cosmos DB
- Indexing and Performance Tuning
- Tips and Best Practices
- Chapter Summary

NoSQL Databases and Global Distribution

As our digital world expands, the types of data we generate and need to manage have become increasingly diverse. Traditional relational databases, with their rigid structures, are not always the best fit for modern applications that deal with large volumes of unstructured or semi-structured data. This is where NoSQL databases step in, offering a flexible and scalable alternative.

NoSQL Databases: Breaking the Mold

NoSQL (Not Only SQL) databases are designed to handle a wide range of data models beyond the traditional tables, rows, and columns of relational databases. These models include:

- **Document:** Data is stored as JSON-like documents, ideal for semi-structured data with varying attributes.
- **Key-Value:** Data is stored as simple key-value pairs, perfect for fast lookups and caching scenarios.
- **Graph:** Data is stored as nodes and edges, ideal for representing relationships between entities.
- **Column-Family:** Data is stored in columns grouped by families, suitable for large-scale distributed storage.

This flexibility makes NoSQL databases well-suited for handling unstructured and semi-structured data, which often doesn't fit neatly into predefined schemas.

Global Distribution: Taking Your Data Worldwide

One of the most powerful features of many NoSQL databases, including Azure Cosmos DB, is global distribution. This involves replicating your data across multiple Azure regions around the world. The benefits of this approach are significant:

- **Low Latency:** By storing data closer to users, you can reduce the time it takes for data to travel between the client and the database, resulting in faster response times and a better user experience.
- **High Availability:** With your data replicated across multiple regions, even if one region experiences an outage, your application can still access data from another region, ensuring continuous availability.

- **Disaster Recovery:** Global distribution provides built-in disaster recovery. If an entire region becomes unavailable, your data is still accessible from other regions, protecting you from data loss.

Multi-Model Databases: The Swiss Army Knife of Data

Some NoSQL databases, like Azure Cosmos DB, are multi-model. This means they can support multiple data models within the same database. For example, you could have one container storing data as JSON documents and another container storing data as key-value pairs.

This flexibility allows you to choose the most appropriate data model for each type of data you need to store, all within the same database system. This can simplify your application development and eliminate the need to manage multiple database technologies.

Choosing the Right NoSQL Database

When selecting a NoSQL database, consider the following factors:

- **Data Model:** What type of data are you storing? Choose a database that natively supports your data model (e.g., document, key-value, graph).
- **Scalability:** Do you need to handle large volumes of data or high traffic loads? Choose a database that can scale horizontally to meet your needs.
- **Global Distribution:** Do you need to serve users around the world? Choose a database that offers global distribution for low latency and high availability.
- **Consistency Model:** What level of consistency do you require? NoSQL databases offer different consistency models to balance consistency, availability, and performance.
- **Integration:** Does the database integrate with other services and tools you use? Choose a database that fits well into your existing technology stack.

In the following sections, we'll delve deeper into Azure Cosmos DB, a globally distributed multi-model NoSQL database that offers a powerful solution for modern application development.

Introducing Azure Cosmos DB

In the ever-evolving landscape of data storage and management, Azure Cosmos DB emerges as a trailblazing solution for modern applications. Think of it as the Swiss Army knife of databases – versatile, adaptable, and ready to tackle diverse data challenges.

Azure Cosmos DB: A Global Powerhouse

Azure Cosmos DB is Microsoft's globally distributed, multi-model database service. That's a mouthful, so let's break it down:

- **Globally Distributed:** Cosmos DB can replicate your data across multiple Azure regions around the world, ensuring that your data is close to your users and accessible with low latency, regardless of their location.
- **Multi-Model:** Cosmos DB supports a variety of data models, including document, key-value, graph, and column-family. This flexibility allows you to choose the best model for your specific application requirements.
- **NoSQL:** Cosmos DB is a NoSQL database, meaning it doesn't adhere to the rigid schema of traditional relational databases. This makes it ideal for handling flexible data structures and evolving schemas.

Built for Modern Applications

Azure Cosmos DB is designed from the ground up to meet the demands of modern applications. It's a perfect fit for applications that require:

- **Low Latency:** Cosmos DB guarantees single-digit millisecond latency for both reads and writes at the 99th percentile, ensuring a responsive and snappy user experience.
- **High Availability:** With automatic and transparent multi-region replication, Cosmos DB provides high availability and resilience to failures. Your data remains accessible even if a region experiences an outage.
- **Scalability:** Cosmos DB can scale seamlessly to handle massive amounts of data and traffic. You can easily adjust throughput and storage capacity as your application grows, without downtime or disruptions.

Use Cases: A Wide Spectrum

Azure Cosmos DB is a versatile tool that can be used for a wide range of applications, including:

- **Web and mobile applications:** Cosmos DB can store and manage user data, product catalogs, social media feeds, and other types of semi-structured data.
- **IoT and telematics:** It can handle the massive influx of data generated by IoT devices and sensors, providing real-time insights and analytics.
- **Gaming:** Cosmos DB can store game state data, player profiles, leaderboards, and other game-related information, ensuring low latency and high availability for a smooth gaming experience.
- **Retail and e-commerce:** It can handle product catalogs, inventory data, customer reviews, and order history for online stores.

In the following sections, we'll delve deeper into the reasons why you might choose Azure Cosmos DB over other database options and explore its unique features and capabilities.

Why Choose Azure Cosmos DB?

Azure Cosmos DB is a compelling choice for modern applications due to its unique combination of features that cater to the demands of today's data-intensive and globally distributed systems. Let's delve deeper into why you might choose Cosmos DB, starting with its exceptional capabilities in global distribution and high availability.

Globally Distributed and Highly Available

Imagine your users are scattered across the globe, from New York to London to Tokyo. How do you ensure that your application responds quickly to their requests, regardless of their location? Cosmos DB addresses this challenge with its globally distributed architecture.

You can replicate your Cosmos DB data across multiple Azure regions around the world. When a user makes a request, Cosmos DB automatically routes the request to the nearest replica, ensuring minimal latency and optimal performance. This global reach means your application can deliver a consistent and responsive experience to users no matter where they are.

High Availability: Always On, Always Accessible

With its multi-region replication, Cosmos DB provides unparalleled high availability. Even if one region experiences an outage, your application can seamlessly continue operating using replicas in other regions. This built-in redundancy ensures that your data is always accessible, minimizing downtime and maximizing business continuity.

Multi-Region Writes: Taking Collaboration to the Next Level

Cosmos DB goes beyond read-only replicas with its multi-region writes feature. This allows you to write data to any region where your database is replicated. This enables active-active replication, where multiple regions can serve both read and write requests.

The benefits of multi-region writes include:

- **Lower Write Latency:** Users can write data to the nearest region, reducing the time it takes for data to be committed.
- **Improved Availability:** Even if a region experiences a write failure, your application can continue writing to other regions.
- **Enhanced Collaboration:** Users in different regions can collaborate on data in real time.

How It Works Under the Hood

Cosmos DB achieves global distribution and high availability through a sophisticated replication mechanism. When you create a Cosmos DB account, you can associate it with one or more Azure regions. Cosmos DB then automatically replicates your data to all associated regions.

Each region has its own set of replicas, which are synchronized using a consensus protocol. This ensures that all replicas have the same data, even if writes are happening in multiple regions simultaneously.

Cosmos DB also provides flexible consistency models, allowing you to choose the right trade-off between consistency, availability, and performance for your application. We'll discuss consistency models in more detail later in this chapter.

The Global Advantage

By harnessing the power of Cosmos DB's global distribution and high availability features, you can build applications that are:

- **Globally Accessible:** Serve users around the world with low latency and high availability.
- **Resilient:** Withstand regional outages and ensure business continuity.
- **Collaborative:** Enable real-time collaboration on data across different regions.

Multi-Model Database

One of the most remarkable aspects of Azure Cosmos DB is its ability to embrace multiple data models, giving you the freedom to choose the best fit for your application's unique requirements. Think of it as a multi-tool that you can use to handle different types of screws – you wouldn't use a flathead screwdriver for a Phillips head screw, would you? Similarly, different data models excel in different scenarios.

Cosmos DB achieves this multi-model magic through APIs (Application Programming Interfaces). Each API provides a way to interact with Cosmos DB using a specific data model and query language. Let's explore the main APIs and their corresponding data models:

- **SQL (Core) API:** This is the default and most widely used API in Cosmos DB. It allows you to work with data as JSON documents and query them using a familiar SQL-like syntax. This is ideal for scenarios where you need a flexible schema, rich querying capabilities, and transactional consistency.
- **MongoDB API:** If you're already familiar with MongoDB, this API will feel right at home. It allows you to use your existing MongoDB skills and tools to interact with Cosmos DB. The data is still stored as JSON documents, but you can use the MongoDB query language and drivers to work with it.
- **Cassandra API:** This API enables you to migrate your existing Apache Cassandra applications to Cosmos DB with minimal code changes. You can leverage your Cassandra expertise and use the CQL (Cassandra Query Language) to query your data.

- **Gremlin API:** For graph databases, the Gremlin API allows you to store and query data as vertices (nodes) and edges (relationships). This is perfect for applications that deal with complex relationships between entities, such as social networks, recommendation engines, or fraud detection systems.
- **Table API:** This API provides a key-value interface similar to Azure Table Storage, but with the added benefits of Cosmos DB's global distribution and automatic indexing.

Choosing the Right API and Data Model

Selecting the most suitable API and data model depends on your application's requirements and your development team's expertise:

- **SQL (Core) API:** Ideal for general-purpose applications that need a flexible schema and rich querying capabilities.
- **MongoDB API:** A good choice for applications that are already using MongoDB or want to leverage the MongoDB ecosystem.
- **Cassandra API:** Suitable for migrating existing Cassandra applications or building new ones with Cassandra-like requirements.
- **Gremlin API:** Perfect for applications that deal with graph data and relationships.
- **Table API:** A simple and scalable option for key-value data storage, especially when you don't need complex querying capabilities.

By offering a variety of APIs and data models, Cosmos DB empowers you to choose the best tool for the job, enabling you to build modern, scalable, and globally distributed applications with the flexibility to adapt to your evolving needs.

Flexible Consistency Models

One size does not fit all when it comes to data consistency. Different applications have varying requirements for how quickly they need to see the most recent updates to their data. Azure Cosmos DB recognizes this and offers five distinct consistency models, each striking a different balance between consistency, availability, and performance. Let's explore them:

1. Strong Consistency:

- **Guarantee:** This is the most stringent consistency model, guaranteeing that all reads will reflect the most recent write, even across multiple regions.
- **Trade-off:** Achieving strong consistency requires additional time for data to propagate across all replicas, potentially leading to slightly higher latency.
- **Ideal for:** Applications where absolute consistency is critical, such as financial systems or inventory management systems.

2. Bounded Staleness:

- **Guarantee:** Guarantees that reads will reflect a write within a specified time interval ("K" versions or "T" time duration).
- **Trade-off:** Offers a balance between strong consistency and availability, with potentially lower latency than strong consistency.
- **Ideal for:** Applications that can tolerate some staleness in their data, such as social media feeds or product catalogs.

3. Session:

- **Guarantee:** Guarantees that all reads within a single session will reflect the most recent writes made within that session.

- **Trade-off:** Offers a good balance between consistency and availability, with lower latency than strong consistency.
- **Ideal for:** User-centric applications where users need to see their own updates immediately, such as shopping carts or personal dashboards.

4. **Consistent Prefix:**

- **Guarantee:** Guarantees that all reads will see the writes in the order they were committed, but may not see the most recent write immediately.
- **Trade-off:** Offers good availability and performance, but sacrifices some consistency for applications that don't require strict ordering of writes.
- **Ideal for:** Applications like social media feeds where new updates are more important than the exact order in which they appear.

5. **Eventual:**

- **Guarantee:** Guarantees that all writes will eventually be reflected in all reads, but there is no guarantee on the order or timing.
- **Trade-off:** Offers the highest availability and performance, but sacrifices consistency.
- **Ideal for:** Applications where data consistency is not critical, such as analytics or logging scenarios.

Choosing the Right Consistency Model

The choice of consistency model depends on your application's specific requirements:

- **Strong Consistency:** Choose this if your application requires absolute consistency, even at the cost of higher latency.
- **Bounded Staleness or Session:** Choose one of these if your application can tolerate some level of staleness, but still needs to maintain consistency within certain bounds or sessions.
- **Consistent Prefix or Eventual:** Consider these if your application prioritizes high availability and performance over strict consistency.

The Flexibility Advantage

Azure Cosmos DB's flexible consistency models allow you to fine-tune the balance between consistency, availability, and performance to perfectly match your application's needs. This means you can optimize your database to deliver the best possible user experience without sacrificing data integrity or performance.

Guaranteed Low Latency

In today's fast-paced digital world, speed is everything. Users expect applications to be responsive and snappy, and even a slight delay can lead to frustration and abandonment. Azure Cosmos DB understands this need for speed and has built its foundation on low latency.

Single-Digit Millisecond Latency: A Commitment to Speed

Cosmos DB offers a Service Level Agreement (SLA) that guarantees single-digit millisecond latency for both reads and writes at the 99th percentile. This means that 99% of your read and write operations will complete within a few milliseconds, ensuring a highly responsive experience for your users.

Global Replication: Bringing Data Closer to Users

To achieve such low latency, Cosmos DB leverages its global distribution capabilities. By replicating your data across multiple Azure regions around the world, Cosmos DB ensures that your data is physically closer to your users, minimizing the distance data needs to travel and reducing latency.

Optimized Data Access: Efficient Routing and Indexing

Cosmos DB also employs various optimizations to streamline data access and further reduce latency:

- **Multi-Homing APIs:** Cosmos DB's APIs are designed to be multi-homed, meaning they can connect to the closest available region automatically, minimizing network latency.
- **Automatic Indexing:** Cosmos DB automatically indexes all properties within your data, enabling fast and efficient queries without requiring you to manually create and manage indexes.
- **Write Optimization:** Cosmos DB's write operations are optimized for speed, ensuring that your data is written to the database quickly and efficiently.

The Performance Advantage

Cosmos DB's commitment to low latency gives you a significant performance advantage, especially for applications that require real-time data access or responsiveness. This can lead to:

- **Improved User Experience:** Faster response times mean a smoother and more enjoyable experience for your users.
- **Increased Engagement:** Responsive applications keep users engaged and reduce bounce rates.
- **Better Conversion Rates:** In e-commerce or other transaction-based applications, lower latency can translate to higher conversion rates.

By choosing Azure Cosmos DB, you're not just choosing a database; you're choosing a platform that prioritizes speed and performance. With its guaranteed low latency, global distribution, and optimized data access, Cosmos DB empowers you to build highly responsive and scalable applications that meet the demands of today's users.

Scalable Throughput and Storage

Imagine your database as a restaurant. As more customers arrive (more data requests), you need more tables and waiters (throughput) to accommodate them. Similarly, as your menu expands (more data stored), you need a bigger kitchen and more storage space (storage capacity). Azure Cosmos DB provides the flexibility to scale both your throughput and storage independently, so you can match your resources precisely to your application's requirements.

Independent Scaling: Tailor Resources to Your Workload

Unlike traditional databases, where you often need to scale compute and storage together, Cosmos DB allows you to scale each independently. This means you can:

- **Scale Throughput:** Increase or decrease the number of request units (RUs) to handle varying levels of traffic and request volume.
- **Scale Storage:** Expand your storage capacity as your data grows, without being tied to a specific compute configuration.

This fine-grained control allows you to optimize costs by only paying for the resources you actually need. You can easily scale up during peak traffic periods and scale down during off-peak hours, ensuring optimal performance and cost-efficiency.

Request Units (RUs): The Currency of Throughput

In Cosmos DB, throughput is measured in **request units (RUs)**. A request unit is a standardized measure of the resources required to perform various database operations, such as reads, writes, and queries. The cost of each operation is expressed in RUs, and you can provision a specific number of RUs for your database or container.

Provisioned Throughput: Predictable Performance

With provisioned throughput, you reserve a certain number of RUs per second for your database or container. This guarantees a predictable level of performance, as you always have the required resources available to handle your requests. This is ideal for applications with predictable or consistent workloads.

Autoscale Provisioned Throughput: Flexibility for Bursty Workloads

For applications with unpredictable or bursty traffic patterns, Cosmos DB offers autoscale provisioned throughput. This feature automatically scales your RUs up or down based on the actual workload, ensuring that your application can handle sudden spikes in traffic without manual intervention. You define the maximum and minimum RU limits, and Cosmos DB handles the rest.

Estimating RU Consumption

Cosmos DB provides a capacity calculator that helps you estimate the RU consumption of your application based on its workload characteristics. This allows you to provision the appropriate amount of throughput and optimize your costs.

By understanding the concepts of independent scaling and request units, you can harness the flexibility and scalability of Azure Cosmos DB to build applications that can handle any workload and deliver a seamless user experience to your users.

Fully Managed Service

One of the most appealing aspects of Azure Cosmos DB is that it's a fully managed service. Think of it as having a dedicated team of experts working behind the scenes to keep your database running smoothly, efficiently, and securely.

No Infrastructure Hassles

With Cosmos DB, you don't have to worry about the underlying infrastructure. Microsoft handles all the nitty-gritty details for you, including:

- **Provisioning:** Azure automatically provisions and configures the necessary hardware and software to run your database.
- **Scaling:** It dynamically scales your resources up or down based on demand, ensuring that your application always has the capacity it needs.
- **Maintenance:** Microsoft takes care of routine maintenance tasks like applying patches, updates, and security fixes, keeping your database secure and up-to-date.

Focus on Your Application, Not Your Database

This fully managed nature of Cosmos DB frees you from the operational burden of managing database infrastructure. You don't have to worry about installing software, configuring servers, or dealing with backups and disaster recovery. Instead, you can focus your time and energy on building and improving your application.

Benefits of a Fully Managed Service

A fully managed service like Cosmos DB offers several key benefits:

- **Reduced Operational Overhead:** You don't need to hire and train specialized database administrators (DBAs) to manage your database. This can significantly reduce your operational costs.
- **Faster Time to Market:** You can get your application up and running faster, as you don't have to spend time setting up and configuring infrastructure.

- **Improved Reliability:** Microsoft has a team of experts dedicated to ensuring the availability and reliability of Cosmos DB. This means you can trust that your database will be up and running when you need it.
- **Enhanced Security:** Azure implements robust security measures to protect your data, including encryption at rest and in transit, network security, and threat detection.

By choosing a fully managed service like Azure Cosmos DB, you can offload the complexities of database management to the experts, allowing you to focus on what you do best – building innovative and impactful applications.

Azure Cosmos DB APIs and Data Models

Azure Cosmos DB's flexibility shines through its multiple APIs (Application Programming Interfaces), each tailored for a specific data model and offering a familiar interface for developers from different backgrounds. Let's start with the most common and versatile option: the SQL (Core) API.

SQL (Core) API

The SQL API is the primary and foundational API for Azure Cosmos DB. It provides a rich and familiar interface for working with document data, allowing you to leverage your existing SQL skills to query and manipulate data in a NoSQL environment.

Document Data Model: Flexible and Schema-less

The SQL API operates on a document data model, where data is stored in JSON (JavaScript Object Notation) documents. These documents are semi-structured, meaning they can have varying attributes and don't require a rigid schema. This flexibility allows your data model to evolve easily as your application's requirements change.

Familiar SQL-like Query Language

The SQL API enables you to query your JSON documents using a SQL-like query language. While it's not exactly the same as traditional SQL used for relational databases, it's designed to be intuitive and easy to learn for developers familiar with SQL. You can use standard SQL keywords like SELECT, WHERE, ORDER BY, and JOIN to filter, sort, and aggregate your data.

Example of a SQL Query in Cosmos DB

```
SELECT c.firstName, c.lastName, c.city FROM c WHERE c.city = "New York"
```

This query would retrieve the first name, last name, and city of all customers located in New York from a container named "Customers".

Advantages of the SQL API

- **Familiarity:** If you're already familiar with SQL, the SQL API offers a smooth transition to working with NoSQL data in Cosmos DB.
- **Rich Querying:** The SQL-like query language provides powerful capabilities for filtering, sorting, and aggregating your data.
- **Transactional Consistency:** The SQL API offers strong transactional consistency, ensuring that your data is always consistent and accurate.

When to Choose the SQL API

The SQL API is an excellent choice for a wide range of use cases, including:

- **Web and mobile applications:** Storing user profiles, product catalogs, and other types of semi-structured data.
- **IoT applications:** Managing device data and telemetry.
- **Gaming applications:** Storing player profiles, game states, and leaderboards.
- **Any application that requires a flexible schema and powerful querying capabilities.**

By understanding the capabilities and benefits of the SQL API, you can leverage the full potential of Azure Cosmos DB to build modern, scalable, and globally distributed applications that can handle the complexities of today's data landscape.

MongoDB API

If you or your team are already proficient with MongoDB, Azure Cosmos DB's MongoDB API is your bridge to the cloud. It allows you to leverage your existing MongoDB skills, tools, and applications with Cosmos DB, making the transition to the cloud seamless and efficient.

Compatibility: Your MongoDB Skills Transfer

Cosmos DB's MongoDB API implements the wire protocol used by MongoDB drivers and tools. This means that your existing MongoDB applications can connect to Cosmos DB without requiring any code changes. You can use the same MongoDB drivers, tools, and libraries that you're already familiar with, such as the MongoDB Shell, MongoDB Compass, and popular MongoDB ORMs.

Beyond Compatibility: The Best of Both Worlds

While providing compatibility, the MongoDB API also gives you access to Cosmos DB's unique features and benefits:

- **Global Distribution:** Take advantage of Cosmos DB's global reach and multi-region writes to create highly available and globally distributed applications.
- **Turnkey Global Distribution:** Your MongoDB application can instantly become globally distributed by simply changing the connection string.
- **Automatic Scaling:** Let Cosmos DB automatically scale your throughput and storage as your application grows.
- **Multiple Consistency Levels:** Choose the consistency model that best suits your application's requirements.
- **Guaranteed Low Latency:** Enjoy single-digit millisecond latency for reads and writes at the 99th percentile.

Scenarios Where the MongoDB API Shines

The MongoDB API is a perfect fit for scenarios where:

- **Migration:** You want to migrate your existing MongoDB applications to the cloud without having to rewrite code.
- **Development Agility:** You want to leverage your team's existing MongoDB expertise to build new applications quickly.
- **Flexibility:** You need a flexible schema that can evolve with your application's requirements.
- **Global Reach:** You want to create globally distributed applications that are accessible to users around the world with low latency.

How It Works: Under the Hood

When your MongoDB application connects to Cosmos DB using the MongoDB API, the requests are translated into Cosmos DB's native operations. This allows you to seamlessly interact with Cosmos DB using the familiar MongoDB query language and drivers, while benefiting from Cosmos DB's underlying architecture and capabilities.

Migrating Data: Easy Transition

Migrating your existing MongoDB data to Cosmos DB is also straightforward. You can use standard MongoDB tools like mongodump and `mongorestore`, or you can use Azure's Database Migration Service (DMS) for a fully managed migration experience.

By choosing the MongoDB API in Azure Cosmos DB, you can unlock the power of cloud computing without sacrificing the familiarity and convenience of your existing MongoDB skills and tools.

Cassandra API

If you're looking to leverage the power of Azure Cosmos DB without abandoning your existing Apache Cassandra investment, look no further than the Cassandra API. It's designed to provide a seamless migration path for your Apache Cassandra applications, minimizing disruptions and accelerating your move to the cloud.

Compatibility: Your Cassandra Knowledge, Retained

Azure Cosmos DB's Cassandra API is wire protocol compatible with Apache Cassandra drivers and tools. This means you can use your existing Cassandra Query Language (CQL) expertise and familiar tools like `cqlsh` (the Cassandra Query Language Shell) to interact with your data in Cosmos DB. In many cases, transitioning involves a simple connection string change, with minimal code modifications required.

Benefits Beyond Compatibility

While offering seamless compatibility, the Cassandra API also unlocks the advantages of Cosmos DB:

- **Global Distribution:** Effortlessly scale your Cassandra application globally with multi-region writes and low latency for users around the world.
- **Turnkey Global Distribution:** Your Cassandra application can instantly become globally distributed by simply changing the connection string.
- **Automatic Scaling:** Cosmos DB automatically handles scaling of throughput and storage as your workload demands change, saving you from manual capacity planning.
- **High Availability:** Enjoy high availability with automatic failover in case of regional outages or other disruptions.
- **Fully Managed:** Offload the burden of managing Cassandra infrastructure, backups, and upgrades to Azure.

Ideal Scenarios for the Cassandra API

This API is perfect if you want to:

- **Migrate existing Cassandra applications to the cloud:** Minimize disruption and reduce migration effort.
- **Leverage Cassandra expertise:** Use your team's existing Cassandra skills to build and manage applications in Azure.
- **Modernize legacy applications:** Benefit from Cosmos DB's scalability, global reach, and managed services without rewriting your Cassandra applications.
- **Build new Cassandra-compatible applications:** Develop cloud-native applications using the familiar Cassandra API and ecosystem.

How It Works: A Smooth Translation

When your Cassandra application interacts with Cosmos DB using the Cassandra API, the requests are translated into Cosmos DB's underlying operations. This allows for seamless compatibility without sacrificing the performance and scalability of Cosmos DB.

A Word of Caution

While the Cassandra API offers high compatibility, there are some differences in features and behavior compared to Apache Cassandra. Be sure to review the Azure documentation to understand these nuances before migrating your applications.

In essence, Azure Cosmos DB's Cassandra API empowers you to leverage your existing Cassandra investments and expertise while enjoying the benefits of a fully managed, globally distributed, and scalable cloud database service.

Gremlin API

Azure Cosmos DB isn't limited to just documents and key-value pairs; it also embraces the world of graph databases through its Gremlin API. This opens up a whole new realm of possibilities for applications that deal with relationships and interconnected data.

Graph Databases: Beyond Tables and Rows

Unlike traditional relational databases that store data in tables, graph databases focus on relationships between data points. They represent data as nodes (entities) and edges (relationships), allowing you to model complex relationships like social connections, product recommendations, or knowledge graphs.

Apache TinkerPop Gremlin: The Language of Graphs

The Gremlin API in Cosmos DB leverages Apache TinkerPop, a popular graph computing framework. Gremlin is the graph traversal language of Apache TinkerPop, designed for navigating and manipulating graphs efficiently. It provides a rich set of operators for traversing, filtering, and transforming graph data.

Building Graph Applications with Cosmos DB

The Gremlin API allows you to build graph database applications on top of Cosmos DB, leveraging its scalability, global distribution, and high availability. You can use the Gremlin query language to perform complex graph traversals, analyze relationships, and uncover hidden patterns in your data.

Use Cases for Graph Databases

Graph databases excel in scenarios where relationships are central to the problem domain. Some common use cases include:

- **Social Networks:** Representing connections between users, analyzing social graphs, and recommending friends or content.
- **Recommendation Engines:** Building personalized recommendation systems based on user preferences and item relationships.
- **Fraud Detection:** Identifying fraudulent patterns by analyzing connections between users, transactions, and entities.
- **Knowledge Graphs:** Representing knowledge domains as interconnected entities and relationships, enabling semantic search and knowledge discovery.

Gremlin Query Example

Let's say you have a graph database of social connections. To find all the friends of a specific user, you could use a Gremlin query like this:

```
g.V('user_id').out('friend')
```

This query starts at the vertex representing the user with the given `user_id`, traverses all outgoing edges of type `friend`, and returns the vertices (friends) connected to the user.

The Power of the Gremlin API

By combining the power of graph databases with the scalability and global reach of Cosmos DB, the Gremlin API opens up a world of possibilities for building sophisticated graph applications that can handle massive amounts of interconnected data.

Table API

The Azure Cosmos DB Table API is a familiar face for those experienced with Azure Table Storage. It offers a nearly identical interface and functionality, making it easy to migrate existing Table Storage applications to Cosmos DB or build new ones using the same key-value approach. However, under the hood, it brings along some powerful enhancements that make it a compelling alternative.

Same Interface, Enhanced Capabilities

The Table API provides a key-value interface where data is stored as entities with properties (key-value pairs), just like in Azure Table Storage. You can use the same SDKs and tools you're accustomed to, with minimal code changes required.

The key difference lies in the underlying architecture. Cosmos DB's Table API leverages the global distribution and multi-model capabilities of the Cosmos DB platform, bringing significant advantages to the table:

- **Turnkey Global Distribution:** Your table data can be replicated across multiple Azure regions with ease, ensuring low latency and high availability for your global users. This is a significant upgrade from Azure Table Storage, which is limited to a single region.
- **Automatic Indexing:** Cosmos DB automatically indexes all properties in your table, eliminating the need for manual index management. This ensures fast and efficient queries, even as your data grows.
- **Guaranteed Performance:** Cosmos DB offers comprehensive SLAs (Service Level Agreements) for throughput, latency, availability, and consistency, ensuring predictable and reliable performance for your applications.

Use Cases for the Table API

The Table API is ideal for scenarios where:

- **You have existing Azure Table Storage applications:** Migrate your applications to Cosmos DB seamlessly to take advantage of global distribution and automatic indexing.
- **You need a simple and scalable key-value store:** The Table API provides a familiar interface for storing and retrieving key-value data.
- **You require low latency and high availability:** Cosmos DB's global distribution and high availability features ensure optimal performance and resilience.
- **You don't need complex querying capabilities:** If your application's query patterns are relatively simple, the Table API's key-value interface is sufficient.

A Familiar Path to Global Scale

In essence, the Azure Cosmos DB Table API is a bridge that allows you to bring your Azure Table Storage experience to a globally distributed, highly available, and performant platform. It's a testament to Cosmos DB's flexibility and commitment to providing a smooth transition for developers from various backgrounds.

Creating a Cosmos DB Account and Database

Let's bring your data to life in Azure Cosmos DB! Creating an account and database through the Azure Portal is a streamlined process that sets the stage for your globally distributed, highly performant application data.

1. Choosing Subscription, Resource Group, and Account Name:

- **Open the Azure Portal:** Head to the Azure Portal (https://portal.azure.com/) and log in.
- **Search for Cosmos DB:** Type "Cosmos DB" in the search bar and select it.
- **Click "Create":** This takes you to the account creation page.
- **Basics Tab:**
    - **Subscription:** Select the Azure subscription where you want to create the Cosmos DB account.
    - **Resource group:** Opt for an existing resource group or click "Create new" to make a fresh one with a descriptive name (e.g., "myCosmosDB-rg").
    - **Account name:** Enter a unique name for your Cosmos DB account. This name will be part of your Cosmos DB endpoint URL (e.g., `<your-account-name>.documents.azure.com`).

2. Selecting an API and Data Model:

- **API:** Choose the API that best suits your application's requirements and your team's skills. The options include:
    - **Core (SQL):** For document data with a SQL-like query interface.
    - **Azure Cosmos DB for MongoDB API:** For compatibility with MongoDB applications and tools.
    - **Azure Cosmos DB for Apache Cassandra API:** For compatibility with Cassandra applications and tools.
    - **Azure Cosmos DB for Apache Gremlin:** For graph databases using the Gremlin query language.
    - **Table API:** For key-value data with a simple interface (similar to Azure Table Storage).
- **For this example, let's select "Core (SQL)" to work with document data.**

3. Configuring Global Distribution and Consistency:

- **Global Distribution (Optional):**
    - If your application requires global reach, enable "Geo-redundancy" or "Multi-region writes." This will replicate your data across multiple Azure regions for high availability and low latency.
    - **If you enable geo-redundancy, you can also choose a default consistency level.** This determines how strict the consistency guarantees are across replicas. Options include strong, bounded staleness, session, consistent prefix, and eventual consistency.
    - **For this example, we'll keep the default of single-region deployment and strong consistency.**

4. Creating the Account and Database:

- **Review + create:** Carefully review your selections. Azure will provide an estimated cost based on your configuration.
- **Create:** Click "Create" to start the deployment process. This may take a few minutes.

After Deployment:

Once your Cosmos DB account is created:

1. **Navigate to the account:** From the resource list or the notification, go to your new Cosmos DB account.

2. **Create a database and container:** Click on "Data Explorer" in the left menu, then click "New Database" to create your first database and container within it.

Key Points to Remember:

- **Location:** Choose a primary region that's closest to your users. You can add more regions later if you need global distribution.
- **Consistency Model:** For most applications, the default strong consistency level is a good choice. However, if you need lower latency or higher availability, you might consider a different model (discussed earlier in this chapter).
- **Throughput:** Consider the expected workload of your application and provision the appropriate amount of throughput (measured in Request Units or RUs). You can always adjust this later if needed.

Congratulations! You've successfully created an Azure Cosmos DB account and database. You're now ready to start adding and querying your data in the cloud!

Working with Containers and Items

Now that you have your Azure Cosmos DB account and database, it's time to start storing your data. In Cosmos DB, data is organized into containers, which are similar to tables in SQL databases or collections in MongoDB. Let's explore how to create containers and work with the data items within them.

Containers: Organizing Your Data

A container is a logical grouping of items (documents, key-value pairs, or graph data) that share a common partition key. You can think of it as a folder for your data, where you store related items together. For example, you might have a container for "Customers," another for "Products," and a third for "Orders."

Each container has its own:

- **Partition Key:** Determines how data is distributed across physical partitions for scalability and performance.
- **Throughput:** Provisioned throughput (measured in Request Units or RUs) that determines the capacity of the container to handle requests.
- **Indexing Policy:** Defines how data is indexed for efficient querying.
- **Unique Key Policy (Optional):** Ensures the uniqueness of certain properties within the container.

Creating a Container in the Azure Portal

1. **Navigate to Your Database:** Open the Azure Portal, go to your Cosmos DB account, and select the database where you want to create a container.
2. **Data Explorer:** Click on "Data Explorer" in the left menu.
3. **New Container:** Click "+ New Container" at the top of the Data Explorer pane.
4. **Container Details:**
   - **Database id:** This is already pre-filled with your selected database name.
   - **Container id:** Enter a unique name for your container (e.g., "Customers").
   - **Partition key:** Choose a partition key path. This is the property in your documents that will be used to distribute data across partitions. (For our "Customers" container, a good choice might be "/customerId".)
   - **Throughput:** Select a throughput provisioning mode (manual or autoscale) and the desired throughput (in RUs/sec).
   - **Unique keys:** (Optional) You can define unique keys to ensure certain properties are unique within a partition or across the entire container.
5. **Create Container:** Click "OK" to create the container.

Adding Items (Documents)

Once your container is created, you can start adding items (documents) to it. Each item is a JSON document containing your data. You can add items through the Azure Portal, SDKs, or REST APIs.

Example (Using the Azure Portal):

1. **Open the Container:** Navigate to your container in the Data Explorer.
2. **Click "New Item":** Click the "+ New Item" button at the top.
3. **Enter JSON:** Enter the JSON document representing your item in the editor.
4. **Save:** Click "Save" to add the item to the container.

Updating and Deleting Items

To update an item, retrieve it, modify its properties, and then replace or merge the updated item in the container. To delete an item, use its ID and partition key.

Best Practices

- **Choose the Right Partition Key:** The choice of partition key significantly impacts performance and scalability. Design your partition key based on your application's query patterns and the expected distribution of data.
- **Optimize Throughput:** Monitor your RU consumption and adjust your provisioned throughput or switch to autoscale if needed.
- **Indexing Policy:** Customize the indexing policy to match your query patterns and optimize query performance.
- **Unique Keys:** If your application requires data uniqueness, consider defining unique keys for certain properties.
- **Bulk Operations:** For large-scale data operations, use the bulk executor library provided by the Cosmos DB SDKs for efficient inserts, updates, and deletes.

By understanding containers and mastering the operations on items, you can effectively store, manage, and query your data in Azure Cosmos DB, building applications that are both scalable and performant.

Querying Cosmos DB

One of the core tasks in any database is querying - fetching the specific data you need from the vast expanse of information stored within. Azure Cosmos DB, with its multi-model capabilities, offers multiple ways to query your data depending on the API you choose. Let's explore how to query data using the SQL, MongoDB, Cassandra, and Gremlin APIs.

SQL API: Familiar SQL-Like Queries

The SQL API in Cosmos DB provides a familiar SQL-like query language for interacting with your JSON document data.

Example: Find all products with a price less than $50:

```
SELECT * FROM products p WHERE p.price < 50
```

This query uses standard SQL keywords like SELECT, FROM, and WHERE to filter the results based on the `price` property of the `products` container.

Filters: You can use comparison operators (=, <>, >, <, >=, <=) and logical operators (AND, OR, NOT) to filter your results based on various criteria.

Sorting: Use `ORDER BY` to sort the results by one or more properties. For example:

```
SELECT * FROM products p ORDER BY p.price DESC
```

This query will sort the products in descending order based on their price.

Pagination: Cosmos DB supports pagination to retrieve results in smaller chunks, which can be useful for large datasets. You can use the `OFFSET` and `LIMIT` keywords to implement pagination.

MongoDB API: Leveraging MongoDB Queries

If you're using the MongoDB API, you can leverage the familiar MongoDB query language to interact with your data.

Example: Find all users named "Alice":

```
db.users.find({ name: "Alice" })
```

This query uses the MongoDB `find` method to search for documents (items) in the "users" collection (container) where the "name" field is equal to "Alice."

Filters, Sorting, and Pagination: You can use the full range of MongoDB query operators, sorting options, and pagination techniques to refine your queries.

Cassandra API: Utilizing CQL

For the Cassandra API, you'll use Cassandra Query Language (CQL) to query your data.

Example: Find all products in the "Electronics" category:

```
SELECT * FROM products WHERE category = 'Electronics'
```

This query selects all rows (items) from the "products" table (container) where the "category" column is equal to "Electronics."

Filters, Sorting, and Pagination: CQL supports various filter and sorting options, as well as pagination through the `LIMIT` keyword and token-based pagination.

Gremlin API: Traversing Graphs

With the Gremlin API, you use the Gremlin graph traversal language to navigate and query your graph data.

Example: Find all friends of a user:

```
g.V('userId').out('friend')
```

This query starts at the vertex with the ID `userId` and follows outgoing edges with the label "friend," returning all the connected vertices (friends).

Filtering, Sorting, and Pagination: Gremlin offers powerful filtering, sorting, and traversal options specific to graph data.

The Right Tool for the Job

Choosing the appropriate query language and API depends on your data model and your team's expertise. The SQL API is a good starting point for most users due to its familiarity and versatility.

However, if you're working with graph data or have existing applications written in MongoDB or Cassandra, the corresponding APIs offer seamless integration and a familiar experience.

Indexing and Performance Tuning

Azure Cosmos DB is designed for speed and efficiency. One of its key features is its automatic indexing capabilities, ensuring that your queries run as fast as possible. However, understanding indexing and applying some performance tuning techniques can further enhance your database's responsiveness.

Automatic Indexing: Your Data's Built-in Accelerator

By default, Cosmos DB automatically indexes every property in your documents. This means that when you execute a query, Cosmos DB can efficiently search through these indexes to quickly find the relevant data, eliminating the need for costly full table scans.

While automatic indexing is convenient, it's not always the most efficient approach for every scenario. If you have a large number of properties that are rarely queried, indexing them all can consume unnecessary resources. That's where customizing indexing policies comes in.

Customizing Indexing Policies: Tailor-Made for Your Needs

Cosmos DB allows you to fine-tune your indexing policies to match your specific workload requirements. You can:

- **Exclude Paths:** Specify which properties or paths within your documents should not be indexed. This can reduce storage overhead and improve write performance.
- **Include Paths:** Explicitly define which properties or paths should be indexed. This can be useful for optimizing queries that frequently filter or sort on specific properties.
- **Composite Indexes:** Create composite indexes on multiple properties to improve the performance of queries that filter or sort on multiple conditions.
- **Spatial Indexes:** Enable spatial indexing for geospatial data to efficiently query for items based on their location.

By customizing your indexing policy, you can optimize query performance while minimizing resource consumption.

Tips for Optimizing Query Performance

Beyond indexing, consider these additional tips for improving query performance:

- **Efficient Queries:**
    - **Use Filters Wisely:** Apply filters that leverage the indexed properties of your data.
    - **Avoid Cross-Partition Queries:** Whenever possible, design your queries to operate within a single partition (i.e., filter by the partition key). Cross-partition queries can be significantly slower.
    - **Limit Results:** Use the TOP or LIMIT keywords to retrieve only the required number of results, reducing the amount of data transferred.
- **Data Modeling:**
    - **Denormalization:** Consider denormalizing your data by embedding related data within a single document. This can reduce the need for joins and improve query performance.
    - **Pre-calculate Aggregations:** If you frequently perform aggregations (sums, averages, counts), consider pre-calculating them and storing the results as properties in your documents.
- **Other Considerations:**

- **Provisioned Throughput:** Ensure you have enough provisioned throughput (RUs) to handle your query workload.
- **Consistency Level:** Choose the appropriate consistency level based on your application's requirements. Strong consistency can impact query performance, while weaker consistency levels can improve performance at the cost of some staleness.

By understanding the indexing mechanisms and applying these performance tuning techniques, you can unlock the full potential of Azure Cosmos DB and ensure your queries run smoothly and efficiently, even at a massive scale.

Tips and Best Practices

Azure Cosmos DB is a powerful tool, but like any tool, it's most effective when wielded with knowledge and finesse. Here are some practical tips and best practices to help you harness the full potential of Cosmos DB:

1. **Choose the Right API and Data Model:**
   Cosmos DB's multi-model capability is a blessing, but it also means you need to choose the right API and data model for your application. Consider these factors:
   - **Existing Skills and Tools:** If your team is already familiar with a particular NoSQL database (MongoDB, Cassandra), using the corresponding API can simplify development.
   - **Data Model:** If your data fits well into a specific model (document, key-value, graph), choose the corresponding API. If you need flexibility, the Core (SQL) API offers a good balance of features and ease of use.
   - **Query Patterns:** The SQL API is versatile for most scenarios, but if you have specific graph or column-family query needs, consider the Gremlin or Cassandra APIs.
2. **Design for Global Distribution:**
   If your application serves users worldwide, leverage Cosmos DB's global distribution capabilities. You can replicate your data across multiple regions to:
   - **Reduce Latency:** Serve data from the nearest region to your users, improving response times.
   - **Ensure High Availability:** If one region goes down, your application can seamlessly continue using a replica in another region.
   - **Scale Read Throughput:** Distribute read requests across multiple regions for improved performance.
3. **Select the Appropriate Consistency Level:**
   Cosmos DB offers five consistency levels, each with trade-offs between consistency, availability, and performance.
   - **Strong:** Highest consistency, but potential for higher latency.
   - **Bounded Staleness:** Provides a balance between consistency and availability.
   - **Session:** Ensures consistency within a user session.
   - **Consistent Prefix:** Guarantees writes are seen in the order they were made, but not necessarily the latest write immediately.
   - **Eventual:** Lowest consistency, but highest availability and performance.

Choose the level that best suits your application's requirements. Most applications can thrive with Session or Bounded Staleness consistency.

4. **Monitor and Scale Throughput:**
   - **Request Units (RUs):** Cosmos DB uses RUs to measure throughput. Each operation consumes a certain number of RUs, and you can provision throughput at the database or container level.
   - **Monitoring:** Use Azure Monitor metrics to track your RU consumption and identify potential bottlenecks.

- **Scaling:** If you're exceeding your provisioned throughput, scale up to avoid throttling or performance degradation. Consider using autoscale for dynamic scaling based on demand.

5. **Security:**
    - **Firewall:** Secure your Cosmos DB account by setting up firewall rules to restrict access to specific IP addresses or virtual networks.
    - **Role-Based Access Control (RBAC):** Use RBAC to grant granular permissions to users and applications, ensuring they can only access and perform actions on authorized resources.
    - **Encryption at Rest:** Cosmos DB encrypts your data at rest by default using Microsoft-managed keys. You can also bring your own keys (BYOK) for additional control.
    - **HTTPS:** Ensure that all communication with Cosmos DB is done over HTTPS to protect data in transit.

By incorporating these best practices into your Cosmos DB strategy, you can unlock its full potential, building globally distributed, highly available, and performant applications that can scale to meet the demands of your growing business.

Chapter Summary

This chapter introduced you to Azure Cosmos DB, a powerful and versatile NoSQL database service that redefines how applications manage data in the cloud. We highlighted its globally distributed architecture, multi-model capabilities, flexible consistency models, guaranteed low latency, and seamless scalability, making it a compelling choice for modern, data-intensive applications.

You learned that Cosmos DB supports various data models, including document, key-value, graph, and column-family, through its different APIs: SQL (Core), MongoDB, Cassandra, Gremlin, and Table. This multi-model approach gives you the flexibility to choose the best data model and API that aligns with your application's requirements and your team's expertise.

We emphasized the advantages of global distribution, such as low latency, high availability, and disaster recovery, along with the unique capability of multi-region writes, enabling active-active replication across regions.

The chapter then explored the concept of flexible consistency models in Cosmos DB, where you can choose the right balance between consistency, availability, and performance. We described the five consistency levels: strong, bounded staleness, session, consistent prefix, and eventual, each catering to different application needs.

We highlighted Cosmos DB's commitment to low latency, with SLAs guaranteeing single-digit millisecond latency for reads and writes at the 99th percentile. You also learned how Cosmos DB achieves this through global replication, multi-homing APIs, automatic indexing, and write optimizations.

We discussed how Cosmos DB allows independent scaling of throughput and storage, providing you with the flexibility to adjust resources based on your application's demands. The concept of request units (RUs) was introduced as a measure of throughput, and we discussed how to provision and autoscale RUs to ensure optimal performance.

We emphasized the benefits of Cosmos DB being a fully managed service, relieving you from infrastructure management tasks and allowing you to focus on your application development.

You were then guided through the steps of creating a Cosmos DB account and database using the Azure Portal, including choosing the right API and data model, configuring global distribution and consistency, and provisioning resources.

The chapter also covered how to work with containers and items, which are the building blocks of your data in Cosmos DB. You learned how to create containers, add items, update them, and delete them.

Finally, we provided an overview of querying Cosmos DB using different APIs and highlighted tips on indexing and performance tuning.

Armed with this comprehensive understanding of Azure Cosmos DB, you're now equipped to leverage this powerful database service to build globally distributed, highly available, and scalable applications that can handle the complexities of modern data management. In the next chapter, we'll turn our attention to another popular database option on Azure: Azure Database for MySQL and PostgreSQL.

Azure Database for MySQL/PostgreSQL: Open-Source Options

Outline

- Overview of MySQL and PostgreSQL
- Introducing Azure Database for MySQL/PostgreSQL
- Benefits of Using Azure Database for MySQL/PostgreSQL
- Creating an Azure Database for MySQL/PostgreSQL
- Connecting to Your Database
- Migrating Your Data
- Managing and Monitoring Your Database
- Tips and Best Practices
- Chapter Summary

Overview of MySQL and PostgreSQL

MySQL and PostgreSQL stand out as two of the most widely used open-source relational database management systems (RDBMS) that empower numerous applications and websites worldwide.

Open-Source Nature:

Both MySQL and PostgreSQL are free and open-source software, meaning their source code is publicly accessible. This has fostered large and active communities of developers and users who contribute to their ongoing improvement, ensuring a robust ecosystem of resources, documentation, and support.

Relational Model:

At their core, MySQL and PostgreSQL adhere to the relational model, a fundamental concept in database management. In this model, data is organized into tables, where each table represents a specific entity (e.g., customers, products). Tables consist of rows (records) and columns (attributes), enabling structured storage and retrieval of information. Both databases utilize SQL (Structured Query Language), a standardized language, for interacting with the data, facilitating tasks like data definition, manipulation, and querying.

Community and Enterprise Editions:

Both MySQL and PostgreSQL offer community editions that are entirely free to use. These editions provide a solid foundation for a wide range of applications. For organizations with more demanding requirements, enterprise editions are available, typically through commercial vendors. Enterprise editions often come with enhanced features like advanced performance optimization, clustering, replication, and dedicated support, making them suitable for large-scale or mission-critical deployments.

In essence, MySQL and PostgreSQL are versatile RDBMS options, catering to diverse needs. Whether you're building a personal website, developing a complex web application, or managing critical enterprise data, these open-source databases offer a powerful and reliable solution.

Introducing Azure Database for MySQL/PostgreSQL

Azure Database for MySQL and Azure Database for PostgreSQL are fully managed database services offered by Microsoft Azure. They bring the power and familiarity of the popular open-source databases MySQL and PostgreSQL to the cloud, simplifying database management and maintenance.

Based on Community Editions:

These Azure services are built upon the community editions of MySQL and PostgreSQL. This ensures compatibility, allowing you to leverage your existing knowledge, tools, and applications seamlessly. If you are already familiar with MySQL or PostgreSQL, you can easily transition to their Azure counterparts.

Benefits of Managed Services:

Choosing Azure Database for MySQL or PostgreSQL frees you from many of the operational burdens associated with traditional database management. Key benefits include:

1. **Automatic Patching:** Azure automatically applies updates and patches to the underlying database software, ensuring your database remains secure and up-to-date without manual intervention.
2. **Automated Backups:** Your data is regularly backed up to protect against data loss. You can easily restore your database to a previous point in time in case of accidental data changes or other issues.
3. **High Availability:** Azure ensures high availability of your database with built-in redundancy and failover mechanisms. This minimizes downtime and ensures your applications remain accessible.
4. **Scalability:** You can easily scale your database resources up or down to meet the changing demands of your applications. This allows you to optimize costs and performance.
5. **Security:** Azure provides a robust security framework with features like data encryption, network security, and threat detection to protect your sensitive data.

In Summary:

Azure Database for MySQL and Azure Database for PostgreSQL offer a convenient and reliable way to manage your MySQL and PostgreSQL databases in the cloud. They provide the benefits of managed services while maintaining compatibility with the community editions, making them a compelling choice for developers and organizations seeking a hassle-free database solution.

Benefits of Using Azure Database for MySQL/PostgreSQL

Fully Managed Service

Azure Database for MySQL/PostgreSQL relieves you of the operational overhead of managing your database infrastructure. Here's how it handles essential database management tasks, freeing you to focus on application development and innovation:

- **Automated Patching:** Azure automatically applies patches and updates to the underlying database software (MySQL or PostgreSQL), including security patches, bug fixes, and new features. This ensures your databases are always up-to-date and protected against vulnerabilities.
- **Automated Backups:** Azure performs regular automated backups of your databases, storing them redundantly in geographically separate locations. These backups can be easily restored in case of data loss or corruption, providing peace of mind and disaster recovery capabilities. You can also configure the backup retention period and create on-demand backups for additional flexibility.
- **High Availability:** Azure automatically replicates your database data across multiple availability zones within a region. This ensures that even if one zone becomes unavailable, your databases remain accessible, providing built-in high availability and business continuity.
- **Scalability:** Azure allows you to easily scale your database resources (compute, storage, memory) up or down based on your application's demands. This eliminates the need for manual provisioning or complex infrastructure changes, allowing you to respond quickly to changing workloads.

- **Monitoring and Alerts:** Azure provides built-in monitoring and alerting capabilities, giving you insights into the performance, health, and security of your databases. You can set up custom alerts for specific metrics, such as high CPU usage or storage consumption, to proactively identify and address potential issues.

By offloading these operational tasks to Azure, you can focus your time and resources on building and enhancing your applications. You can be confident that your databases are secure, available, and performant, while benefiting from the scalability and flexibility of the cloud.

High Availability and Scalability

Azure Database for MySQL/PostgreSQL provides robust high availability and flexible scaling options to ensure your applications remain responsive and resilient even under demanding workloads.

High Availability:

- **Automatic Failover:** Azure Database for MySQL/PostgreSQL automatically creates and maintains replicas of your database within a region. In the event of a primary database failure (e.g., hardware or software issue), Azure automatically initiates a failover to one of the replicas, ensuring minimal downtime and continuous availability of your application.
- **Zone-Redundant High Availability (Optional):** For even higher availability, you can choose the zone-redundant option. This configuration replicates your data across multiple availability zones within a region. Even if an entire zone goes down, your database remains accessible from another zone, providing enhanced protection against regional failures.

Scalability:

- **Vertical Scaling:** You can easily scale up or down the compute and storage resources (vCores, memory, and storage) of your database to match your application's needs. This vertical scaling can be done with minimal downtime, allowing you to adjust your database capacity as your workload changes.
- **Read Replicas:** For read-heavy workloads, you can create read replicas of your database. Read replicas offload read traffic from your primary database, improving performance and scalability. You can have multiple read replicas to distribute the read workload and achieve even higher throughput.
- **Hyperscale (Citus) (PostgreSQL only):** For massive scalability, Azure Database for PostgreSQL offers the Hyperscale (Citus) option. This architecture horizontally scales your PostgreSQL database across multiple nodes, allowing you to handle extremely large datasets and high query volumes with exceptional performance.

Benefits:

- **Reduced Downtime:** Automatic failover minimizes downtime caused by unplanned outages, ensuring your application remains available.
- **Improved Performance:** Vertical scaling and read replicas enable you to adapt to varying workloads and maintain optimal performance.
- **Simplified Management:** Azure handles the complexities of high availability and scaling, allowing you to focus on your application development.

By combining high availability with flexible scaling options, Azure Database for MySQL/PostgreSQL provides a reliable and scalable database platform for your applications. Whether you need to handle sudden traffic spikes or manage large datasets, Azure's capabilities can help you meet your business needs.

Security and Compliance

Azure Database for MySQL/PostgreSQL is designed with a strong emphasis on security, providing a comprehensive set of features to protect your data and help you meet compliance requirements:

Encryption:

- **Encryption at Rest:** Azure encrypts your database data at rest using industry-standard AES 256-bit encryption. This encryption is transparent, ensuring that your data is protected without requiring any changes to your applications.
- **Encryption in Transit:** Azure enforces SSL/TLS encryption for all connections to your database, protecting data in transit over the network.

Network Security:

- **Virtual Networks (VNet):** You can deploy your databases into Azure Virtual Networks, providing an additional layer of network isolation and security. This allows you to control access to your databases using network security groups and route tables.
- **Firewall Rules:** You can define granular firewall rules to control incoming and outgoing traffic to your databases, allowing access only from authorized sources (IP addresses, virtual networks, or Azure services).

Threat Detection:

- **Azure Defender for MySQL/PostgreSQL:** This advanced threat protection service continuously monitors your databases for potential security vulnerabilities and suspicious activities. It provides real-time alerts and recommendations to help you identify and mitigate threats before they can cause damage.

Compliance:

Azure Database for MySQL/PostgreSQL helps you meet various compliance standards and regulations, including:

- **ISO 27001:** Information security management systems
- **ISO 27018:** Protection of personal data in the cloud
- **CSA STAR:** Cloud Security Alliance Security, Trust & Assurance Registry
- **HIPAA/HITECH:** Health Insurance Portability and Accountability Act
- **PCI DSS:** Payment Card Industry Data Security Standard
- **SOC 1, 2, and 3:** System and Organization Controls

Azure maintains these certifications and provides audit reports to help you demonstrate compliance to your customers and stakeholders.

Additional Security Features:

- **Role-Based Access Control (RBAC):** You can grant fine-grained permissions to users and groups, ensuring that only authorized personnel can access and manage your databases.
- **Auditing:** Azure Database for MySQL/PostgreSQL provides detailed audit logs of database activities, allowing you to track changes and detect potential security incidents.
- **Data Masking:** You can mask sensitive data in your database, preventing unauthorized access to confidential information.

By leveraging these robust security features, you can confidently build and deploy applications on Azure Database for MySQL/PostgreSQL, knowing that your data is protected and compliant with industry standards and regulations.

Open-Source Compatibility

Azure Database for MySQL/PostgreSQL is designed to be fully compatible with the respective community editions of MySQL and PostgreSQL. This means you can leverage your existing knowledge, tools, and applications without significant modifications when migrating to Azure.

Key Compatibility Features:

- **Engine Compatibility:** Azure Database for MySQL/PostgreSQL uses the same database engines (MySQL Community Edition or PostgreSQL Community Edition) as you're used to. This ensures that your SQL queries, stored procedures, functions, and other database objects work seamlessly on Azure.
- **Tooling Compatibility:** You can continue using your favorite database management tools, such as MySQL Workbench, pgAdmin, DBeaver, or command-line tools (mysql, psql) to connect to, manage, and administer your databases on Azure.
- **Application Compatibility:** Your existing applications and libraries that connect to MySQL or PostgreSQL databases should work with Azure Database for MySQL/PostgreSQL with minimal or no changes. The standard connection strings and protocols are supported, making the transition smooth.
- **Extension Support:** Azure Database for PostgreSQL supports many popular PostgreSQL extensions, such as PostGIS (for geospatial data), TimescaleDB (for time-series data), and pg_cron (for scheduled jobs), allowing you to extend the functionality of your database as needed.
- **Migration Tools:** Azure provides migration tools and services to help you easily migrate your existing MySQL or PostgreSQL databases to Azure with minimal downtime and disruption.

Benefits of Open-Source Compatibility:

- **Reduced Learning Curve:** You don't need to learn new tools or technologies to work with Azure Database for MySQL/PostgreSQL.
- **Faster Time to Market:** You can quickly migrate your existing applications to Azure without extensive re-engineering.
- **Cost Savings:** You can leverage your existing investments in tools, applications, and training, reducing the overall cost of ownership.
- **Flexibility:** You can choose from various Azure service tiers and deployment options to optimize your database for your specific needs and budget.

By providing full compatibility with MySQL and PostgreSQL community editions, Azure Database for MySQL/PostgreSQL simplifies the migration process and enables you to focus on building and innovating with your applications, not on learning new database technologies.

Cost Optimization

Azure Database for MySQL/PostgreSQL offers several flexible pricing options and features to help you optimize costs while meeting your performance and availability requirements:

Pricing Options:

- **Service Tiers:** Azure provides various service tiers (Basic, General Purpose, Memory Optimized) for both MySQL and PostgreSQL. Each tier offers different levels of compute, memory, and storage resources at varying price points. Choose the tier that best aligns with your workload requirements and budget.
- **vCore Model:** You pay for the number of virtual cores (vCores) you provision, which determines the compute and memory resources available for your database.
- **Storage:** You pay for the amount of storage you use, with options for different types of storage (standard, premium, or ultra disk) based on your performance needs.
- **Reserved Capacity:** You can purchase reserved capacity for your database, committing to a one-year or three-year term in exchange for a significant discount on the vCore price. This is a good option if you have predictable workloads and want to save on costs.

- **Burstable Instances (Flexible Server only):** For less predictable workloads, consider burstable instances. These allow you to use additional vCores when needed, paying for the extra usage only when you exceed your baseline. This provides flexibility and cost-effectiveness for workloads with occasional spikes in activity.

Cost Optimization Features:

- **Automatic Backups:** Azure automatically creates backups of your database, eliminating the need for you to manage and store backups separately. This not only saves you time but also reduces your storage costs.
- **Point-in-Time Restore:** You can restore your database to any point in time within your backup retention period, which can be up to 35 days. This allows you to recover from accidental data loss or corruption without incurring additional costs.
- **Read Replicas:** If you have a read-heavy workload, you can offload read traffic from your primary database to read replicas. This can reduce the load on your primary database and potentially allow you to use a lower-tier service, saving on costs.
- **Autoscaling:** You can set up autoscaling to automatically adjust your database resources (vCores or storage) based on your workload. This helps you avoid overprovisioning resources and paying for unused capacity.
- **Monitoring and Optimization:** Azure provides tools and services to monitor your database performance and identify potential areas for optimization, such as inefficient queries or indexing issues. By addressing these issues, you can improve performance and potentially reduce costs by requiring fewer resources.

By carefully evaluating your workload requirements and leveraging these pricing options and cost optimization features, you can create a cost-effective solution with Azure Database for MySQL/PostgreSQL that meets your specific needs and budget.

Creating an Azure Database for MySQL/PostgreSQL

Here's a step-by-step guide on creating an Azure Database for MySQL or PostgreSQL using the Azure portal, along with explanations to help you understand each decision:

Step 1: Sign In and Start Creation

1. **Sign in:** Open the Azure portal (https://portal.azure.com/) and sign in with your Microsoft account.
2. **Create a resource:** Search for "Azure Database for MySQL" or "Azure Database for PostgreSQL" and click the corresponding service. Then click the "Create" button.

Step 2: Basics

1. **Subscription:** Choose the Azure subscription where you want to create your database.
2. **Resource group:** Select an existing resource group (a logical container for related resources) or create a new one.
3. **Server name:** Enter a unique name for your database server. This will be used to create a subdomain for your database endpoint (e.g., `yourservername.mysql.database.azure.com`).
4. **Server admin login:** Choose a username (e.g., `azureuser`) and a strong password for the server's administrative account.
5. **Location:** Select the region where you want to deploy your database. Choose a region close to your users or application for optimal performance.

Step 3: Compute + Storage

1. **Compute tier:**
    - **Basic:** Ideal for development or testing with light workloads.

- **General Purpose:** Provides balanced compute and memory for most business applications.
- **Memory Optimized:** Best for high-performance database workloads with high memory requirements.
2. **Compute generation:** Choose the latest generation for improved performance and features.
3. **vCores:** The number of virtual cores determines the processing power.
4. **Storage:**
   - **Storage type:** Standard or premium storage (premium is faster and more expensive).
   - **Storage size:** Start with an appropriate size and consider the autoscale option to automatically adjust storage based on usage.
   - **Backup redundancy:** Choose between locally redundant (LRS) or geo-redundant (GRS) storage for backups.

Step 4: Networking

1. **Connectivity method:**
   - **Public endpoint:** Allows connections from any internet-connected device.
   - **Private endpoint:** Securely access the database over your Azure Virtual Network (VNet).
2. **Firewall rules:** (If using a public endpoint)
   - **Allow Azure services to access server:** Enables other Azure services within your subscription to access the database.
   - **Add current client IP address:** Adds your current IP address for development and testing purposes.
   - **Virtual network rules:** (If using a private endpoint) Configure the virtual network where your private endpoint resides.

Step 5: Additional Settings

1. **High availability:** Enable zone redundancy for increased availability.
2. **Advanced threat protection:** Enable this for enhanced security monitoring and threat detection.
3. **Tags:** (Optional) Add tags to your database server for better organization and resource management.

Step 6: Review + Create

1. **Review:** Carefully review all the settings you've configured.
2. **Create:** Click the "Create" button to start the deployment process.

Deployment and Connection

- **Deployment:** Azure will take a few minutes to create your database server.
- **Connection:** Once deployed, you can find connection details (server name, database name, etc.) in the "Overview" section of your database resource. Use these details to connect using a MySQL or PostgreSQL client tool (e.g., MySQL Workbench, pgAdmin).

Important Security Considerations

- **Strong passwords:** Use complex passwords for your server admin login and database users.
- **Firewall rules:** Limit access to your database using firewall rules.
- **Private endpoints:** If security is a high priority, use private endpoints for connections over your VNet.
- **Data encryption:** Ensure data at rest and in transit is encrypted.

Connecting to Your Database

Let's break down how to connect to your Azure Database for MySQL/PostgreSQL using various tools and techniques:

1. MySQL Workbench (for MySQL)

- **Get Connection Details:** In the Azure portal, go to your MySQL database server's "Overview" section and note down the server name, server admin login name, and password.
- **Open MySQL Workbench:** Launch MySQL Workbench and click the "+" icon next to "MySQL Connections".
- **Fill in Details:**
  - **Connection Name:** Give your connection a descriptive name.
  - **Hostname:** Enter the fully qualified server name from the Azure portal (e.g., `yourservername.mysql.database.azure.com`).
  - **Port:** Keep the default port 3306.
  - **Username:** Use the server admin login name from the Azure portal.
  - **Password:** Enter the password associated with the server admin login.
- **Test Connection:** Click "Test Connection" to verify the credentials.
- **Save Connection:** Click "OK" to save the connection settings.

2. pgAdmin (for PostgreSQL)

- **Get Connection Details:** Same as with MySQL Workbench, get the server name, login name, and password from the Azure portal.
- **Open pgAdmin:** Start pgAdmin and right-click on "Servers" in the object browser.
- **Create Server:**
  - **General Tab:** Enter a descriptive name for your server.
  - **Connection Tab:**
    - **Host name/address:** Enter the server name from the Azure portal.
    - **Port:** Keep the default port 5432.
    - **Maintenance database:** Enter `postgres`.
    - **Username:** Use the server admin login name.
    - **Password:** Enter the associated password.
- **Save:** Click "Save" to create the server connection.

3. Command-Line Tools

- **MySQL (mysql client):**
  `mysql -h yourservername.mysql.database.azure.com -u yourusername -p`
- **PostgreSQL (psql client):**
  `psql -h yourservername.postgres.database.azure.com -U yourusername -d postgres`
  (You'll be prompted for the password.)

4. Programming Languages and Libraries

- **Use Appropriate Libraries:**
  - **MySQL:** MySQL Connector/Python, MySQL Connector/J (Java), etc.
  - **PostgreSQL:** psycopg2 (Python), pg (Node.js), Npgsql (.NET), etc.
- **Connection String:** Construct a connection string using the server name, database name, username, and password. For example (in Python using MySQL Connector):
  `import mysql.connector mydb = mysql.connector.connect( host="yourservername.mysql.database.azure.com", user="yourusername", password="yourpassword", database="yourdatabase" )`

5. Azure Portal (Query Editor)

- **Navigate:** Go to your MySQL or PostgreSQL database resource in the Azure portal.
- **Query Editor:** Click the "Query editor" button.
- **Login:** Enter your server admin login credentials.

- **Run Queries:** You can now write and execute SQL queries directly in the browser-based editor.

Important Notes

- **Firewall Rules:** Make sure your IP address or network is allowed in the firewall rules of your database server.
- **SSL/TLS:** For secure connections, configure SSL/TLS settings in your connection tools and libraries.
- **Private Endpoint:** If you are using a private endpoint, you'll need to connect from within your Azure virtual network.

Migrating Your Data

Migrating your MySQL or PostgreSQL databases to Azure can be achieved using various methods, each with its pros and cons:

1. Azure Database Migration Service (DMS)

- **Fully Managed:** DMS handles the entire migration process, minimizing downtime and risk.
- **Multiple Sources:** It supports various source databases (on-premises or cloud-based) and target Azure Database services.
- **Minimal Downtime:** DMS uses a change data capture (CDC) mechanism to keep your target database in sync with the source during migration, allowing for near-zero downtime cutovers.
- **Monitoring and Logging:** Provides comprehensive monitoring and logging for troubleshooting and validation.

How to Use DMS:

1. Create a DMS instance in your Azure subscription.
2. Create a migration project, specifying your source and target databases.
3. Configure the source and target connection details.
4. Select the tables to migrate and start the migration process.
5. Monitor the progress and complete the cutover when ready.

2. Dump and Restore (Native Tools)

- **Simple for Smaller Databases:** Works well for smaller databases and when downtime is not a major concern.
- **Native Tools:**
    1. MySQL: `mysqldump` for creating logical backups
    2. PostgreSQL: `pg_dump` for creating logical backups
- **Process:**
    1. **Export:** Create a dump file from your source database.
    2. **Copy:** Transfer the dump file to a machine that can access your Azure database.
    3. **Import:** Use the corresponding command-line tools (e.g., `mysql` for MySQL, `psql` for PostgreSQL) to import the dump file into your Azure database.

Example (`mysqldump`):

```
mysqldump -h <source_host> -u <source_user> -p <source_database> > dumpfile.sql
```

Example (`pg_dump`)

```
pg_dump -h <source_host> -U <source_user> <source_database> > dumpfile.sql
```

3. **Community Tools**
   - **Flexibility:** These tools often offer additional features and customization options compared to native tools.
   - **Popular Examples:**
     - **MySQL:** mydumper
     - **PostgreSQL:** pgloader

Migration Considerations

- **Database Size:** Large databases might require longer migration times and careful planning to minimize downtime.
- **Schema Compatibility:** Ensure compatibility between your source and target database versions and configurations.
- **Data Validation:** After migration, thoroughly validate your data to ensure accuracy and completeness.
- **Network Bandwidth:** Consider the available network bandwidth for transferring large dump files.
- **Downtime:** Plan for downtime if your migration method requires it.

Recommendation

- For complex migrations or minimal downtime, Azure Database Migration Service (DMS) is a reliable choice.
- For smaller databases or when downtime is acceptable, the dump and restore method using native or community tools can be sufficient.
- Choose the method that best aligns with your specific requirements, resources, and downtime constraints.

Managing and Monitoring Your Database

Let's delve into how you can effectively manage and monitor your Azure Database for MySQL/PostgreSQL to ensure optimal performance, reliability, and security:

Monitoring Metrics

- **Azure Monitor:** The primary tool for monitoring Azure resources. It provides insights into key metrics like:
  - **CPU utilization:** Track how much processing power your database is using.
  - **Memory usage:** Monitor how much memory your database is consuming.
  - **Storage consumption:** Keep an eye on your database's storage usage.
  - **Connection count:** See how many active connections your database has.
  - **Query performance:** Analyze query execution times to identify slow queries.
- **Set Alerts:** Define alert rules in Azure Monitor to get notified when specific metrics exceed predefined thresholds. This allows you to react promptly to potential issues.
- **Diagnostic Settings:** Configure diagnostic settings to send logs to Azure Monitor Logs, a storage account, or an event hub for further analysis and retention.

Scaling Resources

- **Vertical Scaling:** Increase or decrease the compute tier, vCores, and storage size to match your workload requirements.
- **Autoscaling:** Enable autoscaling to automatically adjust storage based on usage patterns, ensuring you have enough space without manual intervention.
- **Read Replicas (MySQL/PostgreSQL):** Create read replicas for read-heavy workloads, offloading read traffic from the primary server and improving performance.

Backups and Restores

- **Automated Backups:** Azure automatically creates full backups of your database and stores them for a specified retention period (7-35 days).
- **Point-in-Time Restore (PITR):** You can restore your database to any point within the backup retention period. This is invaluable for recovering from accidental data deletion or corruption.
- **Long-term Retention (LTR):** For regulatory or compliance requirements, you can configure LTR to store backups for up to 10 years.

Security

- **Firewall Rules:**
  - **Server-level Firewall:** Control access to your database server at the server level by specifying IP addresses or address ranges that are allowed to connect.
  - **Database-level Firewall:** For finer-grained control, set up firewall rules at the database level to restrict access to specific databases within the server.
- **Access Control:**
  - **Server Admin Login:** Ensure you use a strong password for the server admin login and consider enabling multi-factor authentication (MFA) for added security.
  - **Database Users:** Create users with appropriate permissions for specific databases and avoid using the server admin login for routine tasks.
- **Advanced Threat Protection:** Enable this feature to detect and alert you to potential security threats, such as SQL injection attacks.
- **Data Encryption:**
  - **Encryption at Rest:** Azure automatically encrypts your data at rest using Transparent Data Encryption (TDE).
  - **Encryption in Transit:** Enforce SSL/TLS connections for data in transit between your applications and the database.

Additional Tips

- **Query Performance Insights:** Use this feature in Azure Monitor to identify the top resource-consuming queries and optimize them for better performance.
- **Azure Advisor:** Leverage Azure Advisor for personalized recommendations on optimizing your database configuration and improving security.
- **Regularly Update:** Keep your database server and client tools updated with the latest patches and security fixes.

By proactively monitoring your database, scaling resources as needed, managing backups, and implementing robust security practices, you can ensure that your Azure Database for MySQL/PostgreSQL remains healthy, performant, and secure.

Tips and Best Practices

Here are some practical tips and best practices for working with Azure Database for MySQL/PostgreSQL, along with explanations:

Choosing the Right Service Tier

Azure offers various tiers for both MySQL and PostgreSQL, each tailored to different workloads:

- **Basic:** Ideal for development, testing, or small-scale applications with light workloads and predictable usage patterns.
- **General Purpose:** A good balance of compute, memory, and storage, suitable for most production workloads. Offers various options for scaling compute and storage independently.

- **Memory Optimized:** Best suited for high-performance transactional or analytical workloads that require fast response times and high throughput.

Consider your workload characteristics (read/write intensity, concurrency, storage needs) and your budget to choose the most suitable tier. You can easily scale up or down later if your requirements change.

Optimizing Queries

Efficient queries are crucial for database performance. Here's how to optimize them:

- **Indexing:** Create indexes on columns frequently used in WHERE, JOIN, ORDER BY, and GROUP BY clauses. Use EXPLAIN or EXPLAIN ANALYZE to identify potential missing indexes.
- **Query Hints:** Use hints to guide the query optimizer towards better execution plans.
- **Batching:** Group multiple operations into a single request to reduce network round trips.
- **Avoid N+1 Queries:** Fetch related data in a single query using JOIN instead of multiple individual queries.
- **Monitor Slow Queries:** Use the slow query log to identify queries that take longer than expected.
- **Use Parameterized Queries:** Prevent SQL injection attacks and improve performance by reusing execution plans.

Connection Pooling

Creating a new database connection for each request can be expensive. **Use connection pooling to reuse existing connections, reducing the overhead of establishing new ones.** Many programming languages and frameworks offer built-in connection pooling mechanisms or libraries.

Security Best Practices

- **Firewall Rules:** Configure firewall rules to restrict access to your database only from trusted sources (e.g., your application servers).
- **Strong Passwords:** Use complex passwords for database users and regularly change them.
- **Regular Updates:** Apply the latest security patches and updates for both the database server and the underlying operating system.
- **Least Privilege:** Grant users only the minimum permissions needed to perform their tasks.
- **Encryption:** Use SSL/TLS encryption for client-server communication.

High Availability

Azure Database for MySQL/PostgreSQL provides several options for high availability:

- **Read Replicas:** Offload read traffic from the primary server to replicas. Useful for scaling reads and providing some level of failover.
- **Failover Groups:** Automatically fail over to a standby server in another region in case of an outage. Offers higher availability than read replicas.

Additional Tips

- **Monitoring:** Use Azure Monitor to track database performance metrics and set up alerts for potential issues.
- **Backups:** Regularly back up your database to protect against data loss. Azure Database automatically creates backups, but you can also create manual backups.
- **Cost Optimization:** Right-size your database instance, take advantage of reserved capacity, and consider using burstable instances for unpredictable workloads.

Chapter Summary

Azure offers fully managed database services for MySQL and PostgreSQL, catering to developers who prefer these popular open-source relational databases.

Azure Database for MySQL/PostgreSQL Key Benefits:

- **Fully Managed:** Microsoft handles infrastructure management, backups, updates, and security, allowing developers to focus on application development.
- **High Availability:** Built-in replication and automatic failover ensure high availability and business continuity.
- **Scalability:** Easily scale compute and storage resources to meet application demands.
- **Security:** Robust security features, including encryption, firewall protection, and threat detection, safeguard data.
- **Cost-Effectiveness:** Pay-as-you-go pricing and options to optimize costs based on usage patterns.
- **Performance:** Intelligent performance recommendations and tuning options help optimize database performance.

Deployment Options:

- **Single Server:** Ideal for smaller applications or development/testing environments.
- **Flexible Server:** Provides more control and customization options, including custom maintenance windows and zone-redundant high availability.

Choosing the Right Option:

The choice between MySQL and PostgreSQL depends on specific application requirements and developer preferences. MySQL is known for its ease of use and speed, while PostgreSQL offers advanced features and extensibility.

Additional Considerations:

- **Migration:** Azure provides tools and services to simplify migrating existing MySQL or PostgreSQL databases to the cloud.
- **Integration:** Azure Database for MySQL/PostgreSQL seamlessly integrates with other Azure services, such as Azure App Service and Azure Functions.

Azure's open-source database services empower developers to leverage familiar tools and technologies while benefiting from the scalability, reliability, and security of the cloud. Whether you're building a small web application or a large-scale enterprise system, Azure Database for MySQL/PostgreSQL offers a compelling solution.

Section 7:
Azure Identity and Security

Azure Active Directory (AAD): Managing Identities and Access

Outline

- Overview of Azure Active Directory
- Key AAD Concepts and Components
- Managing Users and Groups in AAD
- Implementing Single Sign-On (SSO) with AAD
- AAD Security Features
- Chapter Summary

Overview of Azure Active Directory

Azure Active Directory (AAD) is Microsoft's cloud-based identity and access management (IAM) solution. It serves as the backbone of the Microsoft Azure cloud platform and Office 365, acting as a centralized repository for managing user identities, authentication, and authorization. AAD provides a secure and efficient way to control access to various resources within the Azure cloud environment, including virtual machines, applications, and data.

Role in Identity and Access Management

1. **Centralized Identity Provider:** AAD acts as a single source of truth for user identities. It allows organizations to manage user accounts, groups, and permissions from a central location, simplifying the administration process.
2. **Authentication:** AAD authenticates users who attempt to access Azure resources. It supports various authentication methods, including passwords, multi-factor authentication (MFA), and single sign-on (SSO).
3. **Authorization:** After a user is authenticated, AAD determines what resources the user is allowed to access based on their assigned roles and permissions.
4. **Access Control:** AAD enforces access control policies to ensure that only authorized users can access specific resources. This helps prevent unauthorized access and data breaches.

Benefits of using AAD

1. **Improved Security:** AAD provides robust security features like MFA, Conditional Access, and Identity Protection to safeguard user identities and prevent unauthorized access.
2. **Simplified Access Management:** With AAD, administrators can easily manage user access to Azure resources from a central location, reducing the complexity of managing multiple accounts and passwords.
3. **Enhanced Productivity:** Single sign-on (SSO) enables users to access multiple Azure resources and applications with a single set of credentials, improving productivity and reducing frustration caused by multiple logins.

4. **Hybrid Identity:** AAD supports hybrid identity scenarios, allowing organizations to extend their on-premises Active Directory to the Azure cloud, providing a seamless identity experience for users.
5. **Scalability:** AAD is a cloud-based solution, which means it can easily scale to meet the growing needs of an organization.

How AAD acts as a Centralized Identity Provider

AAD acts as a centralized identity provider by storing user identities and their associated attributes in a secure directory. When a user attempts to access an Azure resource, the following happens:

1. The user provides their credentials (username and password) to AAD.
2. AAD verifies the credentials against the stored user data.
3. If the credentials are valid, AAD authenticates the user and issues a security token.
4. The user presents the security token to the Azure resource they want to access.
5. The Azure resource validates the security token and, based on the user's assigned roles and permissions in AAD, grants or denies access to the resource.

In summary, Azure Active Directory is a crucial component of the Azure cloud environment, providing a comprehensive and secure identity and access management solution. By centralizing identity management, AAD simplifies administration, enhances security, and improves user productivity.

Key AAD Concepts and Components

Let's dive into the core concepts and components of Azure Active Directory (AAD):

Azure Tenants

- An Azure tenant is a dedicated and isolated instance of Azure AD for your organization. Think of it as your organization's private space within the Azure cloud.
- Each tenant has its own set of users, groups, applications, and policies, creating a secure boundary for managing identities and access.
- Organizations typically have one Azure tenant, but there can be scenarios where multiple tenants are used for specific purposes.

Identities in Azure AD

- **Users:** These represent individual people within your organization (employees, partners, customers). Each user has a unique username and password (or other authentication method) to access Azure AD-connected resources.
- **Groups:** Collections of users that simplify the management of permissions. You assign permissions to a group, and all members of that group inherit those permissions.
- **Service Principals:** These are identities representing applications or services that need to access resources in Azure AD. They are often used for automation and integration scenarios.

Authentication Methods

Azure AD supports a variety of authentication methods to verify the identity of users and service principals:

- **Password-based Authentication:** The traditional username and password approach.
- **Multi-Factor Authentication (MFA):** Adds an extra layer of security by requiring a second verification factor, such as a code sent to a mobile device or a fingerprint scan.
- **Federated Identity:** Allows users to authenticate using their credentials from another identity provider (e.g., their corporate Active Directory) through protocols like SAML or WS-Federation.

- **Passwordless Authentication:** Modern methods that eliminate the need for passwords, such as biometrics (fingerprint, facial recognition) or security keys.

Azure AD Connect

Azure AD Connect is a tool that enables seamless synchronization between your on-premises Active Directory (AD) and Azure AD. It does the following:

- **Password Hash Synchronization (PHS):** Securely synchronizes password hashes from your on-premises AD to Azure AD, allowing users to use the same password for both environments.
- **Pass-through Authentication (PTA):** Validates user sign-ins against your on-premises AD in real-time, ensuring that password policies and security measures are enforced.
- **Federation:** Enables single sign-on (SSO) across on-premises and cloud resources by using AD FS (Active Directory Federation Services) or other federation providers.

Key Takeaways

- Azure AD is the central identity and access management system for Microsoft cloud services and many other applications.
- Understanding tenants, identities, authentication methods, and the role of Azure AD Connect is crucial for effectively managing access to your organization's resources in the cloud.

Managing Users and Groups in AAD

Let's break down how to manage users and groups effectively in Azure Active Directory (AAD):

Managing Users in AAD

1. **Create User Accounts:**
    - **Azure portal:** Go to Azure Active Directory > Users > New user. Fill in the required details (name, username, email) and choose a user type (see below).
    - **PowerShell:** Use the `New-AzureADUser` cmdlet with appropriate parameters.
2. **Modify User Accounts:**
    - **Azure portal:** Go to Azure Active Directory > Users, select the user, and click "Edit" to update details like job title, department, or contact information.
    - **PowerShell:** Use the `Set-AzureADUser` cmdlet to modify user attributes.
3. **Delete User Accounts:**
    - **Azure portal:** Select the user and click "Delete."
    - **PowerShell:** Use the `Remove-AzureADUser` cmdlet.

Types of User Accounts

- **Cloud-Only Users:** Accounts created and managed entirely within Azure AD. They don't have a corresponding account in your on-premises Active Directory.
- **Hybrid Users:** Accounts synchronized from your on-premises Active Directory to Azure AD. They exist in both environments, and changes made in one environment are typically synchronized to the other.

Managing Groups in AAD

1. **Create Groups:**
    - **Azure portal:** Go to Azure Active Directory > Groups > New group. Choose a group type (see below) and provide a name and description.
    - **PowerShell:** Use the `New-AzureADGroup` cmdlet.
2. **Modify Groups:**

- **Azure portal:** Select the group and click "Edit" to update the name, description, or other properties.
- **PowerShell:** Use the `Set-AzureADGroup` cmdlet.
3. **Delete Groups:**
   - **Azure portal:** Select the group and click "Delete."
   - **PowerShell:** Use the `Remove-AzureADGroup` cmdlet.

Types of Groups

- **Security Groups:** Used for managing access to resources. You assign permissions to the group, and members automatically inherit those permissions.
- **Microsoft 365 Groups:** Provide collaboration features like shared mailboxes, calendars, SharePoint sites, and Teams. They also have a security group aspect for managing access to the group's resources.

Assigning Users to Groups and Managing Memberships

- **Azure portal:**
  - Go to Azure Active Directory > Groups, select the group, and click "Members" to add or remove users.
  - You can also add users to groups directly from the user's profile page.
- **PowerShell:**
  - Use the `Add-AzureADGroupMember` and `Remove-AzureADGroupMember` cmdlets.

Important Considerations:

- **Delegation:** Assign appropriate administrative roles to allow others to manage users and groups without granting them full global administrator privileges.
- **Dynamic Groups:** Consider using dynamic groups that automatically add and remove members based on user attributes (e.g., department, job title). This can simplify management.
- **Azure AD Premium:** Some advanced group management features, like dynamic groups based on complex queries, may require an Azure AD Premium license.

Implementing Single Sign-On (SSO) with AAD

Let's dive into the world of Single Sign-On (SSO) and how Azure Active Directory (AAD) empowers it:

What is Single Sign-On (SSO)?

SSO is an authentication mechanism that allows users to access multiple applications or resources with just one set of credentials. Instead of remembering separate usernames and passwords for every application, users sign in once and gain seamless access to everything they're authorized to use.

Benefits of SSO

- **Improved User Experience:** Eliminates the frustration of remembering multiple credentials, leading to increased productivity.
- **Enhanced Security:** Reduces the risk of password fatigue and reuse, as users only need to remember one strong password.
- **Streamlined IT Management:** Centralizes authentication, simplifying user provisioning and deprovisioning processes.

How AAD Enables SSO

Azure AD acts as the central identity provider (IdP) for SSO. When a user attempts to access an application or resource, AAD verifies their credentials and, if successful, issues a token that grants them access. The application or resource trusts AAD and accepts the token as proof of the user's identity.

SSO Protocols Supported by AAD

AAD supports several industry-standard SSO protocols:

- **SAML (Security Assertion Markup Language):** Widely used for web-based applications. It relies on exchanging XML-based assertions between the IdP (AAD) and the service provider (the application).
- **WS-Federation:** Similar to SAML, but older and less flexible. It's also based on XML-based assertions.
- **OpenID Connect (OIDC):** A modern and simpler protocol built on top of the OAuth 2.0 authorization framework. It's often used for mobile and web applications.

Configuring SSO for Common Applications

Microsoft 365:

1. **Azure portal:** Go to Azure Active Directory > Enterprise applications > All applications.
2. Search for "Office 365" and select it.
3. Go to the "Single sign-on" tab and choose "Federated" or "Password-based" depending on your requirements.
4. Follow the instructions to configure SAML or password-based SSO.

Salesforce:

1. **Azure portal:** Go to Azure Active Directory > Enterprise applications > All applications.
2. Search for "Salesforce" and select it.
3. Go to the "Single sign-on" tab and choose "SAML."
4. Follow the instructions to configure SAML-based SSO, which involves exchanging metadata between AAD and Salesforce.

Important Considerations:

- **Application Support:** Not all applications support all SSO protocols. Check the application's documentation to determine which protocols it supports.
- **Azure AD Premium:** Some advanced SSO features, like conditional access and risk-based authentication, may require an Azure AD Premium license.
- **Hybrid Environments:** If you have an on-premises Active Directory, you'll need to use Azure AD Connect to synchronize identities and enable SSO for hybrid applications.

AAD Security Features

Let's delve into the robust security features offered by Azure Active Directory (AAD) to protect your organization's identities and resources:

Multi-Factor Authentication (MFA)

MFA adds an extra layer of security beyond just a username and password. It requires users to provide a second verification factor, such as:

- **A code from a mobile app:** Microsoft Authenticator or other authenticator apps.
- **A text message or phone call:** A verification code sent to the user's phone.
- **Biometrics:** Fingerprint or facial recognition.

- **Hardware token:** A physical device that generates codes.

MFA significantly reduces the risk of unauthorized access even if a password is compromised.

Conditional Access Policies

Conditional Access allows you to create granular access policies based on various conditions, including:

- **User or group membership:** Only allow access to specific users or groups.
- **Location:** Restrict access from certain locations or countries.
- **Device platform:** Only allow access from trusted devices or specific operating systems.
- **Sign-in risk:** Block or require additional authentication for suspicious sign-in attempts.

This enables you to tailor security measures to the specific context of each access request.

Identity Protection

AAD Identity Protection uses machine learning algorithms to detect potential identity threats like:

- **Risky sign-ins:** Unusual sign-in locations, times, or methods.
- **Leaked credentials:** Usernames and passwords found in public breaches.
- **Compromised identities:** Accounts exhibiting suspicious activity.

You can configure automated responses to these threats, such as requiring MFA or blocking access.

Monitoring and Auditing

- **Azure Monitor:** Integrates with AAD to collect logs and provide insights into sign-in activities, usage patterns, and potential security issues.
- **Azure Sentinel:** A cloud-native SIEM (Security Information and Event Management) solution that can analyze AAD logs to detect threats and anomalies.
- **Audit Logs:** AAD keeps detailed records of all authentication events and configuration changes, allowing you to track who accessed what and when.

Azure AD Privileged Identity Management (PIM)

PIM helps you manage and protect privileged accounts (e.g., global administrators) by:

- **Just-in-Time (JIT) access:** Granting privileged access only when needed and for a limited time.
- **Approval workflows:** Requiring approval before granting privileged access.
- **MFA enforcement:** Mandating MFA for privileged accounts.
- **Auditing and alerts:** Tracking privileged access and notifying you of suspicious activity.

Regular Review and Updates

AAD security features are constantly evolving. It's crucial to:

- **Review security settings:** Periodically assess your policies and configurations to ensure they align with your security requirements.
- **Stay informed:** Keep up with the latest updates and best practices from Microsoft.
- **Conduct security audits:** Regularly perform audits to identify and address any potential vulnerabilities.

Key Takeaways:

- Azure AD offers a comprehensive suite of security features to protect identities and resources.
- Leveraging MFA, conditional access, identity protection, monitoring, auditing, and PIM can significantly strengthen your security posture.

- Continuous vigilance and regular review of your AAD security settings are essential for maintaining a secure environment.

Chapter Summary

Azure Active Directory (AAD) is Microsoft's comprehensive cloud-based identity and access management (IAM) solution. It serves as the backbone for controlling who can access resources within your organization's cloud environment and beyond. This chapter explores the fundamental concepts, components, and use cases of AAD, demonstrating how it empowers organizations to manage identities securely and efficiently.

Key Concepts and Components

1. **Identity as the New Perimeter:** In the cloud-centric era, traditional network perimeters are fading. AAD shifts the focus to identity as the primary security boundary. By verifying user identities and managing their access rights, AAD ensures that only authorized individuals can interact with sensitive data and applications.
2. **Core Components of AAD:**
   - **Directory:** A central repository for storing and managing user accounts, groups, and other identity-related information.
   - **Authentication:** The process of verifying user credentials (e.g., username and password) to confirm their identity.
   - **Authorization:** The process of determining what resources and actions a user is allowed to access based on their identity and assigned permissions.
   - **Single Sign-On (SSO):** Enables users to access multiple applications with a single set of credentials, enhancing convenience and security.
3. **AAD Use Cases:**
   - **Secure Access to Cloud Resources:** AAD safeguards access to Microsoft 365, Azure services, and other cloud applications.
   - **Hybrid Identity:** Extends identity management to on-premises environments, allowing for seamless integration between cloud and on-premises directories.
   - **External Collaboration:** Enables secure collaboration with partners, customers, and suppliers by managing their access to specific resources.
   - **Conditional Access:** Implements dynamic policies that adjust access permissions based on factors like user location, device type, and risk level.

Benefits of AAD

- **Enhanced Security:** AAD provides robust authentication mechanisms (e.g., multi-factor authentication) and granular access controls to mitigate the risk of unauthorized access.
- **Improved Productivity:** SSO eliminates the need for users to remember multiple passwords, streamlining access and saving time.
- **Simplified Management:** AAD's centralized management console streamlines identity-related tasks, reducing administrative overhead.
- **Flexibility:** AAD supports a wide range of authentication protocols and integration options, accommodating diverse organizational needs.

As organizations increasingly embrace cloud technologies and hybrid work environments, AAD's role in identity and access management will become even more critical.

Azure Security Center: Protecting Your Resources

Outline

- Overview of Azure Security Center
- Key Features and Capabilities
- Setting up Azure Security Center
- Security Policies and Recommendations
- Threat Protection and Detection
- Additional Security Considerations
- Chapter Summary

Overview of Azure Security Center

Azure Security Center is a unified infrastructure security management system designed to strengthen the security posture of your entire IT environment. It serves as a centralized hub for monitoring and protecting your Azure resources, offering a holistic view of your security landscape. By providing advanced threat protection across hybrid workloads, Azure Security Center extends its protection beyond the cloud to encompass both Azure and on-premises resources, creating a comprehensive security solution.

A unified security management system, like Azure Security Center, centralizes security efforts by consolidating security monitoring, threat detection, and remediation into a single platform. This centralized approach simplifies security management, reduces complexity, and enhances visibility across your entire infrastructure. It enables you to efficiently identify vulnerabilities, respond to threats promptly, and implement security best practices consistently.

The ability to protect hybrid workloads is a crucial advantage of Azure Security Center. It bridges the gap between cloud and on-premises environments, ensuring consistent security policies and threat protection across your entire infrastructure. This unified approach simplifies security management, eliminates silos, and ensures that your resources are protected, regardless of where they reside. With Azure Security Center, you can confidently embrace hybrid cloud environments while maintaining a robust security posture.

Key Features and Capabilities

Azure Security Center empowers you with a comprehensive suite of tools and capabilities designed to safeguard your valuable Azure resources. Let's delve into some of its core features:

Continuous Security Assessment

Azure Security Center continuously monitors your Azure environment, evaluating the security configuration of your resources against industry best practices and regulatory standards. This continuous assessment helps identify potential vulnerabilities and misconfigurations, enabling you to proactively address them before they are exploited. Security Center also generates a security score, providing a visual representation of your overall security posture and highlighting areas that need improvement.

Threat Protection

Azure Security Center acts as a vigilant guardian, constantly analyzing security data from your Azure resources to detect and respond to potential threats. It leverages advanced threat intelligence, anomaly detection, and behavioral analytics to identify suspicious activities and security incidents. In the event of a threat, Security Center generates alerts and provides actionable recommendations to help you mitigate the risk and remediate the issue promptly.

Security Recommendations

Azure Security Center goes beyond identifying vulnerabilities by providing actionable security recommendations tailored to your specific environment. These recommendations are based on industry best practices, regulatory compliance requirements, and Microsoft's extensive security expertise. By implementing these recommendations, you can significantly enhance your security posture and reduce the risk of a security breach.

Regulatory Compliance

Maintaining compliance with industry regulations and standards is a critical aspect of security management. Azure Security Center simplifies this process by providing built-in compliance dashboards and reports. It assesses your environment against various regulatory frameworks, such as PCI DSS, ISO 27001, and HIPAA, and helps you identify areas where you need to take action to achieve and maintain compliance.

Vulnerability Assessment

Azure Security Center includes a powerful vulnerability assessment tool that scans your Azure virtual machines for vulnerabilities and misconfigurations. It identifies missing security patches, outdated software, and weak configurations that could be exploited by attackers. The vulnerability assessment results are presented in a prioritized list, allowing you to focus on addressing the most critical vulnerabilities first.

Just-In-Time (JIT) VM Access

Azure Security Center's JIT VM access feature significantly reduces your attack surface by restricting access to virtual machines until it's explicitly requested. This prevents attackers from exploiting open ports or weak credentials to gain unauthorized access to your VMs. JIT VM access only grants access for a limited time window, further minimizing the risk of a security breach.

Setting Up Azure Security Center

To fully utilize the robust security capabilities of Azure Security Center, you'll need to enable and configure it appropriately for your Azure environment. Follow these steps to get started:

1. **Accessing Azure Security Center:**
   - Log in to the Azure Portal.
   - In the search bar, type "Security Center" and select it from the results.
2. **Enabling Azure Security Center:**
   - In the Security Center overview page, you'll see your subscriptions listed.
   - For each subscription, you can choose between the Free or Standard tier. Click on the desired subscription to make your selection.
3. **Selecting a Pricing Tier:**
   - **Free Tier:** Provides basic security hygiene features like security assessments, security recommendations, and limited threat detection.
   - **Standard Tier:** Offers enhanced security features, including advanced threat protection, just-in-time (JIT) VM access, regulatory compliance dashboards, and more.
   - Choose the tier that best aligns with your security needs and budget.
4. **Configuring Data Collection:**
   - After selecting a tier, you'll be prompted to configure data collection.

- Security Center needs to collect security-related data from your resources to perform its assessments and threat detection.
- Choose the appropriate storage account where Security Center will store this data.
5. **Connecting On-Premises Environments (Optional):**
   - For comprehensive security, consider connecting Azure Security Center to your on-premises environment.
   - This allows Security Center to monitor and protect your on-premises servers and virtual machines alongside your Azure resources.
   - You can use Azure Arc to establish this connection, enabling centralized security management across your entire IT infrastructure.

Importance of Connecting to On-Premises Environments

Integrating Azure Security Center with your on-premises environment is crucial for several reasons:

- **Comprehensive Security:** It provides a unified view of security across your entire infrastructure, enabling you to identify and address threats in both cloud and on-premises environments.
- **Consistent Security Policies:** You can apply the same security policies and configurations to both Azure and on-premises resources, ensuring consistent security across your entire IT landscape.
- **Centralized Management:** You can manage and monitor security for all your resources from a single dashboard, simplifying security operations and reducing complexity.

By following these steps and connecting your on-premises environment, you can unlock the full potential of Azure Security Center and establish a robust security posture for your entire infrastructure.

Security Policies and Recommendations

Azure Security Center takes a proactive approach to security by continuously assessing your Azure resources against a set of predefined security policies. These policies are derived from industry best practices, regulatory compliance requirements, and Microsoft's extensive security expertise. By aligning your environment with these policies, you can significantly reduce your risk of a security breach and ensure that your resources are protected according to the highest standards.

Security Policies

Security Center's policies cover a wide range of security controls, including:

- **Identity and Access Management:** Policies related to managing user identities, access controls, and privileges.
- **Network Security:** Policies addressing network configuration, firewalls, and network security groups.
- **Data Protection:** Policies ensuring the protection of sensitive data through encryption, access controls, and backup strategies.
- **Compute Security:** Policies related to the security configuration of virtual machines, app services, and other compute resources.
- **Security Monitoring:** Policies emphasizing the importance of monitoring your environment for security threats and incidents.

Security Recommendations

Based on the security policies and the continuous assessment of your resources, Azure Security Center generates security recommendations. These recommendations are actionable insights that highlight potential vulnerabilities and misconfigurations in your environment. Each recommendation includes a detailed description of the issue, its severity, and step-by-step guidance on how to remediate it. By prioritizing and addressing these recommendations, you can proactively strengthen your security posture and reduce your risk of a security breach.

Common Security Recommendations

Here are some examples of common security recommendations that Azure Security Center might generate:

- **Enable Multi-Factor Authentication (MFA):** MFA adds an extra layer of security by requiring users to provide multiple forms of authentication, such as a password and a code sent to their phone, to access resources.
- **Apply Network Security Groups (NSGs):** NSGs act as firewalls for your virtual networks, controlling inbound and outbound traffic to and from your resources.
- **Encrypt Data at Rest:** Encrypting sensitive data ensures that even if unauthorized access occurs, the data remains unreadable and unusable.
- **Apply System Updates:** Regularly applying system updates and security patches helps protect against known vulnerabilities that could be exploited by attackers.
- **Enable Threat Detection:** Activating threat detection features like anomaly detection and behavioral analytics helps identify suspicious activities and potential threats in real time.

By diligently following these recommendations and regularly reviewing the security state of your resources, you can maintain a robust security posture and proactively protect your valuable Azure assets.

Threat Protection and Detection

Azure Security Center acts as a vigilant guardian, tirelessly monitoring your Azure environment for potential threats and security incidents. By leveraging a combination of threat intelligence, anomaly detection, and behavioral analytics, it proactively identifies and alerts you to suspicious activities, enabling you to respond swiftly and mitigate potential risks.

Threat Intelligence

Azure Security Center taps into a vast network of threat intelligence feeds that provide real-time information about emerging threats, vulnerabilities, and attack patterns. This threat intelligence is constantly updated, ensuring that Security Center stays ahead of the evolving threat landscape. By analyzing this intelligence, Security Center can detect known attack signatures, malicious IPs, and other indicators of compromise, enabling it to raise alerts and block potential threats before they can cause harm.

Anomaly Detection

In addition to threat intelligence, Azure Security Center employs sophisticated anomaly detection algorithms to identify unusual or abnormal behavior within your environment. These algorithms analyze vast amounts of data, including network traffic, system logs, and user activity, to establish baseline patterns of normal behavior. Any deviations from these baselines are flagged as potential anomalies, prompting further investigation. Anomaly detection can uncover hidden threats that may not be detected by traditional signature-based methods, providing an additional layer of protection.

Behavioral Analytics

Azure Security Center also employs behavioral analytics to identify suspicious activities based on user and entity behavior analysis (UEBA). UEBA analyzes the behaviors of users and entities within your environment, such as login patterns, access requests, and data modifications. By establishing normal behavioral profiles, UEBA can detect deviations from these profiles, such as unauthorized access attempts, data exfiltration, or privilege escalation. This helps to identify insider threats and compromised accounts, allowing you to take immediate action to mitigate the risk.

Security Alerts

Azure Security Center generates security alerts whenever it detects a potential threat or security incident. These alerts provide detailed information about the nature of the threat, the affected resources, and recommended remediation steps. Examples of security alerts that Security Center can generate include:

- **Virtual Machine Attacks:** Alerts about suspicious activities targeting your virtual machines, such as brute-force attacks, port scans, or malware infections.
- **SQL Injection Attempts:** Alerts about attempts to exploit vulnerabilities in your SQL databases, such as SQL injection attacks that could lead to data breaches.
- **Brute-Force Attacks:** Alerts about attempts to guess passwords or encryption keys through repeated trial and error.
- **Data Exfiltration:** Alerts about unauthorized attempts to transfer sensitive data out of your environment.
- **Suspicious Network Traffic:** Alerts about unusual network traffic patterns that could indicate a potential attack.

By promptly investigating and addressing these security alerts, you can effectively mitigate risks and protect your Azure resources from harm.

Additional Security Considerations

While Azure Security Center provides a robust foundation for securing your Azure environment, it's crucial to recognize that security is an ongoing process. Implementing additional security measures and adopting a defense-in-depth strategy can significantly enhance the protection of your valuable Azure resources.

Defense-in-Depth

A defense-in-depth strategy involves layering multiple security controls to create a comprehensive security system. Each layer provides an additional barrier to attackers, making it more difficult for them to compromise your resources. Key components of a defense-in-depth strategy for Azure include:

- **Network Security:** Implementing firewalls, network security groups (NSGs), and virtual networks (VNETs) to control traffic flow and protect against unauthorized access.
- **Intrusion Detection and Prevention Systems (IDPS):** Deploying IDPS solutions to monitor network traffic for suspicious activity and block potential attacks.
- **Security Information and Event Management (SIEM):** Utilizing SIEM solutions to collect and analyze security logs from various sources, providing centralized visibility and enabling faster incident response.
- **Endpoint Protection:** Implementing endpoint protection software on virtual machines and other endpoints to detect and prevent malware infections.

Regular Security Assessments

Regular security assessments are essential to identify and address potential vulnerabilities before they can be exploited. These assessments should include:

- **Vulnerability Scanning:** Regular scanning of your Azure resources for known vulnerabilities and misconfigurations.
- **Penetration Testing:** Simulated attacks to assess the effectiveness of your security controls and identify weaknesses that could be exploited by real attackers.

- **Security Audits:** Independent reviews of your security policies, procedures, and controls to ensure compliance with industry standards and best practices.

Complementary Azure Security Services

Azure offers a wide range of security services that can complement and enhance the capabilities of Azure Security Center. Some notable services include:

- **Azure Sentinel:** A cloud-native SIEM and security orchestration automated response (SOAR) solution that provides intelligent security analytics and threat hunting capabilities.
- **Azure Firewall:** A cloud-native firewall service that provides advanced network protection, including application-level filtering and intrusion prevention.
- **Azure Key Vault:** A secure cloud service for storing and managing cryptographic keys, secrets, and certificates.

By leveraging these additional security measures and services, you can create a multi-layered defense system that significantly reduces the risk of a security breach and ensures the continued protection of your Azure environment. Remember, security is an ongoing journey, and it requires constant vigilance, adaptation, and a commitment to staying ahead of evolving threats.

Chapter Summary

In this chapter, we delved into the comprehensive security capabilities of Azure Security Center, a unified infrastructure security management system designed to safeguard your Azure environment. We explored how Security Center continuously assesses the security state of your resources, providing actionable recommendations based on industry best practices and regulatory standards.

Key takeaways from this chapter include:

- The core features of Azure Security Center, such as continuous security assessment, threat protection, security recommendations, and regulatory compliance.
- How to set up and configure Azure Security Center, including choosing the appropriate pricing tier and connecting it to on-premises environments for comprehensive security.
- The importance of security policies and how Security Center generates recommendations to help you identify and address potential vulnerabilities.
- How Security Center acts as a vigilant guardian, utilizing threat intelligence, anomaly detection, and behavioral analytics to protect your resources from potential threats.
- Additional security considerations beyond Azure Security Center, emphasizing the importance of defense-in-depth strategies and regular security assessments.

By leveraging the features and recommendations of Azure Security Center, along with additional security measures, you can create a robust security posture for your Azure environment, ensuring the confidentiality, integrity, and availability of your valuable resources. Remember, security is an ongoing process that requires continuous monitoring, adaptation, and a commitment to staying ahead of evolving threats.

Azure Key Vault: Securely Managing Secrets and Keys

Outline

- What is Azure Key Vault?
- Key Vault Features and Capabilities
- Setting Up an Azure Key Vault
- Storing and Managing Secrets
- Working with Keys
- Access Policies and Security
- Best Practices for Using Azure Key Vault
- Chapter Summary

What is Azure Key Vault?

Azure Key Vault is a cloud-based service offered by Microsoft designed to securely store and manage cryptographic keys, secrets, and certificates. Think of it as a fortified safe deposit box in the cloud specifically for your sensitive information. Its primary purpose is to protect your confidential data, ensuring that only authorized users and applications can access it.

Secrets: In the context of Azure Key Vault, "secrets" refer to any piece of information that you need to keep confidential and protect from unauthorized access. Examples of secrets include:

- **Passwords:** Usernames and passwords for accessing systems and applications.
- **API Keys:** Keys used to authenticate and authorize access to APIs.
- **Certificates:** Digital certificates used for secure communication and authentication.
- **Connection Strings:** Strings that define the connection parameters for accessing databases or other services.
- **Other Sensitive Data:** Any other sensitive information that you want to keep confidential, such as encryption keys, access tokens, or configuration settings.

Benefits of Using Azure Key Vault:

Key Vault offers numerous benefits for organizations seeking to enhance their security posture:

- **Enhanced Security:** Key Vault provides robust security measures to protect your secrets and keys, including encryption at rest and in transit, access controls, and auditing capabilities.
- **Centralized Management:** You can store and manage all your secrets and keys in a single, centralized location, simplifying administration and reducing the risk of accidental exposure.
- **Simplified Access Control:** Key Vault allows you to define fine-grained access policies, specifying who can access which secrets and keys and what actions they can perform.
- **Integration with Other Azure Services:** Key Vault seamlessly integrates with other Azure services, such as Azure App Service, Azure Functions, and Azure Virtual Machines, making it easy to use your secrets and keys within your applications.
- **Reduced Risk of Accidental Leakage:** Storing secrets in Key Vault eliminates the need to hardcode them into your applications, reducing the risk of accidental exposure through source code leaks or configuration files.
- **Compliance:** Key Vault helps you meet regulatory compliance requirements by providing features such as audit logs, role-based access control (RBAC), and integration with Azure Policy.

By leveraging Azure Key Vault, you can significantly improve the security and management of your sensitive data, ensuring that it remains confidential and protected from unauthorized access.

Key Vault Features and Capabilities

Azure Key Vault offers a comprehensive suite of features designed to streamline the management of secrets and keys while ensuring the highest level of security.

Secrets Management

Azure Key Vault provides a secure and user-friendly interface for storing, retrieving, and managing secrets. Secrets can be added to Key Vault manually through the Azure portal or programmatically using the Azure SDKs or REST APIs. You can organize secrets into hierarchical structures, tag them for easy identification, and track their versions for auditing and compliance purposes. Key Vault also provides features like automatic secret rotation and expiration to further enhance security.

Key Management

Key Vault supports a wide range of cryptographic keys, including:

- **RSA Keys:** Used for encryption, decryption, signing, and verifying digital signatures.
- **Elliptic Curve Keys:** Offer similar functionality to RSA keys but with smaller key sizes and faster performance.
- **Symmetric Keys:** Used for encrypting and decrypting data using a single shared key.

You can generate new keys directly within Key Vault or import existing keys from other sources. Key Vault also allows you to control key usage, specifying whether a key can be used for encryption, decryption, signing, or other operations.

Certificate Management

Azure Key Vault simplifies the management of certificates throughout their lifecycle. You can import certificates into Key Vault from various sources, including public certificate authorities and your own internal certificate authority. Key Vault also supports automated certificate renewal, ensuring that your certificates remain valid and up-to-date. By storing certificates in Key Vault, you can easily manage their access and usage, reducing the risk of unauthorized access or misuse.

Hardware Security Modules (HSMs)

For highly sensitive keys that require the highest level of security, Azure Key Vault offers integration with Hardware Security Modules (HSMs). HSMs are specialized hardware devices that provide enhanced protection for cryptographic keys by storing them in a secure, tamper-resistant environment. Key Vault can generate keys directly within an HSM or import keys from an existing HSM. This integration allows you to leverage the security benefits of HSMs while enjoying the convenience and scalability of a cloud-based key management solution.

Setting Up an Azure Key Vault

Creating an Azure Key Vault is a straightforward process that can be completed in a few simple steps:

Step-by-Step Guide:

1. **Log in to the Azure Portal:** Start by logging in to the Azure portal using your Azure credentials.
2. **Create a New Key Vault:**
   - In the search bar, type "Key Vaults" and select it from the results.

- Click on the "+ Create" button to initiate the Key Vault creation process.
3. **Configure Basic Settings:**
    - Provide a unique name for your Key Vault.
    - Select your Azure subscription.
    - Choose an existing resource group or create a new one to organize your resources.
    - Select the region where you want to deploy your Key Vault. Consider factors like proximity to your applications and data residency requirements when making this decision.
4. **Choose a Pricing Tier:**
    - Azure Key Vault offers two pricing tiers:
        - **Standard:** Suitable for most general-purpose scenarios, providing essential features for secret and key management.
        - **Premium:** Offers additional features like hardware security module (HSM) protection for enhanced security of highly sensitive keys.
5. **Configure Access Policies:**
    - **Azure Active Directory (AAD) Authentication:** Enable AAD authentication to control access to your Key Vault based on user identities and group memberships.
    - **Access Policies:** Define granular access policies that specify which users or service principals have permission to perform specific operations on secrets and keys. For example, you can grant read access to one group of users and write access to another.
6. **Review and Create:**
    - Review your configuration settings to ensure they are correct.
    - Click on the "Create" button to deploy your Key Vault.

Additional Considerations:

- **Soft-Delete:** Enable soft-delete to protect your secrets and keys from accidental deletion. Soft-deleted items can be recovered within a specified retention period.
- **Purge Protection:** Enable purge protection along with soft-delete to provide an additional layer of protection against data loss. Purge protection prevents soft-deleted items from being permanently deleted before the retention period expires.
- **Networking:** If you need to restrict access to your Key Vault from specific networks or virtual networks, you can configure network settings accordingly.

By following these steps and carefully configuring your Key Vault settings, you can establish a secure and centralized repository for your sensitive information.

Storing and Managing Secrets

Azure Key Vault offers a straightforward and secure approach to storing and managing sensitive information (secrets) within your Azure environment. This section will guide you through the processes of adding, updating, deleting, and retrieving secrets from Key Vault.

Adding Secrets

You have multiple options to add secrets to your Azure Key Vault:

- **Azure Portal:**
    1. Navigate to your Key Vault in the Azure Portal.
    2. Select **Secrets** under the **Settings** section.
    3. Click on **Generate/Import**.
    4. Enter a name for the secret and its value.
    5. Optionally, you can set an activation date, expiration date, and tags.
    6. Click **Create** to store the secret in your Key Vault.
- **Azure CLI:** Use commands like `az keyvault secret set` to add secrets via the Azure CLI.

- **Azure PowerShell:** Use cmdlets like `Set-AzKeyVaultSecret` to add secrets via Azure PowerShell.
- **Azure SDKs:** Leverage Azure SDKs for your preferred programming language (e.g., .NET, Python, Java) to add secrets programmatically.

Updating and Deleting Secrets

Key Vault allows you to easily update existing secrets with new values. When you update a secret, a new version is created, preserving the history of changes. You can also delete secrets when they are no longer needed. Deleting a secret marks it as inactive, and it can be recovered within a certain retention period (if soft-delete is enabled).

Types of Secrets

Azure Key Vault supports various types of secrets, including:

- **Passwords:** Store usernames and passwords for authentication.
- **Connection Strings:** Store database or service connection information.
- **API Keys:** Store keys required for accessing external APIs or services.
- **Certificates:** Store public and private key pairs for secure communication.
- **Other Sensitive Data:** Store any other confidential information that needs protection.

Retrieving Secrets

To access your secrets securely, you can retrieve them programmatically from your applications using the following methods:

- **Azure SDKs:** Integrate Azure SDKs into your application code to fetch secrets directly from Key Vault. This approach allows you to manage secrets dynamically and eliminates the need to hardcode sensitive information in your application's configuration files.
- **REST APIs:** Use Key Vault's REST APIs to retrieve secrets from any application that can make HTTP requests.

Remember: When retrieving secrets programmatically, ensure that your application has the necessary permissions to access the Key Vault. You can manage access using Azure Active Directory (AAD) authentication and access policies, ensuring that only authorized entities can retrieve secrets.

By following these guidelines and utilizing the various features offered by Azure Key Vault, you can establish a robust and secure system for managing your secrets, ensuring the protection of your sensitive data and enhancing the overall security of your Azure environment.

Working with Keys

Azure Key Vault provides a secure and centralized platform for managing cryptographic keys, allowing you to perform essential cryptographic operations while ensuring the protection and integrity of your sensitive data. Let's explore the different types of keys supported by Key Vault and the processes involved in their generation, management, and usage.

Types of Keys

Key Vault supports a variety of cryptographic keys, each designed for specific use cases:

- **RSA Keys:** RSA (Rivest-Shamir-Adleman) keys are asymmetric keys that utilize two separate keys – a public key and a private key. The public key is used for encryption and verification, while the

private key is used for decryption and signing. RSA keys are widely used for secure communication, digital signatures, and key exchange.
- **Elliptic Curve Keys (ECC):** ECC keys are another type of asymmetric key that offer similar functionality to RSA keys but with smaller key sizes and faster performance. This makes them a popular choice for applications where efficiency is critical.
- **Symmetric Keys:** Symmetric keys use the same key for both encryption and decryption. They are generally faster than asymmetric keys but require secure key distribution. Key Vault supports symmetric keys for scenarios where data confidentiality is the primary concern.

Generating, Importing, and Exporting Keys

Key Vault provides multiple ways to manage your keys:

- **Generation:** You can generate new keys directly within Key Vault. Specify the desired key type, key size, and other parameters based on your security requirements.
- **Import:** If you already have existing keys, you can import them into Key Vault in various formats, such as PEM, PFX, and BYOK (Bring Your Own Key).
- **Export:** You can export keys from Key Vault in a secure format for backup or use in other systems. However, exercise caution when exporting keys, as it increases the risk of unauthorized access.

Using Keys for Cryptographic Operations

Key Vault's cryptographic capabilities allow you to perform essential operations on your data:

- **Encryption and Decryption:** You can use Key Vault keys to encrypt sensitive data, ensuring that only authorized parties with the corresponding decryption key can access it.
- **Signing and Verifying Digital Signatures:** Key Vault keys can be used to create digital signatures, which verify the authenticity and integrity of data.
- **Key Exchange:** Key Vault can facilitate secure key exchange between parties, enabling them to establish secure communication channels.
- **Other Cryptographic Operations:** Key Vault supports various other cryptographic operations, such as key wrapping and unwrapping, which are used to protect keys during transmission or storage.

By utilizing the diverse range of key types and cryptographic capabilities offered by Azure Key Vault, you can establish a robust and flexible key management system that caters to your specific security needs. Whether it's protecting sensitive data, verifying digital signatures, or establishing secure communication channels, Key Vault empowers you to seamlessly integrate cryptographic operations into your applications and processes.

Access Policies and Security

Azure Key Vault prioritizes the security of your secrets and keys by implementing robust access controls and encryption mechanisms. It leverages Azure Active Directory (AAD) for authentication and authorization, ensuring that only authorized entities can access and manage your sensitive data.

Configuring Access Policies

Access policies in Key Vault define granular permissions for users, groups, or service principals. These policies determine who can perform specific operations on secrets, keys, and certificates within a Key Vault. You can grant permissions such as:

- **Get:** Retrieve the value of a secret or key.
- **List:** List secrets or keys.
- **Set:** Create or update a secret or key.

- **Delete:** Delete a secret or key.
- **Other Permissions:** Depending on the resource type (secret, key, or certificate), there are other specific permissions available, like encrypt, decrypt, sign, verify, get certificate, and more.

To configure access policies, follow these steps:

1. Navigate to your Key Vault in the Azure Portal.
2. Select **Access Policies** under the **Settings** section.
3. Click on **Add Access Policy**.
4. Select the principal (user, group, or service principal) you want to grant access to.
5. Choose the specific permissions you want to grant.
6. Click **Add** to save the access policy.

Remember that you can have multiple access policies for a single Key Vault, allowing you to define fine-grained permissions for different entities.

Azure Active Directory (AAD) Authentication

Azure Key Vault integrates with Azure Active Directory (AAD) for authentication and authorization. This means that users and applications must authenticate with AAD before they can access Key Vault resources. AAD provides a centralized identity management system, making it easier to manage access across multiple Azure services. You can use AAD to control who can create and manage Key Vaults, as well as who can access secrets and keys within a vault.

Encryption at Rest and in Transit

Azure Key Vault encrypts your secrets and keys at rest, meaning that the data is encrypted when it's stored in the Key Vault. This encryption is performed using Microsoft-managed keys by default, but you can also choose to use your own keys for additional control. Key Vault also encrypts your data in transit, ensuring that it's protected while being transmitted between your application and the Key Vault service.

By combining robust access controls with encryption at rest and in transit, Azure Key Vault provides a secure environment for storing and managing your sensitive information, giving you confidence that your data is protected from unauthorized access.

Best Practices for Using Azure Key Vault

To maximize the security and effectiveness of Azure Key Vault, consider the following best practices:

1. **Store All Sensitive Information in Key Vault:** Make Key Vault your central repository for all confidential data, including passwords, API keys, certificates, connection strings, and any other sensitive information. Avoid hardcoding secrets into your application code or configuration files.
2. **Rotate Secrets and Keys Regularly:** Establish a regular rotation schedule for your secrets and keys. This minimizes the risk of unauthorized access if a secret or key is compromised. Key Vault offers features like automatic key rotation and scheduled secret rotation to simplify this process.
3. **Enforce Least Privilege Access:** Utilize Azure Active Directory (AAD) authentication and access policies to grant permissions on a need-to-know basis. Assign the minimum necessary permissions to users, groups, or service principals. Regularly review and update access policies to ensure they remain aligned with your organization's security requirements.
4. **Enable Logging and Monitoring:** Key Vault provides comprehensive logging and monitoring capabilities. Enable logging to track access to your secrets and keys, detect anomalies, and gain insights into how your Key Vault is being used. Integrate Key Vault logs with Azure Monitor or a SIEM solution for centralized monitoring and analysis.
5. **Integrate with Other Azure Services:** Key Vault seamlessly integrates with many other Azure services. Leverage this integration to streamline the management of secrets and keys in your

applications. For example, you can use Key Vault references in your Azure App Service or Azure Functions configuration to dynamically retrieve secrets without exposing them directly in your code.
6. **Use Managed Identities:** Managed identities are a secure and convenient way for Azure resources to authenticate to Key Vault. By assigning managed identities to your virtual machines, app services, or functions, you can eliminate the need to manage credentials for these resources.
7. **Soft-Delete and Purge Protection:** Enable soft-delete to protect against accidental deletion of secrets and keys. Soft-deleted items can be recovered within a specified retention period. Additionally, enable purge protection to prevent soft-deleted items from being permanently deleted before the retention period expires.
8. **HSM-Backed Keys:** For highly sensitive keys, consider using HSM-backed keys for enhanced security. These keys are generated and stored within a Hardware Security Module (HSM), providing an additional layer of protection against unauthorized access and tampering.
9. **Regular Backups:** Even with soft-delete and purge protection, it's still essential to regularly back up your Key Vault data. This ensures that you can recover your secrets and keys in the event of a catastrophic failure or accidental deletion.

By adhering to these best practices and utilizing the full range of features offered by Azure Key Vault, you can significantly enhance the security of your sensitive data and ensure its confidentiality, integrity, and availability. Remember, security is an ongoing effort, and it requires constant vigilance and adaptation to protect your valuable assets.

Chapter Summary

In this chapter, we explored the intricacies of Azure Key Vault, Microsoft's cloud-based solution for the secure storage and management of cryptographic keys, secrets, and certificates. We delved into its various features, including the streamlined management of secrets, versatile key management capabilities, and robust certificate handling.

Key takeaways from this chapter include:

- Understanding how Azure Key Vault acts as a secure repository for protecting sensitive information like passwords, API keys, and certificates.
- Recognizing the diverse range of key types supported by Key Vault, including RSA, elliptic curve, and symmetric keys, and how to generate, import, and export them.
- Learning how to create and configure an Azure Key Vault instance, choosing the appropriate pricing tier and setting access policies for enhanced security.
- Grasping the concept of access policies and the role of Azure Active Directory (AAD) in controlling access to your Key Vault.
- Understanding the encryption mechanisms employed by Key Vault to protect your secrets and keys both at rest and during transmission.
- Discovering best practices for using Key Vault effectively, including storing all sensitive information, rotating secrets and keys regularly, and integrating with other Azure services for seamless operation.

By leveraging Azure Key Vault and adhering to these best practices, you can significantly enhance the security posture of your Azure environment. You can rest assured that your sensitive information is safeguarded, access is controlled, and your applications can securely utilize cryptographic operations. Embracing Key Vault empowers you to confidently manage your secrets and keys, providing a solid foundation for a more secure and resilient cloud infrastructure.

Section 8:
Monitoring and Management

Azure Monitor: Gaining Insights into Your Resources

Outline

- Overview of Azure Monitor
- Azure Monitor Components
- Collecting Data with Azure Monitor
- Analyzing Data with Azure Monitor
- Visualizing Data with Azure Monitor
- Alerting and Automation with Azure Monitor
- Chapter Summary

Overview of Azure Monitor

Azure Monitor is a robust and scalable cloud-based monitoring service offered by Microsoft Azure. It serves as the central hub for collecting, analyzing, and acting upon telemetry data generated by your Azure resources and applications. Azure Monitor empowers you with a unified view of your entire environment, whether it's residing in the cloud, on-premises, or even in hybrid configurations.

Azure Monitor's Role in the Monitoring Ecosystem

In the vast Azure ecosystem, Azure Monitor plays a pivotal role as the backbone of observability. It acts as the central nervous system, collecting a wealth of data from various sources, including:

- **Azure resources:** Azure Monitor automatically gathers platform metrics, logs, and diagnostic data from a wide array of Azure services like virtual machines, storage accounts, databases, and app services.
- **Custom applications:** You can instrument your custom applications to send logs and metrics directly to Azure Monitor, providing deeper insights into their performance and behavior.
- **On-premises environments:** Azure Monitor can extend its reach beyond the cloud, collecting data from on-premises servers, applications, and devices through agents and gateways.

Holistic View through Data Collection

The strength of Azure Monitor lies in its ability to collect data from diverse sources, providing a holistic view of your environment. This consolidated data allows you to:

- **Correlate events:** Identify relationships between different events and activities across your entire infrastructure.
- **Identify root causes:** Quickly pinpoint the underlying causes of performance issues or failures.
- **Monitor trends:** Track long-term trends in resource utilization, application performance, and user behavior.

- **Detect anomalies:** Identify unusual patterns or deviations from normal behavior that may indicate potential problems.

Benefits of Using Azure Monitor

Azure Monitor offers a myriad of benefits that empower you to proactively manage and optimize your Azure environment:

- **Proactive Issue Identification:** By continuously monitoring your resources, Azure Monitor can detect issues before they impact your users or business operations, allowing you to take preemptive action.
- **Performance Optimization:** Azure Monitor provides insights into the performance of your applications and infrastructure, helping you identify bottlenecks and optimize resource utilization.
- **Improved Operational Efficiency:** Automated alerting and actionable insights streamline incident response, reducing downtime and minimizing the impact of service disruptions.
- **Cost Optimization:** Azure Monitor helps you understand your resource usage patterns, enabling you to optimize costs by identifying underutilized resources or adjusting your resource allocation.
- **Compliance:** Azure Monitor helps you meet regulatory and compliance requirements by providing audit trails, access controls, and reporting capabilities.

By leveraging the capabilities of Azure Monitor, you can gain a deeper understanding of your Azure environment, make informed decisions, and proactively address issues before they escalate, ensuring the optimal performance, availability, and security of your applications and resources.

Azure Monitor Components

Azure Monitor is comprised of several integrated components that work harmoniously to provide a comprehensive monitoring solution. Each component serves a distinct purpose in the data collection, storage, analysis, and visualization process.

Azure Monitor Metrics

Metrics are fundamental building blocks of Azure Monitor, representing numerical values that are collected at regular intervals. These metrics offer insights into the performance, health, and utilization of your Azure resources. For instance, you can track metrics like CPU usage, memory consumption, network bandwidth, and disk I/O operations. Azure Monitor automatically collects platform metrics from most Azure resources, and you can also define custom metrics to track specific aspects of your applications or services.

Azure Monitor Logs

Logs are text records that capture events and activities generated by your Azure resources and applications. They provide detailed information about system behavior, errors, warnings, and other operational data. Azure Monitor can collect logs from various sources, including Azure platform logs, application logs, and custom logs. These logs can be ingested into a Log Analytics workspace for further analysis and correlation.

Log Analytics Workspaces

Log Analytics workspaces serve as centralized repositories for storing and analyzing log data from various sources, including Azure Monitor logs and custom logs. Within a workspace, you can use the powerful Kusto Query Language (KQL) to perform complex queries, search for specific events, and gain valuable insights from your log data. Workspaces also provide features like alerts, dashboards, and visualizations to help you monitor and troubleshoot your environment effectively.

Application Insights

Application Insights is a feature of Azure Monitor that focuses on monitoring the performance and usage of your web applications. It provides real-time insights into application availability, responsiveness, and user behavior. Application Insights can automatically detect and diagnose performance issues, track user flows, and help you understand how your application is being used. It also integrates with development tools like Visual Studio and Visual Studio Code, making it easy to monitor your applications throughout the development lifecycle.

Collaboration of Components

These components of Azure Monitor work together seamlessly to provide a comprehensive monitoring solution. Metrics provide a high-level overview of resource performance, while logs offer detailed insights into events and activities. Log Analytics workspaces centralize log data and enable powerful analysis, and Application Insights specializes in monitoring web applications. By combining these capabilities, Azure Monitor gives you a holistic view of your environment and helps you identify and resolve issues quickly, ensuring the optimal performance and reliability of your applications and services.

Collecting Data with Azure Monitor

Azure Monitor employs a multi-faceted approach to data collection, enabling you to gain insights from a wide range of sources within your environment. This flexibility ensures that you can monitor the health, performance, and security of your entire infrastructure, whether it's residing in the cloud, on-premises, or a combination of both.

Azure Resources

For most Azure resources, such as virtual machines, storage accounts, databases, and app services, Azure Monitor automatically collects platform metrics and logs. This automatic collection simplifies the monitoring process, as you don't need to manually configure anything to start gathering essential data. The platform metrics cover various aspects of resource performance, such as CPU usage, memory consumption, disk I/O, and network traffic. Azure platform logs capture system events, diagnostic information, and operational data, providing valuable insights into the behavior of your Azure resources.

Custom Sources

In addition to Azure platform data, Azure Monitor enables you to collect logs and metrics from custom sources. This flexibility allows you to monitor a wider range of assets, including:

- **On-premises servers and applications:** By installing the Azure Monitor agent (formerly known as Log Analytics agent) on your on-premises servers, you can collect logs and performance data from them and send it to Azure Monitor for analysis.
- **Third-party applications:** Many third-party applications, such as firewalls, intrusion detection systems, and web servers, can be configured to send their logs to Azure Monitor.
- **Custom applications:** You can instrument your own applications to emit custom logs and metrics, providing deeper visibility into their behavior and performance.

Agents and Extensions

Azure Monitor utilizes agents and extensions to collect data from various resources, including virtual machines and other Azure services.

- **Azure Monitor Agent:** This agent is designed to collect logs and performance data from both Windows and Linux virtual machines. It can be configured to collect specific logs and metrics based on your monitoring requirements.

- **Diagnostic Extensions:** Certain Azure services, such as Azure SQL Database and Azure App Service, offer diagnostic extensions that can be enabled to collect additional logs and metrics specific to those services.
- **Data Collection Rules (DCRs):** DCRs allow you to configure how data is collected from your resources and sent to Azure Monitor. They define which logs and metrics are collected, how often they are collected, and where they are sent (e.g., Log Analytics workspace).

By leveraging these various data collection mechanisms, Azure Monitor ensures that you have a comprehensive view of your environment, allowing you to proactively identify and address issues, optimize performance, and make informed decisions based on real-time data.

Analyzing Data with Azure Monitor

Azure Monitor doesn't just collect data; it empowers you with robust tools and capabilities to dissect and understand the wealth of information gathered from your environment. These tools enable you to transform raw data into actionable insights, facilitating proactive decision-making and effective troubleshooting.

Metrics Explorer

Metrics Explorer is a versatile tool within Azure Monitor that allows you to visualize and analyze metric data in real time. It offers an intuitive interface where you can plot charts, apply filters, and compare multiple metrics across different time ranges. With Metrics Explorer, you can easily identify trends, detect anomalies, and pinpoint performance bottlenecks. For example, you can use it to monitor CPU utilization, memory consumption, network traffic, and other key performance indicators for your Azure resources.

Log Analytics

Log Analytics is a powerful tool that enables you to analyze the vast amounts of log data collected by Azure Monitor. It uses the Kusto Query Language (KQL), a rich and expressive query language designed for analyzing structured and semi-structured data. With KQL, you can write complex queries to search for specific events, correlate data from multiple sources, and gain deep insights into the behavior of your applications and infrastructure. Log Analytics also offers a wide range of built-in functions and operators, making it easy to perform calculations, aggregations, and transformations on your log data.

Insights

Insights in Azure Monitor are pre-built dashboards and workbooks that provide in-depth analysis of specific scenarios or areas of interest. These insights leverage the power of Metrics Explorer and Log Analytics to deliver curated visualizations and reports that focus on specific performance metrics, operational events, or security findings. Azure Monitor offers a growing collection of insights that cover a wide range of use cases, such as:

- **VM Insights:** Provides comprehensive monitoring of virtual machine performance, including CPU, memory, disk, and network metrics.
- **Container Insights:** Monitors the health and performance of containerized applications running on Azure Kubernetes Service (AKS) or other container orchestrators.
- **Application Insights:** Delivers insights into the performance and usage of your web applications, including response times, failure rates, and user behavior.
- **Network Insights:** Monitors the health and performance of your Azure virtual networks, including traffic flow, latency, and connectivity issues.

These insights are designed to be easily customizable, allowing you to tailor them to your specific monitoring requirements.

By leveraging the combined capabilities of Metrics Explorer, Log Analytics, and Insights, you can unlock the full potential of Azure Monitor and transform your monitoring data into actionable insights. Whether you need to troubleshoot performance issues, detect security threats, or optimize resource utilization, Azure Monitor provides the tools you need to gain a deep understanding of your Azure environment and make informed decisions.

Visualizing Data with Azure Monitor

Azure Monitor offers a variety of visualization tools to transform your raw data into meaningful and actionable insights. These tools cater to different needs, from creating quick dashboards for real-time monitoring to generating in-depth reports for analysis and decision-making.

Azure Portal Dashboards

Azure Portal Dashboards provide a customizable canvas for displaying the most relevant metrics and logs from your Azure resources. You can create custom dashboards tailored to your specific needs, choosing from a wide array of visualization options like charts, graphs, gauges, and maps. Dashboards can be shared with team members or pinned to your Azure portal for quick access.

To create a custom dashboard in Azure Portal:

1. Go to the Azure Monitor section in the Azure Portal.
2. Click on the "Dashboards" tab.
3. Click the "+ New dashboard" button.
4. Give your dashboard a name and description.
5. Add tiles to your dashboard. Tiles can display various types of data, such as metrics, logs, and even queries from Log Analytics.
6. Customize the appearance and layout of your tiles.
7. Save your dashboard and share it with others if desired.

Azure Workbooks

Azure Workbooks are interactive documents that combine text, queries, and visualizations to provide a richer and more flexible way to analyze your data. Workbooks allow you to tell a story with your data, guiding readers through your analysis and providing context and explanations alongside visualizations. They are particularly useful for:

- **Incident Investigation:** You can create workbooks to investigate and document incidents, including timelines, affected resources, and mitigation steps.
- **Root Cause Analysis:** Workbooks can help you drill down into the root cause of issues by combining data from multiple sources and visualizing the relationships between them.
- **Capacity Planning:** You can use workbooks to analyze resource utilization trends and forecast future capacity needs.
- **Security Analysis:** Workbooks can help you identify security threats and vulnerabilities by correlating security events and visualizing attack patterns.

Power BI

For advanced visualization and reporting capabilities, you can export Azure Monitor data to Power BI. Power BI is a powerful business analytics service that allows you to create interactive reports, dashboards, and visualizations. You can connect Power BI to your Log Analytics workspace or Application Insights resource to access your Azure Monitor data. Power BI offers a wide range of visualization options, including custom visuals, and allows you to share your reports with others within your organization.

By leveraging these visualization tools, you can gain deeper insights into your Azure environment, identify trends and patterns, and communicate your findings effectively. Whether you need to quickly monitor resource health, troubleshoot performance issues, or create comprehensive reports, Azure Monitor provides the flexibility and power you need to visualize your data in a way that best suits your needs.

Alerting and Automation with Azure Monitor

Azure Monitor empowers you to proactively respond to changes in your environment by setting up alerts and automating actions. This allows you to stay ahead of potential issues, maintain optimal performance, and ensure the availability of your applications and services.

Alerts

Alerts in Azure Monitor act as sentinels, continuously monitoring your resources and notifying you when specific conditions are met. They can be triggered based on various criteria:

- **Metric thresholds:** You can create alerts that fire when a metric value exceeds or falls below a defined threshold. For example, you might set an alert to notify you if the CPU utilization of a virtual machine exceeds 80%.
- **Log queries:** You can define alerts based on the results of log queries. This allows you to be notified of specific events or patterns within your log data, such as errors, warnings, or security incidents.
- **Activity log events:** Azure Monitor tracks events that occur within your Azure subscription, such as resource creation, deletion, or modification. You can create alerts to be notified of specific activity log events, such as when a virtual machine is stopped or restarted.

Action Groups

Action groups are a key component of Azure Monitor's alerting system. They allow you to define a set of actions that should be taken when an alert is triggered. These actions can include:

- **Notifications:** Send email, SMS, or push notifications to designated recipients.
- **Azure Automation runbooks:** Trigger the execution of automated scripts or workflows in Azure Automation.
- **Webhook calls:** Send notifications to external systems or applications via webhooks.
- **ITSM Integration:** Integrate with IT Service Management (ITSM) systems like ServiceNow to create incidents or tickets.

By combining alerts with action groups, you can automate incident response, ensuring that the right people are notified and that appropriate actions are taken promptly to resolve issues.

Autoscale

Azure Monitor's autoscale feature enables you to dynamically scale your resources based on demand. This helps to ensure that your applications and services can handle fluctuating workloads without overprovisioning or underprovisioning resources. Autoscale can be configured based on:

- **Metrics:** You can scale your resources based on metric values, such as CPU utilization, memory consumption, or queue length.
- **Schedules:** You can define schedules to automatically scale resources up or down at specific times of day or days of the week.

For example, you can configure autoscale to add more virtual machine instances to a web application during peak traffic hours and remove them during off-peak hours. This helps you optimize resource utilization and reduce costs.

By leveraging Azure Monitor's alerting and automation capabilities, you can proactively manage your Azure environment, ensuring optimal performance, availability, and cost efficiency.

Chapter Summary

In this chapter, we explored the comprehensive capabilities of Azure Monitor, a powerful toolset for monitoring and analyzing your Azure environment. We learned how Azure Monitor acts as a central hub for collecting, storing, and analyzing telemetry data from various sources, including Azure resources, custom applications, and on-premises environments.

Key Takeaways:

- **Holistic Monitoring:** Azure Monitor provides a unified view of your entire environment, enabling you to correlate events, identify root causes, monitor trends, and detect anomalies.
- **Data Collection:** Azure Monitor automatically collects platform metrics and logs from most Azure resources, and you can also collect data from custom sources using agents and extensions.
- **Data Analysis:** Powerful tools like Metrics Explorer and Log Analytics allow you to visualize and analyze metric and log data, respectively.
- **Insights:** Pre-built dashboards and workbooks offer in-depth analysis of specific scenarios, such as VM performance or container health.
- **Visualization:** You can create custom dashboards in the Azure portal, build interactive workbooks, or export data to Power BI for advanced visualization and reporting.
- **Alerting and Automation:** Set up alerts based on metric thresholds, log queries, or activity log events. Use action groups to trigger automated responses to alerts.
- **Autoscaling:** Dynamically adjust your resources based on demand to optimize performance and costs.

By understanding and leveraging the features and capabilities of Azure Monitor, you can gain valuable insights into your Azure environment, proactively identify and address issues, and optimize your applications and services for maximum performance and reliability. Embrace Azure Monitor as your trusted companion on your observability journey, empowering you to make informed decisions and achieve operational excellence in the cloud.

Azure Advisor: Recommendations for Optimization

Outline

- Overview of Azure Advisor
- Types of Recommendations
- Implementing Azure Advisor Recommendations
- Azure Advisor Score
- Customizing Azure Advisor
- Chapter Summary

Overview of Azure Advisor

Azure Advisor is a valuable tool within the Azure platform that acts as your personalized cloud consultant. Its primary goal is to help you optimize your Azure resources and get the most out of your cloud investment. Advisor does this by continuously analyzing your resource configurations, usage patterns, and telemetry data to identify opportunities for improvement across various aspects of your Azure environment.

How Azure Advisor Works

Azure Advisor employs a combination of intelligent algorithms and heuristics to analyze your Azure deployments. It examines factors such as resource types, configurations, performance metrics, and usage patterns. Based on this analysis, Advisor generates tailored recommendations that are specific to your environment. These recommendations are designed to address potential issues and suggest best practices to help you achieve optimal performance, security, and cost-efficiency.

Benefits of Using Azure Advisor

Integrating Azure Advisor into your cloud management practices can yield numerous benefits:

- **Cost Savings:** Advisor helps you identify idle or underutilized resources, suggesting ways to optimize your usage and reduce unnecessary spending. By implementing these recommendations, you can significantly lower your Azure bill.
- **Improved Performance:** Advisor identifies performance bottlenecks, inefficient configurations, or suboptimal resource allocations. By following its recommendations, you can enhance the speed, responsiveness, and overall performance of your applications and services.
- **Enhanced Security:** Advisor regularly assesses your environment for security vulnerabilities and misconfigurations. It provides recommendations for strengthening your security posture, such as enabling multi-factor authentication, applying network security groups, or encrypting sensitive data.
- **Reliability and High Availability:** Advisor identifies resources that may be prone to failures or outages. It suggests configuration changes or architectural improvements to enhance the reliability and high availability of your applications and services.
- **Operational Excellence:** Advisor provides best practice recommendations to help you adhere to industry standards and optimize your Azure operations. This can streamline your management processes and ensure that your environment is running smoothly.

In essence, Azure Advisor is a proactive tool that empowers you to continuously improve your Azure environment. By taking advantage of its personalized recommendations, you can unlock cost savings, enhance performance, bolster security, and achieve greater operational efficiency in your cloud deployments.

Types of Recommendations

Azure Advisor offers a diverse range of recommendations, each aimed at enhancing specific aspects of your Azure deployments. These recommendations are categorized into several key areas:

High Availability

Azure Advisor analyzes your resource configurations to identify potential single points of failure that could disrupt your applications or services. It provides recommendations for improving the high availability and resilience of your resources, such as:

- **Deploying resources in multiple availability zones:** This ensures that your application remains accessible even if a single zone experiences an outage.
- **Configuring load balancing:** Distributing traffic across multiple resources enhances availability and prevents overload.
- **Enabling disaster recovery:** Setting up backup and recovery mechanisms ensures that you can quickly restore your services in the event of a disaster.

Security

Security is a top priority in any cloud environment. Azure Advisor continuously scans your resources for security vulnerabilities and misconfigurations. It provides recommendations for improving your security posture, such as:

- **Enabling multi-factor authentication (MFA):** Adding an extra layer of security to your user accounts to prevent unauthorized access.
- **Applying network security groups (NSGs):** Filtering network traffic to and from your resources to restrict unauthorized access.
- **Encrypting data at rest and in transit:** Protecting sensitive data from unauthorized access.
- **Regularly patching your systems:** Applying security updates to prevent exploitation of known vulnerabilities.

Performance

Optimal performance is essential for delivering a seamless user experience. Azure Advisor analyzes the performance of your resources and provides recommendations for optimizing them, such as:

- **Right-sizing virtual machines:** Choosing the right size for your virtual machines to ensure optimal resource utilization and cost efficiency.
- **Configuring autoscaling:** Automatically scaling your resources based on demand to handle fluctuating workloads.
- **Optimizing database performance:** Fine-tuning database settings to improve query performance and reduce latency.
- **Caching frequently accessed data:** Implementing caching mechanisms to reduce response times for your applications.

Cost

Azure Advisor helps you manage your cloud spending by identifying cost-saving opportunities. It provides recommendations such as:

- **Resizing or shutting down underutilized resources:** Identifying resources that are not being fully utilized and suggesting ways to reduce their size or shut them down during periods of low demand.
- **Reserving virtual machine instances:** Taking advantage of reserved instances to significantly reduce costs for predictable workloads.

- **Leveraging Azure Hybrid Benefit:** Using your existing on-premises licenses to save on the cost of running Windows Server virtual machines in Azure.
- **Optimizing storage usage:** Identifying unused or underutilized storage accounts and suggesting ways to optimize their usage.

By proactively implementing Azure Advisor's recommendations, you can significantly improve the overall health, security, performance, and cost-effectiveness of your Azure environment.

Implementing Azure Advisor Recommendations

Azure Advisor recommendations are not merely suggestions; they are actionable insights designed to help you optimize your Azure environment. Implementing these recommendations is a straightforward process that can lead to significant improvements in cost, performance, security, and reliability.

Reviewing and Implementing Recommendations

1. **Access Azure Advisor:** You can access Azure Advisor through the Azure portal, Azure CLI, or Azure PowerShell. In the Azure portal, navigate to the Advisor blade to view your recommendations.
2. **Review Recommendations:** Azure Advisor presents recommendations in a clear and concise manner. Each recommendation includes a detailed description of the issue, its potential impact, and the suggested actions to take.
3. **Prioritize Recommendations:** Consider the impact and urgency of each recommendation to prioritize your implementation efforts. Focus on recommendations that address critical issues or offer the greatest potential for improvement.
4. **Implement Recommendations:** Depending on the recommendation, implementation may involve modifying resource configurations, adjusting settings, or deploying additional resources. Azure Advisor often provides step-by-step instructions or links to relevant documentation to guide you through the implementation process. In some cases, you can even implement recommendations directly from the Azure portal with a single click.
5. **Track Progress and Measure Impact:** After implementing a recommendation, Azure Advisor allows you to track the progress of your implementation. You can also measure the impact of the recommendation by monitoring the relevant metrics and logs. This helps you evaluate the effectiveness of the recommendation and make further adjustments if necessary.

Examples of Implementing Recommendations

Let's explore some examples of how to implement Azure Advisor recommendations in different categories:

- **High Availability:** Enable cross-region replication for your storage accounts to ensure data redundancy and protect against regional outages.
- **Security:** Enable multi-factor authentication (MFA) for your Azure administrator accounts to prevent unauthorized access.
- **Performance:** Upgrade your virtual machine to a larger size to address performance bottlenecks caused by insufficient CPU or memory resources.
- **Cost:** Delete unused network interfaces to avoid unnecessary charges.

Tracking Progress and Measuring Impact

Azure Advisor provides a dashboard where you can track the progress of your implementation efforts. You can see how many recommendations have been implemented, postponed, or dismissed. You can also filter recommendations by category, resource type, or impact level.

To measure the impact of recommendations, you can use Azure Monitor to monitor relevant metrics and logs. For example, if you implemented a recommendation to optimize the performance of a virtual machine, you can use Azure Monitor to track the virtual machine's CPU utilization and response times to see if there has been an improvement.

By regularly reviewing and implementing Azure Advisor recommendations, you can continuously optimize your Azure environment, ensuring that your resources are performing at their best, your data is secure, and your costs are under control.

Azure Advisor Score

Azure Advisor Score is a numerical representation of how well your Azure resources align with best practices. It provides a holistic view of your environment's health and helps you track your optimization progress over time.

Calculation of Azure Advisor Score

The Azure Advisor Score is calculated on a scale of 0% to 100%, both in aggregate and for each of the five advisor categories:

- **Reliability:** Assesses the resilience of your resources against failures and outages.
- **Security:** Evaluates the security posture of your resources and identifies potential vulnerabilities.
- **Performance:** Measures the efficiency and responsiveness of your resources.
- **Cost:** Assesses the cost-effectiveness of your resource utilization and identifies potential savings opportunities.
- **Operational Excellence:** Evaluates your operational processes and identifies areas for improvement.

The score for each category is weighted based on the relative importance of that category to your overall Azure investment. For example, if cost optimization is a top priority for your organization, the cost category will have a higher weight than other categories. The aggregate score is then calculated as the weighted average of the category scores.

Significance of Azure Advisor Score

The Azure Advisor Score is a valuable metric that can help you:

- **Understand the current state of your Azure environment:** It provides a quick and easy way to assess the overall health of your environment and identify areas that need improvement.
- **Track your progress over time:** You can monitor your Azure Advisor Score over time to see how your optimization efforts are impacting the health of your environment.
- **Prioritize recommendations:** The score can help you prioritize which recommendations to implement first based on their potential impact on your overall score.
- **Communicate with stakeholders:** You can use the score to communicate the status of your Azure environment to stakeholders and demonstrate the value of your optimization efforts.

Tips for Improving Your Azure Advisor Score

To improve your Azure Advisor Score, consider the following tips:

- **Regularly review and implement recommendations:** The more recommendations you implement, the higher your score will be.
- **Prioritize recommendations with the highest impact:** Focus on implementing recommendations that will have the greatest impact on your overall score.
- **Monitor your score over time:** Track your progress and identify areas where you can make further improvements.

- **Customize Azure Advisor:** Tailor the recommendations you receive to your specific needs and priorities.

By regularly monitoring and acting upon Azure Advisor recommendations, you can significantly improve the overall health and efficiency of your Azure environment, leading to cost savings, enhanced performance, and improved security.

Customizing Azure Advisor

While Azure Advisor's default recommendations offer valuable insights, tailoring them to your specific needs and priorities can further enhance their relevance and actionability. Azure Advisor provides several mechanisms for customization, allowing you to fine-tune the recommendations you receive and even create your own custom recommendations.

Filtering Recommendations

Azure Advisor allows you to filter recommendations based on various criteria:

- **Category:** You can focus on specific categories of recommendations, such as High Availability, Security, Performance, Cost, or Operational Excellence. This allows you to prioritize the areas that are most important to your organization.
- **Resource Type:** You can filter recommendations by the type of Azure resource they apply to, such as virtual machines, storage accounts, or databases. This is useful if you want to focus on optimizing specific types of resources.
- **Severity:** Azure Advisor assigns a severity level to each recommendation (High, Medium, or Low) based on its potential impact. You can filter recommendations by severity to prioritize critical issues.
- **Subscription or Resource Group:** Filter recommendations based on specific subscriptions or resource groups to focus on particular segments of your environment.

You can apply these filters in the Azure portal or through Azure Advisor's API.

Creating Custom Recommendations

If the built-in recommendations don't fully address your specific requirements, you can create custom recommendations. These recommendations can be based on your own internal best practices, compliance requirements, or other specific criteria. You can define custom recommendations using Azure Policy, which allows you to create rules that enforce compliance and governance across your Azure environment.

Automating Recommendation Implementation with Azure Advisor's API

Azure Advisor provides a REST API that allows you to programmatically interact with Advisor's recommendations. You can use the API to:

- **Retrieve Recommendations:** Get a list of all recommendations for your subscription or resource group.
- **Filter Recommendations:** Apply filters to the recommendations based on category, resource type, or severity.
- **Implement Recommendations:** Trigger the implementation of specific recommendations.
- **Track Recommendation Status:** Monitor the status of recommendations and track their implementation progress.

By using Azure Advisor's API, you can automate the process of reviewing and implementing recommendations, saving time and effort. For example, you could create a script that automatically implements all high-severity security recommendations.

Examples of Using Azure Advisor's API

- **Automatically Remediate Security Issues:** Create a script that regularly queries Azure Advisor for high-severity security recommendations and automatically implements them.
- **Generate Custom Reports:** Use the API to retrieve recommendations and generate custom reports tailored to your organization's specific needs.
- **Integrate with Existing Systems:** Integrate Azure Advisor with your existing IT Service Management (ITSM) or DevOps systems to streamline the process of tracking and implementing recommendations.

By customizing Azure Advisor and using its API for automation, you can tailor the service to your organization's unique requirements and achieve greater efficiency in optimizing your Azure resources.

Chapter Summary

In this chapter, we explored the functionalities of Azure Advisor, your dedicated cloud consultant within the Azure platform. We discussed how it analyzes your Azure environment, providing personalized recommendations to optimize your resource utilization across various dimensions, including cost, performance, security, high availability, and operational excellence.

Key Takeaways:

- **Azure Advisor:** A tool that acts as your personalized cloud consultant, offering recommendations to improve your Azure deployments.
- **Recommendations Across Five Areas:** Azure Advisor provides recommendations in five key areas: High Availability, Security, Performance, Cost, and Operational Excellence.
- **Implementation:** You can easily review and implement Azure Advisor recommendations, with step-by-step guidance and the ability to track your progress.
- **Azure Advisor Score:** A numerical representation of your environment's health, which can be used to track your optimization progress and prioritize recommendations.
- **Customization:** Azure Advisor can be customized to filter recommendations based on your specific needs and priorities, and you can even create custom recommendations using Azure Policy.

By actively utilizing Azure Advisor and implementing its recommendations, you can significantly improve the performance, security, and cost-efficiency of your Azure environment, ensuring that you get the most out of your cloud investment. Remember, regular review and implementation of these recommendations is crucial for ongoing optimization and maintaining the health of your Azure deployments.

Azure Cost Management: Understanding and Controlling Costs

Outline

- Introduction to Azure Cost Management
- Azure Cost Management Features
- Cost Analysis
- Budgets and Alerts
- Cost Optimization Strategies
- Chapter Summary

Introduction to Azure Cost Management

Azure Cost Management is a powerful suite of tools provided by Microsoft Azure that empowers you to gain a comprehensive understanding of your cloud spending. It goes beyond simply tracking your bills; it enables you to analyze, manage, and optimize your Azure costs, ensuring you're getting the most value out of your cloud investment.

Purpose of Azure Cost Management

Azure Cost Management serves as your financial compass in the cloud. Its primary purpose is to help you navigate the complexities of cloud spending and make informed decisions that align with your budget and business goals. It provides the visibility and control you need to:

- **Track:** Monitor your Azure usage and spending in real-time, allowing you to identify cost trends and potential anomalies.
- **Analyze:** Deep dive into your cost data to understand your spending patterns, identify cost drivers, and allocate costs to different departments or projects.
- **Optimize:** Implement cost-saving strategies based on actionable recommendations and insights, ensuring you're getting the best value from your Azure resources.

Benefits of Using Azure Cost Management

By incorporating Azure Cost Management into your cloud strategy, you can reap numerous benefits:

- **Gain Visibility:** Understand your spending patterns at a granular level, track costs by resource, service, or department, and identify areas where you can optimize.
- **Identify Cost-Saving Opportunities:** Uncover hidden costs, eliminate wasteful spending, and make informed decisions to reduce your overall Azure bill.
- **Optimize Cloud Usage:** Right-size your resources, identify underutilized assets, and implement cost-effective strategies to maximize your cloud investment.
- **Improve Budgeting and Forecasting:** Create and manage budgets, set spending limits, and receive alerts when you approach or exceed those limits, enabling better financial planning and control.
- **Increase Accountability:** Allocate costs to different departments or projects, ensuring transparency and accountability for cloud spending.

Components of Azure Cost Management

Azure Cost Management is comprised of several integrated components that work together to provide a complete cost management solution:

- **Cost Analysis:** This tool allows you to explore and analyze your cost data using various filters, groupings, and views. You can drill down into specific time periods, resource types, or subscriptions to understand your spending trends and identify areas for optimization.
- **Budgets:** With Budgets, you can set spending limits for your Azure resources and receive alerts when you're approaching or exceeding those limits. This helps you stay on top of your spending and avoid unexpected surprises.
- **Alerts:** Azure Cost Management can send you alerts based on your budget thresholds or other cost-related events. This allows you to proactively manage your costs and take corrective action if necessary.
- **Recommendations:** Azure Advisor integrates with Cost Management to provide personalized recommendations for optimizing your resource usage and reducing costs. These recommendations are based on your usage patterns and Azure best practices.

By leveraging the capabilities of Azure Cost Management and its various components, you can gain a comprehensive understanding of your Azure spending, identify areas for optimization, and implement strategies to control your costs effectively.

This chapter will delve deeper into each of these components, providing step-by-step guidance on how to use them to effectively manage your Azure costs and maximize the value of your cloud investment.

Azure Cost Management Features

Azure Cost Management is a comprehensive suite of tools designed to empower you with the knowledge and control you need to manage your Azure expenses effectively. Let's delve into its key features:

Cost Analysis

Cost Analysis is your primary tool for exploring and understanding your Azure spending patterns. It provides a flexible and interactive interface where you can slice and dice your cost data using a variety of filters, groupings, and views. This allows you to:

- **Understand Spending Trends:** Visualize your cost data over time, identifying trends, seasonal patterns, and potential anomalies. You can see how your spending has evolved over months or years, helping you anticipate future costs.
- **Identify Cost Drivers:** Pinpoint the specific resources, services, or resource groups that are contributing the most to your overall Azure bill. This knowledge allows you to focus your optimization efforts where they will have the greatest impact.
- **Allocate Costs:** Assign costs to different departments, projects, or cost centers within your organization. This helps you track spending against budgets and ensure that costs are accurately allocated.
- **Analyze Cost by Resource Type:** Understand how your spending is distributed across different types of resources, such as virtual machines, storage accounts, or databases. This can help you identify areas where you might be overspending or underutilizing resources.

Budgets

Budgets are a proactive tool for controlling your Azure spending. You can set spending limits for your Azure resources and receive alerts when you approach or exceed those limits. This allows you to:

- **Avoid Unexpected Costs:** Set realistic budgets based on your expected usage and receive timely notifications to prevent unexpected cost overruns.
- **Monitor Spending:** Track your spending against your budget in real time, allowing you to make adjustments as needed.
- **Identify Overspending:** Receive alerts when your spending exceeds your budget, giving you the opportunity to investigate the cause and take corrective action.

Alerts

Alerts go hand-in-hand with budgets, providing you with notifications about various cost-related events. You can configure alerts to notify you when:

- **Your spending approaches or exceeds your budget.**
- **There are unexpected spikes in your spending.**
- **New resources are deployed.**
- **Resources are deleted or modified.**

Alerts can be sent via email, SMS, or push notifications, ensuring that you're always aware of your Azure spending.

Recommendations

Azure Advisor seamlessly integrates with Azure Cost Management to provide personalized recommendations for optimizing your resource usage and reducing costs. These recommendations are based on your usage patterns and Azure best practices. Examples of recommendations include:

- **Right-sizing virtual machines:** Choosing the appropriate size for your virtual machines based on their actual usage.
- **Shutting down unused resources:** Identifying resources that are not being used and recommending that they be shut down to save costs.
- **Reserving virtual machine instances:** Taking advantage of reserved instances to significantly reduce the cost of running virtual machines.

By following Azure Advisor recommendations, you can significantly reduce your Azure costs without sacrificing performance or functionality.

Cost Analysis

Cost Analysis is the cornerstone of Azure Cost Management, empowering you to dissect and understand your Azure spending in granular detail. It equips you with the tools to visualize your cost data, identify trends, and pinpoint areas for potential savings.

Filtering, Grouping, and Visualizing Cost Data

Cost Analysis offers a highly flexible and customizable interface for exploring your cost data. You can apply various filters to narrow down your focus, such as:

- **Time Range:** Select specific dates or predefined time periods to analyze your spending over different durations.
- **Subscription:** Filter by specific subscriptions to isolate costs for different departments, projects, or environments.
- **Resource Group:** Analyze costs at the resource group level to understand spending patterns for related resources.
- **Resource Type:** Filter by specific resource types, such as virtual machines, storage accounts, or databases, to identify which resources are contributing the most to your costs.
- **Meter Category:** Group costs by meter category to understand spending on different Azure services, such as compute, networking, or storage.
- **Tags:** If you've tagged your resources with custom metadata, you can filter by tags to analyze costs for specific projects, departments, or environments.

Once you've applied your filters, you can visualize your cost data in various ways:

- **Accumulated Cost:** View the total cost over the selected time period.

- **Daily Cost:** See a daily breakdown of your costs.
- **Cost by Resource:** View the cost breakdown by individual resources.
- **Cost by Service:** See the cost breakdown by Azure service.

Cost Analysis also allows you to group your data by various attributes, such as resource group, resource type, meter category, or tag. This can help you identify spending patterns and cost drivers more easily.

Analyzing Cost Trends Over Time

One of the most powerful features of Cost Analysis is its ability to visualize your cost trends over time. By plotting your cost data on a graph, you can quickly identify:

- **Seasonal Patterns:** Does your spending fluctuate with the seasons or other recurring events?
- **Unexpected Spikes:** Are there sudden increases in your costs that need investigation?
- **Long-Term Trends:** Is your overall spending increasing, decreasing, or remaining stable?

By understanding your cost trends, you can better forecast your future spending and identify areas where you can optimize your resource usage to reduce costs.

Comparing Costs Across Different Entities

Cost Analysis allows you to compare costs across different subscriptions, resource groups, or resource types. This can be useful for:

- **Identifying Costly Subscriptions:** Determine which subscriptions are contributing the most to your overall Azure bill.
- **Comparing Resource Group Costs:** See which resource groups are the most expensive and identify opportunities for optimization.
- **Evaluating Resource Type Costs:** Compare the costs of different resource types to identify which ones are the most cost-effective for your needs.

Example: You could compare the costs of running your application on virtual machines versus Azure App Service to determine which option is more cost-effective.

By leveraging the various features of Cost Analysis, you can gain a deep understanding of your Azure spending patterns and identify opportunities to optimize your cloud usage. This knowledge empowers you to make informed decisions that can significantly reduce your Azure bill and maximize the value of your cloud investment.

Budgets and Alerts

Budgets and alerts are essential components of Azure Cost Management that empower you to proactively manage and control your Azure spending. They provide a mechanism for setting spending limits, receiving timely notifications, and taking corrective action before costs spiral out of control.

Creating and Managing Budgets

1. **Navigate to Cost Management:** In the Azure portal, search for and select "Cost Management + Billing."
2. **Create a Budget:** Select "Budgets" from the left-hand menu, then click "Add."
3. **Define Budget Scope:** Choose the scope of your budget. You can create budgets at various levels, such as subscription, resource group, or management group.
4. **Set Budget Amount:** Enter the desired budget amount and reset period (monthly, quarterly, or annually). You can also set a start and end date for your budget.

5. **Configure Alerts:** Set thresholds for when you want to receive alerts. You can choose to receive alerts when your spending reaches a certain percentage of your budget (e.g., 50%, 75%, 90%) or when it exceeds your budget.
6. **Choose Alert Recipients:** Specify the email addresses or action groups that should receive the alerts.
7. **Review and Create:** Review your budget settings and click "Create" to save your budget.

To manage your budgets, return to the "Budgets" section in Cost Management. Here you can view the status of your budgets, edit existing budgets, or create new ones.

Configuring Alerts

Alerts are notifications that are triggered when your spending exceeds a specified threshold or meets other predefined conditions. You can configure alerts to be sent via email, SMS, or other notification channels. To configure alerts for your budget:

1. **Edit Your Budget:** In the "Budgets" section, click on the budget you want to configure alerts for.
2. **Click "Edit budget."**
3. **Configure Alert Conditions:** Specify the thresholds at which you want to receive alerts. You can set multiple thresholds for different levels of notification.
4. **Choose Alert Recipients:** Select the email addresses or action groups that should receive the alerts.
5. **Save Changes:** Click "Save" to update your budget with the new alert settings.

Tips for Setting Effective Budgets

- **Analyze Past Spending:** Review your historical spending patterns to determine your average monthly or yearly costs.
- **Set Realistic Goals:** Set budget amounts that are achievable and aligned with your business objectives.
- **Use Multiple Budgets:** Create separate budgets for different resources, services, or projects to track spending more granularly.
- **Regularly Review and Adjust:** Review your budgets periodically and adjust them based on your changing needs and spending patterns.
- **Utilize Budget Alerts:** Leverage budget alerts to stay on top of your spending and prevent unexpected cost overruns.
- **Consider Azure Advisor Recommendations:** Azure Advisor can provide personalized recommendations for optimizing your resource usage and reducing costs, which can help you set more effective budgets.

By utilizing budgets and alerts in Azure Cost Management, you can proactively manage your Azure spending, avoid unexpected costs, and ensure that your cloud budget aligns with your business goals.

Cost Optimization Strategies

Azure Cost Management is not just about understanding your spending; it's about empowering you to make informed decisions that can significantly reduce your Azure bill. This section outlines various strategies you can employ to optimize your cloud costs, ensuring you're getting the most value out of your Azure investment.

Right-Sizing Your Resources

One of the most effective ways to optimize costs is to ensure that your Azure resources are appropriately sized for their workloads. Overprovisioning resources leads to unnecessary spending, while underprovisioning can impact performance. Azure Cost Management provides recommendations based on historical usage data, helping you identify resources that can be downsized or scaled up to match actual demand.

Shutting Down Unused Resources

Azure resources can often be left running even when they're not actively used, leading to unnecessary costs. Azure Cost Management can help you identify idle or underutilized resources, such as virtual machines that are powered on but not being used. By shutting down or deallocating these resources, you can eliminate wasted spending. You can automate this process using Azure Automation or schedule start/stop times for resources to optimize utilization.

Reserved Instances

Reserved Instances (RIs) are a billing discount applied to virtual machines, SQL databases, Azure Cosmos DB, or other resources when you commit to using them for a one-year or three-year term. RIs can significantly reduce your costs compared to pay-as-you-go pricing, making them a great option for predictable workloads. Azure Cost Management provides recommendations for purchasing RIs based on your usage patterns, helping you maximize your savings.

Azure Advisor Recommendations

Azure Advisor is a valuable tool that provides personalized recommendations for optimizing your Azure resources, including cost-saving suggestions. These recommendations can help you identify underutilized resources, suggest more cost-effective alternatives, and highlight opportunities to improve your overall cloud architecture. By regularly reviewing and implementing Azure Advisor recommendations, you can proactively reduce your Azure costs.

Optimizing Cloud Architecture and Design

The way you design and architect your cloud solutions can have a significant impact on your costs. Consider the following tips for optimizing your cloud architecture:

- **Choose the right services:** Azure offers a wide range of services, each with its own pricing model. Carefully evaluate your requirements and choose the services that are the most cost-effective for your needs.
- **Utilize auto-scaling:** Automatically scale your resources based on demand to avoid overprovisioning or underprovisioning.
- **Leverage serverless computing:** Use Azure Functions or other serverless technologies to reduce costs for workloads that have variable demand.
- **Optimize storage:** Choose the right storage tiers for your data and archive or delete unused data to minimize storage costs.
- **Use Azure Cost Management APIs:** Programmatically manage your Azure costs and automate cost optimization tasks.

By implementing these cost optimization strategies and continuously monitoring your Azure spending, you can ensure that you're getting the most value out of your cloud investment while keeping your costs under control. Remember, cost optimization is an ongoing process that requires regular attention and adjustment.

Chapter Summary

In this chapter, we delved into the intricacies of Azure Cost Management, a suite of tools designed to empower you with the knowledge and control needed to effectively manage your Azure spending. We explored the core features of Cost Management, including Cost Analysis, Budgets, Alerts, and Recommendations, and how they work together to provide a comprehensive cost management solution.

Key takeaways from this chapter include:

- **Cost Analysis:** We learned how to use Cost Analysis to gain deep insights into our Azure spending patterns. By filtering, grouping, and visualizing our cost data, we can identify trends, pinpoint cost drivers, and allocate costs effectively. We also discussed how to analyze cost trends over time and compare costs across different entities to uncover potential savings opportunities.
- **Budgets and Alerts:** We explored how to set budgets for our Azure resources and configure alerts to be notified when our spending approaches or exceeds these limits. We discussed tips for setting realistic and effective budgets, and how to use alerts to proactively manage our costs.
- **Cost Optimization Strategies:** We discussed various strategies for optimizing Azure costs, such as right-sizing resources, shutting down unused resources, and taking advantage of reserved instances. We also learned how to leverage Azure Advisor recommendations to identify cost-saving opportunities and explored tips for optimizing our cloud architecture and design to reduce costs.

By mastering Azure Cost Management, you can gain a comprehensive understanding of your Azure spending, identify areas for optimization, and implement strategies to control your costs effectively. This not only helps you save money but also ensures that you're getting the most value out of your Azure investment. Remember, cost management is an ongoing process that requires regular attention and adjustment. By staying proactive and utilizing the tools and strategies discussed in this chapter, you can keep your Azure costs under control and maximize the benefits of cloud computing.

Section 9:
Additional Azure Services

Azure Machine Learning: Building and Deploying ML Models

Outline

- Introduction to Azure Machine Learning
- Key Components of Azure Machine Learning
- Building Machine Learning Models
- Deploying Machine Learning Models
- Chapter Summary

Introduction to Azure Machine Learning

Azure Machine Learning is a cloud-based service offered by Microsoft that serves as a comprehensive platform for accelerating and managing the end-to-end machine learning (ML) project lifecycle. It empowers data scientists, developers, and engineers to build, train, and deploy high-quality machine learning models faster and with confidence.

Purpose in Machine Learning Development

Azure Machine Learning's purpose is to streamline and democratize machine learning development. It aims to remove the complexities often associated with ML projects, making it accessible to a broader audience. By providing a unified platform with a wide array of tools and services, Azure Machine Learning enables you to focus on building and deploying models rather than worrying about infrastructure setup and management.

Advantages of Using Azure Machine Learning

- **Scalability:** Azure Machine Learning allows you to scale your machine learning workloads effortlessly. Whether you're training models on small datasets or massive amounts of data, you can leverage Azure's virtually unlimited compute resources to meet your needs.
- **Collaboration:** Azure Machine Learning fosters collaboration among teams by providing a shared workspace where data scientists, developers, and other stakeholders can collaborate on experiments, models, and deployments. This facilitates seamless communication and accelerates the development process.
- **Automation:** Azure Machine Learning enables you to automate repetitive tasks, such as data preparation, model training, and deployment, through pipelines. This not only saves time but also ensures consistency and reproducibility.
- **Access to Powerful Compute Resources:** Azure Machine Learning integrates with various compute targets, including Azure Machine Learning Compute Instances, Azure Machine Learning Compute Clusters, and Azure Kubernetes Service (AKS). This gives you the flexibility to choose the right compute resources for your specific workload requirements.
- **Open-Source Interoperability:** Azure Machine Learning is designed to work seamlessly with popular open-source machine learning frameworks like TensorFlow, PyTorch, and scikit-learn. You

can bring your existing code and models to Azure Machine Learning or leverage the platform's built-in capabilities.

Personas Who Benefit from Azure Machine Learning

Azure Machine Learning caters to a wide range of users, including:

- **Data Scientists:** Data scientists can use Azure Machine Learning to experiment with different algorithms, train models on large datasets, and track their model's performance over time.
- **Developers:** Developers can leverage Azure Machine Learning to easily integrate machine learning models into their applications, automate deployment processes, and monitor model performance in production.
- **Business Analysts:** Business analysts can use Azure Machine Learning's intuitive interface to explore and analyze data, gain insights, and make data-driven decisions.

By providing a comprehensive and user-friendly platform, Azure Machine Learning democratizes machine learning, making it accessible to users with varying levels of expertise. It empowers individuals and teams to build and deploy powerful machine learning solutions that can drive innovation and transform businesses.

Key Components of Azure Machine Learning

Azure Machine Learning offers a comprehensive suite of tools and services that cater to every stage of the machine learning lifecycle, from data preparation and model training to deployment and monitoring. Let's delve into the key components that make Azure Machine Learning a powerful platform for machine learning development.

Azure Machine Learning Studio

Azure Machine Learning Studio is a web-based visual interface designed to simplify the process of building and deploying machine learning models. It provides a no-code or low-code environment, allowing you to create ML models without writing complex code. Studio offers a drag-and-drop interface with various modules for data preprocessing, feature engineering, model training, and deployment. This visual approach makes it accessible to users with varying levels of ML expertise.

Azure Machine Learning Workspace

The Azure Machine Learning Workspace serves as the central hub for organizing and managing all your machine learning assets. It acts as a collaborative space where data scientists, developers, and other stakeholders can work together on ML projects. Within the workspace, you can:

- **Store and Manage Datasets:** Organize and version your datasets for easy access and reproducibility.
- **Track Experiments:** Keep track of your model training experiments, including the code, hyperparameters, and results.
- **Register Models:** Register trained models for versioning, tracking, and deployment.
- **Deploy Models:** Deploy models as web services for real-time or batch predictions.
- **Monitor Models:** Track the performance and health of your deployed models.

Azure Machine Learning Designer

Azure Machine Learning Designer is a visual interface that allows you to create machine learning pipelines using a drag-and-drop approach. Pipelines are a series of interconnected steps that automate the ML workflow, from data ingestion and preprocessing to model training and evaluation. With Designer, you can visually design and experiment with different pipelines, making it easier to iterate and refine your ML models.

Azure Machine Learning SDK

For users who prefer a code-first approach, Azure Machine Learning provides a robust SDK (Software Development Kit) with libraries and tools for building and deploying ML models using popular programming languages like Python and R. The SDK gives you full control over the ML process, allowing you to customize and extend your workflows to meet specific requirements.

Azure Machine Learning Compute

Azure Machine Learning Compute offers a variety of compute targets for training and deploying your ML models. These compute targets include:

- **Compute Instances:** Fully managed cloud-based virtual machines (VMs) pre-configured for ML development.
- **Compute Clusters:** Scalable clusters of VMs for training large models or running parallel experiments.
- **Azure Kubernetes Service (AKS):** Kubernetes clusters for deploying and scaling containerized ML models.
- **Inference Clusters:** Optimized clusters for real-time or batch model inference.

The choice of compute target depends on the size and complexity of your ML workloads.

Azure Machine Learning Pipelines

Azure Machine Learning Pipelines enable you to automate the end-to-end ML workflow, from data preparation and model training to deployment and monitoring. Pipelines are defined as a series of steps, each representing a specific task in the ML process. You can use the Azure Machine Learning SDK or the Designer to create pipelines. Pipelines can be scheduled to run automatically, triggered by specific events, or run on demand.

By combining these key components, Azure Machine Learning provides a complete and flexible platform for building, training, deploying, and managing machine learning models. Whether you prefer a visual, code-first, or hybrid approach, Azure Machine Learning empowers you to leverage the power of cloud computing to accelerate your ML projects and deliver impactful solutions.

Building Machine Learning Models

Azure Machine Learning provides a variety of approaches for building machine learning models, catering to both beginners who prefer automated solutions and experienced practitioners who need fine-grained control over their model development process.

Automated Machine Learning (AutoML)

Automated Machine Learning (AutoML) is a powerful feature that simplifies the model building process by automating the selection and tuning of the best algorithm for your dataset. You don't need to be an expert in machine learning algorithms to use AutoML. You simply provide your data, specify the type of machine learning task (classification, regression, or forecasting), and set some basic configuration parameters. AutoML then automatically explores different algorithms, hyperparameters, and feature engineering techniques to find the best-performing model. This approach saves you time and effort, allowing you to focus on other aspects of your ML project.

Custom Model Training

For more experienced users who want complete control over the model building process, Azure Machine Learning allows you to train custom models using your preferred machine learning frameworks. Whether you prefer TensorFlow, PyTorch, scikit-learn, or other popular frameworks, you can easily integrate them with Azure Machine Learning. You can write your own training scripts, customize your model architecture, and leverage Azure's powerful compute resources to accelerate your training process.

Hyperparameter Tuning

Hyperparameters are parameters that control the learning process of a machine learning algorithm. Finding the optimal combination of hyperparameters is crucial for achieving the best model performance. Azure Machine Learning offers hyperparameter tuning capabilities that automate the search for the best hyperparameter values. You can define the search space for each hyperparameter, specify the optimization metric (e.g., accuracy, F1 score), and choose a tuning method (e.g., random search, Bayesian optimization). Azure Machine Learning then automatically trains multiple models with different hyperparameter configurations and selects the best-performing one.

Model Evaluation

Evaluating your model's performance is an essential step in the machine learning lifecycle. Azure Machine Learning provides tools and metrics to help you assess how well your model generalizes to unseen data. Common evaluation metrics include:

- **Accuracy:** The percentage of correct predictions made by the model.
- **Precision:** The percentage of positive predictions that are actually correct.
- **Recall:** The percentage of actual positives that are correctly identified by the model.
- **F1 Score:** The harmonic mean of precision and recall, providing a single metric that balances both.
- **Mean Absolute Error (MAE) or Mean Squared Error (MSE):** These metrics measure the average magnitude of errors in regression models.

You can use Azure Machine Learning's model evaluation capabilities to compare the performance of different models, identify areas where your model is underperforming, and make informed decisions about which model to deploy.

Deploying Machine Learning Models

Once you have built and trained a machine learning model that meets your desired performance metrics, the next crucial step is to deploy it so it can start making predictions and adding value to your applications or business processes. Azure Machine Learning simplifies the deployment process, providing multiple options tailored to different scenarios.

Real-Time Deployment

Real-time deployment is ideal for applications that require low-latency predictions, such as fraud detection, recommendation engines, or real-time decision-making systems. In Azure Machine Learning, you can deploy your model as a real-time web service using:

- **Azure Container Instance (ACI):** A simple and cost-effective way to deploy models as containers for development and testing.
- **Azure Kubernetes Service (AKS):** A fully managed Kubernetes service for deploying and scaling containerized models in production.

Real-time deployments typically involve creating an endpoint that exposes your model as a web service. Clients can then send requests to this endpoint to receive predictions in real time.

Batch Deployment

Batch deployment is suitable for scenarios where you need to make predictions on large datasets, such as customer churn prediction or demand forecasting. In Azure Machine Learning, you can deploy your model for batch scoring using:

- **Azure Batch:** A high-performance computing service for running large-scale parallel and high-throughput batch jobs.
- **Azure Databricks:** A collaborative Apache Spark-based analytics platform that can be used for distributed model training and batch scoring.

Batch deployments typically involve submitting a job to a compute cluster that processes your dataset and generates predictions.

Model Monitoring

Once your model is deployed, it's essential to monitor its performance to ensure that it continues to make accurate predictions and remains relevant. Azure Machine Learning offers model monitoring capabilities that allow you to track:

- **Data Drift:** Detects changes in the distribution of input data that could impact model performance.
- **Model Performance:** Tracks key metrics like accuracy, precision, and recall to identify performance degradation.
- **Model Explainability:** Provides insights into the factors that influence your model's predictions, helping you understand why it makes certain decisions.

Azure Machine Learning can automatically alert you if it detects any issues with your deployed model, allowing you to take corrective action promptly.

Model Retraining

Machine learning models can become stale over time as the underlying data changes. To maintain the accuracy and relevance of your models, you need to retrain them on new data regularly. Azure Machine Learning provides tools and automation capabilities to streamline the retraining process. You can set up triggers to automatically retrain your models based on schedules or data changes. You can also manually trigger retraining as needed.

Chapter Summary

In this chapter, we explored the various approaches and tools offered by Azure Machine Learning for building, training, and deploying machine learning models. We learned how Azure Machine Learning caters to both beginners and experienced practitioners by providing both automated and customizable options for model development.

Key Takeaways:

- **Automated Machine Learning (AutoML):** Simplifies model building by automating algorithm selection and hyperparameter tuning.
- **Custom Model Training:** Provides flexibility for training custom models using popular machine learning frameworks like TensorFlow, PyTorch, and scikit-learn.
- **Hyperparameter Tuning:** Automates the process of finding the best hyperparameter values to optimize model performance.
- **Model Evaluation:** Offers tools and metrics to assess model performance and identify areas for improvement.
- **Real-Time Deployment:** Enables deployment of models as real-time web services for low-latency predictions.
- **Batch Deployment:** Facilitates deployment for batch scoring on large datasets.

- **Model Monitoring:** Tracks model performance and data drift in production environments.
- **Model Retraining:** Streamlines the process of retraining models on new data to maintain accuracy and relevance.

Azure Machine Learning empowers you to leverage the power of cloud computing and automation to accelerate your machine learning projects. By combining these capabilities with your domain expertise, you can build, deploy, and manage high-quality machine learning models that deliver valuable insights and drive business innovation.

Azure IoT Hub: Connecting and Managing IoT Devices

Outline

- What is Azure IoT Hub?
- Key Features and Capabilities
- Setting Up an Azure IoT Hub
- Device Provisioning and Authentication
- Device-to-Cloud Communication
- Cloud-to-Device Communication
- IoT Hub Security
- Scaling and Managing IoT Devices
- Chapter Summary

What is Azure IoT Hub?

Azure IoT Hub is a fully managed cloud service offered by Microsoft that serves as the backbone of your Internet of Things (IoT) solutions. It acts as a central message hub, facilitating seamless and secure communication between your IoT devices and your backend applications. Think of it as the central nervous system that connects and orchestrates your entire IoT ecosystem.

The Internet of Things (IoT): A World of Connected Possibilities

The Internet of Things (IoT) refers to a vast network of physical objects, or "things," embedded with sensors, software, and connectivity capabilities. These devices can collect and exchange data over the internet, enabling them to communicate with each other and with central systems. IoT encompasses a wide range of objects, from everyday household appliances like thermostats and refrigerators to industrial equipment like sensors and manufacturing robots. The significance of IoT lies in its potential to transform industries, improve efficiency, and enhance our daily lives.

Azure IoT Hub: The Central Nervous System of Your IoT Solution

Azure IoT Hub plays a pivotal role in IoT solutions by providing the following key functionalities:

- **Device-to-Cloud Communication:** IoT Hub enables devices to securely send telemetry data, such as sensor readings, operational status, and other information, to the cloud.
- **Cloud-to-Device Communication:** IoT Hub enables you to send commands, configurations, and other messages from the cloud to your devices, allowing for remote control and management.
- **Scalability:** IoT Hub is designed to handle millions of devices and messages, ensuring your IoT solution can scale as your needs grow.
- **Security:** IoT Hub provides robust security features, including per-device authentication, encryption, and access control, to protect your devices and data from unauthorized access.
- **Device Management:** IoT Hub allows you to manage your device fleet at scale, including device provisioning, monitoring, firmware updates, and configuration management.

In essence, Azure IoT Hub acts as the bridge between your IoT devices and your cloud-based applications. It enables seamless communication, data exchange, and device management, allowing you to harness the full potential of the Internet of Things.

Key Features and Capabilities

Azure IoT Hub offers a rich array of features that streamline the development, deployment, and management of your IoT solutions. Let's dive into some of its key capabilities:

Device Provisioning

The sheer scale of IoT deployments can make manual device provisioning a daunting task. Azure IoT Hub simplifies this process through the Device Provisioning Service (DPS). DPS automates the provisioning of devices, allowing you to effortlessly register and configure large numbers of devices securely. This eliminates the need for manual intervention and ensures a seamless onboarding experience for your devices.

Bi-directional Communication

Effective communication between devices and the cloud is essential for any IoT solution. Azure IoT Hub enables reliable and secure bi-directional communication through various patterns:

- **Device-to-Cloud Telemetry:** Devices can send telemetry data, such as sensor readings, operational status, or any other relevant information, to IoT Hub. This data can then be processed, analyzed, and acted upon by your backend applications.
- **Cloud-to-Device Commands:** You can send commands from the cloud to your devices to trigger specific actions or control their behavior. This allows for remote control and management of your device fleet.
- **Direct Methods:** Direct methods enable request-response interactions between the cloud and devices, allowing you to invoke specific functions or procedures on devices.

Scalability

IoT deployments can quickly grow to encompass millions of devices generating a massive amount of data. Azure IoT Hub is built to handle this scale, allowing you to connect and manage a virtually unlimited number of devices. It can process millions of messages per second, ensuring that your IoT solution can scale seamlessly as your needs expand.

Security

Security is of paramount importance in IoT, as these devices often handle sensitive data and can be vulnerable to attacks. Azure IoT Hub incorporates robust security measures to protect your devices and data, including:

- **Per-Device Authentication:** Each device is authenticated with a unique identity, ensuring that only authorized devices can connect to IoT Hub.
- **Data Encryption:** Communication between devices and IoT Hub is encrypted using industry-standard protocols like TLS/SSL, safeguarding your data from unauthorized access.
- **Access Control:** IoT Hub provides granular access control mechanisms, allowing you to define permissions for different users and applications.

Device Management

Managing a large fleet of IoT devices can be a complex task. Azure IoT Hub simplifies device management by providing features such as:

- **Device Twins:** A digital representation of each device that stores device state information and desired configurations.
- **Automatic Device Management (ADM):** Enables you to remotely manage and configure your devices at scale, including firmware updates, configuration changes, and device restarts.
- **Device Health Monitoring:** IoT Hub allows you to monitor the health and status of your devices, alerting you to potential issues or failures.

Azure IoT Hub's comprehensive feature set makes it a powerful platform for building and managing scalable, secure, and reliable IoT solutions. By leveraging these capabilities, you can accelerate your IoT development efforts, reduce complexity, and focus on delivering value to your customers and stakeholders.

Setting Up an Azure IoT Hub

Setting up an Azure IoT Hub involves creating the hub instance itself, choosing the right pricing tier for your needs, and registering your IoT devices. Let's walk through the steps:

Step-by-Step Instructions for Creating an IoT Hub

1. **Access the Azure Portal:** Start by logging into the Azure Portal using your Azure account credentials.
2. **Create a New Resource:** Click on the "+ Create a resource" button in the top left corner.
3. **Search for IoT Hub:** Type "IoT Hub" in the search bar and select it from the results.
4. **Configure Basic Settings:**
   - **Subscription:** Choose the Azure subscription you want to use.
   - **Resource Group:** Select an existing resource group or create a new one.
   - **Region:** Choose the Azure region where you want to deploy your IoT Hub. Consider factors like proximity to your devices and compliance requirements.
   - **IoT Hub Name:** Enter a unique name for your IoT Hub. This will become part of the DNS endpoint for your hub.
5. **Select Pricing and Scale Tier:**
   - **Free tier:** Suitable for testing and development with limited features and message quotas.
   - **Basic tier:** Offers essential features for production environments with higher message quotas.
   - **Standard tier:** Provides additional features like device management, message routing, and cloud-to-device messaging with higher throughput and storage capacity.
6. **Review and Create:** Review your configuration and click on the "Create" button to deploy your IoT Hub.

Registering Devices with IoT Hub

Once your IoT Hub is created, you need to register your devices to establish their identities and enable them to communicate securely. There are several methods for registering devices:

- **Manual Registration (Azure Portal):** You can manually add devices one by one in the Azure portal. This method is suitable for small-scale deployments or testing.
- **Bulk Registration (Azure CLI or Azure PowerShell):** For larger deployments, you can use Azure CLI or Azure PowerShell commands to register multiple devices at once using a CSV file or other supported formats.
- **Device Provisioning Service (DPS):** DPS automates the provisioning of devices at scale, simplifying the onboarding process and ensuring zero-touch configuration. It allows devices to automatically register with IoT Hub based on their unique characteristics.

Choosing the Right Pricing Tier

The choice of pricing tier depends on your specific requirements, such as the number of devices, message volume, and required features. The free tier is a good starting point for testing and development, while the basic and standard tiers offer more features and scalability for production environments. Consider the following factors when choosing a tier:

- **Number of devices:** Choose a tier that can accommodate your expected number of devices.

- **Message volume:** Select a tier that can handle the volume of messages your devices will generate.
- **Features:** Consider which features are essential for your IoT solution, such as device management, message routing, and cloud-to-device messaging.
- **Budget:** Choose a tier that fits within your budget constraints.

By carefully considering these factors and following the steps outlined above, you can create an Azure IoT Hub instance that's tailored to your specific needs and start connecting your devices to the cloud.

Device Provisioning and Authentication

Device provisioning is a crucial step in setting up your IoT solution. It is the process of registering and configuring your IoT devices so that they can securely connect to your Azure IoT Hub and start exchanging data.

Importance of Device Provisioning

Device provisioning is essential for several reasons:

- **Simplified Onboarding:** It simplifies the process of bringing new devices online by automating the registration and configuration process. This eliminates the need for manual configuration of each device, which can be time-consuming and error-prone, especially for large-scale deployments.
- **Enhanced Security:** Device provisioning ensures that only authorized devices can connect to your IoT Hub. It helps protect your IoT solution from unauthorized access and potential security breaches.
- **Scalability:** With device provisioning, you can easily scale your IoT solution to accommodate a large number of devices. The automation of provisioning ensures that you can quickly and efficiently onboard new devices as your deployment grows.

Device Provisioning Service (DPS)

Azure Device Provisioning Service (DPS) is a helper service for IoT Hub that automates the device provisioning process. DPS allows you to provision millions of devices in a secure and scalable manner. It eliminates the need for hardcoding device credentials during manufacturing, reducing the risk of security vulnerabilities.

DPS works by associating devices with an IoT Hub based on specific criteria, such as the device's manufacturer, model, or a unique identifier. When a new device connects to DPS, it is automatically authenticated and assigned to the appropriate IoT Hub.

Authentication Mechanisms

Azure IoT Hub supports various authentication mechanisms to ensure that only authorized devices can connect and communicate with it.

Symmetric Key Authentication

In symmetric key authentication, each device is assigned a unique symmetric key that is shared with IoT Hub. The device uses this key to generate a security token, which it presents to IoT Hub during the authentication process. Symmetric key authentication is relatively simple to implement, but it requires careful management of the keys to prevent unauthorized access.

X.509 Certificate Authentication

X.509 certificate authentication is a more secure method than symmetric key authentication. In this approach, each device has a unique X.509 certificate that contains its public key. The device uses its private key to sign a security token, which it presents to IoT Hub along with its certificate. IoT Hub verifies the signature using the device's public key, ensuring that the device is authentic.

Other Authentication Mechanisms

IoT Hub also supports other authentication mechanisms, such as:

- **Trusted Platform Module (TPM) Authentication:** Uses a hardware-based security module to store device credentials and generate security tokens.
- **SAS Token Authentication:** Employs Shared Access Signature (SAS) tokens for temporary and restricted access to IoT Hub.

The choice of authentication mechanism depends on your specific security requirements and the capabilities of your devices.

Device-to-Cloud Communication

Azure IoT Hub serves as a conduit for the flow of data from your IoT devices to the cloud. It supports multiple protocols and message formats, giving you the flexibility to choose the best fit for your specific requirements.

Supported Protocols

IoT Hub provides support for the following protocols for device-to-cloud communication:

- **MQTT (Message Queuing Telemetry Transport):** A lightweight publish/subscribe messaging protocol designed for resource-constrained devices and low-bandwidth networks. MQTT is widely used in IoT due to its simplicity, efficiency, and ability to operate over unreliable networks.
- **AMQP (Advanced Message Queuing Protocol):** A more robust messaging protocol that offers reliable message delivery, advanced routing capabilities, and transactional support. AMQP is suitable for scenarios where message reliability and guaranteed delivery are critical.
- **HTTPS:** The Hypertext Transfer Protocol Secure (HTTPS) is a widely used protocol for secure communication over the internet. IoT Hub supports HTTPS for scenarios where devices have sufficient resources and require a web-standard protocol.

Message Formats

IoT Hub supports various message formats, providing flexibility in how you structure and encode your device data:

- **JSON:** JavaScript Object Notation (JSON) is a lightweight and human-readable data interchange format widely used in web applications and APIs. Its simplicity and ease of parsing make it a popular choice for IoT devices.
- **Avro:** Apache Avro is a binary serialization format that offers compact encoding and efficient data transfer. It is well-suited for scenarios where bandwidth optimization is a priority.
- **Custom Formats:** IoT Hub also allows you to use custom message formats if you have specific data encoding requirements.

Sending Telemetry Data and Device State Information

Devices can send various types of data to IoT Hub, including:

- **Telemetry Data:** This includes sensor readings, operational status, and other time-series data that reflects the current state of the device.
- **Device State Information:** This includes information about the device's configuration, software version, and other relevant details.

- **Event Messages:** These are messages that notify IoT Hub about specific events or occurrences on the device.
- **File Uploads:** Devices can upload files to IoT Hub, such as log files or firmware updates.

To send data to IoT Hub, devices establish a connection using one of the supported protocols and authenticate themselves using a unique device ID and credentials. Once connected, they can send messages to IoT Hub using the appropriate message format.

How to Send Messages from Devices

The specific steps for sending messages from devices to IoT Hub depend on the chosen protocol and SDK. However, the general process involves the following:

1. **Establish a Connection:** The device initiates a connection with IoT Hub using the selected protocol (MQTT, AMQP, or HTTPS).
2. **Authenticate:** The device provides its credentials (e.g., device ID and key) to authenticate with IoT Hub.
3. **Send Messages:** The device sends messages to IoT Hub, specifying the message type, format, and any additional properties.
4. **Receive Acknowledgements (Optional):** Depending on the protocol and configuration, the device may receive acknowledgements from IoT Hub to confirm that the messages were received successfully.

By following these steps and utilizing the appropriate protocols and message formats, you can establish a robust and efficient device-to-cloud communication channel, enabling your IoT devices to seamlessly transmit data to Azure IoT Hub.

Cloud-to-Device Communication

Azure IoT Hub empowers you to not only receive data from your IoT devices but also to send commands and instructions back to them. This bi-directional communication is crucial for managing and controlling your devices remotely, making your IoT solution more dynamic and responsive.

Cloud-to-Device Communication Mechanisms

IoT Hub offers three primary mechanisms for sending messages from the cloud to your devices:

- **Cloud-to-Device (C2D) Commands:** These are simple messages that instruct a device to perform a specific action. They are typically used for immediate, real-time control, such as turning a light on or off or adjusting the temperature of a thermostat. C2D commands can be sent to individual devices or to groups of devices.
- **Direct Methods:** Direct methods are similar to C2D commands but offer a request-response pattern. You send a request from the cloud to a device, and the device can respond with a result. Direct methods are useful for retrieving information from a device, such as its current status or sensor readings, or for triggering a specific action and waiting for confirmation.
- **Desired Properties (Device Twins):** Device twins are JSON documents that store device state information, both reported by the device and desired by the cloud. Desired properties represent the desired state of a device as set by the cloud. When a device connects to IoT Hub, it synchronizes its desired properties with the cloud, and any changes are applied to the device. This mechanism is useful for remotely configuring devices or updating firmware.

Use Cases for Cloud-to-Device Communication

Cloud-to-device communication opens up a wide range of possibilities for managing and controlling your IoT devices. Some common use cases include:

- **Remote Control:** Control devices remotely from the cloud, such as turning lights on or off, adjusting temperature settings, or locking/unlocking doors.
- **Firmware Updates:** Deploy firmware updates to your devices over the air (OTA), ensuring that they stay up-to-date with the latest features and security patches.
- **Configuration Changes:** Modify device settings remotely, such as changing sensor sampling rates or adjusting alert thresholds.
- **Device Diagnostics:** Retrieve diagnostic information from devices to troubleshoot issues or monitor their health.
- **Remote Troubleshooting:** Interact with devices in real time to diagnose and resolve problems remotely.

Implementing Cloud-to-Device Communication

To implement cloud-to-device communication in your IoT applications, you can use the Azure IoT Hub SDKs for your preferred programming language (e.g., C#, Java, Node.js, Python). These SDKs provide convenient APIs for sending C2D commands, invoking direct methods, and updating desired properties in device twins. You can also use the Azure portal, Azure CLI, or Azure PowerShell to send messages to devices directly from the cloud.

Remember that proper error handling and retry mechanisms are crucial for ensuring the reliability and resiliency of cloud-to-device communication, especially in scenarios where devices might be intermittently connected or experience network issues.

By harnessing the power of cloud-to-device communication, you can create more intelligent, responsive, and manageable IoT solutions that adapt to your changing needs and deliver a seamless user experience.

IoT Hub Security

The Internet of Things (IoT) introduces a vast network of interconnected devices, creating immense opportunities for innovation and efficiency. However, this interconnectedness also brings forth significant security challenges. IoT devices often collect and transmit sensitive data, making them attractive targets for cyberattacks.

Importance of Security in IoT Solutions

Ensuring robust security in IoT solutions is paramount for several reasons:

- **Data Protection:** IoT devices often collect sensitive personal, financial, or operational data. Protecting this data from unauthorized access, theft, or manipulation is crucial to maintain trust and comply with data protection regulations.
- **Device Integrity:** Malicious actors can compromise IoT devices, turning them into tools for launching attacks or disrupting operations. Maintaining the integrity of devices is vital to ensure their reliability and functionality.
- **Network Security:** IoT devices are often connected to networks, making them potential entry points for attackers. Securing the communication channels and network infrastructure is essential to prevent unauthorized access and protect against threats like data breaches and denial-of-service attacks.
- **Operational Continuity:** A security breach in an IoT system can disrupt operations, cause financial losses, and damage reputation. Robust security measures help ensure the continuous operation of IoT solutions.
- **Privacy Concerns:** Many IoT devices collect personal data, raising privacy concerns. Protecting user privacy is essential to maintain trust and comply with privacy regulations.

Security Measures in Azure IoT Hub

Azure IoT Hub incorporates several security measures to address the unique challenges of IoT environments:

- **Per-Device Authentication:** Each device that connects to IoT Hub is authenticated using a unique identifier and credentials, ensuring that only authorized devices can communicate with the hub. This prevents unauthorized access and protects against spoofing attacks.
- **Data Encryption:** IoT Hub uses industry-standard protocols like Transport Layer Security (TLS) to encrypt data in transit between devices and the cloud. This ensures that data cannot be intercepted or read by unauthorized parties.
- **Access Control:** IoT Hub provides granular access control mechanisms, allowing you to define fine-grained permissions for different users and applications. This ensures that only authorized individuals or services can access specific devices or data within IoT Hub.
- **Security Monitoring and Threat Detection:** IoT Hub integrates with Azure Security Center to provide threat detection and security monitoring for your IoT devices. This helps identify potential security issues and vulnerabilities, allowing you to take proactive measures to mitigate risks.

Recommendations for Securing IoT Devices and Communication Channels

In addition to the security measures provided by Azure IoT Hub, you should also implement additional best practices to secure your IoT devices and communication channels:

- **Device Hardening:** Ensure that your IoT devices are configured securely. This includes using strong passwords, disabling unnecessary services, and regularly updating firmware and software.
- **Secure Boot:** Implement secure boot mechanisms on your devices to prevent unauthorized code from running at startup.
- **Firewall and Network Segmentation:** Use firewalls and network segmentation to restrict access to your IoT devices and isolate them from other parts of your network.
- **Secure Communication Protocols:** Use secure communication protocols like MQTT over TLS or AMQP over TLS to encrypt data in transit.
- **Regular Security Assessments:** Conduct regular security assessments of your IoT solution to identify vulnerabilities and potential threats.

By implementing these security measures and best practices, you can significantly reduce the risk of security breaches and protect your valuable IoT devices and data.

Scaling and Managing IoT Devices

Scaling and managing a large number of IoT devices can be a complex task. Azure IoT Hub offers robust capabilities to handle millions of devices and messages, ensuring your IoT solution can grow and adapt as your needs evolve.

Device Twins: Digital Representations of Your Devices

IoT Hub employs device twins, which are JSON documents stored in the cloud, to represent each of your IoT devices. Device twins serve two primary purposes:

1. **Device State Information:** They store the reported state of a device, such as its connection status, battery level, sensor readings, and other telemetry data. This allows you to gain real-time insights into the current state of your devices.
2. **Desired Configurations:** Device twins also store the desired configurations for a device, representing the state you want the device to be in. This allows you to remotely control and manage devices by updating their desired properties. The device twin mechanism ensures that devices synchronize their state with the cloud and apply any configuration changes automatically.

Automatic Device Management (ADM)

Azure IoT Hub simplifies device management at scale through Automatic Device Management (ADM). It enables you to remotely manage and update your devices without requiring manual intervention. Some of the key features of ADM include:

- **Firmware Updates:** You can deploy firmware updates to your devices over the air (OTA), ensuring they are always running the latest versions with the latest features and security patches.
- **Configuration Changes:** You can modify device configurations remotely, such as adjusting sensor sampling rates or changing communication settings.
- **Device Restart:** You can remotely restart devices to resolve issues or apply new configurations.
- **Job Scheduling:** You can schedule device management tasks to be executed at specific times or under certain conditions.

Monitoring Device Health and Performance

IoT Hub provides robust monitoring capabilities to track the health and performance of your IoT devices. You can monitor metrics such as device connectivity, message throughput, and error rates. IoT Hub also integrates with Azure Monitor, allowing you to collect and analyze device logs, set up alerts for specific events, and visualize device telemetry data in dashboards. This comprehensive monitoring enables you to proactively identify and address issues, ensuring the smooth operation of your IoT solution.

Scaling Your IoT Solution

IoT Hub is designed to handle massive scale. You can scale your IoT Hub by adding units, which are pre-defined combinations of messaging, storage, and device management resources. As your device fleet grows, you can easily add more units to meet your increasing needs. IoT Hub also supports automatic scaling, allowing it to dynamically adjust its capacity based on demand, ensuring optimal performance and cost-efficiency.

By leveraging the scaling and management capabilities of Azure IoT Hub, you can confidently build and operate large-scale IoT solutions that deliver reliable performance and robust security.

Chapter Summary

In this chapter, we explored the fundamental concepts and capabilities of Azure IoT Hub, a powerful cloud service that empowers you to connect, monitor, and manage your IoT devices at scale. We delved into the significance of IoT and how Azure IoT Hub serves as a central message hub for your IoT solutions.

Key Takeaways:

- **IoT Hub's Role:** We learned that IoT Hub enables seamless and secure bi-directional communication between your IoT devices and your backend applications, acting as the central nervous system of your IoT ecosystem.
- **Key Features:** We explored IoT Hub's rich set of features, including device provisioning, bi-directional communication, scalability, security, and device management.
- **Device Provisioning and Authentication:** We discussed the importance of device provisioning for simplifying onboarding and ensuring security, as well as the various authentication mechanisms supported by IoT Hub.
- **Communication Patterns:** We learned about the different ways devices and the cloud communicate through IoT Hub, including device-to-cloud telemetry, cloud-to-device commands, and direct methods.
- **Security Measures:** We highlighted the robust security features implemented by IoT Hub, such as per-device authentication, data encryption, and access control, to safeguard your devices and data.
- **Scaling and Managing Devices:** We discussed how IoT Hub uses device twins to store device state information and desired configurations, and how automatic device management (ADM) enables remote management of devices, including firmware updates and configuration changes.

We also touched upon monitoring device health and performance using IoT Hub's monitoring capabilities.

By leveraging the capabilities of Azure IoT Hub, you can unlock the full potential of the Internet of Things, enabling you to create innovative solutions that improve efficiency, productivity, and overall business outcomes. With its robust security, scalability, and comprehensive management features, Azure IoT Hub provides a solid foundation for your IoT journey, enabling you to connect and manage your devices with confidence.

Azure Cognitive Services: Adding AI Capabilities

Outline

- What are Azure Cognitive Services?
- Categories of Cognitive Services
- Choosing the Right Cognitive Service
- Integrating Cognitive Services into Your Applications
- Benefits of Using Azure Cognitive Services
- Chapter Summary

What are Azure Cognitive Services?

Azure Cognitive Services are a collection of pre-trained AI models and APIs offered by Microsoft Azure. They empower developers to seamlessly integrate artificial intelligence (AI) capabilities into their applications without the need for deep expertise in machine learning or data science. Think of them as ready-to-use building blocks that you can plug into your applications to enhance them with intelligence.

These services simplify the process of adding AI capabilities by providing a wide range of pre-trained models that can be readily consumed through REST APIs or SDKs. Instead of building complex AI models from scratch, developers can leverage these pre-existing models to perform tasks like image recognition, speech-to-text conversion, language translation, and sentiment analysis, among others.

Azure Cognitive Services can process various types of data, making them versatile and adaptable to different scenarios:

- **Images:** Analyze images to identify objects, people, scenes, and text.
- **Speech:** Convert spoken language into text, synthesize speech from text, and translate speech in real time.
- **Language:** Analyze text to extract sentiment, key phrases, and entities. Build conversational AI applications that understand natural language.
- **Knowledge:** Leverage knowledge bases to create question-and-answer systems or extract insights from structured data.
- **Decision:** Identify anomalies in data, filter out inappropriate content, and personalize user experiences.

By leveraging Azure Cognitive Services, you can infuse your applications with the power of AI, unlocking new possibilities for innovation and creating more intelligent and engaging user experiences.

Categories of Cognitive Services

Azure Cognitive Services are organized into distinct categories based on their functionalities:

Vision

The Vision category of Azure Cognitive Services is a powerhouse of AI capabilities that enables your applications to perceive and understand the visual world. It offers a suite of services designed to extract meaningful information from images and videos, opening up a world of possibilities for applications in various domains.

Computer Vision

Computer Vision is a foundational service in this category that allows you to analyze images and extract valuable insights. It can identify objects, scenes, and concepts within images, making it useful for applications like:

- **Image Tagging:** Automatically tag images with relevant keywords, making them easier to search and categorize.
- **Object Detection:** Identify and locate specific objects within an image, such as people, cars, or animals.
- **Scene Understanding:** Analyze the overall context of an image to determine its scene type (e.g., indoor, outdoor, landscape).
- **Text Extraction:** Extract text from images, such as street signs, product labels, or handwritten notes.

Face API

The Face API is a specialized service focused on detecting and analyzing human faces in images. It can:

- **Face Detection:** Identify the presence and location of faces within an image.
- **Face Recognition:** Recognize and identify individuals based on their facial features.
- **Emotion Recognition:** Detect emotions like happiness, sadness, anger, or surprise in facial expressions.
- **Attribute Detection:** Estimate age, gender, head pose, and facial hair from faces.

This service finds applications in security systems, customer analytics, and even social media platforms.

Custom Vision

Sometimes, you need an image recognition model that's tailored to your specific needs. Custom Vision allows you to create and train your own image classification models with your own data. This flexibility enables you to build models for highly specific use cases, such as:

- **Product Recognition:** Identify specific products in images for inventory management or visual search.
- **Defect Detection:** Identify defects in manufacturing processes or products.
- **Plant Identification:** Recognize different species of plants for agricultural applications.

Form Recognizer

Form Recognizer is designed to automate data extraction from structured and semi-structured documents like invoices, receipts, and forms. It can:

- **Identify Key-Value Pairs:** Extract key information like invoice numbers, dates, and amounts from invoices.
- **Identify Tables:** Extract data from tables, such as product details or line items.
- **Identify Handwritten Text:** Extract handwritten text from forms, making it easier to digitize and process.

This service is invaluable for automating document processing workflows and reducing manual data entry.

By harnessing the power of Azure Cognitive Services' Vision capabilities, you can create applications that see and understand the visual world, opening up a realm of possibilities for innovation and automation.

Speech

The Speech category within Azure Cognitive Services focuses on empowering applications to interact with the spoken word. These services leverage advanced speech recognition, synthesis, and translation technologies to bridge the gap between humans and machines, enabling seamless communication and interaction.

Speech to Text

Speech to Text, also known as speech recognition, is a core service in this category. It converts spoken language into written text, enabling applications to understand and process human speech. This technology is essential for building voice-activated assistants, transcribing audio recordings, and creating accessible applications for people with disabilities.

Text to Speech

Text to Speech, also known as speech synthesis, does the opposite of speech recognition. It takes text input and generates natural-sounding speech in various languages and voices. This capability finds applications in creating voice-overs for videos, building accessible interfaces for visually impaired users, and developing voice-enabled chatbots or virtual assistants.

Speech Translation

Speech Translation is a powerful service that enables real-time translation of spoken language. It can automatically transcribe spoken words in one language and translate them into another language, either in text or speech format. This technology breaks down language barriers, facilitating communication and collaboration across different cultures and regions.

Speaker Recognition

Speaker Recognition is a specialized service that focuses on identifying and verifying individuals based on their unique voice characteristics. It can analyze speech patterns, vocal pitch, and other acoustic features to create a voiceprint that can be used to identify or verify a speaker. This technology finds applications in authentication systems, voice-activated commands, and personalized user experiences.

By incorporating these Speech services into your applications, you can create immersive and interactive experiences that leverage the power of spoken language. Whether you want to build a voice-controlled application, automate transcription tasks, or facilitate real-time communication across languages, Azure Cognitive Services Speech category provides the tools you need to unlock the full potential of speech technology.

Language

The Language category within Azure Cognitive Services is dedicated to empowering applications with the ability to understand, interpret, and respond to human language. It harnesses the power of natural language processing (NLP) to unlock insights from text data and enable more natural and intuitive interactions with users.

Text Analytics

Text Analytics is a fundamental service in this category that allows you to extract valuable information from unstructured text. It can analyze text to determine:

- **Sentiment:** Understand the overall sentiment of a piece of text, whether it's positive, negative, or neutral. This is useful for gauging customer opinions, analyzing social media feedback, or monitoring brand reputation.
- **Key Phrases:** Identify the most important phrases or keywords in a text, helping you summarize content, extract topics, or generate tags.
- **Entities:** Recognize and categorize named entities like people, organizations, locations, dates, and quantities. This is valuable for information extraction and knowledge graph creation.
- **Language Detection:** Automatically detect the language of a text.

Language Understanding (LUIS)

Language Understanding (LUIS) is a service designed for building conversational AI applications. It allows you to create custom language models that can understand natural language intents (what the user wants to do) and entities (the relevant information in the user's request). LUIS can be used to build chatbots, voice assistants, and other applications that interact with users through natural language.

Translator

The Translator service enables you to translate text and documents between multiple languages. It supports a wide range of languages and can be used to:

- **Translate Text:** Translate individual words, phrases, or entire documents.
- **Translate Speech:** Translate spoken language in real time.
- **Transliterate Text:** Convert text from one script to another (e.g., from Latin to Cyrillic).
- **Detect Language:** Automatically detect the language of a text.

QnA Maker

QnA Maker allows you to create question-and-answer pairs from your FAQ pages, documents, or other sources of information. These pairs can then be used to build a knowledge base that can answer questions posed by users in natural language. QnA Maker is a great tool for building chatbots, help desks, and other applications that provide information or support.

By incorporating these Language services into your applications, you can create more intelligent, interactive, and engaging experiences that understand and respond to human language. Whether you're building a customer service chatbot, analyzing social media sentiment, or creating a multilingual application, Azure Cognitive Services Language category provides the tools you need to unlock the full potential of natural language processing.

Decision

The Decision category of Azure Cognitive Services is designed to empower applications with the ability to make intelligent decisions. These services analyze various types of data, providing insights and recommendations to guide decision-making processes, enhance user experiences, and maintain a safe and respectful environment.

Anomaly Detector

Anomaly Detector is a specialized service that excels at identifying unusual patterns or anomalies in time-series data. It analyzes historical data to establish a baseline of normal behavior and then detects deviations from this baseline in real time. This is invaluable for applications that need to monitor and respond to unexpected events, such as:

- **Infrastructure Monitoring:** Detecting anomalies in server performance metrics, such as CPU utilization, memory usage, or network latency, can help identify potential hardware failures or resource bottlenecks.
- **Fraud Detection:** Identifying unusual patterns in financial transactions or user behavior can help detect fraudulent activities.
- **Manufacturing Quality Control:** Detecting anomalies in sensor data from manufacturing equipment can help identify faulty components or process deviations.

Content Moderator

Content Moderator is a service designed to help create safer and more inclusive online environments. It uses AI to detect and filter out inappropriate or offensive content from text, images, and videos. This can be used to:

- **Moderate User-Generated Content:** Filter out offensive language, hate speech, or sexually explicit content from user comments, reviews, or forum posts.
- **Protect Children:** Block access to inappropriate content for minors.
- **Ensure Brand Safety:** Prevent your brand from being associated with harmful or offensive content.

Content Moderator offers various levels of filtering, allowing you to customize the sensitivity to match your specific requirements.

Personalizer

Personalizer leverages reinforcement learning to create personalized experiences for users. It works by taking in information about the user, the context, and the available actions or content. Based on this information, it selects the action or content that is most likely to lead to a positive outcome, such as a user clicking on a link or making a purchase. Over time, Personalizer learns from user feedback to continuously improve its recommendations. This service can be used to personalize:

- **Product Recommendations:** Suggest products that a user is most likely to be interested in based on their browsing history, purchase history, and demographic information.
- **Content Recommendations:** Recommend articles, videos, or other content that a user is likely to find engaging.
- **Personalized Search Results:** Tailor search results to a user's preferences and interests.
- **Personalized User Interfaces:** Adapt the layout and content of a user interface based on their individual preferences.

By utilizing these Decision services, you can imbue your applications with the ability to make informed choices, personalize user experiences, and create a safer online environment.

Choosing the Right Cognitive Service

Azure Cognitive Services offers a wide range of AI capabilities, each designed to address specific tasks and scenarios. Choosing the right service for your application requires careful consideration of your project's requirements, goals, and constraints.

Evaluating Your Application's Requirements and Goals

Start by clearly defining the problems you want to solve or the features you want to add to your application. Consider the following questions:

- **What type of data are you working with?** Images, speech, text, or a combination?
- **What specific tasks do you need to perform on this data?** Image recognition, sentiment analysis, language translation, or something else?
- **How much accuracy do you require?** Do you need a highly accurate model or is a good enough approximation sufficient?
- **How much customization do you need?** Are you looking for a pre-built solution or do you need to train a custom model with your own data?
- **What is your budget?** Cognitive Services are priced on a pay-as-you-go basis, so consider the cost of each service and your expected usage.

Factors to Consider When Choosing a Service

Once you have a clear understanding of your requirements, consider the following factors when choosing a Cognitive Service:

- **Type of Data:** Choose a service that is designed to handle the type of data you are working with. For example, if you need to analyze images, consider using Computer Vision or Custom Vision. If you need to process text, consider using Text Analytics or Language Understanding (LUIS).
- **Level of Customization:** If you need a highly customized solution, consider using a service that allows you to train your own models with your own data, such as Custom Vision or LUIS. If you are looking for a quick and easy solution, consider using a pre-built service like Text Analytics or Translator.
- **Cost:** Cognitive Services are priced on a pay-as-you-go basis. Consider the cost of each service and your expected usage to determine which service fits within your budget.
- **Accuracy:** The accuracy of each service can vary depending on the specific task and the quality of your data. Evaluate the accuracy of different services to choose the one that best meets your needs.
- **Ease of Use:** Some services are easier to use than others. Consider the ease of integration and the availability of SDKs and documentation for your preferred programming language.

Examples of Using Cognitive Services

Here are some examples of how different Cognitive Services can be used to solve specific problems or add new features to applications:

- **Image Recognition:** Use Computer Vision to automatically tag images in a photo library, identify products in images for visual search, or detect defects in manufacturing processes.
- **Sentiment Analysis:** Use Text Analytics to analyze customer reviews, social media posts, or survey responses to understand how people feel about your product or service.
- **Language Translation:** Use Translator to build a multilingual website or application, or to translate customer support requests in real time.
- **Question Answering:** Use QnA Maker to create a chatbot that can answer customer questions about your products or services.
- **Anomaly Detection:** Use Anomaly Detector to monitor time-series data from your applications or infrastructure to detect anomalies that could indicate performance issues or security threats.

By carefully considering your application's requirements and goals, you can choose the right Cognitive Services to build intelligent applications that provide value to your users and your business.

Integrating Cognitive Services into Your Applications

Azure Cognitive Services are designed with developer-friendliness in mind. They provide REST APIs and SDKs for various programming languages, making the integration process relatively straightforward. Let's outline the general steps involved and provide examples for a few popular languages.

Steps for Integration

1. **Obtain API Keys and Endpoint:**
    - Create a Cognitive Service resource in the Azure portal.
    - Retrieve the API key and endpoint for your chosen service from the Keys and Endpoint section.
2. **Install SDK (Optional):**
    - If you prefer to use an SDK (recommended for ease of use), install the appropriate SDK for your programming language. For example, use the `azure-cognitiveservices-vision-computervision` package for Python.
3. **Authenticate:**
    - Authenticate your API calls using the obtained API key. Most SDKs provide helper functions for this.
4. **Construct API Requests:**

- Based on the chosen service, construct the API request with the required parameters, such as image URLs, text input, or audio files.
5. **Make API Calls:**
    - Use your preferred method (e.g., `requests` library in Python, `HttpClient` in C#) to send the request to the service endpoint.
6. **Handle Responses:**
    - Parse the JSON response returned by the API to extract the relevant information or results.

Code Examples

Python (Computer Vision - Analyze Image):

```python
from azure.cognitiveservices.vision.computervision import ComputerVisionClient
from msrest.authentication import CognitiveServicesCredentials # Authenticate
subscription_key = 'YOUR_SUBSCRIPTION_KEY' 
endpoint = 'YOUR_ENDPOINT'
credentials = CognitiveServicesCredentials(subscription_key) # Create client
client = ComputerVisionClient(endpoint, credentials) # Analyze image
image_url = 'https://example.com/image.jpg'
analysis = client.analyze_image(image_url, visual_features=['Description', 'Tags'])
print(analysis.description.captions[0].text)
```

C# (Text Analytics - Sentiment Analysis):

```csharp
using Azure;
using Azure.AI.TextAnalytics;
// Authenticate
string apiKey = "YOUR_API_KEY";
string endpoint = "YOUR_ENDPOINT";
AzureKeyCredential credentials = new AzureKeyCredential(apiKey);
// Create client
var client = new TextAnalyticsClient(new Uri(endpoint), credentials);
// Analyze sentiment
string document = "This is a great product!";
DocumentSentiment documentSentiment = client.AnalyzeSentiment(document);
Console.WriteLine($"Sentiment: {documentSentiment.Sentiment}");
```

Best Practices

- **Error Handling:** Implement robust error handling to gracefully handle API failures, rate limiting, and other potential issues.
- **Caching:** Cache results for frequently used requests to reduce the number of API calls and improve performance.
- **Batching:** Batch multiple requests together to reduce the number of network round trips and improve efficiency.
- **Pagination:** If a service supports pagination, implement it to retrieve large amounts of data in chunks.
- **Rate Limiting:** Be aware of the service's rate limits and adjust your application's behavior accordingly to avoid being throttled.

By following these steps and best practices, you can effectively integrate Azure Cognitive Services into your applications, unlocking the power of AI to enhance functionality and user experiences.

Benefits of Using Azure Cognitive Services

Azure Cognitive Services offer a multitude of benefits that make them a compelling choice for developers and businesses looking to harness the power of AI:

Simplified AI Development

One of the most significant advantages of Azure Cognitive Services is the elimination of the need for extensive machine learning expertise. Developers without a background in data science or AI can still leverage the power of these pre-built models. The services are accessible through simple REST APIs or SDKs, allowing you to integrate AI capabilities with just a few lines of code. This significantly lowers the barrier to entry for AI development and accelerates the time-to-market for your intelligent applications.

Scalability

Azure Cognitive Services are built on the robust and scalable infrastructure of Microsoft Azure. This means that your applications can effortlessly handle fluctuating workloads and scale to accommodate increasing demand. Whether you need to process a few images or millions of documents, Cognitive Services can scale on-demand to meet your requirements, ensuring optimal performance and responsiveness.

Cost-Effectiveness

Azure Cognitive Services follow a pay-as-you-go pricing model, making them highly cost-effective. You only pay for what you use, eliminating the need for upfront investments in expensive infrastructure or specialized AI expertise. This flexible pricing model allows businesses of all sizes to access cutting-edge AI capabilities without breaking the bank.

Continuously Updated Models

Microsoft invests heavily in research and development, constantly improving the AI models behind Cognitive Services. As a user of these services, you automatically benefit from these advancements. The models are regularly updated to incorporate the latest breakthroughs in AI, ensuring that your applications remain at the forefront of technology and deliver state-of-the-art performance.

By leveraging Azure Cognitive Services, you can streamline your development process, reduce costs, and focus on building innovative applications that deliver value to your customers.

Chapter Summary

In this chapter, we explored the exciting world of Azure Cognitive Services, a collection of pre-trained AI models and APIs that enable developers to effortlessly infuse their applications with intelligent capabilities. We delved into the four main categories of Cognitive Services: Vision, Speech, Language, and Decision, discovering how these services can be used to analyze images, process spoken language, understand natural language, and make intelligent decisions.

Key Takeaways:

- **Cognitive Services as AI Building Blocks:** We learned how Cognitive Services simplify AI development by providing pre-trained models that can be easily integrated into applications through REST APIs or SDKs.
- **Vision Category:** Explored services like Computer Vision, Face API, Custom Vision, and Form Recognizer, which enable applications to analyze images, recognize faces, and extract information from documents.
- **Speech Category:** Discussed services like Speech to Text, Text to Speech, Speech Translation, and Speaker Recognition, which empower applications to understand and process spoken language.
- **Language Category:** Examined services like Text Analytics, Language Understanding (LUIS), Translator, and QnA Maker, which enable applications to understand and respond to natural language.

- **Decision Category:** Explored services like Anomaly Detector, Content Moderator, and Personalizer, which help applications make intelligent decisions based on data analysis.
- **Choosing the Right Service:** We discussed the importance of evaluating your application's requirements and goals to select the most suitable Cognitive Services, considering factors like data type, customization needs, cost, and accuracy.
- **Integration and Best Practices:** We outlined the general steps for integrating Cognitive Services into your applications and provided code examples in Python and C#. We also discussed best practices for error handling and optimization.
- **Benefits of Azure Cognitive Services:** We highlighted the advantages of using these services, including simplified AI development, scalability, cost-effectiveness, and access to continuously updated models.

Azure Cognitive Services open up a world of possibilities for building intelligent applications that can see, hear, understand, and make decisions. By harnessing the power of these pre-trained AI models, you can create innovative solutions that enhance user experiences, automate processes, and drive business growth.

Section 10:
Advanced Azure Concepts

Azure Resource Manager (ARM): Infrastructure as Code

Outline

- What is Infrastructure as Code (IaC)?
- Introduction to Azure Resource Manager (ARM)
- ARM Templates
- ARM Deployment Modes
- Best Practices for ARM Templates
- Alternatives to ARM Templates: Bicep
- Chapter Summary

What is Infrastructure as Code (IaC)?

Infrastructure as Code (IaC) is a modern approach to managing and provisioning infrastructure, where you use code to define and automate the creation, modification, and destruction of your resources. Instead of manually clicking through a user interface or running scripts, you define your infrastructure in a declarative or imperative manner, treating it just like any other software code.

Fundamental Principles of IaC

- **Declarative:** In declarative IaC, you define the desired state of your infrastructure, and the IaC tool figures out how to achieve that state. This simplifies the process as you don't need to write the step-by-step instructions yourself.
- **Idempotent:** An IaC operation is idempotent when executing it multiple times results in the same end state. This ensures consistency and prevents unintended changes when the same code is run repeatedly.
- **Version Controlled:** IaC configurations are stored in version control systems like Git. This allows you to track changes, revert to previous states, and collaborate with others effectively.
- **Automated:** IaC enables you to automate the provisioning and management of your infrastructure, reducing manual effort and the risk of human error.

Benefits of IaC

IaC offers several key benefits:

- **Improved Consistency:** IaC ensures that your infrastructure is deployed consistently, eliminating configuration drift and reducing the likelihood of errors caused by manual intervention.
- **Increased Speed and Efficiency:** Automation through IaC significantly speeds up the provisioning process, allowing you to create and manage infrastructure more quickly and efficiently.
- **Enhanced Collaboration:** By storing IaC configurations in version control, teams can collaborate more effectively, track changes, and review each other's work.

- **Reduced Risk of Human Error:** Automating tasks with IaC eliminates the risk of human errors that can occur during manual configuration.
- **Cost Savings:** IaC can help reduce costs by optimizing resource utilization and automating repetitive tasks.
- **Improved Disaster Recovery:** IaC configurations can be easily replicated to recreate infrastructure in the event of a disaster, ensuring faster recovery times.

IaC and DevOps

IaC is a cornerstone of the DevOps methodology, which promotes collaboration between development and operations teams. IaC enables developers to provision their own infrastructure without relying on manual intervention from operations teams. This speeds up development cycles, improves agility, and fosters a more collaborative and efficient workflow between teams.

In summary, Infrastructure as Code revolutionizes the way we manage infrastructure, bringing the benefits of software development practices to the world of infrastructure. By embracing IaC, you can achieve greater consistency, reliability, speed, and efficiency in your Azure deployments.

Introduction to Azure Resource Manager (ARM)

Azure Resource Manager (ARM) is the foundational service within Azure that empowers Infrastructure as Code (IaC) practices. Think of ARM as the brain behind orchestrating and managing all your Azure resources. It's the engine that translates your code into the actual deployment and configuration of your cloud infrastructure.

At its core, ARM provides a consistent management layer that enables you to create, update, and delete resources in your Azure account. It acts as a central interface for interacting with Azure services, allowing you to manage everything from virtual machines and networks to storage accounts and databases.

ARM Templates: Your Blueprint for Azure Infrastructure

ARM templates are the primary tool for defining your Azure infrastructure in code. These templates are written in JavaScript Object Notation (JSON) format and serve as blueprints that describe the resources you want to deploy and their configurations. An ARM template can include details like the type of resources (e.g., virtual machines, storage accounts), their names, locations, and any other relevant properties.

Benefits of Using Azure Resource Manager

Utilizing Azure Resource Manager and ARM templates offers a plethora of benefits for managing your Azure environment:

- **Simplified Deployment:** ARM templates allow you to deploy entire solutions, consisting of multiple resources, with a single command. This eliminates the need for manual configuration and reduces the risk of errors.
- **Improved Reliability:** ARM templates ensure consistent and repeatable deployments. This means that you can confidently deploy your infrastructure across different environments (e.g., development, testing, production) knowing that the resources will be configured in the same way every time.
- **Better Resource Management:** ARM provides a centralized view of your Azure resources, making it easier to manage and track them. You can group resources together, apply tags for organization, and manage access controls for enhanced security.
- **Versioning and Rollback:** By storing your ARM templates in a source control system, you can track changes, revert to previous versions, and collaborate with team members effectively.

- **Cost Savings:** ARM enables you to define dependencies between resources, ensuring that they are deployed in the correct order and preventing unnecessary resource creation. This can help optimize your resource utilization and reduce costs.
- **Integration with Other Azure Services:** ARM integrates with other Azure services like Azure DevOps and Azure Automation, allowing you to incorporate infrastructure provisioning into your continuous integration and continuous deployment (CI/CD) pipelines.

Overall, Azure Resource Manager is a powerful tool that enables you to take full advantage of the Infrastructure as Code paradigm in Azure. By defining your infrastructure in code, you can achieve greater automation, consistency, and control over your Azure deployments. This, in turn, leads to increased efficiency, reduced errors, and faster time-to-market for your applications and services.

ARM Templates

Azure Resource Manager (ARM) templates, the fundamental building blocks of IaC within the Azure ecosystem, are essentially JSON files that act as blueprints for your Azure infrastructure. They provide a declarative way to define the desired state of your resources, outlining their types, properties, dependencies, and configurations.

Structure and Syntax

ARM templates follow a structured format, consisting of several key sections:

- **$schema:** This section specifies the URI (Uniform Resource Identifier) of the JSON schema file that describes the template language's version. It ensures that your template adheres to the correct syntax and structure.
- **contentVersion:** This specifies the version of the template itself, allowing you to track changes and maintain backward compatibility.
- **parameters:** Parameters are placeholders for values that can be provided during deployment, allowing for customization and reusability of templates. You can define parameters for various aspects, such as resource names, sizes, or locations.
- **variables:** Variables are expressions that can be used to simplify your template by storing values that are calculated or derived from parameters. They help reduce redundancy and improve readability.
- **functions:** Functions are built-in expressions that can be used for various operations within the template, such as string manipulation, date calculations, or conditional logic.
- **resources:** This is the heart of the ARM template, where you define the Azure resources you want to create. Each resource has a `type`, `name`, and `apiVersion`, along with additional properties that define its configuration.

Example ARM Template Syntax

```
{ "$schema": "https://schema.management.azure.com/schemas/2019-04-01/deploymentTemplate.json#", "contentVersion": "1.0.0.0", "parameters": { "storageAccountName": { "type": "string", "defaultValue": "mystorageaccount" } }, "variables": { "location": "[resourceGroup().location]" }, "resources": [ { "type": "Microsoft.Storage/storageAccounts", "apiVersion": "2022-09-01", "name": "[parameters('storageAccountName')]", "location": "[variables('location')]", "sku": { "name": "Standard_LRS" }, "kind": "StorageV2" } ] }
```

In this example:

- We have a parameter `storageAccountName` that defines the name of the storage account to be created.
- We have a variable `location` that gets the location of the resource group.
- We have a resource of type `Microsoft.Storage/storageAccounts` representing the storage account.

This template defines a single Azure storage account. When deployed, it will create a storage account with the name specified in the `storageAccountName` parameter (or "mystorageaccount" if no value is provided) in the same location as the resource group. This is just a basic example, and ARM templates can become much more complex, defining intricate relationships between resources and incorporating sophisticated configurations.

Understanding the structure and syntax of ARM templates is crucial for leveraging the power of IaC in Azure. By mastering this declarative approach, you can streamline your deployment processes, ensure consistency, and accelerate the delivery of your Azure solutions.

Parameters, Variables, and Functions

Azure Resource Manager (ARM) templates leverage parameters, variables, and functions to create dynamic and adaptable infrastructure definitions. These elements play crucial roles in customizing deployments, simplifying template code, and incorporating logical operations.

Parameters:

Parameters are placeholders for values that can be provided at deployment time. They make your ARM templates reusable across different environments and scenarios. By using parameters, you can avoid hardcoding values within the template, enabling you to change the configuration without modifying the template itself.

Example:

```
"parameters": { "storageAccountName": { "type": "string", "defaultValue": "mystorageaccount" } }
```

In this example, the "storageAccountName" parameter allows you to specify the desired name for your storage account during deployment. If you don't provide a value, the default value "mystorageaccount" will be used.

Variables:

Variables are used to simplify your ARM templates by storing values that are calculated or derived from parameters. They can also be used to store values that are used multiple times within the template, reducing redundancy and improving readability.

Example:

```
"variables": { "storageAccountEndpoint": "[concat('https://', parameters('storageAccountName'), '.blob.core.windows.net/')]" }
```

This example demonstrates how a variable "storageAccountEndpoint" is created by concatenating the parameter "storageAccountName" with a fixed string, resulting in a valid storage account endpoint.

Functions:

Functions are pre-built operations that you can use within your ARM templates to perform various tasks, such as string manipulation, arithmetic calculations, resource property retrieval, and more. Functions add flexibility and dynamic behavior to your templates.

Example:

`"resources": [ { "type": "Microsoft.Web/sites", "name": "[uniqueString(resourceGroup().id)]", "location": "[resourceGroup().location]" } ]`

In this example, the `uniqueString` function generates a unique name for the web app based on the resource group's ID, ensuring uniqueness and avoiding conflicts during deployment.

Leveraging Parameters, Variables, and Functions

By effectively utilizing parameters, variables, and functions, you can create more flexible, maintainable, and powerful ARM templates. Parameters enable you to customize deployments for different environments. Variables help simplify complex expressions and reduce redundancy. Functions allow you to perform calculations, manipulate strings, and incorporate conditional logic into your templates. Together, these elements empower you to define your Azure infrastructure in a concise, reusable, and adaptable manner.

Resources and Properties

The heart of an ARM template lies in the "resources" section. This is where you explicitly define the Azure resources you wish to deploy, effectively turning your infrastructure vision into reality.

Defining Azure Resources

Each resource within the "resources" section is represented as a JSON object with specific properties:

- **type:** This property specifies the type of resource you want to create, following a hierarchical naming convention. For example, `Microsoft.Storage/storageAccounts` denotes a storage account resource.
- **apiVersion:** This property indicates the API version of the resource provider that you want to use for deployment. It ensures compatibility with the desired functionality and features.
- **name:** This property defines a unique name for the resource within its scope (e.g., resource group or subscription).
- **location:** Specifies the Azure region where the resource will be deployed.
- **properties:** This section contains the configuration settings specific to the resource type. These properties define the characteristics of the resource, such as its size, capacity, or access controls.

Example: Creating a Virtual Machine

`{ "type": "Microsoft.Compute/virtualMachines", "apiVersion": "2023-07-01", "name": "myVM", "location": "[resourceGroup().location]", "properties": { "hardwareProfile": { "vmSize": "Standard_DS1_v2" }, "storageProfile": { "osDisk": { "createOption": "FromImage", "imageReference": { "publisher": "MicrosoftWindowsServer", "offer": "WindowsServer", "sku": "2019-Datacenter", "version": "latest" } } } } }`

In this example, we define a virtual machine named "myVM" with a specific hardware profile and storage configuration.

Resource Properties and Dependencies

Resource properties are used to customize the resource's behavior and configuration. For instance, you can specify the size of a virtual machine, the performance tier of a database, or the access controls for a storage account. Additionally, you can define dependencies between resources, ensuring that they are deployed in the correct order. For example, a virtual machine might depend on a virtual network being created first.

Nested Templates

When dealing with complex deployments that involve numerous resources, nested templates come to the rescue. They allow you to modularize your ARM templates by breaking them down into smaller, reusable components. Each nested template can define a specific part of your infrastructure, and you can then reference these nested templates in your main template. This promotes reusability, improves maintainability, and simplifies the management of large-scale deployments.

By understanding how to define resources, their properties, and dependencies within ARM templates, you gain the power to model your entire Azure infrastructure as code. This approach unlocks automation, consistency, and repeatability, making it easier to manage and scale your Azure solutions.

ARM Deployment Modes

Azure Resource Manager (ARM) offers two distinct deployment modes: incremental and complete. Understanding the nuances of each mode is crucial for effectively managing your Azure infrastructure deployments.

Incremental Deployment (Default)

Incremental deployment is the default mode in ARM. When you deploy a template in incremental mode, ARM focuses on creating or updating resources specified in the template. It leaves existing resources that are not defined in the template untouched. In essence, incremental deployment is like adding or modifying specific pieces of your infrastructure without affecting the rest.

Advantages:

- **Preserves Existing Resources:** This mode is safer, as it avoids accidental deletion of resources that are not included in the template.
- **Faster Deployment:** Since it only focuses on changes, incremental deployments are generally faster than complete deployments.
- **Suitable for Most Scenarios:** Incremental deployment is ideal for adding new resources, updating existing ones, or making minor configuration changes.

Disadvantages:

- **Potential for Configuration Drift:** Over time, incremental deployments can lead to configuration drift if resources are modified outside of the template.
- **May Not Remove Unused Resources:** If a resource is no longer needed but is not explicitly removed from the template, it will continue to exist in the resource group.

Complete Deployment

Complete deployment takes a more aggressive approach. When you deploy a template in complete mode, ARM will delete any existing resources in the resource group that are not defined in the template. It then proceeds to create or update the resources specified in the template. This mode effectively ensures that your resource group's state exactly matches the template's definition.

Advantages:

- **Eliminates Configuration Drift:** Complete deployment eliminates configuration drift by ensuring that all resources in the resource group match the template's definition.
- **Cleaner Resource Group:** It removes unused or outdated resources, keeping your resource group tidy and preventing unnecessary costs.
- **Ideal for Replacing Deployments:** Complete deployment is well-suited for scenarios where you want to completely replace an existing deployment with a new one.

Disadvantages:

- **Risk of Accidental Deletion:** This mode can be risky, as it will delete any resources that are not present in the template, even if they were created outside of ARM.
- **Slower Deployment:** Complete deployments generally take longer than incremental deployments, especially for large resource groups.
- **May Cause Service Interruptions:** Deleting resources can lead to service interruptions if not carefully planned.

Choosing the Right Deployment Mode

The choice between incremental and complete deployment depends on your specific requirements and risk tolerance. Consider the following factors:

- **Desired Outcome:** Do you want to add/update resources or completely replace an existing deployment?
- **Risk Tolerance:** Are you willing to risk accidental deletion of resources in exchange for ensuring consistency?
- **Deployment Speed:** Do you need a fast deployment, or can you afford a slightly longer deployment time?

In general, incremental deployment is the safer and more common choice for most scenarios. However, complete deployment can be useful in specific situations where you need to strictly enforce consistency or replace an entire deployment.

Always exercise caution when using complete deployment and ensure that you have a proper backup of your resources before proceeding.

Best Practices for ARM Templates

While ARM templates are powerful, adopting best practices will make them easier to work with, especially as your projects grow in complexity.

Organization and Naming:

- **Modularize:** Break down large templates into smaller, reusable nested templates. This improves readability and makes troubleshooting easier.
- **Consistent Naming:** Use a clear and consistent naming convention for resources, parameters, and variables. This makes your templates self-documenting.
- **Resource Group:** Organize related resources into resource groups to simplify management and deployment.
- **Template Parameters:** Use parameters to make your templates reusable across different environments and scenarios.

Comments, Formatting, and Modularization:

- **Comments:** Add comments to explain the purpose of different sections, resources, and parameters. This makes your templates easier to understand for yourself and others.
- **Indentation:** Use consistent indentation to make your templates visually appealing and easier to follow.
- **Whitespace:** Use whitespace effectively to separate different sections and improve readability.
- **Nested Templates:** Use nested templates to modularize your templates and reuse common configurations.
- **Parameter Files:** Use separate parameter files for different environments to avoid having to modify the template itself for each deployment.

Linting Tools:

- **ARM Template Toolkit (arm-ttk):** A PowerShell module that provides linting and validation capabilities for ARM templates.
- **Visual Studio Code Extension:** Install the Azure Resource Manager Tools extension for Visual Studio Code to get syntax highlighting, validation, and IntelliSense features.
- **Online Linting Tools:** There are several online tools available that can help you validate your ARM templates.

Source Control:

- **Versioning:** Store your ARM templates in a source control system like Git. This allows you to track changes, collaborate with others, and roll back to previous versions if needed.
- **Branching:** Use branches to develop and test changes to your templates in isolation before merging them into the main branch.

By following these best practices, you can ensure that your ARM templates are well-structured, maintainable, and easy to troubleshoot.

Alternatives to ARM Templates: Bicep

Bicep is a newer domain-specific language (DSL) designed for deploying Azure resources declaratively. It offers several advantages over ARM templates:

- **Improved Readability:** Bicep has a more concise and intuitive syntax compared to JSON, making your templates easier to read and write.
- **Enhanced Tooling:** Bicep is integrated with popular IDEs like Visual Studio Code, providing features like syntax highlighting, auto-completion, and type checking.
- **Improved Error Handling:** Bicep provides better error messages and validation, making it easier to troubleshoot deployment issues.
- **Enhanced Modularity:** Bicep supports modules, allowing you to reuse common configurations and simplify your templates.

Learning Resources for Bicep:

- **Microsoft Bicep Documentation:** The official Microsoft documentation provides a comprehensive guide to Bicep, including syntax, examples, and best practices.
- **Bicep Playground:** An online tool that allows you to experiment with Bicep and see how it translates to ARM templates.
- **Bicep GitHub Repository:** The Bicep project is open source and hosted on GitHub. You can find the source code, examples, and community contributions there.

While ARM templates remain a viable option, Bicep offers a modern and improved alternative for deploying Azure resources declaratively. It is well-suited for developers who prefer a more concise syntax and enhanced tooling support. If you're new to IaC in Azure or looking for a more streamlined way to define your infrastructure, Bicep is worth exploring.

Chapter Summary

In this chapter, we delved into the world of Infrastructure as Code (IaC) and its implementation in Azure through Azure Resource Manager (ARM). We explored the core concepts of IaC, its benefits, and how ARM templates serve as the foundation for defining and automating infrastructure deployments in Azure.

Key Takeaways:

- **Infrastructure as Code (IaC):** A paradigm shift in infrastructure management, enabling the definition and provisioning of infrastructure through code, leading to improved consistency, reproducibility, and automation.
- **Azure Resource Manager (ARM):** Azure's native IaC engine, responsible for deploying and managing resources in your Azure account.
- **ARM Templates:** JSON files that act as blueprints for your Azure infrastructure, describing the resources to be deployed and their configurations.
- **Template Structure and Syntax:** The essential sections of an ARM template, including schema, content version, parameters, variables, functions, and resources.
- **Parameters, Variables, and Functions:** How these elements enhance the flexibility and adaptability of ARM templates, allowing for customization, simplification, and logic implementation.
- **Resources and Properties:** Defining different types of Azure resources within templates, setting their properties, and managing dependencies.
- **Deployment Modes:** Incremental and complete deployment modes, their advantages and disadvantages, and when to choose each mode.
- **Best Practices:** Guidelines for organizing, naming, and maintaining ARM templates for better readability and reusability.
- **Bicep:** An alternative to ARM templates, offering a simpler syntax and improved developer experience.

By mastering Azure Resource Manager and ARM templates (or Bicep), you can unlock the full potential of IaC in Azure. This powerful combination enables you to automate infrastructure deployments, enforce consistency, and streamline your development and operations workflows, ultimately accelerating the delivery of your Azure solutions.

Azure DevOps: Continuous Integration and Deployment (CI/CD)

Outline

- What is Azure DevOps?
- Key Components of Azure DevOps
- Setting Up Azure DevOps
- Building CI/CD Pipelines
- Azure DevOps and Agile Development
- Best Practices for Azure DevOps
- Chapter Summary

What is Azure DevOps?

Azure DevOps is an all-encompassing platform offered by Microsoft that provides a unified set of tools and services designed to streamline the entire software development lifecycle (SDLC). It serves as a centralized hub for planning, collaborating, building, testing, and deploying applications, fostering a seamless and efficient workflow for development teams of all sizes.

Role in Software Development

Azure DevOps plays a pivotal role in modern software development by providing a comprehensive toolkit that supports various methodologies, including Agile and DevOps. It empowers teams to:

- **Plan and Track Work:** Azure Boards allows teams to define project goals, create backlogs, prioritize work items, and track progress using various agile tools like Kanban boards and Scrum boards.
- **Manage Source Code:** Azure Repos provides a robust version control system for managing source code, supporting both Git and Team Foundation Version Control (TFVC).
- **Build and Test:** Azure Pipelines enables continuous integration and continuous delivery (CI/CD), automating the build, test, and deployment processes for faster and more reliable software delivery.
- **Test and Release:** Azure Test Plans facilitates comprehensive testing, including manual and exploratory testing, as well as automated testing through integration with popular testing frameworks.
- **Manage Packages:** Azure Artifacts provides a package management solution for sharing and consuming packages from various sources, including public and private feeds.

Evolution from Visual Studio Team Services (VSTS)

Azure DevOps evolved from Microsoft's Visual Studio Team Services (VSTS), a platform that provided similar development tools and services. While VSTS was primarily focused on Microsoft technologies, Azure DevOps expanded its scope to support a wider range of platforms and languages, embracing a more open and flexible approach to software development. The rebranding to Azure DevOps in 2018 reflected this shift towards a broader ecosystem and greater integration with other Azure services.

Benefits of Azure DevOps

Adopting Azure DevOps can bring several significant benefits to your development team and organization:

- **Improved Collaboration:** The platform fosters collaboration by providing a centralized hub where team members can easily share code, track work items, and communicate effectively. This leads to better coordination, faster issue resolution, and increased productivity.
- **Faster Delivery:** Azure DevOps' CI/CD capabilities automate the build, test, and deployment processes, enabling teams to release software updates more frequently and reliably. This accelerates time-to-market and allows for quicker feedback cycles.
- **Higher Quality Software:** Azure Test Plans enables comprehensive testing, ensuring that software is thoroughly validated before deployment. This helps to identify and fix bugs early in the development cycle, resulting in higher quality software.
- **Increased Efficiency:** By automating repetitive tasks and providing a centralized platform for managing the entire SDLC, Azure DevOps frees up developers to focus on innovation and value creation.
- **Flexibility and Scalability:** Azure DevOps is a cloud-based platform that can be easily scaled up or down to meet the changing needs of your organization. It also offers a wide range of customization options and integrations with other tools and services.

By embracing Azure DevOps, you can transform your software development process, empowering your teams to deliver high-quality software faster and more efficiently.

Key Components of Azure DevOps

Azure DevOps is a comprehensive suite of tools designed to streamline the entire software development lifecycle. Let's break down the key components that contribute to its effectiveness:

Azure Boards

Azure Boards is the central hub for agile planning and work item tracking. It provides a visual representation of your project's progress, allowing you to manage work items, track dependencies, and monitor overall team performance.

- **Agile Planning:** Azure Boards supports various Agile methodologies, including Scrum and Kanban. You can create backlogs, prioritize work items, plan sprints, and track progress towards your goals. It offers customizable boards, customizable work item types, and sprint planning tools to facilitate agile planning.
- **Work Item Tracking:** Azure Boards allows you to create work items to represent tasks, user stories, bugs, or any other unit of work. You can assign work items to team members, track their progress, and add comments and attachments.
- **Visualization:** Azure Boards offers various visualizations, such as Kanban boards, task boards, and sprint burndown charts, to provide a clear picture of your project's progress and identify potential bottlenecks.

Azure Repos

Azure Repos is a cloud-hosted version control system that enables you to manage your source code. It supports both Git and Team Foundation Version Control (TFVC) for distributed and centralized version control respectively.

- **Version Control:** Azure Repos allows you to track changes to your code, collaborate with team members, and revert to previous versions if needed. It provides features like branching, merging, and pull requests to facilitate code collaboration.
- **Code Reviews:** You can use pull requests to review code changes before they are merged into the main branch, ensuring code quality and adherence to standards.
- **Branch Policies:** Implement branch policies to enforce quality gates, such as requiring code reviews or passing automated tests, before code can be merged.

Azure Pipelines

Azure Pipelines is a powerful continuous integration and continuous delivery (CI/CD) platform that automates the build, test, and deployment processes. It enables you to:

- **Build:** Compile your code, run unit tests, and package your application for deployment.
- **Test:** Execute automated tests, such as unit tests, integration tests, and UI tests, to ensure the quality and stability of your code.
- **Deploy:** Deploy your application to various environments, such as development, staging, and production, in a consistent and reliable manner.

Azure Pipelines supports a wide range of languages, platforms, and deployment targets, making it a versatile tool for CI/CD automation.

Azure Test Plans

Azure Test Plans provides a comprehensive solution for managing and executing manual and exploratory tests. It allows you to:

- **Manage Test Cases:** Create and organize test cases, including steps, expected results, and attachments.
- **Run Tests:** Execute manual tests and record test results, including screenshots and videos.
- **Track Test Progress:** Track the progress of your testing efforts and identify areas that need more attention.

Azure Test Plans also integrates with Azure Pipelines, allowing you to automate test execution as part of your CI/CD pipelines.

Azure Artifacts

Azure Artifacts is a package management service that allows you to store, share, and consume packages from various sources, including public registries like NuGet and npm, as well as private feeds that you create within your organization. It enables you to:

- **Share Packages:** Create and publish packages that can be consumed by other teams or projects within your organization.
- **Control Access:** Manage permissions to control who can access and publish packages.
- **Versioning:** Track different versions of your packages and roll back to previous versions if needed.

Azure Artifacts helps you streamline dependency management and ensure that your teams are using consistent and reliable packages.

By combining these key components, Azure DevOps provides a comprehensive and integrated platform for managing the entire software development lifecycle. Whether you're using Agile, DevOps, or other methodologies, Azure DevOps offers the tools and services you need to collaborate effectively, deliver software faster, and achieve higher quality results.

Setting Up Azure DevOps

To embark on your Azure DevOps journey, you need to establish an organization and create a project within it. This section provides step-by-step instructions on how to accomplish this, along with guidance on choosing the right project type and connecting it to your preferred code repository.

Creating an Azure DevOps Organization and Project

1. **Sign Up for Azure DevOps:** If you don't have an Azure DevOps account, sign up for a free account at https://dev.azure.com/. You can sign up using your Microsoft account or create a new one.
2. **Create an Organization:** Once you've signed in, you'll be prompted to create an organization. Provide a unique name for your organization, choose your location, and select the desired visibility (public or private). Click on the "Create organization" button to proceed.
3. **Create a Project:** Within your organization, click on the "New project" button.
    - **Project Name:** Provide a descriptive name for your project.
    - **Visibility:** Choose the visibility setting for your project. Public projects are accessible to anyone, while private projects are restricted to members of your organization.
    - **Version Control:** Select your preferred version control system: Git (recommended for most scenarios) or Team Foundation Version Control (TFVC).
    - **Work Item Process:** Choose the work item process that aligns with your team's workflow. The options are Basic, Agile, Scrum, or CMMI.
    - **Click "Create"** to create your project.

Choosing the Right Project Type

Azure DevOps offers different project types, each tailored for specific needs:

- **Public Projects:** Suitable for open-source projects or when you want to collaborate with the wider community.
- **Private Projects:** Best for internal projects where you need to restrict access to your organization's members.

Consider the size of your team, the nature of your project, and your collaboration requirements when choosing the appropriate project type.

Connecting Your Project to a Code Repository

After creating a project, you need to connect it to a code repository to store and manage your source code. Azure DevOps seamlessly integrates with both Azure Repos and GitHub.

- **Azure Repos:** If you're using Azure Repos, your project is already connected to a default repository. You can create additional repositories within your project as needed.
- **GitHub:** To connect your project to a GitHub repository:
    1. Navigate to the "Repos" section of your project.
    2. Click on the "Import" button and select "GitHub."
    3. Authorize Azure DevOps to access your GitHub account.
    4. Select the repository you want to connect.
    5. Choose whether you want to import the entire repository or just specific branches.
    6. Click "Import" to start the import process.

Once your project is connected to a code repository, you can start collaborating with your team, tracking work items, and building CI/CD pipelines to automate your development and deployment processes.

Building CI/CD Pipelines

Continuous Integration and Continuous Delivery (CI/CD) pipelines are the cornerstone of modern software development practices. They automate the process of building, testing, and deploying applications, enabling teams to deliver software changes rapidly and reliably.

Continuous Integration (CI)

Continuous Integration (CI) is a development practice where developers integrate code changes into a shared repository frequently, preferably several times a day. Each integration is then verified by an automated build and test process, allowing teams to detect problems early.

Principles of CI

- **Maintain a Single Source Repository:** All code changes are committed to a single, shared repository, ensuring that everyone works with the latest version of the codebase.
- **Automate the Build:** The process of compiling code, running tests, and creating deployable artifacts is automated, eliminating manual steps and ensuring consistency.
- **Make Your Build Self-Testing:** Automated tests are included as part of the build process to validate the correctness and quality of the code.
- **Everyone Commits to the Mainline Every Day:** Developers frequently merge their code changes into the main branch to avoid complex and time-consuming integration tasks.
- **Every Commit Should Build the Mainline on an Integration Machine:** Ensure that every code commit triggers a build and test process on an integration environment to catch issues early.
- **Keep the Build Fast:** Optimize the build process to ensure it runs quickly, providing rapid feedback to developers.
- **Test in a Clone of the Production Environment:** Test your code in an environment that closely resembles the production environment to ensure that it will work as expected when deployed.
- **Make it Easy for Anyone to Get the Latest Executable:** Ensure that the latest build artifacts are readily available to stakeholders for testing or deployment.
- **Everyone can see what's happening:** Make the build results and any test failures visible to the entire team so that issues can be addressed quickly.
- **Automate Deployment:** Automate the deployment process to streamline the delivery of your software to production or staging environments.

Benefits of CI

- **Early Detection of Issues:** CI helps identify integration issues and bugs early in the development cycle, making them easier and cheaper to fix.
- **Improved Code Quality:** Automated tests and builds help maintain code quality by ensuring that changes don't break existing functionality.
- **Faster Delivery of Software Changes:** By automating the build and test process, CI enables faster and more frequent releases of software updates.
- **Increased Team Collaboration:** CI promotes collaboration between developers by encouraging frequent code commits and providing quick feedback on the impact of changes.
- **Reduced Risk of Release Failure:** By catching issues early and deploying changes more frequently, CI reduces the risk of failures in production environments.

Setting Up a CI Pipeline in Azure Pipelines

1. **Create a Pipeline:** In your Azure DevOps project, navigate to "Pipelines" and click on "Create Pipeline."
2. **Choose Your Repository:** Select the repository where your code is stored.
3. **Configure Your Pipeline:** Define the steps of your pipeline, including build tasks, test tasks, and any other tasks you need to run.
4. **Specify Triggers:** Set up triggers to automatically start the pipeline whenever new code is committed or on a schedule.

Examples of CI Triggers, Build Tasks, and Test Tasks

- **Triggers:**
    - **Code Commit:** Trigger the pipeline whenever code is pushed to the repository.
    - **Pull Request:** Trigger the pipeline when a pull request is created or updated.
    - **Scheduled:** Run the pipeline on a schedule, such as nightly or weekly.

- **Build Tasks:**
    - **Maven:** Build Java projects using Maven.
    - **Gradle:** Build Java or Android projects using Gradle.
    - **npm:** Build Node.js projects.
    - **.NET:** Build .NET applications.
- **Test Tasks:**
    - **Visual Studio Test:** Run unit tests for .NET applications.
    - **JUnit:** Run unit tests for Java applications.
    - **NUnit:** Run unit tests for .NET applications.
    - **Selenium:** Run UI tests.

This section has presented a comprehensive overview of continuous integration (CI) and its significance in modern software development. The subsequent chapters will delve into the details of continuous delivery (CD) and continuous deployment (CD) practices within Azure DevOps.

Continuous Delivery (CD)

Continuous Delivery (CD) is the next evolutionary step after Continuous Integration (CI) in the CI/CD pipeline. While CI ensures that code changes are integrated and tested regularly, CD takes it further by automating the deployment process to various environments, typically starting with a staging environment.

Principles of CD

- **Build Once, Deploy Many:** The artifact produced during the CI process is deployed multiple times to different environments without being rebuilt, ensuring consistency and reliability.
- **Automate Deployments:** The deployment process is fully automated, eliminating manual steps and reducing the risk of human error.
- **Deployment Environments:** Create separate environments for different stages of the deployment process, such as development, staging, and production. This allows for thorough testing and validation before deploying to production.
- **Deployment as a Business Decision:** While deployments are automated, the decision to deploy to production is a business decision, often requiring approval from stakeholders.
- **Production-Like Environments:** Ensure that your staging and testing environments closely resemble the production environment to minimize surprises during deployment.

Benefits of CD

- **Faster Time to Market:** CD enables rapid deployment of new features and fixes, shortening the feedback loop and allowing for quicker iterations.
- **Reduced Risk of Deployment Failures:** Automated deployments with comprehensive testing in pre-production environments help identify and address issues before they reach production, reducing the risk of costly failures.
- **Increased Confidence in Deployments:** With automated tests and validations in place, teams gain greater confidence in their deployments, leading to improved reliability and customer satisfaction.
- **Improved Collaboration between Teams:** CD fosters collaboration between development, testing, and operations teams by creating a standardized and automated deployment process.

Setting Up a CD Pipeline in Azure Pipelines

1. **Create a Release Pipeline:** In your Azure DevOps project, navigate to "Releases" and click on "New release pipeline."
2. **Select a Template:** Choose a template based on your deployment target (e.g., Azure App Service, Azure Kubernetes Service).
3. **Link Artifacts:** Link your release pipeline to the build artifact produced by your CI pipeline.

4. **Define Stages:** Create stages for each environment (e.g., Dev, QA, Staging, Production) and add deployment tasks to each stage.
5. **Configure Approval Gates:** Add approval gates before deploying to sensitive environments like production, ensuring that stakeholders review and approve changes before they are deployed.
6. **Set up Triggers:** Configure triggers to automatically start the release pipeline when a new build artifact is available or based on a schedule.

Examples of Deployment Tasks and Approval Gates

- **Deployment Tasks:**
    - **Azure App Service Deploy:** Deploys a web application to Azure App Service.
    - **Azure Kubernetes Service Deploy:** Deploys a containerized application to Azure Kubernetes Service (AKS).
    - **Azure Virtual Machine Deploy:** Deploys a virtual machine or a virtual machine scale set to Azure.
- **Approval Gates:**
    - **Pre-Deployment Approval:** Requires approval from stakeholders before deploying to an environment.
    - **Post-Deployment Approval:** Requires approval after deployment to confirm successful deployment and testing.
    - **Manual Intervention:** Allows for manual intervention during the deployment process, such as running additional tests or performing manual checks.

By implementing Continuous Delivery (CD) with Azure Pipelines, you can significantly streamline your software delivery process, enabling faster and more reliable deployments while reducing the risk of errors and failures.

Continuous Deployment (CD)

Continuous Deployment (CD) is the final stage in the CI/CD pipeline, taking the automation one step further by automatically deploying every change that passes all stages of your production pipeline directly to your end users.

Principles of CD

- **Automated Release to Production:** CD removes the manual approval step present in continuous delivery. Once code changes pass all automated tests in the staging environment, they are automatically deployed to production.
- **Frequent Releases:** CD encourages smaller, more frequent releases, reducing the risk associated with each deployment and allowing for faster feedback from users.
- **Production-Ready Environments:** To succeed with CD, your production environment must be well-maintained and highly reliable. This involves having automated testing and monitoring in place to detect issues quickly.
- **Feature Flags:** Feature flags are mechanisms to enable or disable features in production without deploying new code. This allows for controlled rollouts and testing in production.
- **Monitoring and Observability:** Continuous monitoring of the production environment is crucial to identify and address any issues that arise from deployments quickly.

Benefits of CD

- **Accelerated Time to Market:** CD allows for the fastest possible delivery of new features and improvements to users.
- **Reduced Risk:** Smaller, more frequent deployments reduce the risk associated with each release. Any issues that arise can be quickly identified and rolled back.
- **Improved Feedback Loop:** CD accelerates the feedback loop with your customers, allowing you to learn quickly and iterate on your product based on real-world usage.

- **Increased Team Efficiency:** By automating the deployment process, CD frees up developers from manual tasks, allowing them to focus on building new features and improving the product.

Setting Up a CD Pipeline in Azure Pipelines

Setting up a CD pipeline in Azure Pipelines is similar to setting up a CD pipeline. The key difference is that the final stage of the pipeline automatically deploys the code to production, bypassing any manual approval gates.

1. **Create a Release Pipeline:** In your Azure DevOps project, navigate to "Releases" and click on "New release pipeline."
2. **Select a Template:** Choose a template based on your deployment target (e.g., Azure App Service, Azure Kubernetes Service).
3. **Link Artifacts:** Link your release pipeline to the build artifact produced by your CI pipeline.
4. **Define Stages:** Create stages for each environment, including production. Add deployment tasks to each stage.
5. **Remove Manual Approval Gates:** Since CD is about automated deployment, remove any manual approval gates before the production stage.
6. **Set up Triggers:** Configure the pipeline to trigger automatically whenever a new build artifact is available that has passed all tests in the previous stages.

Examples of Production Deployment Tasks and Monitoring

- **Deployment Tasks:**
  - **Azure App Service Deploy:** Deploy the application package to Azure App Service.
  - **Kubernetes Manifest Task:** Apply Kubernetes manifests to deploy containers in AKS.
  - **Azure SQL Database Deployment:** Update the database schema or deploy new database changes.
- **Monitoring:**
  - **Application Insights:** Collect telemetry data from the application, including logs, exceptions, and performance metrics.
  - **Azure Monitor:** Monitor the health and performance of the underlying Azure resources.
  - **Log Analytics:** Analyze log data to identify any potential issues or errors caused by the deployment.
  - **Azure Alerts:** Set up alerts to notify you of any performance degradation or errors in the production environment.

Continuous deployment is a powerful practice that can significantly accelerate your software delivery process and improve the quality of your software. By automating the entire pipeline from code commit to production deployment, you can deliver value to your customers more quickly and with greater confidence.

Azure DevOps and Agile Development

Azure DevOps is a natural fit for agile development methodologies, offering a comprehensive set of tools that seamlessly integrate with Agile practices, fostering collaboration, visibility, and rapid iteration.

Azure Boards for Agile Planning and Management

Azure Boards is the epicenter of Agile planning and management within Azure DevOps. It provides a flexible platform that can be tailored to various Agile frameworks, including Scrum and Kanban. Here's how it supports key Agile practices:

- **Sprint Planning:** Azure Boards allows teams to create sprints, define sprint goals, and assign work items to sprints. It facilitates collaborative sprint planning sessions, allowing team members to estimate effort, prioritize work, and create a sprint backlog.

- **Backlog Management:** Azure Boards provides a backlog view to manage the entire list of work items. You can create user stories, bugs, tasks, or other types of work items, prioritize them, and organize them into a hierarchical structure. This allows you to maintain a clear view of the work ahead and easily track its progress.
- **Kanban Boards:** For teams that prefer a Kanban-style workflow, Azure Boards offers customizable Kanban boards. These boards visualize the flow of work, allowing you to see which items are in progress, which are blocked, and which are ready for review. This promotes transparency and helps identify bottlenecks early on.

Azure Pipelines for Automating Agile Workflows

Azure Pipelines plays a crucial role in automating the build, test, and deployment processes within an Agile workflow. By automating these tasks, you can achieve:

- **Faster Feedback Loops:** Automated builds and tests provide rapid feedback to developers, allowing them to catch and fix issues early in the development cycle.
- **Continuous Integration:** Azure Pipelines enables continuous integration, where code changes are frequently integrated into a shared repository and automatically tested. This ensures that the codebase remains stable and that integration issues are identified promptly.
- **Continuous Delivery and Deployment:** You can set up pipelines to automatically deploy your application to staging or production environments after successful builds and tests. This facilitates rapid and reliable delivery of new features and fixes to users.

Integrating Azure DevOps with Other Agile Tools

Azure DevOps is designed to integrate with a wide range of tools commonly used in Agile environments:

- **Collaboration Tools:** Integrate with Microsoft Teams or Slack for seamless communication and collaboration.
- **Project Management Tools:** Connect with project management tools like Jira or Trello to synchronize work items and track progress.
- **Automated Testing Tools:** Integrate with automated testing frameworks like Selenium or JUnit to run tests as part of your CI/CD pipelines.
- **Code Analysis Tools:** Use code analysis tools like SonarQube or Checkmarx to identify code quality issues and security vulnerabilities.
- **Monitoring Tools:** Integrate with monitoring tools like Application Insights or Azure Monitor to track the performance and health of your applications in production.

By leveraging the flexibility and integration capabilities of Azure DevOps, you can create a tailored Agile environment that aligns with your team's specific workflows and preferences, boosting collaboration, accelerating delivery, and ensuring the quality of your software.

Best Practices for Azure DevOps

To maximize the benefits of Azure DevOps and ensure a smooth and efficient development process, adhering to certain best practices can significantly impact your team's productivity and the quality of your software.

Use a Suitable Branching Strategy

A well-defined branching strategy is essential for maintaining a clean and organized codebase. Choose a branching strategy that aligns with your team's workflow and project requirements. Popular options include:

- **Trunk-Based Development:** In this strategy, all developers work on a single branch ("trunk"), and changes are merged frequently. This approach promotes continuous integration and reduces the risk of merge conflicts.
- **Gitflow:** A more structured approach with separate branches for development, features, releases, and hotfixes. This strategy provides better isolation of features and allows for controlled releases.
- **Release Flow:** A simplified version of Gitflow designed for teams that release frequently. It focuses on using release branches for stabilizing features and hotfixes.

Automate Testing and Deployment

Automation is key to achieving the benefits of CI/CD. Invest in automated testing to ensure that code changes are thoroughly validated before deployment. Utilize Azure Pipelines to create automated build, test, and deployment pipelines that streamline your workflows and reduce manual effort.

Leverage Work Item Tracking

Azure Boards' work item tracking feature is a valuable tool for managing tasks, user stories, bugs, and other work items. Assign work items to team members, track their progress, and link them to commits, pull requests, and builds for traceability and accountability. Use work item queries to filter and analyze your work items, gaining insights into your team's productivity and identifying areas for improvement.

Embrace Release Management

Azure Pipelines' release management features enable you to manage the deployment of your applications across multiple environments. Define release pipelines that automate deployment steps, configure approvals and gates for controlled rollouts, and track deployment history. By utilizing release management, you can ensure that your deployments are consistent, reliable, and compliant with your organization's policies.

Monitor Pipelines and Deployments

Continuous monitoring is crucial for identifying and addressing issues promptly. Monitor your pipelines for build failures, test errors, and deployment issues. Use Azure Monitor to track the performance and health of your deployed applications. Set up alerts to be notified of any anomalies or failures, allowing you to take corrective action before they impact your users.

Utilize Azure DevOps Extensions

Azure DevOps offers a vast marketplace of extensions that can enhance your workflows and integrate with other tools and services. Explore the marketplace to find extensions that can add value to your development process, such as code quality tools, security scanners, and productivity enhancements.

By embracing these best practices and utilizing the full capabilities of Azure DevOps, you can transform your software development process, enhance collaboration, accelerate delivery, and achieve higher quality results.

Chapter Summary

In this chapter, we explored the comprehensive capabilities of Azure DevOps, Microsoft's cloud-based platform designed to streamline the entire software development lifecycle. We delved into its key components—Azure Boards, Azure Repos, Azure Pipelines, Azure Test Plans, and Azure Artifacts—and how they seamlessly integrate to foster collaboration, automation, and efficiency in your development process.

Key Takeaways:

- **Azure DevOps:** A powerful, unified platform that empowers teams to plan, collaborate, build, test, and deploy applications effectively.
- **Agile Planning and Tracking:** Azure Boards serves as your central hub for agile planning, work item tracking, and visualization, supporting various agile methodologies like Scrum and Kanban.
- **Version Control:** Azure Repos offers robust version control capabilities, allowing you to manage your source code using Git or TFVC and collaborate seamlessly with your team.
- **CI/CD Automation:** Azure Pipelines enables you to automate your build, test, and deployment processes, ensuring faster and more reliable software delivery.
- **Comprehensive Testing:** Azure Test Plans facilitates manual and exploratory testing, along with integration with automated testing frameworks, ensuring the quality and reliability of your software.
- **Package Management:** Azure Artifacts provides a central repository for storing, sharing, and consuming packages, streamlining dependency management and promoting code reusability.

By embracing Azure DevOps and adhering to best practices such as choosing an appropriate branching strategy, automating testing and deployment, leveraging work item tracking, and utilizing release management features, you can elevate your development process to new heights. Azure DevOps empowers your team to collaborate seamlessly, deliver software faster, and achieve higher quality results.

Azure Policy: Enforcing Governance and Compliance

Outline

- What is Azure Policy?
- Policy Definitions and Structure
- Policy Assignments and Scope
- Policy Effects
- Initiative Definitions
- Azure Policy Compliance
- Azure Policy and Regulatory Compliance
- Best Practices for Using Azure Policy
- Chapter Summary

What is Azure Policy?

Azure Policy is a robust governance tool within Microsoft Azure that empowers organizations to enforce organizational standards and ensure compliance across their cloud environment. It acts as a vigilant guard, evaluating your Azure resources and actions against a set of predefined rules and configurations. This policy-based approach to management establishes guardrails and ensures that your resources adhere to your organization's security, regulatory, and operational requirements.

Policy-Based Management

At its core, Azure Policy embodies the concept of policy-based management. This approach involves defining rules and conditions that dictate how resources should be configured and used within your Azure environment. These rules, known as policy definitions, are written in a declarative language and can be applied to various scopes, such as subscriptions, resource groups, or even entire management groups.

Policy-based management offers several advantages:

- **Consistency:** It ensures that resources are consistently configured and deployed according to your organization's standards, reducing the risk of human error and configuration drift.
- **Automation:** Azure Policy automatically evaluates your resources against your defined policies, reducing the need for manual checks and audits.
- **Enforcement:** You can configure policies to enforce compliance, either by preventing non-compliant resources from being created or modified or by automatically remediating existing resources to meet your standards.
- **Visibility:** Azure Policy provides a centralized dashboard where you can view the compliance status of your resources and track your progress towards achieving compliance.

Importance of Governance and Compliance in the Cloud

In a cloud environment, where resources can be easily provisioned and modified, governance and compliance become paramount. Azure Policy addresses these critical needs by:

- **Enforcing Organizational Standards:** You can define policies that align with your organization's security, regulatory, or operational standards, ensuring that all resources adhere to these requirements.

- **Assessing Compliance at Scale:** Azure Policy can automatically scan your entire Azure environment, evaluating thousands of resources against your defined policies. This provides you with a comprehensive view of your compliance posture and helps identify any non-compliant resources.
- **Simplifying Remediation:** Azure Policy can automatically remediate non-compliant resources, bringing them into compliance without manual intervention.
- **Meeting Regulatory Requirements:** Azure Policy can help you meet various regulatory compliance requirements, such as HIPAA, PCI DSS, and ISO 27001, by enforcing policies that align with these standards.
- **Reducing Risk:** By proactively enforcing compliance and identifying security vulnerabilities, Azure Policy helps you mitigate risks and protect your Azure environment from potential threats.

In essence, Azure Policy acts as a guardian of your Azure environment, ensuring that your resources are configured and used in a manner that aligns with your organization's goals and regulatory requirements. It provides a powerful and flexible framework for establishing guardrails and maintaining control over your cloud infrastructure.

Policy Definitions and Structure

Azure Policy definitions are the foundation of Azure Policy, representing the rules and conditions that dictate how resources should be configured and managed in your Azure environment. Each policy definition acts as a blueprint for evaluating the compliance state of your resources.

Structure of a Policy Definition

A policy definition in Azure Policy consists of two main blocks:

- `if` **block:** This block defines the condition or set of conditions that trigger the policy evaluation. It specifies the resource types, properties, and values that the policy will check for compliance. You can use logical operators like "and," "or," and "not" to create complex conditions.
- `then` **block:** This block defines the effect that the policy will take if the condition in the `if` block is met. There are several types of policy effects, including "Audit" (log an event), "Deny" (prevent non-compliant resources from being created), "Modify" (modify non-compliant resources to make them compliant), and others.

Types of Policy Definitions

Azure Policy offers two types of policy definitions:

- **Built-in Policy Definitions:** These are pre-defined policies provided by Microsoft that cover a wide range of common governance and compliance scenarios. They are readily available for use and can be easily assigned to your resources.
- **Custom Policy Definitions:** You can create your own policy definitions to address specific requirements that are not covered by built-in policies. Custom policies offer greater flexibility and control over your governance rules.

Examples of Common Policy Definitions

Here are a few examples of common policy definitions:

- **Enforcing Resource Naming Conventions:** You can create a policy that enforces a specific naming convention for your resources, such as requiring all virtual machine names to start with "vm-".

```
{ "if": { "allOf": [ { "field": "type", "equals":
"Microsoft.Compute/virtualMachines" }, { "not": { "field": "name",
"like": "vm-*" } } ] }, "then": { "effect": "deny" } }
```

- **Restricting Resource Types:** You can create a policy that denies the creation of specific resource types, such as restricting the creation of virtual machines with certain SKUs.

    ```
    { "if": { "allOf": [ { "field": "type", "equals":
    "Microsoft.Compute/virtualMachines" }, { "field":
    "properties.hardwareProfile.vmSize", "in": ["Standard_DS1_v2",
    "Standard_DS2_v2"] } ] }, "then": { "effect": "deny" } }
    ```

- **Enforcing Tag Usage:** You can create a policy that requires all resources to have specific tags, such as a department tag or a cost center tag.

    ```
    { "if": { "field": "tags.Department", "exists": "false" }, "then": {
    "effect": "deny" } }
    ```

These are just a few examples of how Azure Policy definitions can be used to enforce governance and compliance in your Azure environment. By understanding the structure of policy definitions and creating custom definitions tailored to your needs, you can effectively manage and control your Azure resources at scale.

Policy Assignments and Scope

Policy assignments are the bridge that connects policy definitions (the rules) to your Azure resources. In essence, a policy assignment applies a specific policy definition to a particular scope within your Azure hierarchy, ensuring that the resources within that scope adhere to the defined rules.

Policy Assignment and its Relationship to Policy Definitions

- **Policy Definitions:** These are the blueprints that define the rules and conditions for your Azure resources. They outline what should be allowed or denied, modified, or deployed.
- **Policy Assignments:** These are the actions of putting those blueprints into effect. A policy assignment associates a policy definition with a specific scope, such as a subscription, resource group, or management group.

Different Scopes of Policy Assignments

You can assign Azure Policies at various hierarchical levels, each with its own implications for inheritance and enforcement:

- **Management Group:** This is the highest level in the Azure hierarchy. Assigning a policy at the management group level enforces the policy on all subscriptions and resource groups within that management group.
- **Subscription:** Assigning a policy at the subscription level applies the policy to all resource groups and resources within that subscription.
- **Resource Group:** Assigning a policy at the resource group level applies the policy to all resources within that group.
- **Resource:** While not directly assigning, policies can be tailored to target specific resource types within the assigned scope.

It's important to understand that policy assignments are inherited down the hierarchy. For example, a policy assigned at the subscription level will automatically apply to all resource groups and resources within that subscription, unless explicitly excluded.

Assigning Policies: Azure Portal, Azure CLI, and ARM Templates

Azure Policy provides multiple ways to assign policies:

Azure Portal:

1. Go to the Azure Policy service in the Azure portal.
2. Click on "Assignments" and then "Assign Policy."
3. Select the scope (management group, subscription, or resource group) where you want to apply the policy.
4. Choose the policy definition you want to assign.
5. Optionally, configure any parameters required by the policy definition.
6. Click "Review + create" and then "Create" to create the policy assignment.

Azure CLI:

```
az policy assignment create --name <assignment_name> --scope <scope> --policy <policy_definition_name_or_id>
```

ARM Templates:

```
{ "type": "Microsoft.Authorization/policyAssignments", "apiVersion": "2021-06-01", "name": "enforceTagging", "properties": { "policyDefinitionId": "/subscriptions/<subscriptionId>/providers/Microsoft.Authorization/policyDefinitions/enforceTagging", "scope": "/subscriptions/<subscriptionId>" } }
```

In this example, the ARM template assigns a policy definition named "enforceTagging" to the subscription level.

By understanding the concept of policy assignments and their different scopes, you can effectively apply policies to your Azure resources and ensure that they adhere to your organization's standards and requirements.

Policy Effects

Policy effects are the heart of Azure Policy's enforcement mechanism. They dictate the actions that Azure Policy will automatically take when a resource either violates or is in compliance with a policy definition. Understanding the different policy effects available allows you to tailor your governance strategies to your specific needs.

Different Policy Effects and Their Outcomes

- **Audit:** The "Audit" effect is non-intrusive. It logs a warning message in the Activity Log when a resource is non-compliant but doesn't prevent the resource creation or modification. This is useful for monitoring compliance and identifying potential issues.
- **Deny:** The "Deny" effect blocks the creation or modification of a resource if it doesn't adhere to the policy rules. This is the strictest enforcement option and ensures that only compliant resources are allowed in your environment.

- **Modify:** The "Modify" effect automatically modifies the resource to bring it into compliance with the policy. For instance, it can add tags, update properties, or append values to arrays. This is a proactive approach that ensures your resources adhere to your standards.
- **DeployIfNotExists:** This effect deploys a specified template if a condition is not met. This can be used to ensure that required resources, like monitoring agents or security configurations, are deployed alongside other resources.
- **Append:** The "Append" effect adds additional fields or values to the requested resource during creation or update. This is useful for adding extra tags, metadata, or other properties to resources for tracking or management purposes.

Choosing the Right Policy Effect

The choice of policy effect depends on your governance goals and the specific scenario. Here's a general guideline:

- **Audit:** Use for monitoring and reporting compliance violations.
- **Deny:** Use when you want to strictly enforce compliance and prevent non-compliant resources from being created or modified.
- **Modify:** Use when you want to automatically remediate non-compliant resources to bring them into compliance.
- **DeployIfNotExists:** Use to ensure the presence of essential resources or configurations.
- **Append:** Use to add additional information or metadata to resources for tracking or management.

Examples of Policy Effects in Action

- **Audit:** A policy with an "Audit" effect could be used to track the creation of virtual machines in unauthorized regions. It would log a warning when a VM is created in a disallowed region, but it wouldn't prevent the creation itself.
- **Deny:** A policy with a "Deny" effect could prevent the creation of storage accounts without encryption enabled. This ensures that all storage accounts comply with your organization's security standards.
- **Modify:** A policy with a "Modify" effect could automatically add a specific tag to all resources, such as a department or cost center tag. This simplifies resource management and tracking.
- **DeployIfNotExists:** A policy with this effect could deploy a Log Analytics agent on every newly created virtual machine, ensuring that all VMs are monitored for security and performance.
- **Append:** A policy with an "Append" effect could automatically add a network security group (NSG) rule to newly created virtual networks to restrict inbound traffic.

By strategically using these policy effects, you can create a comprehensive governance framework that ensures your Azure environment remains secure, compliant, and aligned with your organizational standards.

Initiative Definitions

While individual Azure Policy definitions are powerful in enforcing specific rules, managing numerous policies across your Azure environment can become cumbersome. Initiative definitions come to the rescue by grouping related policy definitions together, simplifying their management and assignment.

What are Initiative Definitions?

An initiative definition is essentially a collection of Azure Policy definitions that are bundled together to achieve a common goal or enforce a set of related standards. You can think of an initiative as a policy package that contains multiple policies tailored to a specific objective, such as ensuring compliance with a regulatory standard or implementing a company-wide security baseline.

Simplifying Policy Management with Initiative Definitions

Initiative definitions offer several benefits for simplifying policy management:

- **Easier Assignment:** Instead of assigning individual policy definitions one by one, you can assign a single initiative definition that encompasses all the relevant policies. This reduces the manual effort and potential for errors associated with managing multiple assignments.
- **Centralized Management:** Initiative definitions provide a centralized location to manage and update related policies. Any changes made to the initiative definition automatically propagate to all the policy assignments linked to it, ensuring consistency across your environment.
- **Improved Readability:** Initiative definitions make it easier to understand the overall purpose and intent of a group of policies. This improves clarity and simplifies communication with stakeholders.

Creating and Assigning Initiative Definitions

You can create initiative definitions in the Azure portal, Azure CLI, or through ARM templates. The process typically involves:

1. **Defining the Initiative:** Give your initiative a name, description, and optionally a category.
2. **Adding Policy Definitions:** Select the policy definitions that you want to include in the initiative.
3. **Configuring Parameters (Optional):** If the policy definitions have parameters, you can provide values for those parameters at the initiative level.
4. **Assigning the Initiative:** Assign the initiative to the desired scope (management group, subscription, or resource group), just like you would with individual policy definitions.

Enforcing Complex Compliance Requirements

Initiative definitions are particularly useful for enforcing complex compliance requirements that involve multiple policies. For example, to comply with the PCI DSS (Payment Card Industry Data Security Standard), you might need to enforce a combination of policies related to data encryption, network security, and vulnerability scanning.

By creating an initiative definition that includes all the necessary PCI DSS-related policies, you can easily assign and manage them as a single unit. This simplifies the compliance process and ensures that all relevant policies are applied consistently across your Azure environment.

In conclusion, initiative definitions play a crucial role in streamlining policy management in Azure Policy. They allow you to group related policies, assign them with ease, and enforce complex compliance requirements effectively. By leveraging initiative definitions, you can simplify your governance efforts, maintain consistency across your Azure environment, and ensure that your resources adhere to your organizational standards.

Azure Policy Compliance

Maintaining compliance with organizational standards and industry regulations is a critical aspect of cloud governance. Azure Policy provides a robust compliance dashboard that acts as your window into the compliance posture of your Azure environment. This centralized hub empowers you to assess, track, and remediate compliance issues effectively.

Azure Policy Compliance Dashboard

The compliance dashboard in Azure Policy offers a holistic view of your environment's adherence to assigned policy and initiative definitions. Its key features include:

- **Overall Compliance Summary:** Provides a high-level overview of your compliance posture, showing the percentage of compliant and non-compliant resources.
- **Compliance by Policy/Initiative:** Drill down into specific policy or initiative assignments to see detailed compliance information for each.
- **Non-compliant Resources:** Quickly identify non-compliant resources, view the specific policy or initiative they violate, and access remediation options.
- **Compliance Trends:** Track your compliance progress over time through historical graphs and reports.
- **Exporting Compliance Data:** Export compliance data in CSV or Excel format for further analysis or reporting.

Identifying Non-compliant Resources and Tracking Progress

The compliance dashboard makes it easy to pinpoint non-compliant resources and track your progress towards achieving compliance. Here's how:

1. **Filter and Sort:** Use the filters and sorting options to narrow down the list of non-compliant resources based on criteria like resource type, location, or policy assignment.
2. **Investigate Details:** Click on a non-compliant resource to view the specific policy or initiative it violates. You can also see detailed information about the resource, such as its properties and tags.
3. **Take Action:** Azure Policy offers various options for remediating non-compliant resources, such as:
   - **Manual Remediation:** You can manually modify the resource to bring it into compliance.
   - **Automatic Remediation:** For some policies, Azure Policy can automatically remediate resources by applying the necessary changes.
   - **Exemptions:** You can grant temporary exemptions to non-compliant resources if you need more time to bring them into compliance.

By regularly reviewing the compliance dashboard and taking appropriate actions, you can continuously monitor and improve your compliance posture.

Creating Custom Compliance Reports

Azure Policy allows you to create custom compliance reports tailored to your specific needs. You can define filters, select specific policies or initiatives, and choose the desired output format (CSV, Excel, or PDF). These custom reports can be used for:

- **Auditing:** Providing evidence of compliance to auditors or regulators.
- **Management Reporting:** Sharing compliance information with stakeholders and management.
- **Trend Analysis:** Identifying patterns and trends in compliance data over time.

In conclusion, the Azure Policy compliance dashboard is a powerful tool for managing and maintaining compliance in your Azure environment. By leveraging its features, you can proactively identify and remediate non-compliant resources, track your progress towards compliance, and create custom reports that meet your specific needs.

Azure Policy and Regulatory Compliance

Azure Policy is a valuable tool in your arsenal for achieving and maintaining regulatory compliance in the cloud. It enables you to enforce policies that align with specific regulatory standards, ensuring that your Azure resources adhere to the necessary security and operational controls.

Enforcing Compliance with Azure Policy

Azure Policy simplifies compliance by offering the following capabilities:

- **Built-in Regulatory Compliance Definitions:** Azure Policy provides a library of built-in policy definitions that map to specific regulatory standards such as HIPAA, PCI DSS, ISO 27001, and others. These definitions encapsulate the necessary controls and configurations required by these standards, allowing you to quickly apply them to your resources.
- **Custom Policy Definitions:** In addition to built-in definitions, you can create custom policy definitions to address unique compliance requirements specific to your industry or organization. This flexibility ensures that your policies align precisely with your compliance needs.
- **Initiative Definitions:** Initiative definitions bundle multiple policy definitions together, enabling you to easily apply a set of policies relevant to a specific compliance standard with a single assignment. This streamlines the process of enforcing comprehensive compliance.
- **Compliance Dashboard:** Azure Policy provides a compliance dashboard that gives you visibility into the compliance status of your resources. You can easily identify non-compliant resources, track your progress towards compliance, and generate reports for auditors or regulators.

Examples of Policy Definitions for Common Compliance Requirements

Let's look at some examples of policy definitions that can help you meet common compliance requirements:

- **HIPAA (Health Insurance Portability and Accountability Act):**
    - "Ensure that all storage accounts have encryption enabled" to protect sensitive patient data.
    - "Require that all virtual machines have network security groups (NSGs) applied" to restrict access and secure network communication.
    - "Audit the logging of Azure SQL database activities" to track access and detect potential security incidents.
- **PCI DSS (Payment Card Industry Data Security Standard):**
    - "Require that all virtual machines are patched with the latest security updates" to protect against known vulnerabilities.
    - "Ensure that all network traffic is filtered through a firewall" to prevent unauthorized access to cardholder data.
    - "Enforce strong password policies for all user accounts" to secure access to sensitive data.
- **ISO 27001 (International Organization for Standardization 27001):**
    - "Require that all resources have appropriate tags for identification and classification" to facilitate asset management and risk assessment.
    - "Implement access controls for all Azure resources" to ensure that only authorized personnel can access sensitive data and systems.
    - "Regularly review and update security policies and procedures" to maintain a strong security posture.

By utilizing these policy definitions and creating custom definitions where necessary, you can leverage Azure Policy to automate compliance checks, enforce security controls, and streamline your compliance management process. Regularly monitoring your compliance dashboard and taking proactive measures to address any non-compliant resources will ensure that your Azure environment remains secure and compliant with industry standards and regulations.

Best Practices for Using Azure Policy

Azure Policy is a versatile tool, but its effectiveness can be maximized by adhering to certain best practices that ensure smooth implementation, prevent disruptions, and enhance your overall governance strategy.

Start with Built-in Policy Definitions

Azure Policy offers a vast library of built-in policy definitions covering a wide range of common scenarios. These definitions are well-tested and curated by Microsoft, adhering to industry best practices and regulatory standards. Begin by exploring these built-in policies and utilize them as the foundation for your governance framework. This allows you to quickly implement common controls without the need to create custom policies from scratch. As you gain more experience and identify specific requirements not covered by built-in policies, you can gradually introduce custom policy definitions tailored to your organization's unique needs.

Test Policies in a Development Environment

Before applying any policy definition to your production environment, thoroughly test it in a development or sandbox environment. This practice helps you identify any potential issues, unintended consequences, or conflicts with other policies. Testing in a controlled environment allows you to refine your policies and ensure they work as expected before deploying them to critical production resources.

Utilize Tags and Resource Groups for Effective Scope Management

Azure Policy allows you to assign policies at different scopes, such as management groups, subscriptions, and resource groups. Utilize tags and resource groups to effectively scope your policies to the relevant resources. For instance, you can assign policies to specific resource groups based on their purpose (e.g., development, testing, production) or apply policies based on tags that categorize resources by department, project, or environment. This ensures that your policies are applied precisely where they are needed, minimizing the risk of over- or under-enforcement.

Leverage Exemptions for Flexibility

In some scenarios, you might encounter situations where a resource needs to deviate from a policy temporarily. Azure Policy provides an exemption mechanism that allows you to grant temporary exemptions to non-compliant resources. This flexibility can be helpful during migrations, testing, or when dealing with legacy systems. Exemptions can be time-bound and should be used judiciously to maintain the integrity of your governance framework.

Integrate with Other Azure Services

Azure Policy seamlessly integrates with other Azure services, creating a comprehensive governance and security ecosystem. Consider integrating Azure Policy with:

- **Azure Monitor:** Leverage Azure Monitor to collect logs and metrics related to policy evaluation and compliance. This enables you to track policy changes, identify non-compliant resources, and create alerts for potential violations.
- **Azure Security Center:** Integrate with Azure Security Center to leverage its security recommendations and threat detection capabilities, enhancing the overall security posture of your Azure environment.
- **Azure DevOps:** Incorporate Azure Policy into your CI/CD pipelines to ensure that new resources deployed through your pipelines adhere to your governance standards.

By following these best practices, you can harness the full power of Azure Policy to establish a robust governance framework, enforce compliance, and safeguard your Azure resources while maintaining the flexibility and agility required for your business operations.

Chapter Summary

In this chapter, we explored Azure Policy, a powerful tool for enforcing governance and compliance in your Azure environment. We learned how Azure Policy allows you to define and enforce rules for resource configurations, ensuring that your cloud environment adheres to your organizational standards and regulatory requirements.

Key Takeaways:

- **Azure Policy:** A policy-based management tool that helps you maintain control and compliance in your Azure environment.
- **Policy Definitions:** The building blocks of Azure Policy, defining the rules and conditions that resources must adhere to.
- **Policy Assignments:** The mechanism through which you apply policy definitions to specific scopes within your Azure hierarchy.
- **Policy Effects:** The actions Azure Policy takes when resources are non-compliant, ranging from simple auditing to automatic remediation.
- **Initiative Definitions:** Collections of policy definitions that simplify the management and assignment of complex compliance requirements.
- **Compliance Dashboard:** A centralized view of your Azure environment's compliance status, helping you identify and address non-compliant resources.
- **Regulatory Compliance:** How Azure Policy can assist you in meeting various regulatory compliance standards like HIPAA, PCI DSS, and ISO 27001.
- **Best Practices:** Recommendations for using Azure Policy effectively, including starting with built-in definitions, testing in development environments, using tags for scoping, and leveraging exemptions.

By understanding and applying the concepts discussed in this chapter, you can leverage Azure Policy to establish a robust governance framework in your Azure environment. This will not only ensure compliance with organizational and regulatory standards but also improve the security, stability, and cost-effectiveness of your cloud resources. Remember, Azure Policy is a powerful tool that, when used effectively, can significantly enhance your cloud governance capabilities.

Appendices

Appendix A: Glossary of Azure Terms

This glossary provides concise definitions of essential Azure terms used throughout this book, helping you grasp the fundamental concepts and navigate the Azure landscape with confidence.

Active Directory (AD): Microsoft's directory service that provides authentication and authorization for users and computers within a network. Azure Active Directory (Azure AD) is Microsoft's cloud-based identity and access management service.

App Service: A fully managed platform for building, deploying, and scaling web apps, mobile back ends, and RESTful APIs.

Azure: Microsoft's public cloud computing platform that offers a wide range of services, including compute, storage, networking, databases, and analytics.

Azure CLI: A command-line interface for managing Azure resources.

Azure Portal: The web-based user interface for managing Azure resources.

Azure Resource Manager (ARM): The deployment and management service for Azure. It provides a consistent management layer for creating, updating, and deleting resources in your Azure account.

Azure Virtual Machine (VM): A scalable computing resource that you can use to run applications and workloads in the cloud.

Blob Storage: A scalable object storage service for storing large amounts of unstructured data, such as text or binary data.

Cloud Computing: The on-demand availability of computer system resources, especially data storage and computing power, without direct active management by the user.

Container: A lightweight, standalone, executable package of software that includes everything needed to run an application: code, runtime, system tools, system libraries, and settings.

Cosmos DB: A globally distributed, multi-model database service that supports NoSQL data models such as document, key-value, graph, and column-family.

DevOps: A set of practices that combines software development (Dev) and IT operations (Ops). It aims to shorten the software development life cycle and provide continuous delivery with high quality.

Infrastructure as Code (IaC): The process of managing and provisioning computer data centers through machine-readable definition files, rather than physical hardware configuration or interactive configuration tools.

IoT (Internet of Things): The network of physical devices, vehicles, home appliances, and other items embedded with electronics, software, sensors, actuators, and connectivity which allows these things to connect, collect and exchange data.

IoT Hub: A managed service that enables reliable and secure bi-directional communications between millions of IoT devices and a solution back end.

Kubernetes: An open-source platform for automating deployment, scaling, and management of containerized applications.

Load Balancer: A device that acts as a reverse proxy and distributes network or application traffic across a number of servers.

Machine Learning: A branch of artificial intelligence (AI) and computer science which focuses on the use of data and algorithms to imitate the way that humans learn, gradually improving its accuracy.

Managed Disk: A managed hard disk in Azure that provides a simple and scalable way to store data.

Microservices: An architectural style that structures an application as a collection of loosely coupled services, which implement business capabilities.

NoSQL Database: A non-relational database that does not use the tabular schema of rows and columns found in most traditional database systems.

Region: A geographical area in Azure where you can deploy your resources.

Resource Group: A container that holds related resources for an Azure solution.

Resource Manager Template (ARM template): A JavaScript Object Notation (JSON) file that defines the infrastructure and configuration for your Azure solution.

REST API: A Representational State Transfer (REST) Application Programming Interface (API) is an architectural style for an application program interface (API) that uses HTTP requests to access and use data.

Role-Based Access Control (RBAC): A system that provides fine-grained access management of Azure resources.

SDK (Software Development Kit): A set of software development tools that allows the creation of applications for a certain software package, software framework, hardware platform, computer system, video game console, operating system, or similar development platform.

Serverless Computing: A cloud computing execution model in which the cloud provider allocates machine resources on demand, taking care of the servers on behalf of their customers.

SQL Database: A relational database service in Azure that provides a fully managed platform for building, deploying, and managing relational databases.

Storage Account: A unique namespace in Azure for your data.

Subscription: A logical unit of Azure services associated with an Azure account.

Virtual Network (VNet): A representation of your own network in the cloud.

Appendix B: Azure Certifications

Azure certifications are industry-recognized credentials that validate your skills and knowledge in Microsoft Azure technologies. They demonstrate your expertise to potential employers and can help you advance your career in cloud computing. Microsoft offers a wide range of Azure certifications across various roles and skill levels, providing a clear path for professional development.

Why Get Azure Certified?

Earning an Azure certification offers numerous benefits:

- **Validation of Expertise:** Certifications validate your skills and knowledge in specific Azure technologies, boosting your credibility and confidence.
- **Career Advancement:** Certifications can open doors to new job opportunities and help you negotiate higher salaries.
- **Industry Recognition:** Azure certifications are recognized worldwide, demonstrating your commitment to staying current with the latest cloud technologies.
- **Personal Growth:** The process of preparing for and passing an Azure certification can help you deepen your understanding of Azure and improve your skills.

Azure Certification Paths

Microsoft organizes Azure certifications into different paths or roles based on your areas of interest and expertise. The main certification paths include:

- **Azure Fundamentals:** This foundational certification validates your understanding of core cloud concepts and Azure services. It is a good starting point for beginners who are new to Azure.
- **Azure Administrator Associate:** This certification is designed for those responsible for managing and maintaining Azure infrastructure. It covers topics such as resource management, storage, networking, and virtual machines.
- **Azure Developer Associate:** This certification is geared towards developers who build and deploy applications on Azure. It covers topics such as cloud-native development, serverless computing, and containerization.
- **Azure Solutions Architect Expert:** This advanced certification validates your ability to design and implement end-to-end Azure solutions. It covers a wide range of topics, including infrastructure, security, data storage, and networking.
- **Azure Data Scientist Associate:** This certification focuses on the skills required to design and implement machine learning and data science solutions on Azure. It covers topics such as data ingestion, data preparation, model training, and deployment.
- **Azure AI Engineer Associate:** This certification is designed for engineers who work with artificial intelligence and machine learning on Azure. It covers topics such as building and deploying AI models, creating custom vision solutions, and using Azure Cognitive Services.
- **Azure Data Engineer Associate:** This certification validates the skills needed to design and implement data platforms and pipelines on Azure. It covers topics such as data storage, data processing, and data warehousing.
- **Azure Security Engineer Associate:** This certification focuses on securing Azure environments and protecting data. It covers topics such as identity and access management, network security, and threat protection.

Preparing for Azure Certifications

Microsoft offers various resources to help you prepare for Azure certifications:

- **Microsoft Learn:** This online learning platform provides free, interactive training courses for all Azure certifications.
- **Microsoft Official Courseware (MOC):** Instructor-led training courses offered by Microsoft Learning Partners.
- **Practice Tests:** Take practice tests to assess your knowledge and identify areas where you need more preparation.
- **Community Resources:** Join online forums and study groups to connect with other Azure professionals and get support.

Tips for Passing Azure Certifications

- **Start with Azure Fundamentals:** If you're new to Azure, begin with the Azure Fundamentals certification to build a solid foundation.
- **Choose the right path:** Select the certification path that aligns with your career goals and interests.
- **Create a study plan:** Develop a study plan that includes a mix of online courses, instructor-led training, and practice tests.
- **Join a study group:** Connect with other Azure professionals to discuss concepts, share resources, and get support.
- **Practice, practice, practice:** Hands-on experience with Azure is essential for passing the certifications. Create a free Azure account and experiment with different services.
- **Stay up-to-date:** Azure is constantly evolving, so make sure to stay current with the latest updates and features.

By following these tips and utilizing the resources available, you can increase your chances of success in your Azure certification journey.

Appendix C: Additional Resources for Learning Azure

As you continue your journey into the world of Microsoft Azure, expanding your knowledge and skills is key to unlocking its full potential. This appendix provides a curated list of valuable resources that can further enhance your understanding of Azure concepts, technologies, and best practices.

Official Microsoft Resources:

- **Microsoft Learn:** The official learning platform from Microsoft offers a vast collection of free, self-paced online courses and modules covering various Azure services and topics. It's a great place to start for beginners and experienced professionals alike. You can find Azure-specific learning paths and certifications here.
- **Azure Documentation:** Microsoft's comprehensive documentation provides detailed information about Azure services, features, and APIs. It's a valuable reference for understanding how to use different Azure services and troubleshoot issues.
- **Azure Blog:** Stay up-to-date with the latest Azure news, announcements, and technical deep dives by following the official Azure blog.

Community Resources:

- **Microsoft Tech Community:** This online community is a hub for Azure users and professionals to connect, share knowledge, and discuss Azure-related topics. You can find forums, blogs, and Q&A sections where you can ask questions and get help from other Azure enthusiasts.
- **Stack Overflow:** This popular Q&A platform for developers is a great resource for finding answers to technical questions related to Azure. Many Azure experts actively participate in this community.
- **GitHub:** Many open-source projects and sample code repositories related to Azure are hosted on GitHub. Exploring these repositories can give you hands-on experience and practical insights into Azure development.

Blogs and Websites:

- **Azure DevOps Blog:** This blog focuses on Azure DevOps and provides tutorials, best practices, and updates on new features and releases.
- **Serverless Notes:** This blog covers serverless computing on Azure, including Azure Functions, Logic Apps, and Event Grid.
- **Build Azure:** This website offers a collection of learning resources for Azure, including tutorials, videos, and podcasts.

Books and eBooks:

- **Azure in Action:** This book provides a comprehensive overview of Azure, covering everything from the basics to advanced topics.
- **Architecting Microsoft Azure Solutions:** This book focuses on designing and implementing cloud solutions on Azure.
- **Exam Ref AZ-900 Microsoft Azure Fundamentals:** This book is designed to help you prepare for the AZ-900 certification exam.

YouTube Channels and Video Resources:

- **Microsoft Azure Channel:** The official YouTube channel for Azure provides a wealth of video content, including tutorials, demos, and customer stories.
- **John Savill's Azure Academy:** This YouTube channel offers in-depth Azure tutorials and demonstrations.

- **Cloud Academy:** This online learning platform offers video courses on various Azure topics, including certifications.

Additional Tips:

- **Hands-on Practice:** The best way to learn Azure is through hands-on practice. Create a free Azure account and experiment with different services.
- **Certifications:** Consider pursuing Azure certifications to validate your skills and demonstrate your expertise to potential employers.
- **Networking:** Attend Azure conferences and meetups to connect with other Azure professionals and learn from their experiences.

By exploring these resources and actively engaging with the Azure community, you can continue your learning journey and stay ahead of the curve in the ever-evolving world of cloud computing.

Conclusion

Congratulations on completing your journey through "Microsoft Azure Made Easy: A Beginner's Roadmap." You have now gained a solid foundation in the fundamentals of Microsoft Azure and are well-equipped to embark on your cloud computing adventures.

We began by demystifying the concept of cloud computing and exploring the compelling reasons why Azure stands out as a leading cloud platform. You learned about the core building blocks of Azure, including subscriptions, resource groups, and regions, and how to navigate the Azure portal to manage your resources effectively.

We then dove into the practical aspects of getting started with Azure, guiding you through the process of creating your first Azure account, navigating the Azure portal, and exploring the vast offerings in the Azure Marketplace.

Next, we explored the diverse range of Azure services, covering compute, storage, networking, databases, identity and security, monitoring and management, and additional services like machine learning, IoT, and cognitive services. We provided a beginner-friendly roadmap for each service, explaining the key concepts, features, and use cases, empowering you to harness their power for your own projects.

In the advanced concepts section, you delved into the realms of infrastructure as code with Azure Resource Manager, continuous integration and deployment with Azure DevOps, and policy-based governance with Azure Policy. These concepts lay the groundwork for building scalable, reliable, and compliant cloud solutions.

Throughout this book, we've emphasized the importance of hands-on practice. We encourage you to continue exploring Azure, experimenting with different services, and applying your newfound knowledge to real-world scenarios. Remember, the cloud is a dynamic and ever-evolving landscape, so embrace a lifelong learning mindset and stay curious.

As you continue your Azure journey, remember that the resources listed in Appendix C are invaluable tools for expanding your knowledge and skills. Engage with the Azure community, participate in forums, and seek out additional training materials to stay at the forefront of cloud computing.

With dedication and perseverance, you can unlock the full potential of Microsoft Azure and build a successful career in the cloud. We hope this book has served as a valuable guide, and we wish you all the best in your future endeavors!

www.ingramcontent.com/pod-product-compliance
Lightning Source LLC
Chambersburg PA
CBHW082104220526
45472CB00009B/2033